MULTIPLE LITERACIES FOR THE 21ST CENTURY

RESEARCH AND TEACHING IN RHETORIC AND COMPOSITION

Michael M. Williamson and David L. Jolliffe, series editors

Basic Writing as a Political Act: Public Conversations About Writing and Literacies
Linda Adler-Kassner and Susanmarie Harrington

New Worlds, New Words: Exploring Pathways for Writing About and In Electronic Environments
John F. Barber and Dene Grigar (eds.)

The Rhetoric and Ideology of Genre: Strategies for Stability and Change
Richard Coe, Lorelei Lingard, and Tatiana Teslenko (eds.)

Teaching/Writing in the Late Age of Print
Jeffrey Galin, Carol Peterson Haviland, and J Paul Johnson (eds.)

Multiple Literacies for the 21st Century
Brian Huot, Beth Stroble, and Charles Bazerman (eds.)

Identities Across Text
George H. Jensen

Against the Grain: Essays in Honor of Maxine Hairston
David Jolliffe, Michael Keene, Mary Trachel, and Ralph Voss (eds.)

Classroom Spaces and Writing Instruction
Ed Nagelhout and Carol Rutz

Unexpected Voices
John Rouse and Ed Katz

Directed Self-Placement: Principles and Practices
Dan Royer and Roger Gilles (eds.)

forthcoming

Black Letters: An Ethnography of a Beginning Legal Writing Course
Randolph Cauthen

Marbles, Cotton Balls, and Quantum Wells: Style as Invention in the Pursuit of Knowledge
Heather Graves

Remapping Narrative: Technology's Impact on the Way We Write
Gian S. Pagnucci and Nick Mauriello (eds.)

Tech Culture: Internet Constructions of Literacy and Identity
Gian S. Pagnucci and Nick Mauriello (eds.)

Who Can Afford Critical Consciousness
David Seitz

Principles and Practices: New Discourses for Advanced Writers
Margaret M. Strain and James M. Boehnlein (eds.)

MULTIPLE LITERACIES FOR THE 21ST CENTURY

edited by

Brian Huot
University of Louisville

Beth Stroble
The University of Akron

Charles Bazerman
University of California-Santa Barbara

Printed in the United States of America

Library of Congress Cataloging-in-Publication Data

Multiple literacies for the 21st century / edited by Brian Huot, Beth Stroble, Charles Bazerman

p. cm. -- (Research and teaching in rhetoric and composition)
Papers presented at the Second Watson Conference.
Includes bibliographical references and indexes.
ISBN 1-57273-536-8 (cl) -- ISBN 1-57273-537-6 (paper)
1. Literacy--Social aspects--United States--Congresses. 2. English language--Rhetoric--Study and teaching--United States--Congresses. I. Title: Multiple literacies for the twenty-first century. II. Series

LC151.M86 2003
302'2'244--dc22

2003056626

Hampton Press, Inc.
23 Broadway
Cresskill, NJ 07626

This book is dedicated to the memory of Dr. Thomas R. Watson, a Louisville physician, banker, and entrepreneur, born August 16, 1935, in Graves County, Kentucky; he died January 15, 1996. He was married to Sylvia Watson and had two daughters, McCall Watson Eng and Emily Watson Ragan.

Dr. Watson was a board certified gynecologist, active in his profession. In concert with his career in the medical field, he served on civic and charitable boards, including the University of Louisville Board of Overseers, and was involved with Magnolia Bancorp, Commonwealth Bank, Bankers' Mortgage, Health Care Partners, and Celsus, Inc.

In 1995, Dr. Watson gave $1.2 million to the English Department of the University of Louisville to endow a biennial International Conference in Rhetoric and Composition and a Visiting Distinguished Professorship of Rhetoric and Composition. This gift is a mark not only of Dr. Watson's extraordinary generosity, but also of his imaginative and far-sighted vision. It attests to his understanding of the fundamental importance of a literate citizenry, and of the vital task faced by the liberal arts, particularly Composition studies, in educating students to become critical, active, and engaged readers and writers. This volume would not be possible without Dr. Watson's generosity and vision.

CONTENTS

LITERACY AND SCHOOLING

LITERACY AND TECHNOLOGY

LITERACY AND OTHER SENSES/CAPACITIES

CRITICAL LITERACIES AND CRITICAL THINKING ABOUT LITERACIES

REFLECTIONS

INTRODUCTION

Brian Huot
University of Louisville
Beth Stroble
University of Akron

Multiple Literacies for the 21st Century, the title of the Second Watson Conference, and this volume implies that literacy is not one thing and that time changes what is meant by literacy. Although these two assumptions are central to this volume and to much of the current scholarship about literacy and its study, it would be misleading and reductive to assume that this volume or the study of literacy is limited to these two elements. In fact, it has been our attempt to look as expansively as we can in selecting and editing the chapters for this volume. If the scholarship about literacy has taught us anything at all in the last several years, it is that literate behavior like all behavior associated with language is diverse and human, containing the potential to not only create meaning and identities for individuals and groups but to become meaningful in and of itself. In other words, we cannot separate the ways in which people read and write from the ways in which they think about the world and identify themselves in it.

As a field of study, literacy has undergone radical changes over the last two decades. As late as the 1960s and 1970s, certain kinds of literacy like that associated with the Western alphabet were privileged over others. Within this framework, there is a clear distinction between orality and literacy. Basically, the argument went that the advent of literacy played a major role in the development of culture, government, business, law, and other institutions. The strong version of this argument is best seen in the early work of Goody and Watt (1968), who proposed that alphabetic literacy allowed the development of a specific consciousness that promoted the cultural achievements of Western society. Walter Ong's (1982) *Orality and Literacy* went so far as to propose that people who were not literate were limited in the level of cognitive development and their ability to perform certain tasks. Ong's ideas were translated into literacy education by Farrell (1983) who advocated that African-American students be taught the full complement of the verb *to be* in order that they could achieve the raised consciousness afforded by alphabetic literacy. Once these ideas about literacy entered the literature on the teaching of writing they were soundly critiqued by Bizzell (1998) and others. Daniel (1986) has called this version of literacy the great leap theory because its proponents ascribe such profound effects for those people and cultures who are literate. Street called this version of literacy autonomous because it focuses on literacy's technical aspects and ignores the importance of social context, as if literacy or any other language practice can exist independently of the culture and people within which it occurs. Several studies of literacy from people like Heath (1983), Ogbu (1988) and Street all address the culturally situated nature of literacy.

Scribner and Cole's (1981) study of the Vai in North Africa most directly looks at the great leap or autonomous theory of literacy. Since the Vai people are potentially tri-literate in Arabic, English, or Vai, they are a potentially very interesting group of people to study. Scribner and Cole conducted a series of experiments as well as an ethnographic study. They found that there were no measurable differences in cognitive abilities between those who were literate or not, regardless of the various languages involved. What they did find, however, was that many of the cognitive effects discussed by Ong and others could be observed among those people who had received a formal education. Scribner and Cole concluded that the effects on people's ways of reasoning and expressing themselves could more accurately be attributed to formal schooling rather than to their ability to read and write in a specific language or script. As Heath (1983) illustrated in her landmark study of working-class people in the Piedmont Carolina area, formal schooling is best understood as a set of practices rooted within a specific cultural context. In this way, the types of effects Goody and Watt and Ong and others observed are no more than cultural differences. Various types of literacies affect different people and groups of people in different ways, depending on the ways in which a specific culture is disposed to use them.

The upshot of the repudiation of earlier notions of literacy that emphasized the oral literate dichotomy and accorded literate behavior special status and consciousness has been a focus on the social aspects of literacy and its teaching. This social turn for literacy scholarship has helped us begin to focus not only on the ways in which individuals and groups are affected by literacy but also on the ways in which groups and individuals affect literacy. Brandt's (1998) study involving interviews from people who have lived throughout the 20th century demonstrates how important a factor the historical moment can be, as literate behavior has undergone radical changes within the state of Wisconsin over the last 100 years. Besnier's (1995) study of the Nukulaelae, who use literacy for a very narrow range of communication, illustrates the importance of place and the host culture in terms of the forms literacy might eventually take. These kinds of studies and the overall emphasis of culture in the study of literacy provides us with a broader sense of literate behavior than what might have been thought possible even a few short decades ago.

As the 20th century fades into memory, we are reminded of the radical changes the last 100 years and its continuing march of technologies have brought not only to the acts of reading and writing but to what it means to be literate now and what it might mean to be literate in the next hundred years. Although concepts like the continuing perception of a literacy crisis have remained with us from the last century, literacy itself has never been a static concept. The use of computers and the proliferation of computer-mediated communication in the schools, on the job, and in the private lives of more and more millions of people continues to not only change the shape of literate behavior, but to change the shape of people's lives. These changing aspects of literacy continue to complicate our understanding of literacy as it expands into more and more aspects of they way we live. Truly, at this point in time, literacy has become an ever complex concept meaning many different things to various groups of people. In this context, it is important to recognize and respect the range of literacy practices that are not only indicative of individuals and groups but which practices serve to provide personal, ethnic and cultural identities for those who use written language in specific ways.

The concept of *multiple literacies* is certainly not novel. The earliest use of the term *multiple literacies* that we have found comes from Patrick Hartwell's landmark essay "Grammar, Grammars and the Teaching of Grammar." Hartwell's reference and this volume point to the movement over the last 20 to 30 years in which we have seen the recognition of multiple literacies first as an idea and later as a term. Certainly, multiple literacies is a widely accepted way of thinking about literacy, and its substance is supported by a wide range of research that has looked at the literate practices of different people and of people in different sites. This research has begun to help us recognize that school-sponsored literacy is but one way of being literate in our society and around the world. Freeing literacy from a specific site or set of practices allows us to see it as generative, as a way to consider and recognize the experiences, memories, and histories of those who use literacy to make meaning in their lives, regardless of their group or personal identities. In its multiplicity, literacy and its various practices are constantly in tension with the range of centrifugal and centripetal forces that have always surrounded it. One only has to consider the history of the literacy crises to realize that literate practices have always been a site for struggle and conflict.

With the range of literacy and literate behavior being widely known and recognized, we face new challenges as this recognition becomes increasingly codified. It is quite common to speak of various kinds of literacy. For example, a quick browse of the Web informs us of cultural literacy, critical literacy, information literacy, computer literacy, functional literacy, quantitative literacy, numeracy, prose literacy, document literacy, personal literacy, multicultural literacy, academic literacy, ethical literacy, media literacy, adult literacy, technological literacy, family literacy, cyber literacy, and workplace literacy. This proliferation of various kinds of literacy, as far as we can tell, was an invention of the late 20th century. Some kinds of literacy like workplace, family, or adult refer to the specific sites groups or individuals. Other kinds like critical, information, and cultural refer to a cluster of skills centered around reading and writing that are valued by a group of people who have some recognized authority or whose assignment of value appeals to some recognized authority.

It should be clear that just recognizing and cataloging a range of literate practices does not in and of itself help to represent all peoples and their use of literacy. It is important to distinguish between multiple literacies that are generative, reflective, and descriptive of the way people actually read and write and those that merely codify how some authority believes literacy should function and people should act with written language in specific contexts and sites. To understand this distinction, it might be helpful to borrow from the way linguists distinguish between descriptive and prescriptive forms of grammar study. It is one thing to recognize that different groups of people or different sites in which people interact require specific and distinct forms of written communication and to describe this way of using written language. It is quite another matter to decide that a specific site or activity requires specific language conventions and to develop assessments and other means for enforcing specific literate practices and the attitudes that inform them. This distinction between describing and prescribing literate practices is crucial because of the way power is exercised in and outside of school concerning literacy. As Foucault (1979) and others have noted, various social institutions have provided themselves with ways to discipline individuals and to manipulate individuals to discipline themselves. This self-disciplining power of literacy is all too evident to any of us who having introduced ourselves as English teachers and have received the predictable response: "I'll have to watch my grammar."

It is important in celebrating the literate practices of various groups and individuals that we not fail to cast a critical eye at literacy itself. Critiques of literacy and its position in schools and other institutions have come mainly from Marxism, cultural studies and other disciplines devoted to cultural critique. One of our favorite reminders about the negative potential of literacy comes from singer-songwriter and Nashville Bad Boy Steve Earle (1993): "They teach you how to read and write/So you can go down to the county bank and sign away your life." Earle's point about the role of literacy, in his song about the shackles of small town life, reminds us that we must question literacy as we would any other cultural practice and be unwilling to accept it as universally good or useful activity. This critical, self-reflexive view for literacy seems especially important, considering that certain forms of literacy like Hirsch's (1987) *Cultural Literacy* advocate a fairly fixed version of not only literate behavior but of the ways in which people think about and relate to each other their worlds. As Bizzell (1998) noted, "In short, Hirsch's candidate for a privileged ideology of literacy is not as context-free as he claims: it is an academic ideology" (p. 143). In reality, Hirsch's cultural literacy lists are a collection of texts, definitions, and ideas that reflect Western, European canonical understandings of history, art, and literature. The question about this or any other notion of cultural literacy ought to be "whose culture?" More broadly, attempts by Hirsch and others to codify or prescribe literate behavior should be understood as an attempt to mandate ideology and prescribe cultural behavior.

Farr (1993), who has studied the ways in which Hispanics use literacy and how these ways distinguish and disadvantage them from the majority of Americans, pointed out that "although literacy *in itself* does not require or reflect a certain style of thinking, *specific* literacies, including essayist literacy and, for that matter specific oralities as well, do" (pp. 11-12). *Essayist literacy*, a term coined by Scollon and Scollon (1981) in the 1980s refers to a way of communication that emphasizes logic over emotion and depersonalizes communication as if to make the language itself language autonomous. Farr made the point that essayist literacy is a natural extension of the home language of upper middle-class White people and to determine language ability and even intelligence based on the use of a specific type of literacy promotes the hegemony and inequality that schools and literacy instruction are supposed to overcome. Whether we refer to essayist literacy, cultural literacy, or other forms of language that attempt to privilege one form of literacy over the other, the intent and results are the same. What also remains the same is that just recognizing that there are multiple literacies does not mean that the literacy of various people and groups of people are automatically respected and celebrated. This volume attempts to do just that—to respect and celebrate the various kinds of literacy used by various people and groups of people. Although this respect and celebration are important in understanding the value of various kinds of literacies, they are also important in understanding the ways in which literacy has evolved and is likely to evolve in the future.

Chapter authors were presenters at the Second Watson Conference, a biannual conference hosted by the Department of English at the University of Louisville. The conference and a visiting professorship are endowed by funds from the estate of Dr. Thomas A. Watson. This second conference, titled Multiple Literacies for the 21st Century, resulted from multiple years of planning and discussion of the conference topic, culminating in conference presentations and now in these chapters selected from among those presentations.

This volume is divided into six sections, beginning with four literacy narratives from a variety of settings and moving to four studies of schooling as one site for literate practices. Part III includes five chapters that examine the complex interactions between technology and literacy. Five chapters in the fourth section of this volume expand our definitions of literacies and the pathways by which they are reached. The authors of three chapters in the final section consider rhetorical dimensions of multiple literacies. To conclude the volume, two authors reflect on themes of the second Watson conference.

LITERACY NARRATIVES/LITERACY AND LIVES

Branch, Gleason, Bell, and Hogg contribute narratives from school, community, and the workplace. Branch's chapter focuses on the stories and experiences of adult literacy learners. In bringing the stories of unsuccessful literacy learners to light, he reminds us of the ways in which disadvantaged people are forced away from literacy learning. This stark view of literacy education also has its bright side in that Branch is able to give voice to those who finally do learn to read and write for themselves and those they love.

Gleason describes methods for helping her older, returning, working students use their life experiences to understand the role of literacy in their lives and to develop their ability to acquire academic literacy. Through writing ethnographies about their lives and workplaces, these students understand the cultural worlds they inhabit, use their skills in speaking, develop academic research skills, and produce an extensive academic assignment through smaller manageable tasks. Interestingly, students often notice and comment on the uses of and beliefs about language in their workplaces and other social worlds.

Bell's chapter about teacher portfolios illustrates the ways in which collecting, selecting, and reflecting on literacy artifacts helps new teachers develop their ideas about the teaching of writing. She demonstrates the interconnected nature of lived experience, teacher education, and literacy. Her chapter provides a useful model for those interested in teacher education and new models for considering literate behavior.

Hogg's literacy narrative shows how literacy shaped and was shaped by the women of her grandmother's generation in a western Nebraska town. She explores these women's roles as *sponsors of literacy*, to use Brandt's terms, and thus challenges limited definitions of public and private literacies through the examples of their public and private writings and roles. As a result, we see literacies of women in a site little explored by previous researchers.

LITERACY AND SCHOOLING

Wardle; Leki; Beach, Eddleston, and Philippot; and Patton and Nagelhout focus on schooling as one site of literacy education and associated definitions of literate practices in their studies of school settings. Wardle's study shows that authority in producing, examining, and discussing text is related to students' knowledge about the genre of the texts in which they are working. When students understood the genre of the assignment, they were able to provide their peers appropriate rhetorical feedback. But when the genre was unfamiliar, their feedback was limited to minor technical issues. On the other hand, when students were allowed to puzzle through their understanding of an unknown genre in a group workshop, they were able to gain some understanding of their task.

In her chapter, Leki sensitizes us to second-language speakers' reactions to the ways they are typically treated within writing classes. She then reveals the great variety of meaning students find in literacy instruction by providing a cross-cultural look into the meanings of academic literacies in relation to cultural values.

Because large group discussions are an ongoing reality in U.S. classrooms, it is important to consider the ways in which skilled teachers can create dialogic exchange in large-group literature discussions. Beach, Eddleston, and Philippot study two large-group literature discussions in high school classrooms and through their comparisons of low and high levels of student participation, provide teachers with strategies for facilitating greater student involvement.

Patton and Nagelhout explore the complexities of introducing literacy as meta-understanding in science classrooms. They describe the efforts and difficulties of "reforming" science education through integration of science facts and rhetorical processes. As they report their study of classroom settings and a graduate/mentor relationship, they urge us to consider the complex ways in which rhetorical insights and understanding of science concepts must interact for successful learning.

LITERACY AND TECHNOLOGY

Tannacito; Schendel, Neal, and Hartley; Ramey; Wysocki; and Pence examine complex interactions between technology and literacy that often blur the traditional lines between reading and writing and speaking and listening as technology enables collaboration and social constructions. Tannacito's chapter details the benefits of electronic response for students, for both their writing process and the products of their writing. She contends that electronic peer response is an increasingly important literacy because of its interactive nature. The students profiled in this chapter provide an encouraging example of how electronic response can work well to support a social view of learning and writing.

Schendel, Neal, and Hartley describe their own process as they collaborated to co-author this chapter and another article online. They contribute to a study of multiple literacies by considering the intersections between collaboration within composition studies and research into online spaces. They examine the field's assumptions about collaboration and computer-mediated communication and make theoretical assertions about online collaboration.

Ramey, in analyzing the rhetoric of a military Web site, shows that the analytical concepts designed for older forms of communication also serve to understand the new literacies of new media. Classical concepts of ethos, logos, pathos, and *kairos* reveal much about the way the *MarineLINK* Web site is constructed. Even more interestingly, the new technologies bring back into focus the much neglected canons of memoria and delivery.

Wysocki's study of a children's software packages uses feminist/psychoanalytic film theory to consider the construction of gender as expressed in the content and form of the computer-based interactive multimedia. She considers the literacies we need to understand and teach the relations between the visual representations and identity developed on computer screens. She offers hope that, with careful embodiment of the spaces on screens, visual spaces can be created for child's play that are not rigidly gender-bound.

Using as a model a software program available to new teachers, Pence provides insight not only into the ways in which we can help new teachers learn but into the ways in which teachers need to learn. Set within the context of helping Europe-American teachers work with Hispanic American and Native American children, Pence's chapter blends a reconsideration of literacy with the use of technology to create culturally aware support systems for new teachers.

LITERACY AND OTHER SENSE/CAPABILITIES

Sohn, Langstraat, Swiencicki, Cheville, and Johanek explore the multiple pathways by which literacies may be developed and thus expand our conceptions of literacies. Sohn starts from what her students report about the role of music in their personal and intellectual development to consider how deeply music and literacy may be linked. Music is deeply embedded in the lives of her Appalachian students and forms a deep bond of family and communication. Using this reported material, she explores the similarities, parallels, and concrete interactions of music and literacy development, and she explores what this means for pedagogy and our attitudes toward the experiences of our students.

Langstraat examines the ways in which composition has historically considered issues of affect in writing. In particular, she considers the role of the emotional style of cool constraint that came to be entrenched in composition by the 1950s to remain dominant to the present day. By examining an influential programmatic document of the 1960s, she shows this style of literate participation became associated with reason, democracy, and cultural attainment.

Swiencicki demonstrates how visual representations can speak more forcefully and directly than words, if you know how to read the images. She shows how the *Chicago Defender* in the early 20th century educated its readers into skilled visual literacy and at the same time helped them understand the world around them more deeply. The visual and social literacy advanced in the paper helped form the political consciousness of African Americans during the period just prior to the major urban migration.

Cheville extends the notion of literacy to include the experiences of college athletes. She reveals that people who have a hyper-awareness of their physical identities often learn and relate to the world in different ways than those of us who teach and study literacy. Focusing on college athletes on and off the court, Cheville illustrates the embodied nature of knowledge that for some people cannot exist outside of the physical understandings of their own bodies.

Johanek's chapter invites us to reconsider our beliefs and assumptions about numbers and mathematics. She illustrates that like literacy, numeracy is an abstract system of representation that allows human beings to create and discover meaning. Johanek's treatment of numeracy demands that we reconsider not only our own attitudes about numbers and mathematics, but that we also reconsider our relationship as teachers and scholars toward teaching and writing as well.

CRITICAL LITERACIES AND CRITICAL THINKING ABOUT LITERACY

Ball; Bruch, Kinloch, and Marback; and Gray-Rosendale look at multiple literacies from a rhetorical viewpoint, provoking thought about literacies and critical agencies. Kevin Ball examines media reporting of the 1997 manhunt for Alis Ben Johns, a murder suspect, to reveal the way the trope of illiteracy is used differently to serve interests of regional and national communities. Local Ozark reporting treats Johns' lack of schooling as a sign of savagery in order to distance the community from what they treat as traditional regional stereotypes. National reporting used the stereotype of the uncivilized but savvy woodsman to tantalize the readers with the wild creature who must be hunted down and vanquished. The way we reject the outsider reveals the way we construct the inside of literate culture.

Bruch, Kinloch, and Marback write about the Heidelberg Project—a found art installation in Detroit. They focus on the use of signs by the residents of Detroit's Eastside protesting the use of their neighborhood as a site for art and visitation. Theorizing this resistance, Bruch, Kinloch, and Marback argue about the ways in which literacy illustrates privilege and distance in this particular site.

Gray-Rosendale details how visual literacy can strengthen and enrich written literacy within the classroom. She does this by examining graphic design and written text in the Harlem Renaissance journal *The New Negro*. She then describes how she uses the combination of text and graphics with her classes to help them see the complexity of meaning that can be created by playing word and image off against each other.

REFLECTIONS

The final section includes two pieces written in response to the themes of the Watson Conference. Pfeffer describes the literacy journey she undertook in her doctoral study. Linked to her own journey is that of the participants in a case study she conducted, the professors, and English education students in a graduate teacher preparation program. Like Pfeffer, these professors and students considered how to define literacy and what it meant for their teaching. Finally, Pfeffer reflects on the meanings of her literacy journey for her and for her own students. Bazerman, holder of the Watson Professorship in Rhetoric and Composition for the 1997-1998 year prior to the Watson Conference, reflects on this collection of meaning-making about multiple literacies as a moment in the history of literacy. Bazerman brings to the task of reflection the sensibilities of writer, reader, rhetorician, scholar, historian, and teacher. In this final chapter, he contemplates the significance of this moment in the 5,000-year history of literacy and imagines the future for literacy and its educators.

REFERENCES

Besnier, N. (1995). *Literacy, emotion and authority: Reading and writing on a polynesian atoll*. Cambridge: Cambridge University Press.

Bizzell, P. (1998). Arguing about literacy. *College English, 50*(2), 141-153.

Brandt, D. (1998). Sponsors of literacy. *College Composition and Communication, 49*(2), 165–185.

Daniel, B. (1986). Against the great leap theory of literacy. *Pretext, 7*(3-4), 181-194.

Earle, S. (1993). Someday. *Essential Steve Earle*. Universal City, CA: MCA Records.

Farr, M. (1993). Essayist literacy and other verbal performances. *Written Communication, 10*(1), 4-38.

Farrell, T.J. (1983). IQ and standard English. *College Composition and Communication, 34*(4), 470-484.

Foucault, M. (1979). *Discipline and punish: The birth of the prison*. New York: Vintage.

Goody, J., & Watt, I. (1968). The consequences of literacy. In J. Goody (Ed.), *Literacy in traditional societies* (pp. 27-84). Cambridge: Cambridge University Press.

Hartwell, P. (1985). Grammar, grammars and the teaching of grammar. *College English, 47*(1), 105-127.

Heath, S.B. (1983). *Ways of words: Language life and work in communities and classrooms*. Cambridge: Cambridge University Press.

Hirsch, E.D., Jr. (1987). *Cultural literacy: What every American needs to know.* Boston: Houghton/Mifflin.

Ogbu, J.U. (1988). Literacy and schooling in subordinate cultures: The case of Black Americans. In E.R. Kintgen, B.M. Kroll, & M. Rose (Eds.), *Perspectives on literacy* (pp. 227-242). Carbondale: Southern Illinois University Press.

Ong, W.J. (1982). *Orality and literacy: The technologizing of the word.* London & New York: Routledge.

Scollon, R., & Scollon, S. (1981). *Narrative, literacy and face in interethnic communication.* Norwood, NJ: Ablex.

Scribner, S., & Cole, M. (1981). *The psychology of literacy.* Cambridge, MA: Harvard University Press.

Street, B.V. (1984). *Literacy in theory and practice.* Cambridge, UK: Cambridge University Press.

I

LITERACY NARRATIVES: LITERACY AND LIVES

1

IN THE HALLWAYS OF THE LITERACY NARRATIVE

Violence and the Power of Literacy

Kirk Branch
Montana State University

> *I remember if I couldn't get the lesson the teacher would put me in the hallway.*
>
> —Al[1]

Following a series of interviews with William, part of a larger project of collecting the literacy narratives and educational autobiographies of seven adults at Rainier Community Learning Center in Seattle, he and I discussed the stories he had told me. Throughout the interviews, William repeatedly stressed that he almost never attached a purpose to the literacy education he received from childhood to the present. At a community college adult basic education class, for example, he learned to identify verbs, adverbs, and adjectives, "I used to know all that junk, but I don't know it now, though." He summarized his years of schooling as such: "I just did whatever they had me to do, I would do it . . . I ain't never found nothin' interestin' so I just do whatever." Near the end of our interview, however, William emphasized his current practice of reading the Bible several times a week, a recent and, by his account, his first literate habit. This struck me as a way in which he was finally developing his own purpose for literacy, and in reference to that, I told him, "I find your story to be inspiring." William smiled at me and said, "Well, I don't."

The meaning I strain to make of William's story highlights my desire, a desire also visible in popular and academic discourse on education, to find such stories about literacy inspiring. I use William's troubled narrative to bolster my own expectations about literacy's transformational power. That this reading makes no sense to William, has no connection to his own experience, in fact negates his interpretation of that experience, emphasizes a vast difference in perspective between how I read literacy as a scholar and teacher, and how William understands literacy as an adult with limited reading and writing skills. Miller (1996) argued that "the solicitation of one kind of narrative simultaneously prohibits the production of other kinds of narratives, for this is what allows one to accrue cultural capital within a given institutional context" (p. 280). So it is, I argue, with the interpretation of literacy narratives, as in the way my reading of William's story, professionally rendered and supported, disallows his own.

In this chapter, I examine the literacy narratives students bring with them when they return to school as adults, and I examine the myriad ways students have experienced and come to define literacy throughout their lives. I make available alternative approaches to literacy that stem from my interviews with adults who have limited reading and writing skills. These perspectives typically have little or no cultural capital in conversations dominated by literate professionals who speak and write about what nonliterate adults need and why they need it and who definitively proclaim the uses of learning and the function of literacy. As my story with William indicates, it is possible to focus their interpretations solely on the inspirational, to fit them into what Eldred and Mortensen (1988) have called the "disciplinary romance" (p. 513) of literacy teachers, for these students did share experiences with and notions about literacy that match public and professional expectations of such stories, stories that, at least for me, are inspiring. Stopping there, however, romanticizes the experiences of these students beyond recognition.

I take my title from a story Al told about his childhood schooling in a coal mining town in the Washington Cascades. Al's experience, echoed in several other accounts I collected from students, suggests that the failure to live up to a narrative of educational progress has consequences that go beyond having one's story silenced:

> I remember if I couldn't get the lesson the teacher would put me in the hallway . . . I don't know what the reason was. Maybe she figured you were stopping everybody else from learning or something. I guess that's what it was all about. I remember that, in fourth grade. I was

> there by myself. And that, that was many years ago and they still do it the same way now. They go the same process as they did years ago. If you don't seem to keep up, if you don't seem to understand, they want to put you in the hall, or something like that. 'Cause I had the same experience with my son, here in Seattle.

Michael reported being sent to run errands in grade school: "Go to the store for the teacher, go around to a different classroom, give other teachers some note an' stuff, what they need, bring back stuff for three or four teachers . . . Mostly because I wasn't able to do the work, so you know, I'd be outta the class." William reported being sent to study in the kitchen at another learning center while the other students, more advanced, prepared for the GED test. These experiences suggest an effort to remove from the classroom—the central cultural site of education—students who disrupt the visions of possibility and progress, the utopia, that exist in any syllabus, curriculum, or assignment.

I emphasize these removals because they help make clear the potential physical consequences of adherence to a progress plot for education; not only are stories forced into an inspirational coda that crowds out other less laudatory interpretations, but students themselves become threatened for failing to meet these expectations. Interpretive violence and the violence of physical removal and punishment, I argue, are intricately connected. By spending time in what I call the hallways of the literacy narrative, listening to versions of literacy narratives as told by these adult students, I argue that undereducated adults, and children, commonly experience the power of literacy as a violent force that enacts physical and social injuries, injuries that ultimately lead to their exclusion from the classroom. This is, of course, a significant inversion of the "power of literacy" as it appears in the often told and intentionally moving story of the adult learning to read and write.

In that familiar narrative, an adult realizes that she needs to learn to read and write, whether for work or family or personal esteem. Some crisis or meeting provides her with impetus to return to school or find a teacher, and doing so, after the requisite struggle and conflict, leads her to a successful resolution of the crisis, through learning. Literacy (and its teacher) saves the day again, giving birth to another productive adult. Or, if "productive" is too pragmatic, another engaged learner, another informed parent, another empowered citizen. The classroom, or its narrative equivalent, holds an almost sacred power, the ritualized site of moral, psychological, and intellectual development, a place of growth and nearly unbounded potential. And within that classroom, the student–teacher relationship works toward its inevitable outcome: The student becomes educated, the teacher educates, everyone is inspired.

Especially in discussions of adult literacy education, where students are assumed to come freely to this idealized classroom, the only barrier to the story's positive conclusion appears to be the student. Rockhill noted that a lack of motivation commonly appears as "a major explanation for adult non-participation in literacy programmes" (p. 156) in the United States:

> Thus, as the argument goes, freedom is increased through the social provision of more educational opportunities from among which the individual, as agent, is morally obligated to choose. The adult educator's responsibility is clear—to fight for the provision of more education—and once this is accomplished, to mobilise and motivate adults to participate in the opportunities so provided. (p. 162)

Provide the space, that is, and the students will, or rather should, follow. In this model, uneducated adults have only to make the right choice.

Invert the "power of literacy," however, into a potentially violent force, and the goals of education become at once more urgent and less transformative. Rather than allowing students to experience literacy's transformative powers, education becomes instead a struggle against those powers as they act upon students by, say, removing them from the classroom. These adults described much more harrowing forms of violence related to literacy, as I describe, and overall their stories demand that we curb the interpretive power of the traditional literacy narrative over their own self-represented lives. Although nearly all of the students interviewed here proclaim their present return to school as a strongly positive experience, and I certainly do not want to deny their real power to inspire, theirs are also narratives fraught with problems and challenges and very real pain. Stepping into the hallways of the literacy narrative honors the complexity of the perspectives and experiences undereducated adults have regarding literacy.

INTERVIEWING FOR LITERACY NARRATIVES: PROBLEMS AND POSSIBILITIES

Because one of my concerns has to do with the ways in which, as Stuckey (1991) wrote, "literacy oppresses" (p. 64), it is important to reflect on my own position and process as hyper-literate researcher soliciting and interpreting highly personal narratives from undereducated adults. In seven tape-recorded interviews, all conducted at Rainier, I asked questions about and encouraged students to reflect on their educational biographies. Interviews lasted from 45 minutes to 3 hours each. We spoke about literacy in their homes, their earliest memories of education and reading and writing, their experiences with schooling as children up to the present, and their lives outside of school—work, family, social—as they involved literacy and education. In some cases, they struggled to remember experiences they had not considered for years; on the whole, however, most of them had already thought extensively about their educational histories, so they had much to tell me. My relationship to Rainier is also very important: I began this project after having worked as a volunteer teacher and tutor at the center for several years. I have described the center and my relationship to it elsewhere in more detail (Branch, 1998), but I must note here that I believed firmly in the center's commitment to participatory education and that I learned about and applied the practices and theories of educators like Paulo Freire and Myles Horton there long before I encountered them in the academy. At the time of the interviews, I considered myself an active part of the community established there. I had known many of the students for several years, and some had been students in classes I taught there.

Linde's (1993) description of the anthropological interview provides some useful qualifiers for my study. These interviews, she noted, are not spontaneous, but rather structured by the questioner's point of view:

> The intentions and questions of the anthropologist, the effects of an interpreter or of the anthropologist's imperfect command of the subject's language, the differences between the discourse forms appropriate in the subject's culture and those that the anthropologist expects, and the possible interpolations and deletions of editors all mean that this type of life history cannot be considered purely as the speaker's self-report. (p. 47)

Although mine are not strictly anthropological interviews, these qualifiers became issues both during the interviews and in the analysis in this chapter. My intentions were to elicit literacy histories, and although the interviews were largely unstructured, the particular ordering of events and situations had everything to do with the direction in which I steered the conversation. I also shape the narratives simply by taking comments out of context and placing them next to other comments. In many ways, then, these interviews become my story. And of course my subjects did not just approach me and begin to discuss some of their literacy experiences that they thought I might want to hear. I sought them out and focused their stories toward the issues and details that I wanted to examine.

Also, studying the transcripts, I find my more-than-occasional attempts to direct the students or their own responses at times awkward and embarrassing. This excerpt from my interview with June, similar to the earlier example cited with William, shows me ardently reproducing a version of the traditional literacy narrative even in the face of her own interpretation, so forcefully that she capitulates somewhat. I am guiding the interview here toward a reflection on how she influenced her children's and grandchildren's educations:

> *Me:* *Your grandchildren, though, have graduated?*
>
> *June:* *Oh yeah. All four. My daughter that passed, her two graduated high school, and my youngest daughter's.*
>
> *Me:* *Did you have any influence in that happening?*
>
> *June:* *No. My daughter, her daughter told her that she wanted to go, to finish high school. There's no reason for her not to finish, she said. But just for her to finish high school. But now she's goin' to college to be a ticket agent or somethin'. And her son, there's just nothing for either of them did not want to finish high school.*
>
> *Me:* *It sounds like you got the ball rolling. . . . In your family you got things moving.*
>
> *June:* *Yeah. Now, like, I'm going to school and my two grandkids, I come home talkin', and they so happy for me, that I'm goin' to school.*

Undaunted by June's refusal to take credit, I turn my hopeful question into a declaration of her agency that ignores her own assessment. In the process, this clearly becomes something other than June's own "self-report." In some ways, too, it was a priority to me that these interviews be informal, more like conversations, because I was uncomfortable with simply asking one question after another; but perhaps as a consequence, there are moments when my teaching voice threatens to dominate the "conversation." And of course, any notion that these were just "conversations" is a fiction.

Still, my intention (although at the time I did not name it this) was to initiate what Portelli (1997) has called (presumably following Geertz's "thick description") a "thick dialogue," which he opposed to a questionnaire: "In a judicial interrogation or a sociological questionnaire, the informant's answer to a given question may not influence either the form or the order of the questions to follow, but in a thick dialogue, questions arise dialectically from the answers" (p. 11). In my interviews, I did not sit down with a scripted list of questions I wanted to ask, although I ended up asking many of the same questions; rather, I felt that it was important to let our dialogue guide the discussion. This meant that I participated in the interviews not only by asking questions but by responding to them as well, by engaging during the interviews with the stories the adults told me. If it is safe to say that this has its perils (as seen in the excerpt with June), I agree with Portelli (1997) that "what the interviewer reveals about him or herself is ultimately relevant in orienting the interview toward monologue or self-reflexive thick dialogue" (p. 12); if I expect my students to be forthcoming with me, I must also be forthcoming with them. What keeps this from being a conversation comes, I think, from the way authority is derived in this setting:

> By opening the conversation, the interviewer defines the roles and establishes the basis of narrative authority. In fact, although an oral autobiographical narrative may look on the surface very much like any other autobiographical *text*, it constitutes a very different autobiographical *act*, because the basis of authority is different. Autobiography (especially if written for publication) begins with a person's decision to write about herself or himself, but in the interview, the initiative is taken by the interviewer, from whom the legitimacy to speak is ostensibly derived. (Portelli, 1997, p. 9)

In other words, I decided that these stories had authority, and I granted them that authority by asking for and recording them, and later, now, by presenting them in an academic chapter.

My transcriptions of course affected their speech and their stories; as I transcribed the several hours of taped conversations, I gradually began to edit out the "uh"s and the repeated words. I did this in part because all of the students requested copies of the transcripts, and exact transcripts of the interviews proved almost unreadable for beginning and struggling readers; also, I was examining these narratives for content, not linguistic features. Whatever the reasons, the transition from tape to transcript clearly influenced the structure and the content of the interviews.

Linde's (1993) note about the appropriate discourse forms also reflect difficulties I had in collecting the interviews. I began the process by working with a colleague at the center to identify students we thought would provide interesting interviews. We selected students whom we knew had a fairly sophisticated level of reflection and an interest in talking about their own education. After I had conducted my initial interviews, my friend suggested that I visit some classes, describe my project, and ask any students if they might be interested in participating. Although I found one excellent source—Arlene—I also ran into some difficulties doing this. In one class, I knew that two of the students who volunteered would be inappropriate subjects; one was a recent immigrant from Somalia with extremely limited English skills, and the other could not reflect on his experiences when I asked him to elaborate or supply more details. And although I knew this about both of them when they volunteered, having solicited student participation in this way, I felt obliged to carry out the interviews. Neither of them appears in this study, but I describe this here to include another note about how I shaped these narratives by selecting and including students who met a particular set of criteria, thus excluding others. Finally, all of these students made the very difficult decision to return to school as adults, which meant a public acknowledgment of their "illiteracy".[2] Their simple and determined presence in an educational institution suggests a sometimes surprising belief (in light of their stories) in the positive powers of education, and so I imagine that similarly skilled adults who never return to school would present very different perspectives.

I also do not want to claim that this study is statistically relevant. I am not trying to make grand claims about the adult literacy population when I describe similarities or themes that I saw appearing throughout these interviews. All seven of my subjects are African American,[3] four women and three men, six of them older than 40 years, four from either Texas or Louisiana. I cannot generalize from them about the experience of adult literacy students or on the basis of age or race. Nor am I attempting here to be comprehensive. Indeed, part of my claim here is that discussions of literacy must be contextualized, and such contextualization defies generalizing. Although I highlight similarities across these interviews, I do so more to suggest the complicated ways that students have experienced literacy and literacy education throughout their lives than to make universal claims about their stories.[4] And although the experiences of students at centers in different parts of the country, even in Seattle, would no doubt raise other issues, they would be similar to the students represented in these interviews simply because all adult students have extensive histories with literacy that predate their return to school. If these interviews allow any generalization, it is that adult literacy students bring with them, in their return to school, vast and varied experiences with literacy. These experiences must be taken into account in their education, of course, but we should also recognize these stories as lived correctives to the bliss of the literacy narrative. Literacy narratives, as these interviews suggest, are not necessarily so easily redemptive, nor are the powers of literacy described within them experienced only in positive ways.

VIOLENCE AND THE FUNCTION OF LITERACY

Brodkey (1989) suggested one way that the power of literacy functions in her description of a letter writing project between graduate students training to teach adult basic education (ABE) and actual ABE students. Brodkey noted that the graduate students often read past the words of the ABE students as they related to class and gender. The prospective teachers ignored references to social or financial problems, for example, or they abruptly shifted the topic of conversation in the letters away from class-related issues. For Brodkey, this represents the discursive power that teachers have over their students, a power that attempts to create the classroom as a space free of class and prohibits students from defining identity in their own terms. This power, she claimed, also has the potential to alienate students whose identities are not acknowledged in the classroom:

> Discursive hegemony of teachers over students is usually posed and justified in developmental terms—as cognitive deficits, emotional or intellectual immaturity, ignorance, and most recently, cultural literacy—any one of which would legitimate asymmetrical relationships between its knowing subjects, teachers, and its unknowing subjects, students . . . the teachers frenetically protected educational discourse from class, and in their respective refusals to admit class concerns into the letters, they first distanced and then alienated themselves from their correspondents. (p. 139)

Echoing Miller's claim about how one narrative approach drowns out another, Brodkey (1989) argued that educational discourse "insists that [students] articulate themselves as the subjects teachers represent, or not at all" (p. 140). In adult literacy education, the self-articulations of students appear most commonly in speeches and media portrayals which highlight the rebirth through literacy those students have experienced. Beyond that, however, students have little or no effect on the determination of curricular theories, goals, and approaches. This too is a kind of "discursive hegemony," one I call here a *power of literacy* exercised over others.

This use of the power of literacy immediately contrasts, I hope, to the more common usage suggested in the ways literate professionals define the use of learning, definitions that suggest the beneficial and intrinsic power of literacy. Thus, depending on the theoretical and political approach, literacy has the power to make a person employable and the nation economically competitive; literacy has the power to raise the self-esteem of an individual; literacy has the power to allow equal participation in a cultural conversation; literacy has the power to reveal the oppressive codes that structure one's life and to change that oppression. In all cases, the power of literacy rests in its positive transformational effect, and this transformation is one way of describing the use of literacy.

The idea of a functional literacy, for example, holds out the acquisition of basic literacy skills as the primary way that adults will gain a level of status as social participants. Functional literacy, as Levine (1986) noted, is typically understood as "a level of literacy less rudimentary than the capacity to provide a signature and read a simple message, but less than full fluency" (p. 25). Levine traced the term's first appearance to concerns during World War II that an alarming number of troops were, in the words of the army, illiterate, "incapable of understanding the kinds of written instructions that are needed for carrying out basic military functions and tasks" (cited in Levine, 1986, p. 26). Levine argued that over the past 50 years, this term has prioritized employment as a primary goal of literacy instruction and remains a powerful concept "largely because it promises substantial collective and personal returns from equipping individuals with an ill-defined but relatively modest level of competence" (p. 35). Functional literacy, that is, appears as an achievable goal with the widespread and positive effect of improving individual employment opportunities and national economic competitiveness.

This approach to functional literacy is compelling in its practicality and its transformative power; it appeals to a literate person's perception of the overwhelming centrality of print in everyday life and work. And, it is an emphasis, certainly, that appears throughout the interviews I conducted. June, for example, an African American in her 60s from Louisiana, sees literacy as useful in part because it allows her to be a smart and safe consumer:

> I guess when you go to the store and see how they, they don't mean to cheat you . . . but if you don't know how to read, you don't know how to read your slips from the store. An' I don't shop unless I see a sale paper. I wouldn't even be able to see the prices in the sale paper. Might know the numbers but I wouldn't know the name.

Like June, Al, an African American in his 70s from a coal-mining town in the Washington Cascades, emphasizes the function of literacy and the difficulty of being nonliterate in day-to-day activities. Here he describes a visit to the doctor's office where he first had to fill out a medical information form:

> It was a big, big application. They wanted to know everything. Your medical history, what did your mother die from, what did your great-grandmother die from, how long did she live an' all that junk. An' you'd fill it out the best you could an' you'd take it back up there an' they'd just, "Hey, that's gotta be filled out, that's gotta be filled out," an' they wouldn't try to help you at all. I guess they say, "Well, I got my education. You're gonna have to get yours." I said, "Well, I done it the best I could" an' then they'd finally, somebody would help you with this.

Both of these activities, shopping and filling out forms, regularly appear in curricula emphasizing functional literacy, and both are clearly a priority to June and Al. In a sense, then, these statements could be used as support for prioritizing functional literacy, for making it the centerpiece of adult literacy education.

It is important, however, to note the emphases of June and Al's statements, up against an official proclamation of functional literacy. Here, for example, is a recent definition by the UNESCO Institute for Education (1998): to be *functionally literate* means "being able to make sense of the increasingly complex messages that need to be understood if one is to participate actively in the societies of today—for instance, the ability to communicate, to understand printed instructions, to use basic numeracy skills in daily life and, more importantly, to be able to go on learning through written media." The focus in this definition, as in most approaches to functional literacy, is on empowering adults to be more active social participants, which emphasizes the positive transformational powers of literacy. June and Al, however, present an approach to functional literacy that highlights a less salutary power, that of literates over nonliterates. The exercise of this power can be unintentional, as in June's concerns over being short-changed while shopping, or intentional, at least perceived as such, as in Al's example of the condescension he experienced in the doctor's office. But in both cases, June and Al highlight Stuckey's (1991) claim that "In American society the struggle is between those who can read and write and those who cannot or have no opportunity to, and struggle is over who is entitled to negotiate" (p. 65). Functional literacy, approached from this side, could thus be conceived as a literacy gained in order to claim the right to negotiate against the exercise of the power of literacy.

A further example might clarify what I mean by this shift in perspective. Barbara, an African American in her 70s, said that she wanted to learn to read and write ever since she witnessed people losing their land to oil companies in her east Texas farming community:

> I needed to learn something. That's how so many peoples back there got cheated outta their land. Because they couldn't read an' write and they'd think they was doin' one thing and they was signin' papers, signin' everything they had away, because they didn't know how to read and write. See [the oil companies] knew that, so that's how they did it. . . . For them to get on the property to drill, then they would have to lease the land for so many years. An' you would have to sign their lease paper. In place of them signin' the lease paper for release they were signin' a paper for sellin' because they knew they didn't know any better. . . . Takin' the land. They wasn't leasin' it. They was buyin' it, instead of leasin' it.

As Barbara describes it here, these farmers needed literacy in order to save their land, to negotiate against the exercise of the power of the oil companies from acting negatively on them. The function, the use of literacy, in these examples, is less about becoming empowered or active social participants than about limiting the extent of literate power over nonliterates.

The situations I described thus far—being removed from school, being cheated, having land stolen—describe an economic and cultural violence, but participants also directly linked physical violence to their literacy experiences, as in William's primary years in central Louisiana:

> Miss Cunningham, she'll whup you, . . . if you flunked somethin' or if you made a bad grade or didn't do your work, you got a whuppin', an' she had a strap they called Doc, a leather strap . . . that come around with a hand like that, and in the middle it had holes in it, and she would tell you, say, like you didn't pass or something like that, she'd say, "William, go in the bookroom"—a little closet where they kept the books—"reach up on to that top shelf an' get me the such-a-colored book" . . . I couldn't reach it so what I did, . . . I got up on the shelf tiptoe. As I tiptoed, she walked in behind me, put her hand up against me, I was on my toes, and she got the whuppin'. . . . An' every time that strap hit, you'd feel it suckin' the meat of your clothes when it come loose.

As with the experiences of being removed from the classroom, students repeatedly describe a violent lack of physical agency in relation to their own learning. Although I never asked about this specifically, students repeatedly recounted experiences of being beaten in school as punishment for failing one or another literacy requirement. And several of the students described being unable to attend school, first as children and later as adults, because of the economic priority of work over education. I want to spend some time citing and examining these stories, because they suggest the power of schooled experiences to significantly shape literacy practices that can last a lifetime.

Street (1995) developed the idea of literacy practices from Heath's (1982) notion of a literacy event. Heath defined a literacy event as "any occasion in which a piece of writing is integral to the nature of a participant's interactions and their interpretive processes" (p. 93). A discussion of literacy practices, however, refers "not only to the event itself but to the conceptions of the reading and writing process that people hold when they are engaged in the event" (Street, 1995, p. 133). For these students, familiar schooled literacy events surrounding spelling and reading (and occasionally writing) often became skewed into literacy events involving physical and mental abuse, which in turn encouraged literacy practices involving deception and absence. Students experience here the power of literacy not as a tool for agency; rather, the "powers of literacy" have acted on these students physically in ways that, for much of their lives, effectively alienated them from full literacy.

These experiences once again provide a way of understanding literacy as more than simply a cognitive or intellectual issue; because students' loss of physical agency is intrinsically linked to power dynamics in and out of the classroom, literacy can be understood as physical and an ideological issue as well. As Shapiro (1999) argued, attending to the body in relation to schooling provides a perspective in which a "specific social reality emerges, expressing a distinct set of social relations and assumptions about the world, and how one lives in that world. The child learns these in that which is most visibly controlled—the body. Therefore, the effects of such a process come to be associated, in the early years, in the way curriculum is geared to 'body management'" (p. 86). For many of the students I interviewed, beating became the most obvious form of "body management," and they responded by developing ways to fake their way through or avoid literacy events altogether.

For several of these students, learning in school quickly became associated with pain, fear, and avoidance; the most vivid memories are often of punishment. Students remember the rods teachers used, the various reasons for and the rituals of punishment; for some, this discipline became the defining aspect of their education. Punishment drove students from school and encouraged them to devise strategies for hiding their inabilities. In all cases, however, punishment became a central part of particular literacy events.

Arlene, an African-American woman in her early 60s from a small farming community outside of Dallas, describes her education at an all-Black school in terms that make beatings the central emphasis:

> When I went to school, when you didn't know something, you got whuppin's on your hand, and some of them, you got strappin's, because you didn't know something. So I got where I didn't like school real early, because there was a lot of stuff that I didn't know, and there was nobody to teach me because my parents didn't know. But the teachers didn't see that, they just thought, well, you didn't know, so they whupped you. . . . You'd have to read, you'd have to spell, and learn words to spell. And if you didn't know them, and how to spell them when you came back to class, you got a whupping.

Arlene's memories of punishment in school center on literacy events; students were meant to demonstrate knowledge of some sort—in this case, spelling—and in her description, "whuppings" are as much a part of the literacy event as the spelling words themselves. She describes school as primarily emphasizing "when you didn't know something," which she describes in community terms. What schools do, in this description, is ferret out and punish not only an individual's but a family's lack of knowledge. Arlene is "whupped" because neither she nor her parents have the literacy skills that school demands.

Ironically, Arlene specifically remembers a traumatic beating in direct response to a demonstration of her literacy. Following one incident where a student was beaten so harshly that he died, Arlene's father told school authorities that if his daughter needed disciplining, he, and not they, would do it.

> And then I got a whupping at school 'cause some boy and me was playing. He was writing stuff on the desk and I wrote stuff on the desk and some of the stuff we shouldn't have been writing on the desk. So he called the teacher, and the teacher seen what I wrote on the desk and the teacher whupped me. He whupped me with the strap that had holes in it. When I went home I had all these welts on me, little holes . . . so they was trying to doctor me at home 'cause I had these great big old welts and whips on me and my daddy didn't know whether I was gonna live or die either. They were really big, and it was really scary. It scared me and it scared him too.

Arlene is once again disciplined as part of a literacy event here, but in this case it is for "writing stuff on the desk" in violation of school rules. Arlene connects both a dislike for school and a tendency to miss a lot of classes with these beatings. Although she continued in school until she married, she says her parents, only briefly educated themselves, allowed her to stay home when she wanted. "[My mom] wouldn't make me go back if they was gonna beat me." Understandably, such experiences made school alienating and frightening, especially within classes such as English where failure was justification for harsh punishment.[5]

As with Arlene, punishment for Michael was a ritualized aspect of literacy events in school, and failure meant the paddle. For Michael, regularly missing school was directly connected with the literacy event of spelling tests; I would go so far as to argue that these absences themselves are properly considered literacy events, using Heath's definition, because a piece of writing is central to them. Michael, now in his 40s, describes avoiding his Detroit area school from fear of punished failure: "The school used to have spelling tests on Friday and each word you'd miss you'd get a whack with the paddle. I would skip school on Fridays sometimes to keep from having to take the test. I'd play sick at home, you know, all kinds of ways to get around it." We can also see how these literacy events helped to shape the students' literacy practices: The beatings that Arlene and Michael describe here shaped their view of schooled literacy as something to avoid; reading and writing were tightly connected with "the strap" or "the paddle." For these students (and for Arlene's family), beatings associated with literacy events became legitimate reasons for skipping school, an early shaping of their literacy practices.

Another manifestation of the ways these literacy events shaped literacy practices comes in the specific and often intricate strategies these students devised to keep from being beaten by avoiding failure in the classroom. In order to distract her teacher from recognizing her poor spelling, for example, Arlene remembers devising a plan that almost backfired:

> One time I copied [the spelling words] frontwards and I copied 'em backwards. And I was hopin' she'd do one of those. . . . She called 'em, and then I had turned 'em in and I made a good mark. She says "Oh that's good." Said "Arlene you get up, stand up here an' you spell all them words" cause I made a good mark. An' I couldn't spell any of 'em, actually. I just was tryin' to keep from getting' a whuppin'. . . . She said "Well, how did you do them if you couldn't spell 'em?" And I never did tell her why. I just didn't want to get a whuppin' and that was one of the ways.

William's strategy for spelling tests involved a complicated process of memorizing letters in each word on a list by rolling his eyes once for each letter. During the test, the rolling of his eyes would trigger the correct spelling, but recall depended on knowing the exact order the teacher would use to call words, and he quickly forgot one list in memorizing another. Here, students fake ability in a particular literacy event in order to avoid being beaten, a literacy practice that emphasizes deception over performance, and recalls the ways that adults described hiding their inability to read later in life. Success in these literacy events is contingent not on learning the spelling words, but on escaping unharmed from the threatening situation.

It is notable in these stories of punishment that most of them involve the literacy event of spelling tests, especially since adults who write in class for the first time in several years commonly worry about their spelling, using it as an excuse for not being able to write. At the same time, then, that these rituals of punishment can drive students to turn away from school, they also reinforce the idea that literacy is about correctness, and that correctness is everything, crucial enough to demand punishment. These stories also highlight the academic ritual of the examination, which Foucault (1977) called "a perpetual comparison of each and all that made it possible both to measure and to judge" (p. 186). Beating, certainly, is one way of enacting judgment, but in its very brutality it is easy to brush aside as a practice of the past, one that only older students have experienced. Sarah, a 19-year-old working toward her GED, suggests that although in-school beatings may be mostly of the past, other methods of measuring and judging carry a similar public weight and provide ways of dividing students that have their own, more subtle, physicality. She describes

> knowing as if you're competing to get a good grade like everyone else. . . . I felt more embarrassed because I was getting low grades, and then I felt humiliated when the teachers would announce your grade. . . . When they're reading off the grades that everyone got, they'll tell everyone what their grade was. Or passing the papers around face up, so I felt ashamed . . . for me I felt humiliated, embarrassed, ashamed, wanted to be more quiet . . . the students with the high grades would say "I got this and this and this" and you would automatically feel bad.

Although Sarah is not beaten for failure, she is still singled out physically and psychologically within the classroom. I include this here to suggest that even if the overt physicality of beatings no longer occur within classrooms, other practices exist that have similar effects on students. Sarah's discussion highlights the ways that examination works to make students constantly visible to one another and to the institutions. Her lifelong near hatred for school suggests that literacy events such as the examination, even without beatings, have the power to profoundly and adversely shape individual literacy practices.

Foucault (1977) showed how a procedure like the examination remains physical; that is, how this type of examination separates individuals one from another. In fact, the examination Sarah describes, in which the outcomes are made public in one way or another, seems almost innovative in the terms Foucault used here:

> It is the fact of being constantly seen, of being able always to be seen, that maintains the disciplined individual in his subjection. And the examination is the technique by which power, instead of emitting the signs of its potency, instead of imposing its mark on its subjects, holds them in a mechanism of objectification. In this space of domination, disciplinary power maintains its potency, essentially, by arranging objects. (p. 187)

In other words, the examination as Sarah experienced it becomes a more efficient, although less brutal, method of subjecting students. Her description may not evoke the same wince of imagined pain that William's recounting of "Doc" causes, but it is a physical memory of literacy, perhaps even of punishment, nonetheless. I want to suggest, then, that one function of literacy in the classrooms these students describe was immediately practical: knowing how to spell, or getting a good grade, functioned to keep one from getting hit with the strap, the paddle, the power of literacy.

Although I do not have the space to detail this fully here, many of these students, especially the older ones who grew up in the south, described not being able to attend school as children because they had to work. Barbara's experience indicates the extent that work could disrupt schooling. Now in her 70s, Barbara attends two classes a week in addition to working as a cook in an elementary school cafeteria. Originally from a tiny town in east Texas, she has never known the experience of attending school when she didn't have to work. As a child in that community, Barbara went to school in a church with other Black children only when they could not work; for most of the year, however, they could work:

> We would pick cotton September and October and November, the last of November, sometime in November we'd go to school. December, and January, February, long in there we'd get to go to school. You put all them months together and you may get three good months, maybe four. Because they start plowin' ground and the next you know that corn be poppin' up, the next thing you know you be thinnin' corn. Next thing choppin' cotton. So you just didn't have much chance of goin' to school.

At the age of 12, Barbara quit completely, forced by economic circumstances to work as a way of helping her family survive: "Why I had to quit, I had to eat. If you don't work you don't eat. You don't have no place to live. My mom didn't have no husband, and I had three brothers and one sister and she had to pay rent, she had to buy groceries, we had to buy clothes." After she quit, "the learnin' I got was through work. Whatever anybody tell me or show me, I do it." She describes an economy organized around the primacy of Black labor, where children's value as workers made schooling secondary.

Not surprisingly, the priority of work over school became more common for adults, who work inside and outside of the home. Arlene describes passing up an opportunity to go in order to take care of her family:

> I kinda wanted to go [to school], but I couldn't because I had a child, I had to take care of the child. I had to more or less think about how to survive than going to school, so I did that. Then, I had the chance when I coulda went back to school, but I had got married and had kids, and that meant that I would have to leave my kids for long periods of time and I wouldn't do that, because I thought they needed more attention. I stayed with them and got them off to school and did this, that and the other and was back home by the time they were to cook dinner, stuff like that.

Here, "this, that and the other" described Arlene's house cleaning jobs. Al also had ambitions to return to school which were unattainable because of work: "You think about goin' back. At that time, you workin' so hard 'bout all you can do is just work and try to make it. You think about it, tryin'. But you don't get around to it." Again the priority of work—rather than lack of ambition or motivation to better oneself—determines the ability of these students to attend school.

Each of these students connects their lack of literate success to continued and in some cases lifelong pressures from working. I argue for a conception of these experiences again as related to the physical experience of literacy. For these students, literacy existed quite literally in a separate place, a place where they could not be because their productive bodies were needed elsewhere. Thus, these work experiences also directly shaped literacy practices. Because economic conditions demanded an understanding of reading and writing as less important than working, these experiences reinforce the notion that literacy is less important than earning a living; thus, the necessity of working had direct implications for understanding literacy.

Listen to these adults speak of their own experiences with literacy—their experiences of being beaten, of being removed from classrooms, of being compelled to work instead of going to school—and literacy takes on a physical and ideological presence. Physical, because students experience it acting on their own bodies; and ideological, because their relation to literacy, like all relations to literacy, is intricately connected to power relations in and out of school, to the teacher's and the school's ability to control their future and to the necessity to work instead of attend school as a way of providing for themselves and their families. These students help us understand better a process of alienation and separation, literacy narratives in which literacy is physically absent and unattainable. They also remind us that, more often than not, the ideological has physical manifestations.

In light of these reflections, I want to suggest that one way of understanding functional literacy is as a literacy in reaction to violence, what nonliterate people, that is, need in order to avoid being acted on negatively by and negotiate against the power of literacy. This is, I think, a critical distinction to the idea of functional literacy as a tool of social empowerment. Although a literacy gained in order to stave off the powers of literacy may have some real and valued effects (i.e., keeping your family's land, not getting hit with a strap) and so should remain a focus of literacy education, a literacy defined primarily in opposition to violence is in effect a reactionary literacy and thus severely limited. Under these circumstances, any movement beyond this narrow approach must be recognized as both creative and political, because it acts in defiance to this powerful norm.

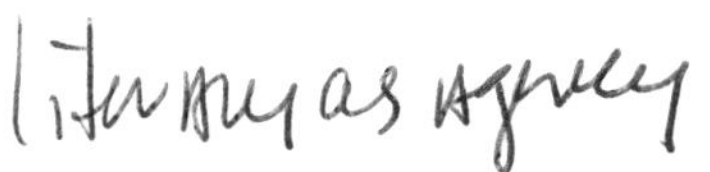

"WHAT'S THE USE OF LEARNIN'?" BEYOND THE FUNCTIONAL

Powell's (1999) perspective on what she called a "transformative literacy" emphasizes that "students must believe that their words will be heard, and that the hearing of their words will have the potential not just to inform, but also to inspire." Students, she claimed, need "to feel the authority of language for their own lives, and to trust in the power of their words to affect change" (p. 100). I read her vision, in light of my reflections, as a call to remember that literacy scholars and teachers cannot dismiss notions of transformation, power, and inspiration in relation to literacy, however vexing they may be. Instead, we need to ask questions of agency: Who is transformed? By what power and for what purpose? And on what do we base our inspiration? Making agency a central issue provides a way of starting to move beyond a literacy in reaction to power and toward a literacy as a claiming of power.

I turn now to two students, Michael and June, whose statements about their goals and experiences suggest a literacy that transcends a reaction to violence, one in which they not only "feel the authority of language for their own lives," but claim it. Michael, who had been a student at Rainier for 4 years at the time of our interview, said that his goals for learning had not changed since he started at the center: "I want a GED, and I want to attend college. Them are my goals. . . . Hasn't changed. I still have the same goals, and one day they gonna happen." Michael cited his most important goal as "to be able to be productive, and in order for me to be productive I have to be fluent in readin' and writin'. . . . I still have one goal at the top of my list, and that's to better myself. However long it takes, that's what I've gotta do, and that's what I'm gonna do." But what does this mean, "to better myself," "to be more productive"? In a more recent conversation I had with Michael, he stated that he did not mean by this that literacy would make him a better person than a nonreader; to better yourself in this context meant to become an asset to one's community. And Michael addresses this clearly in our interviews. Here, he describes work he currently does for the King County Literacy Coalition, speaking to solicit both more students and more money for literacy programs:

> I usually tell the life experience part and there usually be another speaker speak about the money expenses, the part they need for donations. We're usually workin' with a team. I do a five or ten minute speech, and then the other person do a five or ten minute speech. It works like that. That makes me feel like I have some worth as bein' a student here. I'm not givin' nothin' but a little of my time, but it still makes me feel good to know that, by me goin' out to different places we may get a

> couple more students in here that needs some help, or we might get some tutors to come in. We're asking for tutors and students. I feel that somebody has to do it.

For Michael, this already begins to address his goal of bettering himself and of being more productive; after he has gained fluency in reading and writing, he plans on continuing this work as a tutor too:

> I'm tryin' to give something back, because if we learn something and don't do anything with it, what's the use of learnin'? I'm tryin' to work at that, put that thought in my mind too. That's somethin' I've learned from bein' a kid, 'cause a lot of the things that I know how to do came from peoples takin' the time to show me. Like when I used to work in the gas station; the mechanics would take time and show me how to do certain things, and that's how I became mechanical.

I argue this as a clear distinction from literacy in reaction to violence and as such a creative and critical use of literacy. By defining betterment and productivity not in economic terms—"The main motive is not for money," Michael insisted—but in terms of working within the community, Michael appropriates the notion of literacy as power as a personally and socially relevant idea. He also creates a space where he can pursue that vision.

June told a story about her literacy that suggests another kind of power. Throughout much of her life, June felt bitter toward her mother for denying her the opportunity to attend school; literacy became for her the central tool in productively dealing with that anger:

> I learned my name and how to write it. That's all [my mother] thought I need to know. And I resented her for that for a while. . . . Other girls was learning, going to school, most of them. All she wanted us to do was to learn to write our name. And get married. And then after I kept with the learning, I said, "All she wanted us to do was to learn to write our name and we need more in life." But she didn't think that day was gonna be . . . what it is today. Life. I think she just thought it would stay the same. And I resented her until I wrote a letter to her in a class. And that helped. It just like it lifted something. It made me feel that she didn't know no better.

June reacts here to the narrowest kind of functional literacy: knowing how to write your name. June wrote and published the piece she described, the letter to her mother, in a book produced in a class I taught several years ago:

Being Without a Mother

My Dear Mother,

I wish you was here with me and my family. You would be proud of me your daughter. I am in school. I think about you, when we didn't get to school very much. We had to work. Mother, if you was here to see the change in me. When I asked you about going you would say I had to work in the field. I would cry. You just didn't know what was ahead for your children. It is sad I didn't get my education. Mother, I am in school now learning and having fun. It is a wonderful place to be, in school. Mother, I am not the only one trying. I am proud of myself and the people around me, my friends. Mother, I have written a book. I am just getting started. It is hard being of age and still in school. Mother, I will make it something I always wanted to do. I have five grandchildren and one great grandchild. If you was here you would have a wonderful time with your family. I get so much out of life now, talking, reading, writing, and just listening. I enjoy just sharing it with you.

With love, your daughter

For June, writing this piece was clearly an experience in moving beyond literacy in reaction to violence, experienced by June as a denial of her right to receive an education. Literacy here became a psychological tool, a way of working through personal pain. Although this is quite a different movement than the one Michael makes, I claim it here as both a creative and a critical move; in an educational milieu dominated by a literacy in reaction to power, June explicitly uses literacy to move beyond her anger at that power, in this case experienced through her mother. In creating and enacting her own uses for literacy, June rejects the more limited version of literacy, just as Michael does. From the distance of the academy, it is easy to note the limitations in an act like June's—it appears, for example, solitary, and thus emphasizes the individual instead of the social—but in lives that have experienced education primarily in terms of frustration, absence, and bitterness, this personal use of literacy must also be considered politically significant. As Yagelski (2000) reminded us, such acts of literacy "amount to the very kind of political and economic participation about which Friere writes; they are local manifestations of the broader ideological struggles inherent in literate acts" (p. 7). And furthermore, June's piece, published in a book distributed through the center, heeds Powell's (1999) criteria for a transformative literacy as a social statement that wields an authority in language and that takes as its own the power to inspire.

van Maanen (1988) noted that the process of writing up site-based research "is often an unbalanced one, so far as the final representation is concerned: informants speak, ethnographers write" (p. 137).[6] I recognize that by collecting, transcribing, excerpting, organizing, and analyzing these interviews, I cannot honestly claim that these experiences speak for themselves or that they are unmarked by my influence and the academy's. I exercise my literate power over these stories with the knowledge that my representations of them are partial and limited, but for these stories to acquire cultural capital, for these students' experiences to matter in educational and institutional settings, to somehow a claim a power of literacy for themselves, they must first somehow be heard, and heard in unfamiliar ways that move beyond our interpretive expectations. I argue that we should resist persistent and easy readings of adult literacy narratives, for it is difficult to understand the point of our inspiration in the face of many students' ongoing frustration. Reading from the hallways of the literacy narrative means refusing to banish the stories that challenge prevailing ideologies about literacy, and it requires an acknowledgment that literacy has many more powers than the inspirational.

ENDNOTES

1. The names of all the students have been changed.
2. I typically do not use this word to describe people, because of the negative moral weight it carries. I use it here because it is precisely that moral weight that makes returning to school so difficult to do: It can become on the order of a confession.
3. Although I do not have statistics from Rainier available, I taught individuals and classes there for 8 years. In those classes, of students born in the United States, I can remember two white students and one Latina student. Although a sizable portion of the students were immigrants, primarily from Asia and East Africa, I did not include these students in my study, because second-language learning and literacy is not my primary area of interest. Of my students born in the United States, almost all were African American, as were most of the U.S.-born students at Rainier. Rainier itself is located in a neighborhood with a large African-American and immigrant population, which may account for this representation, which is not reflective of literacy programs nationwide, or even statewide in Washington. Thus, the available students for my study at Rainier were almost entirely African American. I make no claims in this study about the literacy experiences of the general population of African Americans, and I focus on race only insofar as it comes up in individual oral histories. This study was approved by the Human Subjects Division at the University of Washington.
4. I have been highly influenced in my methods by oral history theory and practice, and am particularly interested in a central question of the field, which

Portelli (1997) phrased this way: "What do we recognize in the stories with which we work that makes them relevant beyond the immediate sphere of their individual narrators, the way a literary work is relevant to literature or a hagiography to church history and religion?" (p. 82) He argued the danger of attempting to interpret oral histories only through "the necessary abstraction of the social science grid" (p. 88):

> the actual world is more like a mosaic or patchwork of countless different shapes, touching, and overlapping, and sharing, but also cherishing their irreducible individuality. As sciences of the individual, oral history and literature deal with the portions of the mosaic that cannot be subsumed under the grid. They give us unwieldy representations, often harder to handle and work with, but perhaps more consistent, not only with the presence of subjectivity but also with the objective reality of things. (p. 88)

Portelli (1997) emphasized not how to turn subjective accounts into valid evidence under objective criteria, but how to understand the significance of a subjective account. He argued that as texts, "the representative quality of oral sources and life histories is related to the extent to which they open and define the field of expressive possibilities . . . it is measured less by the reconstruction of the average experience, than by the subjective projection of imagined experience: less by what materially happens to people, than by what people imagine or know *might* happen" (p. 86).

Portelli's description here applies to my interpretation of these oral histories in that I have tried to honor their "irreducible individuality" by quoting from them at length and by providing as much context for them as is possible in the space I have. These oral histories are valuable not because they represent the experience of statistically representative numbers of adult literacy students, nor simply because they are, individually, compelling stories: They are valuable because they present another way of imagining and understanding the power of literacy, as described through subjective accounts of lived experience. Just as I recognize that the act of interviewing and transcribing comes layered with several levels that make the data unreproducable and thus not "objective," so does the act of story-telling these subjects engage in during the interviews, and I am interpreting them as stories, as subjective and interested accounts. I read these histories in particular for places in which informants discussed what they saw as the individual and social consequences of having low literacy skills, as well as any explanations they had for their low literacy skills. I also examined closely accounts of individual educational experiences, especially as they focused on literacy.

5. Arlene also notes that she was rarely punished in her cooking and sewing classes, both emphasizing skills intended for domestic use, and both traditionally regarded as women's work. This lack of punishment in these settings becomes interesting in light of my discussion of student's "productive bodies."

6. As this project came to a conclusion, I sat down with six of the seven students I interviewed for this chapter to show them what I was doing, reading to them the sections I had excerpted and getting their feedback. I learned from this that these students thought that I had represented them fairly and accurately and that I was the one doing the representing, not them. My text was only available to most of them with me as an interpreter.

REFERENCES

Branch, K. (1998). From the margins at the center: Literacy, authority, and the great divide. *College Composition and Communication, 50*(2), 206-231.

Brodkey, L. (1989). On the subjects of class and gender in the literacy letters. *College English, 51*(2), 125-141.

Eldred, J.C., & Mortensen, P. (1988). Reading literacy narratives. *College English, 54*(5), 512-539.

Foucault, M. (1977). *Discipline and punish: The birth of the prison.* London: Penguin.

Heath, S.B. (1982). Protean shapes in literacy events: Ever-shifting oral and literate traditions In D. Tannen (Ed.), *Spoken and written language: Exploring orality and literacy* (pp. 91-117). Norwood, NJ: Ablex.

Levine, K. (1986). *The social context of literacy.* London: Routledge & Kegan Paul.

Linde, C. (1993). *Life stories: The creation of coherence.* Oxford: Oxford University Press.

Miller, R. (1996). The nervous system. *College English, 58*(3), 265-286.

Powell, R. (1999). *Literacy as a moral imperative: Facing the challenges of a pluralistic society.* Lanham, MD: Rowman & Littlefield.

Portelli, A. (1997). *The battle of Valle Giulia: Oral history and the art of dialogue.* Madison: University of Wisconsin Press.

Rockhill, K. (1993) Gender, language, and the politics of literacy. In B.V. Street (Ed.), *Cross-cultural approaches to literacy* (pp. 156-175). Cambridge: Cambridge University Press.

Shapiro, S. (1999). *Pedagogy and the politics of the body. A critical praxis.* New York & London: Garland.

Street, B.V. (1995). *Social literacies: Critical approaches to literacy in development, ethnography, and education.* London & New York: Longman.

Stuckey, J.E. (1991). *The violence of literacy.* Portsmouth: Heinemann.

UNESCO Institute for Education. (1998). Homepage. Retrieved October 2, 1998, from the World Wide Web: http://www.education.unesco.org/unesco/eduprog/uie/

Van Maanen, J. (1988). *Tales of the field: On writing ethnography.* Chicago: University of Chicago Press.

Yagelski, R. P. (2000). *Literacy matters: Writing and reading the social self.* New York & London: Teachers College Press.

2

CONNECTED LITERACIES OF ADULT WRITERS

Work Ethnography in College Composition

Barbara Gleason
City College of New York, CUNY

When mature adults enter college, they are often more motivated and focused on educational goals than they were as younger students. Years of experience managing households and jobs lend older students habits of mind, organizational abilities, and communication skills that enhance their chances of academic success. Moreover, adult workers entering college are likely to bring with them workplace literacies that support their learning of academic literacies, especially when their instructors are alert to this possibility (Popken, 1999; Strom & Belanger, 1996; Uehling, 1996). However, as a result of being away from school for 5, 10, or even 20 years, adults are less familiar with school-based literacies than are 18-year-olds. Test-taking and essay writing, for example, can be sources of intense anxiety for older students. For all of these reasons, adult workers entering college are not particularly "well served by a traditional model of education that assumes a student body of eighteen-year olds" (Belanger & Strom, 1999, p. 104). As Belanger and Strom suggested in their book on worker education writing courses, adult students are more likely to benefit from curricula that account for their complex histories and current lives as workers, family members, community volunteers, and church members.

I teach at the Center for Worker Education, a bachelor's degree program housed in City College, one of the senior colleges within the City University of New York. The Center offers two degrees, a BA in liberal arts and a BS in early childhood education, along with a substantial academic advisement program. Students who attend the evening and weekend classes offered at the Center generally work in civil service jobs, in the private sector, in day-care programs, or in elementary school classrooms as paraprofessionals. Students' ages range from 25 to 55, although there are exceptions at both ends. And most of these students are women (85% in my courses). Their diversity of age is matched by a similar diversity of culture: Many are native-born U.S. citizens who are African American or Hispanic. Most who are immigrants come from Central America, South America, or the Carribean, and a few are from other parts of the world such as China, Ireland, or Nigeria.

Students at the Center for Worker Education (CWE) are among the growing population of mature working adults who started attending college in significant numbers during the 1970s although their presence was felt during the 1950s and the 1960s.[1] The characteristics of older adults in U.S. colleges vary from region to region and from college to college, as even a cursory glance at the five worker education programs portrayed by Belanger and Strom (1999) would indicate. However, the description of adult college students that Cross (1981) published still holds for a substantial number of CWE students:

> The great majority of degree-seeking adults come from working-class backgrounds; most are first-generation college students whose parents did not attend college. At the same time, the students themselves tend to be better educated and to hold better jobs than their age counterparts in the general population. The one phrase that might best describe them better than any other is "upwardly mobile." They seem determined to rise above the socioeconomic level of their parents, largely through the route of advanced education. (p. 67)

Many scholars would, like Cross, classify CWE students as "working class"; however, these students are less likely to view themselves as working class due to certain connotations, such as being poor, that they may attach to this term.[2] In any event, "class" is not the distinguishing characteristic of this group of students, nor is age, race, gender, or sexual orientation even though all these categories are useful for understanding this highly diverse population. What is distinctive about this group of people is that they have decided to enter or reenter college while working fulltime and balancing other obligations.

The curriculum for the worker education writing course that I teach invites students to use their own life experiences, language forms, and literacies as resources for acquiring academic literacy. Inspired by Freire's (1972) problem-posing approach to literacy education, this curriculum encourages students to "develop their power to perceive critically *the way they exist* in the world *with which* and *in which* they find themselves" (pp. 70-71). One writing assignment that goes a long way toward encouraging critical perception is the ethnographic research that Heath (1983) introduced in *Ways with Words* and that others have since developed and refined (Chiseri-Strater & Sunstein, 1997; Kutz, Groden, & Zamel, 1993; Zebroski, 1996). This writing project involves student writers in investigating communities of their own choosing.

I assign ethnographic research to adult writers for three principal reasons: first, to guide students through a sequence of manageable writing tasks that culminates in one long report; second, to allow students use of their oral fluencies and spoken language abilities as a way into academic research and writing (Elbow, 1985); and third, as a way for me to learn from my students about the specific social and cultural worlds that they inhabit. Like the teachers at the Bryn Mawr Summer School for Working Women of the 1920s and 1930s, my first concern is to "discover the special interests and occupational backgrounds of . . . [my] students" (Smith, 1941, p. 25; cited in Hollis, 1994, p. 36).

This focus on learning about the lives of my adult students has led me to realize that many returning adults are already confident, proficient language users at work. My CWE colleague, Barbara Omolade (1994), observed that Black adult women in college "can and do express themselves within their families and community groups, at work, and when negotiating complex bureaucratic systems" (p. 148). However, in academic settings these same women often feel silenced, especially in traditionally patriarchal classrooms, and they sometimes "freeze up" during exams. Black women students' educational insecurities, Omolade argued, can lead them to produce writing that is superficial, noncommunicative, and too focused on pleasing the teacher. In short, the rhetorical competencies these women exhibit in familiar environments are sometimes vastly superior to their *apparent* abilities in college classrooms, and in my experience this holds true for women of other ethnic groups as well as for men.

This difference in persona and apparent competency was brought home to me most forcefully by Gail, a student who enrolled in two classes that I taught at CWE.[3] An African-American woman in her early 40s, Gail entered CWE to complete a bachelor's degree that she had begun many years earlier. During her first semester at CWE, she enrolled in a required introductory literature course (Core Humanities 1) that I was teaching and then consistently declined my invitations to read orally or to voice her views in class. Nearly every week, Gail would remind me that she did not like to speak in public, that she "hated" reading, and that she could not write. The writing that she produced for this class was usually brief and uninvolved, earning low grades that frustrated and angered her. One day, Gail brought to class some poems written by children in the shelter for homeless families where she worked. Our mutual interest in those poems induced me to use one as a prompt for response writing in that class. Gail's written response to these poems was far more articulate and passionate than her prior writing had been. A year later, Gail enrolled in my elective introductory writing course, where she began using academic writing to examine her literacies, her language, and her work community.

Because she spoke so enthusiastically about the residence shelter for homeless families where she was working, I asked Gail if I could visit her at work. Gail graciously invited me to the city-sponsored program where she was working as a case manager. After a subway ride to Manhattan's upper west side, I found the eighty year old building—formerly a residence hotel—and entered its spacious high-ceilinged lobby. A security guard (and doorman) called Gail, who came to the lobby to greet me. Together, we took the elevator to an upper floor that housed the offices of many workers (e.g., nurses, psychologists, and client case managers). As we visited a classroom for young children, Gail described some of the program's educational opportunities for adolescents and adults. From the first moment that we began this visit, Gail appeared relaxed, confident, and articulate. Introducing me to her colleagues and her clients as her "professor," Gail switched back and forth continuously from a conversational "street talk" style marked by humor, witty repartee, and a few nonprestige grammatical forms to a more formal register marked by professional jargon, a sober tone, and standardized language. Among the literacies Gail practices at work are interviewing her clients and taking notes, filling out forms, conversing with clients in all sorts of informal situations, reading institutional manuals and guidelines, and writing client case reports. In a "by-the-way" message conveyed while we conversed with her supervisor, Gail revealed for the first time that she routinely revises and proofreads her client case reports at the behest of her supervisor. A pie-shaped chart on the wall of her office showed Gail to have had more success than any other case manager at placing clients in their own homes during the previous month.

The contrast in competence between the "in-class" and the "at-work" Gail has been replicated by many of my students, leading me to the obvious conclusion: to try to exploit the skills and the confidence that adult students have acquired at work for their literacy learning in a college writing course. To this end, I have recently begun encouraging students to research and write about their working communities, just as Gail did in a research project about the residence shelter for homeless families that she wrote in spring 1999. Cynthia, a student in my fall 1996 CWE writing course, first showed me how a mature working adult could turn a class writing project toward her own professional interests and aims.

CYNTHIA'S STUDY OF WEP WORKERS

She grew up in an African-American family, the middle child in a family of eight children. Early on, Cynthia recognized that educational success was the key to competing for her mother's attention. And Cynthia was successful: Learning came easily for her—so easily that even cutting classes could not prevent her from earning good grades. But at the end of her junior year, she left high school, gave birth to a child, and later returned to earn her high school diploma. At the age of 33, she registered for my 100-level writing course as an elective even though college composition is not required for liberal arts majors at CWE. Cynthia had come to college principally to "become a more professional speaker and writer" at work, but with one semester left before graduating, she remained dissatisfied with her writing abilities.

Employed as a supervisor in the Special Programs Unit of the New York City Housing Preservation and Development office, Cynthia's job responsibilities included supervising three women enrolled in a new and controversial Work Experience Program (WEP) in New York City. In a proposal essay that she wrote before beginning her research, she describes the community she plans to study and her aims. Here are the first two paragraphs of that essay:

> "Me can't take dis shit no more, dem people don went tan tut me food stamps again," Marcia said. "Tat's why me gon get all ta work experience me tan dit from tis assignment, den me gon get me a real job and faget tis welfare shit," Joan responded.
>
> Marcia and Joan come from the community of people I would like to observe. It is the Work Experience Program Community which consists of people on Public Assistance (welfare) that have to work in city agencies to continue receiving their welfare benefits. I would like to base my observation on three women (Marcia, Joan, and Kathy) from the WEP community assigned to work in NYC Housing Preservation and Development. This is where most of the observation will take place.

Cynthia represents Marcia and Joan speaking Jamaican English because she has perceived that their common use of this language binds them closer together while also separating them from other workers. As I later learned in our conversations, Cynthia understood that "a country accent or dialect" could "shut out a person from certain institutions or groups of people" (Key, 1998, p. 11). Her focus on language also derives from the language awareness component of my curriculum: register, dialect, standard English, and spoken versus written language forms are all topics for reading, class discussion, and writing in this curriculum.

Cynthia's use of dialogue in the opening of this essay reflects another issue as well: her interest in learning to quote sources in her writing. Until enrolling in this class, Cynthia simply avoided quoting: She didn't understand how paraphrasing and quoting differ or how to introduce and punctuate quotes. As a result, her writing was "just okay" but not "good or excellent" as she explains in her portfolio cover letter.

Cynthia entered into her research with the idea of using this class project to learn about the people she supervised and to improve her abilities as a supervisor. In her proposal essay, Cynthia explains her intentions:

> I plan to share all my information from this project with Marcia, Joan, and Kathy to help them better understand their financial situation, and to help them get off welfare. If I could accomplish this, then my Ethnographic Research Project will be more than a class project, but rather a blessing in disguise. Because I will have a better understanding of the WEP population, which will allow me to better address their needs, I can then be a more effective and efficient WEP supervisor.

After submitting a research proposal essay, Cynthia observed these three women at work, described their actions and communications in her fieldnotes, conducted an interview with Marcia, and then wrote an interview report entitled "Circles: Picking Up the Pieces." She begins that report with a brief description of Marcia as a "middle-aged Jamaican born woman" who "works 55 hours in a 2-week period in order to continue receiving public assistance." In preparing for this interview, which took place in an outdoors market area away from the office, Cynthia scripted a list of 14 questions about Marcia's past, her present status as a recipient of public assistance and a participant in the WEP, and her future plans.

Cynthia learned how Marcia came to be on public assistance, how she felt about that status, and how she planned to increase her employability with a college education. Cynthia discovered that three personal traumas in close succession had led to Marcia's having to apply for public assistance: first, the apartment she shared with her husband caught fire and she "lost everything"; 1 year later, her husband died suddenly of a heart attack; and 6 months after the death of her husband Marcia was laid off from her bank job. In her report, Cynthia records her response to learning of these personal tragedies. Here is what she writes: "As Marcia was speaking I felt myself being drawn into these incidents and had to step back and ask myself if I could survive such hardships. I honestly don't know if I could." At the end of the interview Cynthia found herself "moved to tears" but also grateful to have learned about Marcia's personal history and to have established a foundation for a more personal relationship.

Throughout her report, Cynthia quotes Marcia speaking in a Jamaican dialect. Commenting on Marcia's language use, she notes that Marcia's dialect becomes more pronounced when she speaks of her Jamaican culture and of events in Jamaica. During the interview, Marcia herself makes reference to her dialect: she states that with "better grammar" and with "writing skills" she might have had more job opportunities and thus would have avoided having to apply for public assistance benefits.

Despite her belief that "better grammar" would make her more employable, Marcia appears to enjoy using her Jamaican dialect to speak with a fellow WEP worker. This cultural and linguistic tie may explain why "Marcia and Joan are very close," as Cynthia states in the ethnographic report that she titled "The Ties that Bind: The Work Experience Program Community." Cynthia also reports that Marcia can be heard to begin speaking Jamaican English in the middle of a conversation. Cynthia writes, "At times I will hear them speaking and all of a sudden Marcia's dialect will switch from American to Jamaican and Joan will follow in a Jamaican accent."

In her analysis of this community of three WEP workers, Cynthia concludes they are strongly supportive of one another because they "communicate well" and because they "have this special bond" as women on public assistance participating in the Work Experience Program. Referring to the language issues that we had read about and discussed in class, Cynthia writes of Marcia's ability to code-switch, of these women's common use of Jamaican English, and Marcia's tendency to use Jamaican English when talking about events in Jamaica. Cynthia's attentiveness to her co-workers' language forms and communicative practices signals her own growing awareness of language—a process that, according to Pattison (1982) and many other scholars, underlies literacy development—as well as her desire to communicate more effectively with the women she supervises at work.

At the end of her report, Cynthia remarks on her new appreciation of how catastrophic situations can cause people to have to apply for public assistance benefits. She reflects on how she has learned from Marcia that the experiences people have as recipients of welfare benefits can be "demeaning" and can cause them to "lose self-esteem [and] motivation." And she reports on how this research will affect her work as a supervisor of WEP workers: At the time she wrote her report, Cynthia had already invited Marcia to speak to groups of new WEP workers about her goal of completing a 4-year college degree—an opportunity that Marcia was looking forward to. Summing up, Cynthia says, "I now have a better understanding of this community and great respect for the three women I observed."

TEACHING ETHNOGRAPHIC WRITING IN A WORKER EDUCATION CLASS

Cynthia is one of many students who have chosen to study their workplace communities. In four classes that I taught between 1996 and 1998, 31 of 59 students, or 53%, studied their own work communities. A sampling of their titles indicates the wide range of jobs that they hold and some of their work-related concerns: "Erasing Bureaucracy at What Used to Be the PVB [Parking Violations Bureau]"; "The Diversities of Room 101"; "Legal Technicians' Job Problems: An Ethnographic Report"; "Understanding Homelessness"; "The Office Social Club"; "A Financial Community and Its Culture"; "Traveling through a Penal Institution"; "Difficulties of the Hispanic Students"; "Riverbank State Park's Lap Swimmers"; "Daily Life at Good Council Home"; "Employee Morale at the Environmental Protection Agency."

Student ethnographers embark on their research by selecting a community that they find particularly compelling. This choice is guided principally by a student's interests, as in the case of a woman who studied an animal shelter in order to deepen her understanding of the animal rights movement. However, accessibility and time constraints necessarily restrict choices: Many working adult students decide to embed their research within daily routines at work in order to avoid spending time commuting to and from some other place.

A primary reason for the suitability of ethnography to a writing course is the opportunities it affords for studying language forms, language practices, and communication in actual contexts of use. By observing and describing people interacting with one another, students create texts depicting complex relationships among speakers, utterances, responses, meanings and situations. Questions of interpretation arise (e.g., questions of how specific comments are "heard" by others and responded to). As they examine recorded comments of the people they have observed, students can reflect on the various meanings that their words may suggest, both to listeners in live situations and to readers of a written report. An added benefit is that by observing and writing about how people use spoken language in communicative situations, student writers are invited to reflect on how they themselves use language and to notice that language is available to be examined, learned, and used consciously for intended purposes. Because many of these students are acquiring standard written English or the conventions of academic writing, language learning is an aspect of their writing development and therefore a key feature of my curriculum.

To bring language forms, attitudes, and practices into sharp focus, I distribute essays and stories to introduce concepts such as "jargon," "dialect" and "standard English" during class. One example of an essay I use is "Vertamae Grosvenor—The Shame and Pride of Speaking Gullah" by Burkhalter (1995). When Vertamae Grosvenor moved to Philadelphia at the age of 10, she spoke Gullah—a creolized form of English spoken in regions of South Carolina and Georgia. Although she acquired standard English and later became a published writer and National Public Radio commentator, Grosvenor had felt ashamed of the Gullah she spoke as a child: "Those of us who moved north realized very early that we had to talk a different way . . . but the damage was done . . . you were led to believe that somehow you were inferior" (Burkhalter, 1995, p. 4). After reading essays and stories such as this one, students discuss their attitudes toward language and how these attitudes can affect them as writers. We then turn to the themes of "community" and "work," which also become topics for reading and discussion.

By choosing their own work communities for a class writing project, these very busy students make good use of the limited time that they have for work, school, and family. Some, like Cynthia, have special interests and problems at work that this class assignment allows them to explore. A third reason for these students' choosing to focus on their own work communities is one described by Goodman (1985):

> In the past, most Americans lived in neighborhoods. We were members of precincts or parishes or school districts. My dictionary still defines community, first of all, in geographic terms, as "a body of people who live in one place." But today fewer of us do our living in that one place; more of us use it just for sleeping. . . . It's not that we are more isolated today. It's that many of us have transformed a chunk of friendship, a major portion of our everyday social lives, from home to office . . . [and] the workplace becomes our neighborhood. (Goodman, cited in Evans et al., 1992, p. 182)

Goodman's observation that workplaces are supplanting neighborhoods as primary communities certainly holds true for many of the working adult students in my classes, who often write about their co-workers not just as colleagues but also as friends and mentors. My students and I discuss Goodman's argument about work communities in class while reading and discussing other authors' views on the nature of "community."

As is true of all communities, co-workers' relationships can be collegial and even familial but can also be sites of tension and conflict, especially when people work in stressful conditions. Employees' health and well-being can be affected by difficult work environments, as can be seen in an ethnography written by Jessie, a 30-something Brooklyn-born woman of Irish descent.

JESSIE'S STUDY OF NEW YORK CITY TITLE EXAMINERS

For Jessie, writing a workplace ethnography provided an opportunity to reflect on her own experiences as a title examiner and the conditions in which she was working. In her research proposal, Jessie explains that she works in the Register's Office, which is housed in Surrogate's Court located in downtown Manhattan. Her job as title examiner involves researching "the full history of an assigned property, including a 50-year deed search, all open mortgages, an interpretation of legal documents, and a search for numerous liens against the premises and owners."

In the process of researching property titles, as Jessie explains in her final report, title examiners look for existing "covenants and restrictions"; for example, covenants dated in the 1800s might include "no bone boiling, slaughter houses, or tanneries," whereas modern covenants may involve prohibitions against "medical research on fecal tissue" or restrictions on "building height." As a title examiner, Jessie searches for and interprets a variety of documents to verify the status of a property title for a company that insures titles. She reports the results of a search on a standardized form that requires routine writing of short responses.

One feature of Jessie's written report distinguishes it from most others: Jessie uses particularly effective descriptions of place to further her thesis about the high degree of stress experienced by New York City title examiners. This thesis is suggested in her title—"The Cycle of Stress: The Life of a Title Examiner"—and developed throughout the entire essay by Jessie's use of interviews, descriptive field notes, and personal experience as a title examiner.

In her final report, Jessie describes the office in which she works as "old, decrepit and cluttered." Making effective use of contrast to advance her point about "inadequate conditions" in this office, Jessie describes the building's entrance as modeled on the Paris Opera House, "a mixture of colorful mosaic tiles, carved arched doorways and an incredible double marble staircase that leads to the second floor." However, inside the title examiners' office the ceiling is scarred by hanging "chunks of plaster and paint chips" that appear to "compete" with fluorescent lights. An open doorway is decorated with "dozens of wires intertwined [and] hanging down as if this is the city's version of drapes." Using metaphor (hanging wires perceived as "drapes") and contrasting descriptions of place, Jessie underscores her point about how visually unappealing and unhealthy this title examiners' office is, at least as seen through her eyes. Additionally, Jessie creates vivid images: In her office you can see "a beautiful spiral marble staircase with a wrought iron handrail that leads to nowhere" and "two huge marble fireplaces, one on each side of the room, covered with about an inch of dust, assorted papers, and old forgotten books."

The hodge-podge, unkempt appearance of this office suggests an environment that is colorful but that may pose health hazards for workers. Here, title examiners (who are self-employed or employed by private companies) compete with one another for limited work spaces and "antiquated" equipment. Access to document printers, copy machines, and microfiche machines is limited to regular work day hours. Since only 7 of the 10 document printers are typically functioning at one time, examiners must stand in "long, time-consuming lines," as one examiner that Jessie interviewed explains; this informant then adds that sometimes there is no paper, so examiners must "dig used paper out of the garbage and feed it into the computer backwards." An examiner named Jen tells Jessie of how a co-worker had become so frustrated at having to stand in line that he "vented his frustrations in an earsplitting diatribe of atrocities against him caused by Jen and her company." In addition to competing for work space and equipment, examiners and their companies compete for clients, which "fosters feelings of suspicion, paranoia, and a sense of rivalry."

The stress of being a title examiner is represented particularly well by the case of Allan—a middle-aged man who had had three heart attacks in the previous 6 years. In her interview with Allan, Jessie learned that he begins his workday "at 3 a.m. while still at home" and returns at the end of the day "to put in another 4 or 5 hours of work." Allan has built an "empire" matched by no other examiner, but his "workaholic trait" Jesse finds to be a "common characteristic among title examiners."

In a conference on her first draft, I asked Jessie why title examiners remain in this line of work when the job is so stressful. Jessie explained that examiners typically earn $50,000 or more a year and that no college degree, certification, or license is needed. Although Jessie herself was earning much less than $50,000, she could look forward to this earning potential in the future. However, Jessie had good cause to be concerned about a highly stressful work environment: She is a recent survivor of cancer. Although she did not write about her illness in her ethnography, she had disclosed this information about herself in a literacy autobiography that she had written earlier in the semester. Jessie very clearly inscribed her concerns about her own health between the lines of her workplace ethnography. When I later asked Jessie if her health had played a role in her analysis of title examiners' working conditions, she assured me that indeed this had been true.

The treatments she had been forced to undergo had been painful and debilitating: chemotherapy, full body radiation, and a bone marrow transplant. The transplant Jessie describes as "the apex of my affliction" but also "the turning point in my life." It was at this time that Jessie decided to confront her "academic demons"—including severe writing anxiety—by returning to college. She writes, "With all that I have been through, it's hard to believe that my fear of writing could be so intense." Despite her fear of academic failure and her anxiety-ridden experiences as a writer, Jessie worked effectively all semester long to produce high-quality essays that earned her a strong "A" for this course.

In response to questions that I posed on the last day of class, Jessie wrote that the field research project had been her "most difficult assignment"—in part because she had already begun reassessing her decision to work as a title examiner. As she explained, "Writing about the place I may return to . . . caused personal problems to arise." When I later inquired about the nature of these "personal problems," Jessie told me that writing about her office environment forced her to examine a part of her life that was very sensitive and even painful for her. As a self-employed title examiner, Jessie had had to decide between buying a car and paying for her own health insurance. She had bought a used car and then found herself in the midst of a life-threatening health crisis with no health insurance. This unexpected turn of events had resulted in strong feelings of anger and resentment toward an industry Jessie had been part of for 15 years. The last comment she wrote on the questionnaire was this: "Basically, I have realized that I need to reevaluate the field of work I have chosen." We had discussed some of her concerns about work when reviewing a first draft of her workplace ethnography; I suggested that these were ideas that she could include in her conclusion.

After our conference about her first draft, Jessie went on to write this final paragraph for her report:

> I myself have had difficulties with the high stress levels created in and by this line of work. As a result, I have questioned my participation in staying within this line of work. This research is part of a journey as to what kind of work I want to explore for my future. This is embedded in

> a longer journey that questions where I want to go professionally. Should I become a teacher? Or should I continue examining? Although at present time I have no conclusive answers to these questions, this paper has enabled me to explore future job opportunities for myself.

Among the options Jessie was considering were working for a private title insurance company (rather than remaining self-employed) and becoming a teacher. Just after the end of spring 1999 term, she was hired by a private title insurance company and now enjoys all the benefits of a full-time employee—including health insurance. But despite this clearly advantageous shift in her professional status, Jessie is still considering teaching as a future profession.

HOW WRITING ABOUT WORK BENEFITS RETURNING ADULTS

When I started teaching writing to working adults 4 years ago, I looked for ways of teaching to strength. I took into account that these students—like their younger peers enrolled in our college's regular curriculum—could build academic literacies on one or more of the following: oral fluencies; pleasure reading; journal writing; expertise in two or more dialects; proficiency in two or more languages; conversational storytelling abilities; and code-switching competencies. However, I did not foresee the importance of literacies acquired at work.

By choosing to write about their own workplace communities, my adult students began informing me of their lives as workers and of their workplace literacies. I came to understand that each student might already possess specific workplace literacies that could serve as a scaffold for acquiring academic literacy. Jessie is a good case in point: As a title examiner, Jessie searches for documents and interprets them in order to trace the histories of property titles. She knows how to find documents, interpret technical and archaic language, synthesize information gleaned from her searches, and use evidence to form conclusions which she reports in writing.

My increased understanding of adults in my own classes motivated me to begin reading the adult education scholarship, which offers various theories about adult learning and how it differs from the learning of children and adolescents (Cross, 1981; Knowles, 1984; Sutherland, 1997). Adults, some scholars argue, are more likely than younger students to question the practical value of what they're learning. They are also prone to take good advantage of student-centered teaching and self-directed inquiries such as field research projects. Cynthia is a good example of a student who used a class-assigned writing project to pursue her own interests at work. She explains in her report how this task benefited her at work:

> I now have a better understanding of the WEP community on a personal level, thanks to Marcia. I know that people are on public assistance for many reasons—some may be tragedies. I also know that Marcia has a lot to offer as a person who has suffered many tragedies. She has a great deal of life experience and is full of potent information. I have an abundance of respect for her now that I know how she came to be on public assistance.

By studying her own workplace, Cynthia learned about the histories of three women she was supervising, increased her understanding of their points of view, and changed her own perspective on welfare recipients generally. These learning experiences (increased understanding and change of perspective) exemplify attitudes toward learning that some scholars associate with mature phases of intellectual development (Beaty, Dall'Alba, & Marton, 1997; Belenky, Clinchy, Goldberger, & Tarule, 1986).

To learn more about the experiences of returning adults, I also surveyed the composition scholarship. A special issue of *The Writing Instructors* (*TWI*) proved especially helpful (Aronson, Hansen, & Nerney, 1996). In this *TWI* issue, Popken reported on how adult writers can recognize and use relationships between genres they already write at work and genres they are expected to write at school. To illustrate, he described the case of a student who transferred her ability to write straightforward prose that makes a point quickly in business letters to her writing of essay exams.

Popken's research on how adult writers transfer genre knowledge acquired at work to their academic writing prompted me to consider similar transferrals I have observed in my adult students' writing. Gail, for example, relied heavily on her professional jargon when writing her ethnography, as is evident in the opening of her report:

> Volunteers of America is a non-profit organization that is partially funded by the city of New York. It is dedicated to restoring hope, dignity and self-reliance to individuals and families in a crisis or distress. I now work with Volunteers of America as a case manager for three years, and we provide help to those in need.
>
> When families arrive at this facility they are assigned a case manager. This is the job that I have and my caseload is anywhere from 15 to 25 families. A case manager's job is to address the underlying causes of homelessness, identifying the families needs and providing information, referrals, advocacy and follow-up to ensure effective service linkage. The case manager's analysis is based on sessions that are conduct-

> ed with residents on a bi-weekly basis. The case manager interviews the residents, completes the intake package (see attachment I), assesses the family needs and makes the necessary referrals for the family.

Using the language of her workplace enabled Gail to write with confidence and authority—features that were not present in her writing 1 year earlier.

Gail's emotional investment in her work ethnography stemmed in part from a desire to pursue a masters in social work and achieve professional advancement. Gail's identity had become closely tied to her work as a case manager for homeless families. Her high level of involvement in this writing project led Gail to spend more time on her writing and to produce better writing than she had when writing about literature 1 year earlier. As a result, her grades improved: in the introductory literature class she had earned a "C"; however, in this college composition class, Gail earned a grade of "A". Because Gail had decided to continue on to graduate school, earning good grades and developing confidence as a writer had both become priorities. In short, Gail's growing identity as a professional social worker motivated her to become a more proficient writer.

CONCLUSION

Gail, Cynthia, and Jessie are representative of many adult students that I have met: They have used an academic writing project to strengthen their own writing abilities (Gail), to understand and learn from their co-workers (Cynthia), or to examine a problem they are encountering at work (Jessie). Equally important, these mature women undergraduates discovered how to unify their complex lives by combining work experience with academic writing. In so doing, they helped me to understand the learning experiences of my older adult students—most of whom are women who work full time while attending college classes.

Adult writers such as Gail, Cynthia, and Jessie reverse the traditional developmental model: Rather than learning academic literacies as younger college students do at the ages of 18 through 21, in preparation for their professional futures, these older students have acquired workplace literacies as young adults and then reentered the classroom after having worked at full-time jobs for several years. These students' lives are generally "interrupted and conflicted . . . not narrowly focused or permanently pointed toward a single ambition" (Bateson, 1990, p. 9). In analyzing the trajectories of five adult women's lives, Bateson portrayed an approach to living that resembles the paths of many mature workers who seek an undergraduate college education: these lives "are not without commitment" but involve "commitments [that] are continually refocused and redefined" (p. 9). By reversing the traditional high school–college–career developmental model and by bridging their own work lives and literacies with their academic learning, adult undergraduates such as Gail, Cynthia, and Jessie are forging a new, nontraditional pathway—a route that often entails earning a GED rather than a high school diploma, entering the workforce, and then registering for college classes. By observing their progress and talking with adults who enter college as undergraduates, we can all gain new perspectives on the teaching and learning of academic literacy.

ACKNOWLEDGMENTS

I would like to thank Edward Quinn for responding to several different versions of this essay and Charles Bazerman for his tactical and tactful suggestions. I am very grateful to "Gail," "Cynthia," and "Jessie" for allowing me to quote their writing and for sharing their stories with readers of *Multiple Literacies for the 21st Century*. And, I thank Robin Weisberg of Hampton Press for editing the final version of this essay.

ENDNOTES

1. In *Adults as Learners*, Cross (1981) described demographic changes in college student populations and several profiles of adults enrolling in courses for academic credit. In *Adult Learning: State Policies and Institutional Practices*, Cross and McCartan (1984) described several laws, policies, and services that have encouraged adults to enter college.
2. Linkon provided a useful discussion of "working class" for educators in her introduction to *Teaching Working Class*.
3. The students mentioned in this chapter have selected their own pseudonyms. All students' names have been changed. All students have granted permission to quote their writing.

REFERENCES

Aronson, A., Hansen, C., & Nerney, B. (1996, Winter). Undergraduate learners and the teaching of writing. *The Writing Instructor, 15* , 51-58.

Bateson, M. C. (1990). *Composing a life*. New York: Penguin.

Beaty, E., Dall'Alba, G., & Marton, F. (1997). The personal experience of learning in higher education: Changing views and enduring perspectives. In P. Sutherland (Ed.), *Adult learning: A reader* (pp. 33-43). Sterling, VA: Stylus.

Belanger, K., & Strom, L. (1999). *Second shift: Teaching writing to working adults.* Portsmouth, NH: Heinemann/Boyton/Cook.

Belenky, M. F., Clinchy, B. M., Goldberger, N. R., & Tarule, J. M. (1986). *Women's ways of knowing: The development of self, voice, and mind.* New York: Basic Books.

Burkhalter, N. (1995). Vertamae Grosvenor—The shame and pride of speaking Gullah. *NCTE Council Chronicle, 4*(5), 4.

Chiseri-Strater, E., & Sunstein, B. S. (1997). *Fieldworking: Reading and writing research.* Upper Saddle River, NJ: Prentice-Hall.

Cross, K.P. (1981). *Adults as learners.* San Francisco: Jossey-Bass.

Cross, K.P., & McCartan, A.M. (1984). *Adult learning: State policies and institutional practices* (ASHE-ERIC Higher Education Research Report No. 1). Washington, DC: Association for the Study of Higher Education.

Elbow, P. (1985). The shifting relationships between speech and writing. *College Composition and Communication, 36*, 283-303.

Freire, P. (1972). *Pedagogy of the oppressed* (M. B. Ramos, Trans.). New York: Herder & Herder.

Goodman, E. (1985). A working community. In E. Goodman (Ed.), *Keeping in touch.* New York: Simon and Schuster. Reprinted in Evans, F. B., Gleason, B., & Wiley, M. (Eds.). (1992). *Cultural tapestry: Readings for a pluralistic society* (pp. 181-183). New York: HarperCollins.

Heath, S.B. (1983). *Ways with words: Language, life, and work in communities and classrooms.* New York: Cambridge University Press.

Hollis, K. (1994). Liberating voices: Autobiographical writing at the Bryn Mawr Summer School for Women Workers, 1921-1938. *College Composition and Communication, 45*, 31-60.

Key, D. (1998). *Literacy shutdown: Stories of six American women.* Newark, DE: International Reading Association.

Knowles, M.S. (1984). *The adult learner: A neglected species* (3rd ed.). Houston, TX: Gulf.

Kutz, E., Groden, S.Q., & Zamel, V. (1993). *The discovery of competence: Teaching and learning with diverse student writers.* Portsmouth, NH: Heinemann/Boynton/Cook.

Linkon, S.L. (1999). Introduction: Teaching working class. In S. L. Linkon (Ed.), *Teaching working class* (pp. 1-11). Amherst: University of Massachusetts Press.

Omolade, B. (1994). *The rising song of African American women.* New York: Routledge.

Pattison, R. (1982). *On literacy: The politics of the word from Homer to the age of rock.* New York: Oxford University Press.

Popken, R. (1996). A study of the genre repertoires of adult writers. *The Writing Instructor, 15*, 85-93.

Popken, R. (1999). Adult writers, interdiscursive linking, and academic survival. In M.H. Kells & V. Balester (Eds.), *Attending to the margins: Writing, researching, and teaching on the front lines* (pp. 56-73). Portsmouth, NH: Heinemann/Boynton/Cook.

Strom, L., & Belanger, K. (1996). Teaching on "turns": Taking composition courses to a union hall. *The Writing Instructor, 15*, 71-82.

Sutherland, P. (Ed.). (1997). *Adult learning: A reader.* Sterling, VA: Stylus.

Uehling, K. (1996, Winter). Older and younger adults writing together: A rich learning community. *The Writing Instructor, 15*, 51-58.

Zebroski, J. (1986). The uses of theory: A Vygotskian approach to composition. *The Writing Instructor, 5*(2), 71-84.

3

WHERE TO PLACE THE LECTERN

How GTA Literacy Portfolios Inform Writing Pedagogy

Kathleen Bell
University of Central Florida

In the postmodern 21st century world of multiple images delivered by multiple technologies, students entering university have already used a range of literacies far different from the traditional measures of reading and writing used to determine their entry into first-year composition courses. As a literacy site, first-year composition classes seek to strengthen traditional literacies and to cultivate new directions in literacy, that is to address the effects expanding delivery systems and the bombardment of information have on making language choices. To teach these students and courses a majority of large institutions rely on graduate teaching assistants (GTAs), or adjunct faculty. As a writing program administrator (WPA) responsible for preparing GTAs to teach first-year composition, I needed to know how well these novice teachers' understanding of their own literacy would guide them in developing a conscious literacy in others. Could I assume that being English majors and having passed the GRE requirements were enough to intuit and accommodate the literacy needs of first-year students adjusting to a new culture? This chapter attempts to answer that question.

THE OCCASION

Not long ago, a composition student asked to interview me for her research paper. Her topic was "Is it appropriate for graduate teaching assistants to teach first-year classes?" Fearing a potential problem with one of the GTAs, I immediately asked her if she had had an experience that led her to choose the topic. She quickly recounted her problems with a GTA in math who "hadn't a clue what to do." When I asked what her expectations are for teachers, she answered, "Someone who knows *what* we're supposed to be learning and *how* to learn it." Confidently I replied that the GTAs who teach composition receive training to meet those expectations. Still, she pointed out, "Receiving training is not the same as having experience."

She was right. GTA preparation programs often begin with 1 to 2 weeks of "basic training"—the distribution and discussion of recommended or required texts, model or required syllabi, sample annotated student essays and assignments from experienced teachers, and testimonies from tenured faculty and veteran GTAs—before the fall semester starts. Even when this orientation is more extensive in time and content, the primary focus remains on the *what* and *how* of teaching based on the experience of others. For most institutions, the financial constraints of funding GTAs makes it impossible to hold an orientation until the contract year begins just prior to classes. Consequently, the initial, abbreviated preparation is based on the underlying assumption that new GTAs will draw on their experiences as learners, particularly on their engagement with language and their achievements as English majors, to translate training into quality teaching.

The WPAs responsible for overseeing this training know well the great leap of faith involved in making this assumption. Afterall, most GTAs were exempt from taking the very course they will be teaching, and few, if any, have any teaching experiences or methods courses. To cushion that leap of faith, most institutions require a one-semester graduate seminar on the theory and practice of teaching composition that attends to the *why* underlying pedagogical choices GTAs are making concurrently while taking the course. This baptism-by-fire approach, usually supplemented with mentoring, listserv discussions, and classroom observations, generates an urgent survival level of dialectic.

High on the GTAs' list of concerns is how to get students more involved in class discussion of writing, how to stimulate more enthusiasm for the subject. In typical postmodern fashion, the arguments the GTAs put forth to solve this problem formed a complex set of competing discourses, but what fascinated me most was how the way they valued the physical distance and posture teachers chose in proximity to their students defined the lectern as a critical signifier. For example, some argued that an instructor who stood behind the lectern in front of the class could be perceived as authoritative, impersonal, and often too intimidating for students to risk being wrong; others thought that stance professional and knowledgeable, thereby instilling trust in students to respond; still others perceived the behind-the-lectern stance as one that conveyed insecurity—the need to hold on to something. Likewise, some viewed an instructor who removed the lectern and sat on the table as comfortable, knowledgeable, and conversational—a close on-level proximity that will elicit more response—whereas others perceived the stance as too nonchalant, unfocused, or even unprofessional. Similarly, some argued that an instructor who ignored the lectern to sit at the same level with the students was either professionally secure or unprofessional.

As much as I enjoyed this range of arguments, I was surprised that this basically homogeneous group of English majors (95% White, aged 22–28) viewed teaching behavior so diversely. Knowing that I could no longer assume that the GTAs' experiences as learners could be used as a foundational narrative on which to build the seminar, what I needed to know was the process by which these views were formed, the cultural codes and the signifying practices involved. What was the source of their beliefs and how would those beliefs affect their pedagogy?

THE SEARCH FOR CONNECTIONS

In designing the required Theory and Practice seminar, I always attempted to use a pedagogy that allowed the GTAs to experience many of the same processes the basic curriculum requires of first-year students, such as multiple drafts and peer responses. And, to demonstrate how to test assumptions they may have about their students' writing experiences, I required GTAs to compose a brief writing history, an assignment that later transformed into a narrative based on a single, pivotal writing experience that contributes significantly to their definition of writing. Although these two assignments informed me on writing products and attitudes toward writing, they did little to provide background on how the GTAs' beliefs about how learning takes place were formed. When we incorporated portfolios into the first-year composition curriculum, I, too, incorporated the portfolio process into the GTA seminar. In this way, using the theme of literacy for the portfolios, I could gain some insight into the experiences and beliefs GTAs brought to their teaching pedagogy—not only where they might place the lectern, but why.

In his *Rhetoric Review* article, "Narratives of Knowledge," Kail (1988) said that "when we teach, we tell a story to our students and to ourselves, a story about the acquisition of knowledge. The telling of this tale is what we refer to as pedagogy" (p. 179). That tale, Kail contended, is represented in the syllabus as the "plot" of a journey often codified into a textbook resembling "something akin to what Jean-Francois Lyotard calls a 'master narrative,' a story around which other stories are constructed" (p. 179). Here lies the crux of the dilemma for most institutions and specifically the WPA: The institution depends (particularly financially) on the retention of in-coming freshmen. To be successful academically, in-coming freshmen need an enriching and supportive general education program, one based on the institution's mission statement designed for a particular population. This unified "master narrative" of what it means to receive an education at University X then becomes the dominant force in curriculum design. Consequently, the WPA must accept the responsibility for overseeing the development of a curriculum and pedagogy complementary to the institution's master narrative.

As many of us in this position know, striking a balance between supporting the academic/political stability the institution wants to achieve and constructing a curriculum based on the praxis that allows pedagogy to respond to changing literacy needs is our most formidable challenge. I argue that one approach to striking that balance is to examine more closely "the proliferation of little narratives" that Daniell (1999) contended "have influenced and continue to shape the images we have of who we are, what we do, and how we do it" (p. 394). If these "little narratives" have replaced the master narratives of modernism, and if, as Daniell contended, "literacy—the term and the concept—connects composition, with its emphasis on students and classrooms, to the social, political, economic, historical, and cultural" (p. 393), then knowing GTAs' literacy narratives should reveal how their how-to-learn knowledge is established and possibly transmitted in teaching college-level, academic literacy to others.

The documentary power inherent in portfolios should enable students to generate complex narratives of involvement, not only with texts but with people. As Berlin (1994) explained, "The portfolio in a postmodern context enables the exploration of subject formation. As students begin to understand through writing the cultural codes that shaped their development, they are prepared to occupy different subject positions, different perspectives on the person and society" (p. 65). The challenge, then, was to design the literacy portfolio project for a full exploration of personal literacy that would allow the complexity of the GTAs' development to emerge.

THE PORTFOLIO PROJECT

The context for this project is the Theory and Practice in Teaching Composition seminar required of all new GTAs, graduate students pursuing their master's degree in literature, creative writing, or technical writing. In addition to the GTAs, students new to the graduate program in English and doctoral candidates from the College of Education also populate the course. Approximately 90% or more of the class has no teaching experience; the emphasis is on teaching first-year college composition.

My first reason for incorporating portfolios into the Theory and Practice seminar was for GTAs in particular to experience the process of developing a portfolio similar to the one required of their composition students. Rather than using portfolios for large-scale assessment, the composition program uses portfolios at the local, classroom level to stimulate dialogue and develop growth in student writers through self-reflective practices. For the four required core essays, students *collect* all documents (i.e., drafts, peer responses, teacher conference notes, writing lab consultations) contributing to the development of each completed essay. Students write a *self-reflection* on each essay both before and after the essay is graded. Finally, students select documents from the portfolio to use in support of an argument on their own growth as a writer in their final in-class essay. In some way, I wanted to simulate that process for the GTAs.

The second reason for incorporating portfolios was for all class members to discover the story/narrative that informs their definition of literacy—an experience I expected to deepen our sense of community and our understanding of the expectations we have of our students. These goals are merged and embedded in the following excerpts from the assignment sheet:

Purpose:

1. to compile a portrait of yourself as a literate person
2. to identify your assumptions about what constitutes literacy
3. to generate an operational definition of literacy
4. to evaluate yourself as a literate person
5. to understand the possibilities for using portfolios pedagogically

Process:

- Collect a range of documents/items associated with your literacy during the next 2–3 weeks.
- Examine the documents/items as a group; in your Reflection Log, analyze their relationship and begin describing your emerging profile. From this reflection determine in what direction(s) you need to add and/or delete items to refine your personal profile.

- Continue this process at least two more times until you have made your final selection of 5–10 documents/items and have entered three or more informal responses in your Reflection Log (date response entries).
- Using your final document/item selections, develop a formal 2–3 page self-evaluation of your literacy profile; address purposes 2, 3, and 5 stated above in your evaluation.

In the beginning, I expected the artifacts students collected to be fairly traditional for English majors: influential books, exceptional academic papers, achievement recognition, short stories and poems, published work. These experiences, afterall, contributed to their graduate degree ambitions. In fact, in response to the graduate students' need to know if they "were doing it right," I held a group sharing *after* everyone had made the first reflection log response. Each person identified one item from his or her respective first round of collection that surprised her or him. Although most of the items they selected did fall into expected categories, those that didn't—the sheet music, coin, ballet slipper, and passport—expanded the group's perception of the narrative possibilities in more personal directions.

THE DISCOVERIES

The portfolio assignment focused on purpose and process but did not stipulate how to present the portfolios, so imagine the collective amazement the night the assignment was due as class members entered the room with suitcases, backpacks, baskets, artist-sized zippered portfolios, scrapbooks, and mailing tubes in addition to the typical accordion-style portfolio. One shoebox portfolio even included a cassette tape with instructions for experiencing the "literacy portrait," complete with candle, a bottle of wine, a small box of truffles, and background music complementing each literacy item. What became evident as class members inspected each other's portfolios is that, intrigued first by the external, physical diversity, they recognized a sense of agency in the portfolio they developed. As Berlin (1994) pointed out:

> Since we all occupy a unique position in relation to the discourses around us, we all bring a slightly different perspective to our common experience. Thus, while we are not totally autonomous subjects, a certain measure of originality in human action is possible as we engage in the interchange of conflicting perspectives on experience. (p. 63)

I was hopeful that the contents of the portfolios contained that same element of diversity and originality.

The Contents

Each portfolio contained 5 to 10 items selected to form a profile of personal literacy, a reflection log documenting the process of selection, an operational definition of literacy, and an evaluation of the personal and pedagogical discoveries revealed in using the portfolio process. From the 60 teaching assistant (TA) portfolios I catalogued over 3 years, the following artifact categories that appear in Table 3.1 emerged.

The first three categories in the table—reading influences, writing influences, recognition/awards—epitomize the standard dictionary definition of literacy: the ability to read and write. The recognition of that accomplishment, especially for English majors, conveys a sense of power beyond that of the status quo. Although not surprising as categories, I find the emphasis on product not process disturbing with respect to pedagogy. Will many of the GTAs expect students to be already knowledgeable of their own writing and reading processes? Will the 50% who noted personal, self-sponsored writing as an influence expect students to also be self-sponsored writers?

The remaining categories of influence—family, travel, multidisciplinary—offer pedagogical hope that GTAs might instill the need for interaction in keeping with Brandt's (1990) definition of *literacy* as "one's involvement with other people—rather than with texts" (p. 32). The subcategories

Table 3.1. Artifact Categories from 60 TA Portfolios

Category	%
Reading Influences	
Preschool books	35%
School-age books	20%
Postsecondary texts	50%
Writing Influences	
Elementary/high school	30%
Academic writing	35%
Personal writing	50%
Published/professional	34%
Recognition/Awards	
School-based writing	25%
Diplomas; academic honors	34%
Family Influences	
Photos, history, objects	35%
Family writing	30%
Travel Influences	
Passports, postcards photos, objects	35%
Multidisciplinary Influences	
Ballet slippers, CDs, sheet music, museum brochures, baseball cards, oil paints	65%

Note. Only one person included oral experiences—achieving speaking fluency in a foreign language.

under each of these three influences indicate both a process and a cultural context associated with the items that contributed to the GTA's becoming literate, promising components in support of a process-based curriculum.

Overall, 60% of the GTAs included artifacts covering childhood experiences to the present, whereas 40% focused on their adult, postsecondary life. These two different starting points for profiling literacy raise basic questions about how these GTAs perceive the nature of literacy development: Is the development merely a step-by-step progression of skills marked by chronological stages of completion or is it a recursive, dialectic process constantly in motion over a lifetime? Interestingly, both perspectives view literacy development as having a cumulative effect, a commonality that may lead the product-based, step-model GTAs to a fuller understanding of how those skills factor into what Brandt (1995) called accumulating literacy, "the way individuals transform and amalgamate literacy practices in response to—or as part of—rapid social change" (p. 653).

The range of items these GTAs included to capture their sense of being a literate person followed, for the most part, traditional, dictionary definitions of literate: "able to read and write; knowledgeable or educated in several fields or a particular field; a well informed, educated person" (*The American Heritage Dictionary*, 3rd ed.). I had hopes, however, that as individual portraits, their narratives would illuminate the path of their development in ways that could be translated into teaching practice.

The Literacy Constructs

"Narratives," Lyotard (1984) explained, "determine criteria of competence and/or illustrate how they are to be applied. They thus define what has the right to be said and done in the culture in question." (p. 23). The culture in question for the literacy portfolio project was the graduate seminar context in which the narrators, the GTAs, were studying the theory and practice of teaching composition. As narrators constructing a personal portrait of themselves as literate people, their stories were theirs alone to recall, beginning at whatever point they thought their portrait started to take shape; the criteria of competence would be implied by the collection of artifacts and explained in their operational definitions of literacy. Would similar criteria of competence emerge from these portraits of literacy constructed by apprentice members of the same culture? Given their shared goal (to become successful teachers of writing), their similarity in age (range 23–42; majority 26–28), and academic background as English majors, I expected their criteria and definitions to be closely aligned. Instead, their narratives and definitions surprised me in the ways they both competed with and complemented each other.

The discussion that follows presents a range of sample portfolios categorized by three theoretical constructs, each characterized by a type of boundary implicit in the artifact narratives and operational definitions of literacy. The first category I label *skill-based*, a construct with constraining boundaries and that resembles the autonomous model championed by Ong (1988) and Havelock (1982). The second category, the *contextual* construct, reflects the community boundaries and layered interaction found in Brandt (1995) and Brice-Heath's (1993) work. Finally, the *conceptual* construct relies on the open boundaries characteristic of Bizzell (1988) and Brodkey's (1994) arguments against single or dichotomous conceptions of literacy. The analysis of the range of portfolios within each construct is intended to explain how the artifacts and operational definitions work together to shape the boundaries of "learning how."

Skill-Based Construct. The artifacts in these portfolios are characterized by closed, static boundaries; most items represent products or symbols of legitimation, particularly postsecondary academic achievement. For these GTAs, literacy resides in the individual who achieves a transferrable set of hierarchically developed skills recognized in the products they create. Formal education is the key to achieving literacy (see Table 3.2).

The artifact narratives from this sample range of portfolios convey a noticeable emphasis on progress, competition, production, recognition, and publication. Implicit are the ground rules that must be followed and acceptable standards that must be achieved in performance, an extrinsically imposed standard for which a person should accept responsibility. The prevalence of school-sponsored assignments, experiences, and recognition reveals a dependency on the academic context to sanction and determine literacy. In this way, these skill-based artifacts fall within the vertical view of Brandt's (1995) "accumulating literacy" theory. As Brandt explained, the effects of changes in the twentieth century have resulted in both a vertical (piling up) and horizontal (a spreading out) accumulation of literacy (pp. 651–652).

One form of "piling up" Brandt noted is "in the levels of formal schooling that begin to accumulate (albeit inequitably) in families" (p. 652). Although the narrator of Portfolio 4 is the only one who directly identifies "how far [the generations of his family] have come," the implication is evident in Portfolio 2's diploma artifacts and Portfolio 3's transcript and summa cum laude status. I argue that this group of narrators also display signs of "piling up" in the layers of proof of achievement they include: academic assignments, library card, recommendations, and published works—not just one artifact but several in each portfolio. Another form of "piling up" that Brandt (1995) noted is "residual . . . materials and practices from

Table 3.2. Skill-Based Construct: GTA Literacy Portfolios

Portfolio 1 Published articles Recent personal reading list Published report writing manual "Volunteer" certificate from Literacy League	**Definition***:* I think of myself as literate in that I am a good reader and writer, and I share my literacy with others.
Portfolio 2 High school & undergraduate diploma Personal childhood writing Voter registration card; library card Military identification card Family history scrapbook Newspaper	**Definition***:* To be literate is to gain knowledge in order to make oneself a more well-rounded, informed person who is then qualified to make rational decisions and improve society.
Portfolio 3 Kozol's *Death at an Early Age* Three published newspaper articles; published poems Rejection slips Three academic papers; MA reading list Transcript; summa cum laude status; scholarships	**Definition***:* Literacy begins with the desire to have it . . . to attain understanding, to use that understanding, and to continuously strive for it. And the cyclical movement toward literacy creates a desire to help others. Evaluations; recommendation letters toward literacy.
Portfolio 4 Family history documents; baby photos of self Photos of grandfather; grandfather's dictionary Grandfather's Mass book Annotated bibliography; academic essays Photos from Cambridge study abroad program Comic books; *Hardy Boys* Script of old radio show father listened to	**Definition***:* My literacy is a result of many generations of my family and every friend that I have ever had. I see in my great-great-grandfather's enlistment package an "X" where he was required to sign his name and think how far we have come. How far I have come.
Portfolio 5 "Twilight early," a personal poem "Whither wanderest thou," e-mail "The dividing line," e-mail "The Ivory Tower," personal parodic poem Academic essay Annotated bibliography of criticism on William Gibson	**Definition***:* To be literate, in its best and fullest sense, one needs an understanding and intuitive feel for the complexities, subtleties, and evolution of one's language and its literature. In essence, a literate person is one who realizes that he or she is playing very sophisticated language games whenever writing or reading occurs . . . and plays these games very well.

earlier times [that] often linger at the scenes of contemporary literacy learning" (p. 652). Portfolios 4 and 5 indicate the transformation of literacy practices in which emergent forms (e-mail; study abroad programs) take their place alongside residual ones, such as the script of an old radio show.

When the operational definitions of literacy are merged with these primarily skill-based artifacts, however, the closed, static criteria boundaries show signs of broadening applications into social contexts. For example, Portfolios 1 and 3 indicate a need to help others attain literacy, Portfolio 2 expresses interest in using the "qualification" of literacy to "improve society," Portfolio 4 includes "friends" as part of developing literacy (although no contribution is identified), and Portfolio 5 implies that "sophisticated language games" will be played with others. Granted, for each of these GTAs the meaning of literacy resides in the self and primarily in an academic or educated context. In this way, the plot of the skill-based narrative construct follows the modernist master narrative construct. As Lyotard (1984) explained, "The [narrative] of legitimation . . . an take two routes, depending on whether it represents the subject of the narrative as cognitive or practical, as a hero of knowledge or a hero of liberty" (p. 31). The GTA skill-based narrators follow a journey of acting on their desire to be literate by acknowledging and accepting the standards that lead to achievement that, when recognized, leads to the power invested in a hero of knowledge, a person presumably prepared to give knowledge to others.

Contextual Construct. The artifacts in these portfolios emphasize social practices in a wide array of contexts as constituting literacy. The more varied the contexts, the more literate and richer life can be. Inherent in the flexible boundaries that characterize this group is the element of *choice* (see Table 3.3).

In contrast to the skill-based portfolios, the artifacts in the portfolios in Table 3.3 express a strong, personal interaction with contexts, with an emphasis on the process of development rather than on products proclaiming achievement. Although a few academic references appear—teaching certification (Portfolio 7), MA thesis prospectus (Portfolio 8), Chaucer's *Major Poetry* (Portfolio 9), and MA exam reading list (Portfolio 10)—all of the portfolios contain at least four different self-defining contexts, from running in the New York City marathon to performing in a play, from playing music to understanding the legal citation system, experiences in which the participant learned more about his or her self as a literate, knowledgeable person. Literacy, as viewed from these context-based artifacts, resides in what a person *does*, not what a person *is*. Characteristic of Brandt's (1995) horizontal view of accumulating literacy, the flexible boundaries in these GTA artifact narratives portray literacy as a work in progress.

Table 3.3. Context-Based Construct: GTA Literacy Portfolios

Portfolio 6 *Critic's Ink,* self-published high school magazine Journalism career folder; lists (from daily use) National Audubon membership NYC marathon entrant list Resumes composed for self and family "The Rubber Man," first published story Cassette tape of own college band Personal video collection annotations	**Definition***:* Being literate is being able to use accumulated information and experience in your daily life, in all kinds of company and various situations. It is letting the literacy become self-perpetuating, with each learning experience leading to another. It is molding that literacy, taking care of it, giving it purpose and direction and discipline . . . and it is giving back, too.
Portfolio 7 Pictures of family; voter registration card *Generation of Swine* by Hunter Thompson Teaching certification; 8th grade poem Grateful Dead and Doors (CDs) *Patrick Will Grow* (childhood book) Copy of *Men's Health*	**Definition***:* Literacy is not static, nor is it always measurable. It is an evolving and holistic working knowledge: it is intellectual, it is philosophical, it is emotional, it is sociological. It is far beyond the three R's.
Portfolio 8 Photos of daughter; passport MA thesis prospectus E-mail server instructions Legal citation system Cultural Literacy Scale tone seventh chords Spanish class notes in Spanish *Le Petite Prince* Gamache family photo, 1959	**Definition***:* It is important for me to remember to put literacy in a cultural context. Whereas I may believe that an understanding of Dante's *Commedia* is essential to a comprehension of Western culture, my students may feel the same way about the lyrics of a particular song or the premise of a certain film. I must be careful not to equate literacy with cultural elitism. After all, the level of literacy a person chooses to attain will have much to do with the culture in which they choose to live.
Portfolio 9 Dictionary inscribed by grandmother Grandfather's Audubon engagement book Music: Miles Davis; Charlie Parker; scales book *Chaucer's Major Poetry* *Rackety Boom* (children's book) *The Best Loved Poems* (read to by parents) *Playbill* citing performance in Shakespeare *Guitar Player* and *Surfer* magazines *Pieces of the Frame* by John McPhee	**Definition***:* Obviously, one's personal literacy is a compendium of one's personal history. No two people share exactly the same literacy. Each aspect of one's literacy ties a person to other people, to a subculture. . . . There are too many choices, and our backgrounds are too diverse, to share one literacy.

(cont.)

Table 3.3. Context-Based Construct: GTA Literacy Portfolios (cont.)

Portfolio 10 *Read Aloud Poems* (children's book) *The Borrowers* *The Little Prince* Letters from mother Postcards (family correspondence, 1940) Khachaturian's "Toccata" Rachmaninoff's "Prelude" Opus 23, No. 6 Family recipes Reading list for MA exams	**Definition:** I see literacy as a connector. Literacy connects me to my discovering, creative, analytic self. Literacy provides a medium for my reticent rural family to communicate. Literacy links me to the larger communities of formal education and the networks that include work, organizations, and social ties.

The operational definitions of literacy accompanying these lists of artifacts add considerable dimension and texture to the horizontal, "spreading out" view of accumulating literacy. For these GTAs, a person's history of literacy nurtures the willingness to explore new contexts, but actually achieving literacy—a "self-perpetuating," "evolving" understanding of oneself—from those contexts is a matter of *choice*, not just agency. Thus, the person who visits 10 countries in 2 weeks will gain little more than a stamped passport unless the person consciously chooses to learn from the experience. Literacy, although not always measurable, develops a consciousness of experience which allows learning to take place for these GTAs, and when applied to diverse contexts, that level of interaction apparently forms a memorable connection to the "self," "a subculture," and "larger communities." In turn, the connections breed the confidence to explore new contexts.

This "plot" of the context-based narrative produces the adaptability to address rapid changes in literacy demands. As Brandt (1995) explained, "The transformation of literacy obtained in one context for use in another was a principal strategy of literacy learning . . . and a hallmark of advancing literacy"; "literacy in an advanced literate period requires an ability to work the borders between tradition and change, an ability to adapt and improvise and amalgamate" (p. 660).

Conceptual Construct. The lists of artifacts in these literacy portfolios are open, responsive to experience. Characterized by fluid boundaries, this group draws attention to the world of imagination and metaphor in its view of literacy as a means of seeking and interpreting experience (see Table 3.4).

Ranging from the static boundaries of achievement recognition and academic products to the flexible boundaries of music and art beyond to hand tracings, fossils, and incense, the artifacts in the portfolios in Table 3.4 appear to defy classification. Yet, the eclectic nature of each list compels us to use the same level of imagination that informs the perspective on literacy this group of portfolios represents. The individual artifacts are simple and comprehensible, but scrolling down each list forces us to contemplate the changing position of the GTA narrator in relation to the item, context, or event. Whereas an entry such as "certificate of appreciation" (Portfolio 11) identifies the narrator as the recipient, the juxtaposition with the "box of Trappist incense" cues us to consider symbolic, metaphoric, or perhaps spiritual relationships. This movement convinces us that the boundaries are open and fluid, and as such, they encourage others to enter.

Although obvious in the horizontal, spreading out view of accumulating literacy these artifact narratives project, their diversity becomes clearer in intent when viewed through the lens of the operational definitions. Although these GTAs acknowledge the functional value of achieving the

Table 3.4. Concept-Based Construct: GTA Literacy Portfolios

Portfolio 11 Passport; postcard of Moreau's 1865 *Young Thracian Women . . . Head of Orpheus* Botticelli's *Primavera* as humans, My library, itemized Subscription list of journals/periodicals Box of Trappist incense (Abbatial) Volunteer certificate from Dept. of Corrections	**Definition:** I see literacy, this mysterious ability to read and write, as a pathway to *helping us realize our greatest potential as* a tool for helping us understand ourselves and the world in which we live. My understanding of literacy may best be described as a cultural literacy, implying cultivation, growth, fecundity, a refinement of the mind, an expansion of awareness.
Portfolio 12 Photos of grave site, cave paintings, storyteller at Renaissance Fair Shopping bag full of assorted poems, letters, fragments "Ancient Daemon," poem always in progress Collection of German beer drinking songs Atlas; encyclopedia; fossil ammonite Collection of "dismissed" artifacts: library card, ads, legal documents, money	**Definition***:* Language must function imaginatively and metaphorically to affirm the potential self at the same time it functions literally and compliantly to communicate the existent self. Literacy must dance with illiteracy.
Portfolio 13 College anthropology paper on endangered Amazon languages "Brer Rabbit and the Tar Baby" Child's hand tracings (from working as nanny) Grandfather's copy of *Merchant of Venice* quarto VIP Shakespeare Festival member card Title page of undergraduate honors thesis	**Definition***:* Literacy is the ability to make metaphor . . . the ability to take experiences and images not coded in language and internalizing the image by relating it to his or her own world. Literacy is interactive . . . teaching others how to *participate in humanity through the process of literacy.*

(cont.)

Table 3.4. Concept-Based Construct: GTA Literacy Portfolios (cont.)

Portfolio 14 Photos of string bass and various performances "Reflections on a Dairy Farm," personal poem Program from own classical music performance First graduate essay (unsuccessful) Baby book; school days book John Berryman poems Souvenir from Dickinson's home Jaco Pastorius debut album "The Morning Bed," poem in-progress	**Definition**: It's not what you know, but what you're knowing. Literacy is taking what was, combining it with what is, and throwing it at what will be. Literacy is an ever evolving, inclusive, and diverse process of melting, molding, and making of the intangible whole.
Portfolio 15 *Anna's Birthday Book* (poems and drawings created for young niece) Book of poems written in elementary school Response letter from congressional representative English Dept. student recognition banquet program Collection of author autographs *Fiddler on the Roof* program attended with family Huntington Library ticket stub and brochure Photo with friends on European bike tour	**Definition**: Clearly, even if there is a basic agreed-upon literacy threshold, it is apparent that some are more literate than others. Fluency and adaptability characterize this "advanced literacy," both in thought and the expression of that thought. Literate thinkers (and writers) have developed a capacity for abstraction, for understanding and utilizing the complex relationships between things and ideas. It is an attitude . . . we must embrace it. . . . We must constantly re-invent ourselves and our ways of looking at the world.

ability to read and write, that "basic agreed upon literacy threshold" (Portfolio 15) that "functions literally and compliantly to communicate the existence of self" (Portfolio 12), they have reached the realization that literacy is a recursive process of self-affirmation (Portfolio 12), "an expansion of awareness" (Portfolio 11), an evolving process of knowing "what you're knowing" (Portfolio 14). And, as they state or imply, "the ability to make metaphor" (Portfolio 13), both in internalizing experience and externalizing it in expression is the process through which they achieve self-actualization.

The plot of this conceptual narrative relies on the dialectic process to stimulate self-reflection and recursiveness. Witness in Portfolio 12, for example, the Ongian insistence of "must function" juxtaposed with "imaginatively and metaphorically" and the initial paradox of "literacy must dance with illiteracy"; note also the inclusion of an unsuccessful graduate essay in the Portfolio 14 artifacts. Zebroski (1994), in his "tidal wave" representation of Vygotsky's model of higher mental function development, illustrated how the dialectic process depends on the clash of competing forces to initiate the reconstruction of past experiences in terms of new experiences. It is the oscillating movement of this dialectic that generates the fluid boundaries of the conceptual construct of literacy development.

Where to Place the Lectern

What I wanted to know from the GTAs' literacy portfolios was how their experiences in developing their own literacy might affect their pedagogical stance and, consequently, their placement of the lectern as a signifier of that pedagogy. From the narrative constructs that emerged from the GTA portfolios, I discovered that the simple act of positioning a lectern requires a heightened awareness of the complex ways in which literacies develop for both the instructors and the students. To assume that pursuing a graduate degree in English creates an instinctive, homogeneous foundation for teaching writing is as erroneous as assuming that all first-year composition students have the same writing needs.

For the majority of us teaching in process dominant composition programs, the context-based literacy narrative that emerged from the GTAs' portfolios appears most compatible. The teacher/narrator placing him or herself eye to eye with the students (unconcerned with the placement of the lectern), the theme of conscious choice, the collaborative, interactive process of knowing, the application to diverse contexts—all features of this narrative align with process theory and the social constructionist view which underlies it. If that context-based construct becomes the equivalent of a master narrative that informs and legitimates the pedagogy of the entire program, then should we directly teach/require that pedagogy in the Theory and Practice seminar or do we allow the competing narratives held by the other GTAs to, in essence, dialectically construct the novice community? From my experience with the GTA literacy portfolios I argue that in order for the study of theory to have a meaningful context, GTAs first need to know what they *already* know about learning literacies and through sharing those "little narratives" to build the kind of "metanarratives" Berlin (1993) advocated as heuristics for shaping their understanding of what they believe their students need to know. From that community-based, socially constructed knowledge, GTAs can identify the theoretical assumptions they plan to test through their pedagogical practices.

For Lu (1999), reaching that heightened awareness involves a form of literacy she joined Cornell West in naming *critical affirmation,* which she described as a trope that "mark[s] writing, especially personal narratives, as a site for reflecting on and revising one's sense of self, one's relations with others, and the conditions of one's life" and "as a possible site for critical intervention on the formation of one's self" (pp. 173-174). In particular, she identified the gap between her theoretical stance and actual practice as an important site for reflection and revision. In her provocative demonstration of using this narrative process to combat her own level of "teacher illiteracy," Lu confirmed the need for "self education on how we read and write the personal when conducting critical exchanges" (p. 193). Indeed, in Lu's view, unless teachers engage regularly in the critical affirmation process, they will have difficulty helping students gain fluency in critical affirmation.

For GTAs, as apprentice teachers, compiling a literacy portfolio offers one of the best means to identify sites where the gap between the theory they are learning/constructing and the practices they are attempting reveal the need for reflection and revision. As Belanoff (1994) explained, "Portfolios engender the literacy within which they are created and evaluated; like language, portfolios both reflect and create the culture within which they communicate"; and as our institutional missions and our own aims become more diverse, and students and faculty more heterogeneous, "portfolios allow us to make our complexity—or confusion—manifest" richly shaping, contextualizing the concept of literacy (pp. 21-24). As the narratives emerge, revealing their competing discourses and complex power relations, then the critical affirmation process can begin and, through the same process, continue as the GTA's pedagogy develops.

Daniell (1999) explained that these

> little narratives are marked by a tension between Foucauldian determinism and human agency, showing the power of institutions to control people by controlling their literacy and the power of individuals and groups to use literacy to act either in concert with or in opposition to this power . . . [they] make clear that literacy can oppress or resist or liberate, and the best of [them] present the simultaneity of these ideological contradictions. (p. 406)

Can our composition program narratives also allow for the contradictions inherent in the little narratives to reside together and in doing so stimulate the possibilities for negotiating variance among narrative boundaries and the construction of diverse student narratives? Such an amalgamation might better serve the rapid changes in materials, tools, and social relationships propelling the 21st century and better prepare both GTAs and undergraduates to "develop the capacity to become active agents of their own histories rather than unreflective products of the cultural codes that ha[ve] shaped them" (Berlin, 1993, p. 265).

If, as Brandt (1995) stated, "literacy is always in flux; learning to read and write necessitates an engagement with this flux, with the layers of literacy's past, present, and future" (p. 666), then using literacy portfolios to collect both GTA and student literacy narratives may be the most relevant means of understanding how to revise our program narratives and training programs to meet that challenge, to examine the connection of writing, literacy and culture, and to keep the issue of where to place the lectern negotiable.

REFERENCES

Belanoff, P. (1994). Portfolios and literacy: Why? In L. Black, D. Daiker, J. Sommers, & G. Stygall (Eds.), *New directions in portfolio assessment* (pp. 13-24). Portsmouth, NH: Boynton/Cook.

Berlin, J. A. (1993). Literacy, pedagogy, and English studies: Postmodern connections. In C. Lankshear & P. L. McLaren (Eds.), *Critical literacy* (pp. 247-269). Albany: State University of New York Press.

Berlin, J. A. (1994). The subversion of the portfolio. In L. Black, D. Daiker, J. Sommers, & G. Stygall (Eds.), *New directions in portfolio assessment* (pp. 56-67). Portsmouth, NH: Boynton/Cook.

Bizzell, P. (1988). Arguing about literacy. *College English, 50*, 141–153.

Brandt, D. (1990). *Literacy as involvement: The acts of writers, readers, and texts.* Carbondale: Southern Illinois University Press.

Brandt, D. (1995). Accumulating literacy: Writing and learning to write in the twentieth century. *College English, 57*, 649-668.

Brice-Heath, S. (1993). *Identity and inner-city youth: Beyond ethnicity and gender.* New York: Teachers College Press.

Brodkey, L. (1994). Writing on the bias. *College English, 56*, 527-547.

Daniell, B. (1999). Narratives of literacy. *College Composition and Communication, 50*, 393-410.

Havelock, E. (1982). *The literate revolution in greece and its cultural consequences.* Princeton, NJ: Princeton University Press.

Kail, H. (1988). Narratives of knowledge: Story and pedagogy in four composition texts. *Rhetoric Review, 6*, 179-189.

Lu, M.-Z. (1999). Redefining the literate self: The politics of critical affirmation. *College Composition and Communication, 51*, 172-194.

Lyotard, J.-F. (1984). *The post modern condition: A report on knowledge* (G. Bennington & B. Massumi, Trans.). Minneapolis: University of Minnesota Press.

Ong, W. J. (1988). *Orality and literacy: The technologizing of the word.* London: Routledge.

Zebroski, J. T. (1994). *Thinking through theory: Vygotskian perspectives on the teaching of writing.* Portsmouth, NH: Boynton/Cook.

4

THE SPACE BETWEEN PUBLIC AND PRIVATE

Women's Literacy in Rural Nebraska

Charlotte Hogg
Texas Christian University

In the small town where I grew up in western Nebraska (with a population of 563), the boundaries between public and private are malleable. I moved there at age 12, and my grandma Dorlis was president of the Paxton Library Board at the time.[1] She would lend me the key to the library when I was bored or lonely, the new student in a class of 14. The library, smaller than many living rooms, held a new leather-bound book, *Early Paxton*, in which my grandma and other older women had written down memories of their families, town, and ways of life on the rural Great Plains. I remember specifically reading Elsie's piece. She was familiar—my grandma's next door neighbor. I discovered that, like me, she had moved to Paxton in the sixth grade and didn't like it. I don't think Elsie ever knew I read her pages down at the library, that they brought me solace after a move I didn't want to make. Somehow, reading her memoir felt quite intimate, despite the fact that I was in the public library and that Elsie had known her writing would be put in a "public" space.

Years later, my literacy study of these women who contributed to *Early Paxton* has that same feel. I cannot write about women like my grandma or Elsie for a public audience without acknowledging—sometimes foregrounding—the private, the personal, and its significance to my research.

As I continue to think about literacy practices in the lives of Paxton women, I am understanding that my desire to relay the private in what I write for others mirrors the ways public and private is convoluted for them.

In this chapter, I describe how women in Paxton, shaped by their rural lifestyle and its pervasive agrarian ideology, challenge limited definitions of public and private. I believe Paxton women model the face of women's literacy studies to come, showing us how women in sites currently unseen by researchers allow us access to the complicated ways literacy can shape—and is shaped by—women.

I first need to clarify how I am conceiving of public and private in this piece. At its most basic, the difference between public and private has to do with audience, or the absence of one. Private writings by women are thought to be diaries, journals, and letters written for a very specific person or group of persons. Public writing is written with the intent to be published in some form, such as magazine articles. However, the spheres of public and private also represent a more complex discussion of gender and the kinds of activities and lifestyles available to women and men. In her book, *Public Man, Private Woman*, Elshtain (1993) made the caveat that "to tell the full story of the public and the private would be the work of a lifetime" (p. 4). Many scholars have described the ways in which men created and had access to the public sphere while women were relegated to the domestic or private sphere and denied a public voice on many levels, from being withheld the right to vote to being kept out of the workplace (Elshtain, 1993; Glenn, 1997, among many others). Although the well-known feminist phrase, "the personal is political," inherently suggests a collapse of the dichotomy or an overlapping of the spheres in academic scholarship, the terms *public* and *private* often hold fast and simplify lives more complicated than these definitions. As we continue researching literacies of women in varying contexts, the binary terms *public* and *private* finally limit the ways we can see women's literacy at work in their lives and communities.

Other scholars have also called for researchers to question assumptions about the "separate spheres" as they have come to be known in academic writing and the tendency to view "public" and "private" as monolithic ideas (Friend, 1999; Gere & Schutz, 1998). Gere (1997) explained in *Intimate Practices: Literacy and Cultural Work in U.S. Women's Clubs, 1880-1920* that she identifies women's clubs as "one of the *competing* publics at the turn of the century," a move that "calls into question the category of 'separate spheres' common in academic feminism, urging instead more complex interpenetrations of women's clubs and other social formations" (p. 13). In the introduction to *Recipes for Reading: Community Cookbooks, Stories, Histories*, Bower bolstered Gere's argument: "What we may designate as fairly private activity or discourse (sewing, the writing of letters, contributing to a cookbook) may actually have been seen by women of the past as forms of public participation" (p. 6). Even academic feminists, then, have not always fully appreciated how women's literacy practices and contexts surpass and subvert the confines of the labels academicians have bestowed, despite, as Davidoff (1998) explained, the fact that scholars know the constraints of public and private.

In her piece on 19th-century correspondence between two women, "Writing Themselves into Consciousness: Creating a Rhetorical Bridge Between the Public and Private Spheres," Gring-Pemble described what she termed a "pre-genesis": "a transitional space between private and public expression in which women, who were largely excluded from public discussion, shared, tested, and refined their ideas in a manner that compelled them to articulate their views in a powerful public document" (p. 44). Gring-Pemble is quick to complicate her own definition, however, by noting that to discuss the few public acts of courageous women in history only serves to "highlight an artificial dichotomy between the public and the private and to ignore intermediary and highly significant processes of transformation" (p. 44). I would also argue that the terms *transitional* and *transformation* suggest a hierarchy between the two spheres, that to move from private into public suggests a kind of positive evolution, and that the "private" work done to move to the "public" space is valued for its eventual public result, not for the private rhetorical processes and contexts that enabled that result. To emphasize women's moves *toward* public spaces throughout history continually privileges the public sphere and implies that the private is less valuable.

In fact, for many, defining the private has come from examining what the public isn't. Habermas, an instrumental figure on theories of public space, articulates the public sphere as one where "access is guaranteed to all citizens. A portion of the public sphere comes into being in every conversation in which private individuals assemble to form a public body" (cited in Gring-Pemble, 1998, p. 43). Many theorists who address the notion of separate spheres draw extensively on Habermas as an authority regarding public space, but as scholars like Fraser (1994) argued, his theories of the bourgeois public stem from a particular context that may not always usefully transfer to discussions of the separate spheres. Fraser, although noting that Habermas' theories are "indispensable," contended that his failure to examine multiple public spheres leads to an idealized liberal public sphere and that ultimately "the bourgeois public's claim to full accessibility was not in fact realized" (1994, pp. 75, 80). There is no doubt that feminist theorists must continue to work within and against complicated issues like public space, as Fraser and others do, to illuminate gender inequities and provide alternatives for richer, more inclusive theories. Yet, considerations of the private by way of the public can also give credence to one sphere at the expense of analysis of another (when they are talked about as distinct realms). In the important anthology, *Feminism: The Public and the Private* (Dietz, 1998), three of four sections of the book are categorized by gender/feminism in the public sphere. The second part from the title—the private—receives much less critical attention.[2] Rather than acknowledging and existing within the tension between "public" and "private," it seems that much of the scholarship on this issue, while calling for greater nuances within the spheres, still devotes its pages to traditional theories of public space (although often to critique it).

For those who conduct the important recovery of women's lives that is commonly categorized as "private" writing or art—diaries, letters, quilts, recipes—the act of providing access to these documents and artifacts alone does not necessarily work against the common assumption that to move from the private to public is growth. This is certainly not to say that defining and critiquing traditionally male spaces and celebrating women's movement into public positions of power is not valid use of scholarship; rather, ideas like Gring-Pemble's "pre-genesis" and others that work against the dichotomy of the spheres but ultimately privilege what has been considered public do only part of the job of unsettling the spheres.

As I analyzed the writing of Paxton women, I kept trying to find theoretical models, examples, and/or abstractions that applied to my study of women in Paxton, but kept falling short. The women I know differed from historical examples of women who created public spaces in the face of sexism. The dense abstractions about publics and politics did not describe life in Paxton. I suspect this could have a great deal to do with the fact that many feminists who refer to Habermas—even if it is to challenge his theories from a feminist perspective—keep his "strong appreciation for the role performed by a new set of cultural institutions that flourished in *urban* centres: coffeehouses, clubs . . . and above all, journals and the commercial press" (Landes, 1998, pp. 138–139; italics added). It's no wonder I can't figure Paxton into these theories. So rather than use the language of other publics—alternative publics, counter publics, local publics—which I think only reinforces a hierarchy of the spheres, I imagine an elasticity between public and private that allows for a range of possibilities that don't use a monolithic concept as the touchstone or standard.

THE SCOPE (AND SITES) OF WOMEN'S LITERACY

As we move into the next century and continue to research women's literacies, it is important to examine not only who still needs to be considered, but how those we study influence and shape our conceptions of literacies. The field of composition and literacy studies would be best served by continuing to recognize and emphasize the impact of literacy on gender and vice versa. In the introduction to *Nineteenth Century Women Learn to Write*, Hobbs (1995) contended: "We will not be able to deal responsibly with contemporary issues of women's literacy either at home or abroad without historical knowledge of our own literacy, its contradictory assumptions and differential processes" (p. 4). Only in the relatively recent past have scholars highlighted the dangers in thinking of literacy in neutral (or neutered) terms when gender, class, race, and religion (among other things) impact the kinds of access people in this country have had to literacy learning. It is in the much more recent past that studies of women's literacies have added to the important and painstaking recovery work of finding out who, when, how, and where women did and did not have access to literacy. Again, from Hobbs (1995), the question is not just "'how did literacy affect women?'"—although this is also a critical question to answer—but "'how did women change literacy?'" (1995, p. 3). In the future, the focus of literacy research should enact this reciprocity between gender and our conceptions of literacy.

Meanwhile, we must be mindful of who and what has been privileged in our field; research must allow for greater latitude in time, region, and our conceptions of what constitutes "nontraditional." As Harmon (1995) reminded, "a substantial portion of the literature of the history of women's education in the United States centers on higher education, especially on elite, eastern women's colleges" (p. 84). We know much more about the women enrolled at the Seven Sisters institutions than we do of women at other colleges or not in college at all. Although this has to do in part with the logistics of conducting research—the archives at these institutions are intact—the emphasis on eastern college women privileges, among other things, traditional notions of literacy that occur in institutional settings.

As I write these words, recent works come to mind that challenge this statement, signaling to me our scope is broadening. Works such as Gere's (1997) *Intimate Practices*, Bower's (1998) *Recipes for Reading*, Heller's (1997) *Until We Are Strong Together*, and Horsman's (1990) *Something on My Mind Besides the Everyday* explore literacy practices outside of the traditional (and often masculinist) realm of institutional settings and conventional sites. Certainly, these texts signify how far the field of literacy studies has come in its exploration of women's literate lives as it has expanded beyond statistical figures of rudimentary literacies or published documents by women. More importantly, these works supply us with not only a growing body of knowledge regarding women largely ignored by researchers but also substantial theories about the use of that knowledge to consider literacy in more complicated ways. But we are only beginning, however richly, to understand the ways women in this country influenced and were influenced by literacy.

A MATTER OF SCALE: PAXTON WOMEN'S LITERACY

Much of the scholarly and literary work written about Euro-American women living in the Great Plains is lodged in the era of settlement. The enduring and quintessential prairie women from literature existed during the late 1800s: Laura Ingalls Wilder, O.E. Rölvaag's Beret, or Willa Cather's Ántonia. Historical work done on plainswomen has emphasized Oregon Trail journals and diaries from the early years of settlement. Just as the image of Lakotas using teepees and hunting bison has become the too often unquestioned image of American Indians on the Plains, the image of the 19th-century prairie woman clad in a bonnet outside her soddie has not adequately moved forward into and through the 20th century. In terms of studying the ways in which women's literacies and language have been at work in the Plains at any time in its history, particularly the 1900s, we know much less.

Not coincidentally, rural experiences on the Great Plains have been overlooked since the country embraced urbanization in the 20th century; thus, the Plains are recognized problematically when acknowledged at all. After all, according to geographer Shortridge (1997), "Plains people, with their small populations, have never had much control over how others have seen them. The possibilities for distortion, misunderstanding, and general mythmaking are enormous" (p. 115). I contend that women's experiences have also been neglected because of the ideologies working within and perceived outside the region. Anthropologist Deborah Fink (1992) argued that "common consensus associates rural areas with farming and farming with men; concomitantly, most rural studies have been about male farmers" (pp. 7-8). As Fink explained, because rural women define(d) themselves and others define(d) them as "farm wives," the difficult work they did on the farm was viewed as just "helping out," because it was the male's farm. In her second book, *Agrarian Women*, Fink delineated the agrarian ideology that began with Thomas Jefferson and persists today. Agrarianism, "the belief in the moral and economic primacy of farming over other industry," romanticizes the rural in part as a balance to the cosmopolitan city. The middle of the country has become the Heartland and breadbasket to the world, the "center of the nation's morality, the social foundation, [and] the source of all wealth" (p. 28). Against the urban cultural heartbeat, rural America is to be its quiet conscience. But Jefferson did not include women into the agrarian ideology except as nurturers to sustain husbands' needs so they could continue to feed the world.

It is important to recognize that Fink's observation extends beyond studies done about people in rural areas to include the perceptions *within* the rural culture as well. Fink wrote that "rural people have concurred in attributing greater importance to men than to women" (p. 8). The scant attention women on the Plains have received by researchers only perpetuates the agrarian ideology prevalent in rural areas.

From living in Paxton and knowing the women now involved in my research study, I argue that, even while they condone and sometimes even embrace agrarian ideologies, older women in the community complicate this ideology through their literacy practices. Furthermore, I believe the way women in Paxton think of and use literacy in their rural setting can enrich our conceptions of women's literate lives.

The women in Paxton I am working with are between the ages of 79 and 103 and have lived all of their lives in and around the town first settled by whites in the 1860s during the building of the railroad. Many of the women are second- or third-generation family members of the community; my grandma Dorlis writes that her grandfather bought land sight unseen before he moved from Wisconsin. Of the nine older women I spoke to, one never married and the remainder are widowed. All who married had children. All are White, some live on farms, some on ranches, and each attends one of the churches (Methodist, Lutheran, Catholic) in or around Paxton. A few worked outside the home as telephone operators or grocery store clerks. I had known all but one long before I began asking them about their literate lives for the purpose of research. All of them contributed to the *Early Paxton* book in the library.

The older women in Paxton have accommodated the ideology of their region insofar as they appear to maintain the belief in the designated roles assigned to men and women within the framework of agrarianism. Most of them did not have jobs outside the home, for example, and seemed to define their interests as secondary to or included in their husbands'. Like Julie Roy Jeffrey, a historian who has studied frontier women, I did not find that the women in my study greatly challenged the masculinist belief systems that pervade the western Nebraska region. Yet, through literate acts, these women complicate traditional assumptions of the rural White woman on the Great Plains. We must remember, too, that these women are engaging in acts relegated as service through a patriarchal society that has long withheld women from the public sphere. Yet, when we look at the specific nuances of women who participate in the "private" sphere, we can see how muddled the binary of public and private becomes. In Paxton, the mayor is male and the three major businesses in town are run by men; they hold the typical (and public) positions of power in the community. However, through their "extracurricular" activities involving literacy, the women in my study determined what Keith County citizens read in the Paxton section of the newspaper, composed (and shaped) histories of the town, library, churches, and cemetery, and they have run the public library since the time it was built when they "were found to be very handy with hammer and saw" (Hogg, 1992, p. 5).

The *Keith County News* exemplifies the ways in which conventional notions of public and private are not sustained in this small town. Before I moved to Paxton, my grandma would send me a small newspaper article when I returned to Fargo, North Dakota after visiting her. The article from her local paper told of my family's visit to her house for our vacation. Over the years I lived in Paxton, I saw my name in the paper for everything from riding a float in the Labor Day Parade to winning a Regents' scholarship to the University of Nebraska-Lincoln. The Paxton contributor to the *Keith County News* at this time was usually Marie, one of the older women in my study who, upon turning 100, wrote an article for the newspaper about her birthday party and the Sparkling White Grape Jell-O her guests ate (as she and Jell-O were both turning a century old). Other older women in town occasionally submitted articles to the newspaper as well. My grandma, a founding member of the Paxton Library Board, wrote about the 25th and 50th anniversaries of the library for the newspaper, as well as the history of the Methodist Church in Paxton.

Memoirs in the collection *Early Paxton* also reflect the unique scale of public and private occurring in the context of this small town. The idea for putting the volume together came in 1981 from Joyce, who is a generation younger than the women she asked to contribute to the book. In the foreword, she wrote:

> This notebook is a gathering of writings about early Paxton, Nebraska, before 1925, written for the most part by the ladies who lived here. It seems appropriate to acknowledge these ladies' lives as they lived with inconveniences, deprivation, but also with acceptance by virtue of faith, humanness and ever present humor. . . . This book is presented to the Paxton Library in appreciation of the kindness and happiness the women of Paxton have extended to their community. (Lierley, 1982, p. 1)

While doing research, I came across two interesting and useful books on writing done by rural women that illuminated the unique positioning of the *Early Paxton* memoirs. *Writings of Farm Women 1840-1940*, edited by Fairbanks and Haakenson, contains memoirs and histories written by women, including authors such as Laura Ingalls Wilder and Elinore Pruitt

Stewart. Nearly all of the women in the anthology were previously published. The editors' analysis of one author who, "like most who recorded their memories, [she] is less interested in a sociological analysis than in describing everyday experiences," exemplifies the kind of writing done by published rural women (p. 79). The other collection, *Read This Only to Yourself: The Private Writings of Midwestern Women, 1880-1910*, by Elizabeth Hampsten (1982), centers on private letters and journals of North Dakota women. The writing in these two books differs: The public writings are descriptive stories of hardship in a rural setting, whereas the private writings are repetitive with little detail, asking more of the reader through silences and gaps in the narrative.

When I compared these collections to *Early Paxton*, it again seemed the older women from my hometown were melding set definitions of public and private. Because they knew others would be reading their memoirs, the women in Paxton constructed their pieces in ways that seem most similar to the published works. Yet much of their memoirs are filled with indexical expressions, which are, to quote Brandt (1990), "liberties that writers take by virtue of an intimate relationship with their readers" (p. 74). One woman begins her narrative with, "I was born about one mile straight north of Paxton, Nebraska, in the first house on the east side of the road, where the Bill Simpson family now lives" (Sedlacek 1982, p. 196). Hence, although the writings are much more similar to the collection of published writings by Fairbanks and Haakensen, the Paxton women appeared to be writing to an intimate audience. Even given the level of perceived intimacy with the reader, their writings contain very little of the kind of narrative in the Hampsten collection.

I asked my grandma about the audience she had in mind when she wrote her 40 pages for *Early Paxton*, pages filled with memories from her childhood as well as of the town itself, as she describes former local preachers from the 1920s, for example. She told me she didn't really have a specific audience in mind, that she wrote the ideas as they came to her, which she states explicitly in her text: "The memories I have of my first years are many, but I have no idea of the chronological order as they come rushing back" (Hogg, 1982, p. 59). Yet contributors to the book did know Joyce's intent to house the collection at the library, that the writing would not be for their eyes only. The characteristics of their memoirs—indexical expressions combined with writing containing stories and rich detail—signify the way these women conceptualized their audience in ways that do not fit into fixed definitions of public and private.

From talking with my grandma, it is clear the agrarian ideology valuing the work and lives of men is a part of her belief system and thus influences her literacy practices. Not only did she put her energy into her husband's genealogy, she wrote a short biography of her grandfather on her father's side. Still, she is aware of not having done more writing about the men in her life, telling me: "I always wanted to write my dad's story, and I always wanted to finish [my husband's] story, and I just didn't do it. I was so busy with other things. Church stuff came up and stuff like that, why I helped out. Course I worked awful hard in Garden Club. . . . I wished I'd done that writing" (Hogg, personal communication, May 12, 1997). Though she did choose to commit to her community clubs rather than finish writing about her father and husband, she conveyed regret for doing so. Significantly, it was only after her husband died that Grandma began to record her own memories in writing, suggesting that somehow she found community and church clubs more acceptable diversions while he was alive than "indulging" in writing about herself. Composing her piece for *Early Paxton*, then, shows how she constructed a kind of public space for writing about herself and her past but still wrote for an audience that was, in a sense, private. From working at the library for years, she most likely assumed who might pick up *Early Paxton* with interest. The library was at once a safe haven with which to display her writing but also a site for marking a kind of authoritative space—it was neither public nor private, but both.

Although most of the women in my study have documented either family or community history in some form, a few other women stand out in particular for their literacy practices that made an authoritative space in their lives and community. Fae, now in her early 80s, compiled and composed the town history for the library. She also single-handedly updated the cemetery records, including the tedious work of researching unmarked graves. She implied that certain (male) town members who should have been in charge of the cemetery records were not doing their job:

> I mean, the dead person isn't going to come to you and say, "hey, my name isn't on the record!" So I told [my husband] that when I quit teaching I'll make a new map. . . . There were 100 people buried out there that were not on our records. . . . I made a map and took it down . . . [to] make copies. (Christensen, personal communication, July 12, 1997)

When I asked these women why it was important to them to write these histories, they simply told me it should be written so it wouldn't be lost. To them, histories of the family, town, and area defined the writing (and speaking) moments they found most valuable, and the purpose was to pass on the heritage of place and the people within that place. For members of the town—the readers of these histories—it is not only the history but the women's constructions of that history that is preserved. These women—who, incidentally, told me they disliked history in high school because it involved tedious memorization of dates—shaped perceptions of their region and community through their historical writings, perhaps as much by the authoritative act of composing history as by what their documents said.

Not only did Paxton women write histories for families or towns that will be read for generations, but they have maintained responsibility for selecting library materials since the town library was created over 66 years ago, because only women have served on the Paxton Library Board (see Passet, 1994, for a discussion on Western women librarians). Because volunteering for the community would sustain the position of women as "helpers," working for the library was another space where women did not tread outside the normative behaviors of the town but still created a space that falls between the boundaries of the private, domestic sphere and the public one. Women on the board served in every capacity of the library, including working at the desk, reading for story hour, and organizing book drives. Members of the library board had control over choosing new books purchased by the library and managed to include some of their own preferences for texts, including regional and Western authors. This group, in effect, created a local canon for the community of Paxton. And some quite obviously exerted control within the library—Gerta, for example, upon reading a book in the library she felt was too risqué for young adult readers, wrote "Muddy" in the inside flap to alert parents of its "dirty" contents.

PAXTON WOMEN AS "SPONSORS" OF LITERACY

What does it matter that these women led literate lives that existed somewhere in the space between public and private? After all, the use of the dichotomous terms in scholarly writing often serves to illustrate the ways in which women were relegated to certain lifestyles and not allowed access into others simply because they were women. The fluidity of public and private I am suggesting is not meant to disable the important lessons we learn by incorporating such terms into our research or even the terms themselves. Rather, I hope to show through my study of older women in Paxton that to think of them as existing in only one sphere limits not only their (literate) lives but the ways they were responsible for transmission of literacy in their homes and community.

I believe the Paxton women are acting as "sponsors" of literacy, which are, among other things: "any agents, local or distant, concrete or abstract, who enable, support, teach, model, as well as recruit, regulate, suppress, or withhold literacy—and gain advantage by it in some way" (Brandt, 1998, p. 166). Brandt's article uses the idea of sponsorship to explore larger issues of "economies of literacy," but her definition is useful in terms of considering the ways in which women benefit others and themselves through their literacy practices (p. 167). Brandt contended that sponsors "lend their resources or credibility to the sponsored but also stand to gain benefits from their success, whether by direct repayment or, indirectly, by credit or association" (p. 167).

Many residents of Paxton have told me that for the older women in town, education was critical not only for themselves—many could be described as "lifelong learners"—but also for subsequent generations. For the older women, work in the library, church clubs, and other organizations served them as they made authoritative spaces in a patriarchal agrarian setting. But when I asked the women or the next generation of club women (who are in their 60s) why it was so important to do this work, the response was nearly always the same: they want to educate Paxton residents in order to keep the community strong. Women (and men) in this area are proud of Nebraska having one of the highest literacy rates in the country. More importantly, in the face of declining rural populations, they are proud of Paxton, and to them, keeping it thriving is a crucial task. Sponsorship by women in this community means literally keeping the town alive for future generations. Transmission of literacy is thus deeply tied to historical and regional knowledge. Many of the Paxton women took on dual responsibilities of working to engage others in literate acts and also regional awareness. These acts also made available models of rural women. Through the insightful work of historian Susan Armitage (1992), I have been able to see how connecting gender to regional studies can broaden and enrich our understanding of region, and in turn, literacy:

> [W]e need to look at women to answer the most basic question of how one develops a sense of regional identity. . . . Surely the development of regional identity must have been a multigenerational experience, and parental transmission of ideology an important aspect of that development. . . . How did western women develop a sense of regional identity and transmit it to their children?. . . . [T]hrough careful study of gender and region, we can understand how regional identity forms, how it is maintained, and why it persists. (p. 97)

Armitage referred here to something beyond the issue of a women's domain or public versus private. She argued that the conceptualization of the West, as an example, must account not only for the ways in which women developed regional identities within/against the dominant identities but also how women influenced subsequent generations—in short, how they shaped their region.

In 1973, my grandma gave me a program booklet from the pageant in which she was nominated for Keith County Pioneer Centennial Queen. In it she had written her own biography (in third person). She closes with: "Her hard-working law abiding ancestors who came to Keith County in their covered wagons with visions of the good life in Nebraska have left her a heritage of which she is proud. By her life she prays that she may pass that same heritage on to her children and grandchildren" (Hogg, 1973, p. 7). Clearly, my grandma has passed a heritage onto me. It is not, perhaps, the heritage she imagined me taking on. Rather, what she and other Paxton women have provided me and many others in the town is a more complex understanding of the lives and identities of rural women on the Plains. The women shaped their regions and the heritage they chose to pass on through their work as sponsors of literacy. I learned from women like my grandma (and not from, say, Willa Cather) what a woman on the rural Plains can be and how that identity challenges masculinist regional constructs. So I gained knowledge from their literacy practices in the traditional sense—I understand quite a bit about rural America in the early 1900s because of their memoirs—but I also learned about the complicated roles women have in Paxton that are often oversimplified by those not from this area. Kruse (1995) reminded that "rural sociologists and education researchers frequently approach the field from a deficit perspective; the investigator describes the rural community in terms of what it lacks in comparison to urban areas" (p. 1). The impetus for this article came when I realized that my perceptions of rural Plains women differed greatly from what has been portrayed in the media and elsewhere (when portrayed at all). My images of rural women come out of their literacy practices—and did so long before these practices became a topic of study for me. While growing up, I saw women writing and I read their writing in the newspaper, public library, and church. I overheard Grandma describing library board conversations over what new books to buy. I was sponsored through literacies neither public nor private but both, thus changing the way I saw rural women. It is my hope that examples from the Paxton women enable us not only to imagine them differently but also to imagine the places and women still unseen in ways that help us continually re-examine and re-consider how we study women's literacies in the 21st century.

ENDNOTES

1. For each interview I conducted, I obtained approval to research human subjects from the University of Nebraska-Lincoln Institutional Review Board, and

each participant signed an informed consent form. At the time I began interviewing older women, very early in my research processes while I was still gaining an understanding of ethnographic methodologies, I used the standard informed consent form that states that names will be kept confidential. Later, I realized that the decision to keep people anonymous is complicated—people then don't get credit for what they have said or done, as one example. Ultimately, I decided to have an addendum to my informed consent form for participants to have the option to sign whose writing I cite in the text. For those who have passed away or who never signed consent forms, I cited them for their written work as I would any author and wanted to keep that consistent with those who were participants in my study. Therefore, the women whose written work I cite, like my grandma Dorlis, have signed the addendum and agreed to the use of their real names so they will receive credit for their written work (although they were given the choice of whether or not to remain confidential). All of the other participants/interviewees have pseudonyms.

2. Social or maternal feminism is one source of inquiry that focuses on the private sphere, but rather than providing a balance to scholarship emphasizing the public, works like Elshtain's *Public Man, Private Woman* risk tipping the scales far the other way so the private is privileged at the expense of the public. See Dietz (1998) in *Feminism, the Public and the Private* for more about this.

REFERENCES

Armitage, S. (1992). Gender and region. In G. Lich (Ed.), *Regional studies: The interplay of land and people* (pp. 85-100). College Station: Texas A&M University Press.

Bower, A. (Ed.). (1998). *Recipes for reading: Community cookbooks, stories, histories*. Amherst: University of Massachusetts Press.

Brandt, D. (1990). *Literacy as involvement: The acts of writers, readers, and texts.* Carbondale: Southern Illinois University Press.

Brandt, D. (1998). Sponsors of literacy. *College Composition and Communication, 49*(2), 165-185.

Davidoff, L. (1998). Regarding some old husbands' tales: Public and private in feminist theory. In J.B. Landes (Ed.), *Feminism: The public and the private* (pp. 164-194). New York: Oxford University Press.

Dietz, M. G. (1998). Citizenship with a feminist face: The problem with maternal thinking. In J.B. Landes (Ed.), *Feminism: The public and the private* (pp. 45-63). New York: Oxford University Press.

Elshtain, J.B. (1993). *Public man, private woman: Women in social and political thought* (2nd ed.). Princeton, NJ: Princeton University Press.

Fairbanks, C., & Haakenson, B. (Eds). (1990). *Writings of farm women, 1840-1940: An anthology*. New York: Garland.

Fink, D. (1992). *Agrarian women: Wives and mothers in rural Nebraska, 1880-1940.* Chapel Hill: University of North Carolina Press.

Fink, D. (1996). *Open country, Iowa: Rural women, tradition, and change.* Albany: State University of New York Press.

Fraser, N. (1994). Rethinking the public sphere: A contribution to the critique of actually existing democracy. In H.A. Giroux & Peter McLaren (Eds.), *Between borders: Pedagogy and the politics of cultural studies* (pp. 74-100). New York: Routledge.

Friend, C. (1999). From the contact zone to the city: Iris Marion Young and composition theory. *JAC: Journal of Advanced Composition, 19*(4), 657-676.

Gere, A. R. (1997). *Intimate practices: Literacy and cultural work in U.S. women's clubs, 1880-1920.* Urbana: University of Illinois Press.

Gere, A.G., & Schutz, A. (1998). Service learning and English studies: Rethinking "public" service. *College English, 69*(2), 129-149.

Glenn, C. (1997). *Rhetoric retold: Regendering the tradition from antiquity through the renaissance.* Carbondale: Southern Illinois University Press.

Gring-Pemble, L.M. (1998). Writing themselves into consciousness: Creating a rhetorical bridge between the public and private spheres. *Quarterly Journal of Speech, 84*, 41-61.

Hampsten, E. (1982). *Read this only to yourself: The private writings of Midwestern women, 1880-1910.* Bloomington: Indiana University Press.

Harmon, S. D. (1995). "The voice, pen and influence of our women are abroad in the land": Women and the Illinois State Normal University. In C. Hobbs (Ed.), *Nineteenth-century women learn to write* (pp. 84-102). Charlottesville: University Press of Virginia.

Heller, C. E. (1997). *Until we are strong together: Women writers in the tenderloin.* New York: Teachers College Press.

Hobbs, C. (1995). *Nineteenth-century women learn to write.* Charlottesville: University Press of Virginia.

Hogg, D. (1973). Biography. *Keith County Pioneer Centennial Queen Pageant program*, pp. 6-7.

Hogg, D. (1982). Untitled. In J. Lierley (Ed.), *Early Paxton* (pp. 59-102). Unpublished anthology.

Hogg, D. (1992, April 16). History of Paxton public library is listed. *Courier Times*, p. 5.

Horsman, J. (1990). *Something on my mind besides the everyday: Women and literacy.* Toronto: Women's Press.

Kruse, M. (1995). *From village to college: Writing the rural experience.* Unpublished doctoral dissertation, University of Nebraska-Lincoln.

Landes, J.B. (1998). The public and private sphere: A feminist reconsideration. In J.B. Landes (Ed.), *Feminism: The public and the private* (pp. 135-163). New York: Oxford University Press.

Lierley, J. (Ed.). (1991). *Early Paxton.* Unpublished anthology.

Passet, J. E. (1994). *Cultural crusaders: Women librarians in the American West, 1900-1917.* Albuquerque: University of New Mexico Press.

Sedlacek, L. (1982). Untitled. In J. Lierley (Ed.), *Early paxton* (pp. 196-206). Unpublished anthology.

Shortridge, J. (1997). The expectations of others: Struggles toward a sense of place in the Northern Plains. In D.M. Wrobel & M. Steiner (Eds.), *Many wests: Place, culture and regional identity* (pp. 114-135). Lawrence: University of Kansas Press.

II

LITERACY AND SCHOOLING

5

"IS THAT WHAT YOURS SOUNDS LIKE?"

The Relationship of Peer Response to Genre Knowledge and Authority

Elizabeth A. Wardle
Iowa State University

Many scholars have argued that understanding genre conventions is essential to academic success. How this relationship works, however, has not been adequately studied, especially among first-year college students. Most of the research discussing how students attain genre knowledge has been conducted among upper level and graduate students (Berkenkotter & Huckin, 1993; Haas, 1994) or is theoretical. Although there are claims that activities common in many first-year writing classrooms can help students attain skills related to genre knowledge, many of these claims are anecdotal; few researchers have studied how peer review activities actually function with regard to genre knowledge and academic literacies in first-year composition classrooms. This exploratory study is a step toward clarifying that relationship. In it, I explore the development of first-year students across two sequenced assignments and other relevant activities within the sequence of an entire semester of a first-year composition course.

The theoretical research about genre suggests that genre knowledge is important because in order to join an unfamiliar discourse community (in this case, achieve "academic literacy," in its multitude of forms), newcomers must learn the knowledge the community values and the language use habits that mediate the community's activity (Berkenkotter, Huckin, & Ackerman, 1988; Bizzell, 1982; Prior, 1998). In part, this requires newcomers to understand the conventions, genres, and codes that are valued in and enacted by that community: They must "expand their involvement with others in the activity system" and "appropriate at least some of these routinized tools-in-use (genres)" (Russell, 1997, p. 521). If, as Bazerman (1994) argued, genres are "forms of life, ways of being, frames for social action," then they cannot be understood without an understanding of the social systems in which they exist. Students can't produce or understand texts in their disciplines "unless they can define their goals in terms of the community's interpretive conventions" (Bazerman, 1994, p. 19; see also Berkenkotter & Huckin, 1993; Berkenkotter, Huckin, & Ackerman, 1988; Bizzell, 1982; Delpitt, 1995; Miller, 1984). "Genre conventions signal a discourse community's norms, epistemology, ideology, and social ontology"; thus, people learn various genres by participating in "the communicative activities of daily and professional life" (Berkenkotter & Huckin, 1993, p. 4).

The theoretical research about genre knowledge is further complicated by its discussion of authority. The research suggests that students cannot learn the necessary conventions unless they are participating—at some level—in the community. How does this happen? The researchers who attempt to answer this question turn to authority: students must take or be given positions of authority and privilege before they actually have them. They must "imagine for themselves the privilege of being 'insiders'—that is, of being both inside an established and powerful discourse community and of being granted a special right to speak." In effect, students "have to assume privilege without having any" (Bartholomae, 1985, p. 412). Others have echoed Bartholomae's sentiments about the importance of authority, arguing that students must have "authority to generate knowledge as well as possess it" (McCarthy & Fishman, 1991, p. 466). How this happens is not clearly outlined and few studies have specifically attempted to document it. Russell (1997) noted this is a difficulty, writing that one of the major challenges for researchers has been to understand "*how* writers develop and exert agency, identity, voice—and power—in the face of what appear to be hegemonic social forces or social language" (p. 533; italics added).

Adding to the complication is the fact that researchers have written about this process of gaining authority differently. Some have described it as an active process wherein the student takes on a voice of authority, locates him or herself within a discourse, and assumes the right to participate (Geisler, 1990). Others have suggested that perhaps it is not the student who must actively take on this role, but the teacher who must give the student the right to claim authority: "students must be given the opportunity to listen to themselves and their classmates . . . they must be given authority to generate knowledge" (McCarthy & Fishman, 1991, p. 466). Bazerman (1988) obliquely suggested that perhaps authority must be earned, rather than simply given or assumed; he argued that a kind of negotiation goes on between the novice and the more accomplished member of the community "until the beginner produces an utterance recognized as bearing meaning within the socially shared system." When things go well, "the neophyte becomes socialized into the semiotic-behavioral-perceptual system of a community" and develops "the scripts, schema, and plans appropriate to participation in the community" (p. 307).

All of this theoretical work raises important empirical questions for researchers and difficult pedagogical questions for teachers: How do students acquire genre knowledge? How can instructors teach (or at least facilitate) students' ability to start learning it (if they can; see Dias, Freeman, Medway, & Pare, 1999). How do instructors handle the important concept of authority—do they give it, force students to take it, make students earn it? These questions must be explored in order for the theoretical work about genre knowledge to be put to use; for, as Baltasar Gracian asked four centuries ago, "Of what use is knowledge unless it be made to function?"

Many composition researchers have discussed day-to-day activities in the first-year classroom, but few have explicitly studied how genre conventions are taught or learned there. Despite this lack, the literature does provide hints that perhaps peer response in its various forms might serve some function in teaching students genre conventions. For example, it suggests that peer response has benefits such as sharpening critical thinking skills (Brissland, 1980; Bruffee, 1973; Butler, 1981; Gebhardt, 1980; Hughes, 1991; James, 1981; Lagana, 1973; Lamberg, 1980; Marcus, 1984; Sager, 1973), helping students see writing as social rather than isolated (Berlin, 1987; Forman & Cazden, 1985; Gere & Abbott, 1985; Harris, 1989; Holt, 1992), and encouraging students to become authorities on various aspects of reading and writing (Herrington & Cadman, 1991).

If this is the case, then peer response may hold the potential for providing students with a number of ingredients needed for attaining academic literacies. Within first-year writing classrooms, peer response groups may serve as what Russell (1997), following Gieryn (1983), called a "stabilized-for now site of boundary work between the activity system of a discipline/profession . . . and that of the educational institution"—in this case, the composition classroom (p. 530). However, very little research describing benefits of peer response specifically examines what happens during peer response activities that might help first-year students begin to understand the genre conventions of their new academic activity system(s).

If peer response can help first-year students begin to learn new genre conventions and gain academic literacies, what are the specific activities that promote this learning? First-year composition classrooms are often the smallest classrooms of which students are a part during their first year at the university. The peer-response groups within those classrooms are even smaller. The two together might provide a less threatening door—or at least window—into the strange new discourse communities and genres of the university. Many first-year writing classrooms explicitly try to teach some of the many genres and conventions students will encounter at the university and peer-response activities require students to actively think about and discuss those new genres and conventions. Within the context of peer-response activities, students are forced to take a position of authority to some degree, to figure out what they know that other people do not and then pass that information along. At the same time, students in many first-year writing classrooms are being taught useful strategies that advanced members of university discourse communities use in order to read and write new kinds of texts, especially strategies regarding how to consider a text (their own or others) rhetorically, taking into account the context that influences a text, previous texts that are related, the varying audiences for a text, and so on. Finally, peer-response groups explicitly provide students the opportunity to work in a zone of proximal development (Vygotsky, 1978), pooling what they know in order to accomplish more as a group than they would have as individuals.

Because of the importance of genre knowledge to academic literacies and the lack of clear research detailing how first-year students do or do not begin learning new genre conventions, I designed an exploratory study that would allow me to closely observe the efforts of first-year students participating in peer-response activities. Specifically, this study enabled me to watch how students assumed (or did not assume) authority while gaining new genre knowledge. In this exploratory inquiry, I followed two first-year writing students (Josiah and Paul) over the course of the semester, observed classroom and workshop talk, collected written peer-responses, and conducted interviews. I chose this classroom because the teacher, Isabel, focused extensively on peer-response activities and taught several assignments that could safely be considered new academic genres for most of the students. During the course of the semester, I was able to observe as the students wrestled with new genre conventions in their peer-response activities. Although my observation of two participants does not allow for generalizations, it did allow for detailed inquiry and description of the ways these students struggled with—and began to learn—new genre conventions. These descriptions may prove helpful in concretely illustrating the theory about genre knowledge. The written and oral work of these two students suggested that, for them, peer-response activities were integral parts of helping them master new academic genres. My descriptive inquiry also suggests that much of the current literature may not explore fully enough the complicated relationship between genre knowledge and authority. In my study, students were only able to assert authority once they had earned it; workshop sessions created a safe place where students could earn this authority by working together in a dynamic zone of proximal development.

METHODS

I conducted this exploratory study during the spring semester of an intermediate college writing class at an urban university in a large southern city. I served as a participant-observer in this course. Although occasionally the instructor would ask me to help her demonstrate a concept or a student would ask me a question, I spent most of my time silently observing and tape recording.

Intermediate college writing, the course I observed, was required of nearly all first-year students at this school. The goals of the course, as mandated by the composition program, were to teach students to locate, evaluate, read, and comprehend source material; choose appropriate research topics; collect information; and compile their research successfully and appropriately for academic audiences. The primary goal of the course, then, was to teach students to research and write academic texts.

The teacher of this course, Isabel, was a graduate student in her second year of teaching at the time of observation. She received excellent teaching evaluations from her students, who often signed up for her classes again despite the fact that she assigned more work than many other teachers. She consciously attempted to create an atmosphere of trust in her classroom, and her students affirmed that she was successful in this endeavor. However, as my results show, this trust by itself was not sufficient for teaching students genre knowledge or helping them assume authority.

Isabel focused on teaching her intermediate writing students to think about their research topics, work through them in a systematic way, explore them before narrowing them, and produce a number of texts in different academic genres, including annotated bibliographies, précis, literature reviews, abstracts, and research papers. In class she focused on teaching students strategies for close and careful reading of texts, which applied to texts they researched, wrote, and read for others. She often provided students with examples of texts she had written to illustrate points she was making.

There were 26 students in the course I observed, a class that typified the university profile of White, working-class, first-generation college students. On the first day, Isabel explained my research project to the class and asked for volunteers. Five White students, two women and three men, volunteered. However, due to health problems and outside factors, by the end of the semester I only had useable data from two of these students, Josiah and Paul, both of whom had taken Isabel's introductory class the previous semester and earned either grades of A or B. Although attrition among participants may be considered a weakness of the study, the close observation I was able to make of these two students allowed me to achieve a useful descriptive inquiry. Clearly, however, there are limitations to what we can infer from any discussion of the activities of these two White, male students.

Josiah was a traditional 18-year-old freshman from a small city only a few minutes from the university. His open, outspoken manner was noticeable from the beginning and he had a good rapport with the instructor. He always spoke out in class and often responded to Isabel's questions humorously or irreverently, telling her, for example, that an assignment she gave was "a pain in the ass." He also showed a high degree of comfort with me, joking with me when I observed workshop group sessions. Both of Josiah's parents were college graduates and expected him to do well in school, which he did. He told me he enjoyed Isabel's class and chose to enroll in it both semesters because her class was "open with the rest of the students" and "really calm," not like high school where "you were always worried about 'was this right' and you couldn't really ask questions."

Paul was a 23-year-old freshman in his first year of college who had just completed 4 years in the military. For Paul, married with a new baby, college was serious business. He took a full load of classes while working 35 hours per week. The two most noticeable traits about Paul were his seriousness and his leadership. Never late or absent, Paul always sat in the front row and had his books open and notes out when class began. He was always prepared, even when no one else was. Paul responded to questions earnestly, choosing his words carefully, often explaining what he thought Isabel was saying to other students who were confused. Although writing was not easy for him, Paul's hard work enabled him to receive high grades in Isabel's courses. In small groups, Paul took a gentle but firm leadership role, asking questions to get the group back on task when they wandered off. This was a conscious decision for him, a logical and necessary result of his years in the military, his strong religious beliefs, and his age. He told me he could remember what it was like to be 18 and think it was fun to get off track but that he also knew what it meant to be "wasting your time when you're spending thousands of dollars." Like Josiah, Paul chose to enroll both semesters in Isabel's class because he enjoyed it. He explained that when he entered her class, "it was like freedom, like she took chains off of people and let them go."

In the class I observed, students were required to complete what Isabel termed "four major writing assignments" and "a series of minor writing assignments." The major writing assignments consisted of a career research paper, an annotated bibliography on a topic of their choice, a literature review to come out of their annotated bibliography, and a final research paper, also to come out of their annotated bibliography. The minor writing assignments included peer critiques, a research proposal, a literature conference précis and reflection, and an abstract for the final research paper. Isabel assigned standard grades on all the assignments with a (recommended) option to revise for the required portfolio at the end of the semester.

Isabel's peer-response system consisted of several components. She scheduled in-class workshops for each assignment, which required students to bring their work to class and receive feedback from their small, three- to four-member group during class time. Isabel did not usually provide written instructions for these in-class workshops; instead, she asked students to read and respond to texts based on what they knew and understood about what made that textual genre successful. At the beginning of the semester, she and I modeled the workshop process for the class, demonstrating the kinds of questions they should be asking and the kinds of feedback they should be giving. Isabel considered workshop participation an essential component of the course.

Isabel also assigned what she called peer critiques, which required the students to send their writing home with a peer who then wrote a two-plus page, prose critique in response to what they read. This assignment included a lengthy assignment sheet with suggested questions for students to ask and answer such as, "Who do you think the intended audience is for this piece? What about this piece interests you as a reader? What is the author trying to do in this piece?" These questions focused largely on the rhetorical situation—the writer, the audience, and the context (including social relationships surrounding the text, history of the discipline for which the text was written, other texts related to the one under consideration, and conventions appropriate to the particular genre of the text). The questions only briefly touched on grammatical concerns and the assignment clearly asked students to focus on "larger" issues before dealing with "smaller" ones.

During the course of the semester I collected data from a variety of sources, including observing, taperecording, and coding workshop sessions; taperecording interviews with Josiah, Paul, and Isabel; reading and coding Josiah and Paul's peer critiques; and observing the classroom and reading Isabel's handouts. By semester's end I had collected peer critiques written by both Paul and Josiah in response to four assignments: a five- to seven-page career research paper, a précis detailing a presentation at the literature conference, an annotated bibliography written in preparation for the final research paper, and a ten-page research paper about any topic or issue the students chose.

Isabel posed questions about rhetorical issues in her peer critique assignment and, as a result, I looked for evidence of rhetorical responses when I read the critiques and workshop transcripts. It seemed to me (and, I think, to Isabel, too) that those contextual features many researchers consider rhetorical (see, especially, Haas, 1994) are directly linked to issues of genre knowledge. If a student can envision the audience for a text and understand what that audience's textual needs are, he or she is well on the way to being able to understand genre features and the activity that helped shaped them.

I analyzed my data continuously during the semester, especially toward the end of the term. I read all data numerous times, formulating tentative coding categories that related to genre knowledge and rhetorical understanding of various texts. I combed through the data repeatedly in order to look for less obvious references to genre conventions or unusual appropriations of authority. This method allowed me to pull from multiple data sources to discuss each issue and support each conclusion with specific references to the data I collected from all participants (Lincoln & Guba, 1985; Merriam, 1998).

RESULTS OF INQUIRY AND OBSERVATION

Although most of the semester's work was completed in anticipation of the final research paper, the précis assignment was the one that proved to be most interesting because it considerably stretched most of the students' genre knowledge. The assignment required that students attend one session of a professional literature conference held at the university and then write a précis of a presentation given by one of the presenters. This assignment caused a huge amount of confusion and dismay among the students. They complained that all the presenters spoke in a manner that was "over their heads," that it was very difficult to write a précis of an oral text to which they could not refer later, and that they didn't understand what a précis was, what it should look like, or what it was supposed to do. In the end, Isabel decided that the peer critiques of the précis were too off the mark to receive a grade. She did, however, give students a chance to revise their incorrect précis in order to write them according to appropriate genre conventions. Isabel told me that she saw the précis assignment as a failure so she moved away from it quickly. However, it provided an excellent opportunity for me to examine how students dealt with an unfamiliar genre, what steps they took to learn the new genre conventions, and how peer response activities helped them in this effort, if at all.

For Josiah and Paul it seemed that different activities, although they were similar, had very different (and important) affordances for learning genre conventions. Workshops served to help students work through confusion together while peer critiques allowed them to demonstrate the concrete knowledge they had about the genre—if they had any. My analysis showed that the students gave each other no appropriate genre feedback whatsoever in their précis peer critiques and they were unable to assume any authority when writing these critiques, despite the fact that the very nature of the activity provided students with the opportunity to do so. The workshop that followed the précis critique helped students gain some genre knowledge by working together in a zone of proximal development, although they still were unable to assume any authority for themselves, because they did not yet have enough genre knowledge to speak with certainty. However, in the peer-response activities surrounding the subsequent assignment—an annotated bibliography—the students demonstrated both appropriate genre knowledge and a clear sense of authority deriving from that knowledge, perhaps partly as a result of the peer workshops.

What I saw when observing Paul and Josiah suggests that the literature may not adequately consider the importance of authority: Authority cannot simply be given or assumed, it must be earned through knowledge. In addition, genre knowledge may at least partially be gained through participating in the work of creating a new genre with the help of a community of supportive peers.

Confusion Demonstrated in Précis Critique

Isabel provided the students with an opportunity to assume authority by assigning them to write peer critiques in which they were forced to give feedback to other students. As I mentioned earlier, her peer critique assignment sheet directed students to consider in their critiques the rhetorical factors so necessary to acquiring genre knowledge: appropriate conventions, intended audiences and their needs, and so on. When Josiah and Paul critiqued genres with which they were familiar (such as research papers), they were able to provide this rhetorical feedback and assume authority. However, when they critiqued the précis genre, with which they were not familiar, they were unable to provide rhetorical feedback or assume authority. For example, most of Josiah's peer critiques provided an average of 6.5 rhetorically related comments (comments such as, "What I think the reader would like is. . . "). However, his précis critique provided his peer with no rhetorical feedback at all (see Table 5.1). In fact, in his précis peer critique Josiah gave only one substantial suggestion for improvement of any kind. Instead, he spent a good amount of time talking about how "weak" his own précis was and how difficult the conference presentation had been to understand. He also spent one fairly lengthy paragraph talking about the way the student writer had included her own opinion in the précis—something he liked and approved of. Unfortunately, in this case, Isabel had emphasized that personal opinion should be excluded from the text because, in her view, a précis should be an objective and impersonal summary. Although she explained this to the students before they wrote their précis or critiques, most students failed to follow (or perhaps understand) her directive. Josiah's critique clearly illustrated a failure to maneuver successfully through a new set of genre conventions, a failure nearly all the students in the class mirrored, either in their own précis and/or in their peer critiques.

Paul's précis critique was similar to Josiah's in that it not only omitted any mention of appropriate genre conventions, but was also the only peer critique in which he showed basically no evidence of rhetorical awareness at all (see Table 5.2). Although he averaged nine rhetorical comments in his other peer critiques, he barely managed to make one in his précis critique.

In the précis critique, the closest Paul came to mentioning any rhetorical element was to tell the student writer to "decide for yourself what information, if any, can be further reduced into one small paragraph. This depends on the end requirements that Isabel wants for this." This comment

Table 5.1. Josiah's References to the Rhetorical Situation in Peer Critiques

Critique	Rhetorical Comments in Critique Related to Genre Knowledge
Critique 1: Career research paper	6
Critique 2: Précis	0
Critique 3: Annotated bibliography	7
Critique 4: 10-page research paper	7

Table 5.2. Paul's References to the Rhetorical Situation in Peer Critiques

Critique	Rhetorical Comments in Critique Related to Genre Knowledge
Critique 1: Career research paper	15
Critique 2: Précis	1
Critique 3: Annotation bibliography	8
Critique 4: 10-page research paper	4

suggested Paul was considering the reader as an important factor in determining appropriate format and that he envisioned the instructor as the reader. However, in his other critiques, he rarely indicated that he envisioned Isabel as the primary audience, perhaps because she encouraged her students to consider who might actually want to read that genre about that particular topic, and then to consider that person or group as their audience. Paul was usually successful in doing this, but in his précis critique he was either confused as to the purpose of the assignment and the intended audience—or else he could not hide his certainty that Isabel was, in the end, the "real" audience. In my view, he was so far removed from an activity system that would value such a genre that he simply could not fathom an audience who would need to read it (Russell, 1997).

The remainder of Paul's critique pointed out misused or misspelled words and minor grammatical problems, items Paul never spent an entire critique discussing when responding to any other genre. In the précis critique, Paul ignored the rhetorical questions he was confused by in order to focus, instead, on what he did know and understand—in this case, grammar, spelling, and sentence structure.

Because Isabel's purpose for assigning peer critiques was to encourage the students to focus on the rhetorical elements necessary for fully understanding many of the genre conventions of academic writing, she was extremely disappointed in the précis critiques and decided not to grade them. However, she did provide students the opportunity to meet in workshop and discuss their précis in order to revise them.

Josiah and Paul's précis critiques suggest that, although it may be necessary for the teacher to provide students opportunities to assume authority, the students may not be able to take on this authority immediately because they do not yet possess enough knowledge to do so. Instead of looking at these peer-response activities as opportunities for the teacher to give students authority, the teacher might better look on them as opportunities for the students to earn authority over a new genre. Additionally, as clear as Isabel's explanation of appropriate conventions might have been, students were simply not able to grasp her directions before they had attempted to write the new genre, although, as is seen, in the subsequent workshops, the zone of proximal development (ZPD) provided new affordances for earning authority by learning genre conventions.

Working Through Confusion in Précis Workshop

The day the students turned in their written précis peer critiques, they met in small workshop groups to discuss their précis. What occurred in this workshop clearly illustrated Vygotsky's (1978) notion of working in a dynamic ZPD. Although the students still did not assume the authority Isabel had provided them the opportunity to assume, they did begin to work through the confusing genre conventions together by pooling their knowledge.

Josiah began the précis workshop (where he was paired with Paul and another student named Cameron) by asking the others to clarify for him what he was supposed to do in the précis because, he said, he was "completely lost." During this workshop, he gave basically no substantial feedback the entire time. Instead, he asked questions of Paul, Cameron, Isabel (when she came by), and even me (which was unusual), and talked mostly about confusion. Cameron and Paul provided most of the substantial comments during this workshop. Rhetorical awareness was obviously difficult for Josiah when he admittedly did not understand the assignment—what it should do, what it should look like, and why it was being asked of him.

On the other hand, Paul took a dual leadership role with Cameron and did refer to rhetorical elements several times in helping the other students understand what the assignment was asking of them. Paul tried to make sense of the précis by explaining a mistake in Josiah's paper this way: "It's still so vague that if I picked it up I wouldn't know if I'd be able to use it in research or not." He tried to envision for the group what some people, in some system of activity (in this case, academic research), might want to see in a précis and why, in order to figure out how one should be written. Although Paul was explicitly concerned about appropriate genre conventions, he did not yet understand them. He could mimic the directions regarding genre conventions that Isabel gave in class, (e.g., "The first thing is watch the 'yous' because [Isabel] just mentioned the 'yous' in there"), however, he couldn't really explain *why* these conventions were appropriate, although he tried.

Workshop group participants voiced their lack of authority continually during the précis workshop, which began with an informal group discussion about lack of authority and knowledge, a discussion that we might be tempted to describe as "commiserating":

C: [to researcher] We went to the literary conference and we have to do this précis over one paper.

J: Is that all we had to do, just talk about that? Because I missed, like, the class that she explained all this and I was completely lost. I went to this thing and just sat there. There was a group of four people—old smart people—and I was kind of like going, "aaaah!"

C: After all three of them spoke I was sitting there and the, uh, chair was like . . .

EW: Were you the only one there to listen?
C: Well, there was another guy from our class, I think, that was there (laughs)
P: There were only two students in ours.
J: Mine was full of braniacs.
C: They all started discussing, they were like, "We have time to discuss" so they got into it.
J: I had no idea what they were talking about.
C: I just took notes.
J: I don't know if I did it right or not.

These "lack of authority" discussions were pervasive in all the workshops I observed and usually lasted for a number of turns, until one of the group members moved on and tried to begin to construct an understanding of the genre conventions. After the preceding discussion, Cameron took a leadership role and turned the conversation in a different direction by making the first substantive statement about the précis genre: "It's just supposed to be a summary." This turned the tide of the discussion from commiserating to working. Josiah read his précis and then asked Cameron, "Is that what yours sounds like, kinda?" Cameron replied by saying, "Sort of" and then giving Josiah some directions for changing his précis.

In all the workshops, including the précis workshop, once a group member turned the conversation in this way, the rest of the group usually followed the example and tried to move from confusion to mastery of whatever was confusing them. Because no one person knew exactly how to achieve the conventions of this genre, they all pooled their information and worked toward an understanding together. For example, when Cameron, Josiah, and Paul were all confused about how to condense a long presentation in the very short space afforded in a précis, they tried to figure it out together. Within the space of only a few minutes, each student spoke, adding to or questioning comments another student made and trying to craft Cameron's précis so that it conformed to appropriate genre conventions. This conversation was fast and collaborative. No one made a directly authoritative statement, but they all managed to pool pieces of correct information in order to help Cameron produce a better précis.

The students worked together like this a number of times, struggling toward what they thought were appropriate conventions. Although they all clearly felt the right to speak—even to make mistakes—they did not pretend an authority over the genre that they had not yet earned. They relied on one another and pooled what they knew to help them achieve knowledge of appropriate genre conventions. These results echo the results of the précis critique, again suggesting that students cannot simply be given authority without actually earning it, in this case, by gaining some mastery of appropriate genre conventions. Additionally, the workshop results suggest that Vygotsky's ZPD can help explain how students acquire genre knowledge and authority to write, by co-constructing knowledge that would earn them the authority to critique and write the genre.

It could be argued that students' confusion in the précis workshop stemmed more from an inability to understand the vocabulary and content of the conference presentations, rather than from a lack of genre knowledge. Although this may be the case, later drafts of the students' précis indicated that they *could* eventually provide a satisfactory (although not sophisticated) account of the conference presentations they saw, once they understood some of the important conventions of the new précis genre. This is evidenced by the grades students received from Isabel on their (much-revised) précis.

It is also possible that confusion about genre conventions—or a lack of ability to learn genre conventions, despite clear explanation—is due not simply to lack of practice writing that genre or to being outside the system of activity that created that genre, but also to complete incomprehension of the vocabulary, knowledge, content, worldview, and ongoing actions of that system, even when directly faced with them. In other words, being present in a system of activity is not the same thing as belonging to it or being enculturated into it.

After the précis workshop, Isabel answered students' questions about appropriate conventions for summary writing and provided students with examples of annotations that she had written, in order to prepare them for their next assignment: an annotated bibliography that was purposely sequenced after the précis assignment so that students could continue to develop their critical summary writing skills.

Improvement in Annotated Bibliography Critique

After the précis workshop and Isabel's additional lecture and handouts, Paul and Josiah asked questions of both Isabel and me, then they revised their précis and began to work on their annotated bibliographies. The peer critiques they wrote for these annotated bibliographies illustrated genre knowledge and an authority about summary writing that had not been present when they began to consider the genre of critical summary writing in their précis critiques and workshop. The précis workshop and the ensuing class discussions had helped students gain enough understanding of appropriate summary conventions so that they could speak about them with some authority in the next peer critique. For example, Josiah's critique of the annotated bibliography confidently addressed wordiness, a problem that had troubled him in the précis workshop only a few weeks earlier. He wrote:

> In the first annotation you give a good short précis on this book but it could be a little shorter. Isabel gives an example of how to do this in her outline on peer critiquing these annotations (which I don't think you received . . .) but it says that instead of writing "a book containing information . . . " you should write, "contains information on narcotics. . . ." That should help. The next three seem fine but the same problem that was in the first annotation occurs in the fourth. That is the one by Kurtland. . . . Just put, "Provides in-depth view."

Josiah's critique of the annotated bibliography made five references to appropriate genre conventions and six references to the context of an annotated bibliography, both of which were entirely absent in his peer critique of the précis (see Table 5.1). These references to appropriate conventions referred almost entirely to guidelines set by Isabel. Josiah repeated, apparently word for word, directions Isabel had given for what the opening to the annotated bibliography should look like and then told his peer that he "did all this." He also referred to examples of annotations that Isabel had passed out and used those examples to suggest (accurate) corrections for five of his peer's annotations. The sequenced experience of writing and responding to a précis had taught Josiah to understand what some of the appropriate genre conventions for objective summary writing were. He had also turned to failproof examples—those given by the teacher—in order to get it right. By doing so, he kept from making the same mistakes twice. He did not appear to understand *why* certain conventions were appropriate (i.e., he did not explain the genre conventions in terms of the activity that shaped them), but now at least he knew what the correct conventions were and talked about them with authority, which he had not been able to do in his précis critique.

Paul's critique of the annotated bibliography was similar to Josiah's in that he, too, spoke with confidence and authority about how to write a concise summary, something he had not been able to do at the time of the précis critique or workshop. But Paul's critique went even further: It demonstrated that he had carefully thought about who the reader of his peer's annotated bibliography might be and what this reader needed to know. Although he never explicitly stated who he saw as the reader, he made numerous statements about who might find that particular annotated bibliography interesting and, thus, why the annotations should be written according to certain conventions. These statements included, "This information may be helpful for someone looking for structural problems in the Statue of Liberty, for example" and "This would help someone looking for information on a certain engineer or comparing two engineers" and "You may want to list a few of the major structural failures in this book to help those researching specific ones." He was stretching himself further, trying to imagine the workings of an activity system that might benefit from this genre that was so foreign to him.

Clearly, between the time of the précis critique and the annotated bibliography critique, both Paul and Josiah managed to master at least some of the appropriate conventions of a new academic genre: summary writing of various kinds. They moved from stated confusion about conventions and a focus entirely on grammar to clear and accurate rhetorical feedback and the ability to assume authority over new genre conventions. This mastery appeared to occur as the result of a workshop discussion and some continued help and examples from the instructor and may be due in no small part to the sequencing of assignments. It is important to note that Josiah and Paul both made strides in gaining genre knowledge and authority through negotiating their understandings in the ZPD. However, Josiah was only able to articulate what the appropriate genre conventions were; Paul was able to explain both *what* the conventions were and *why* they were that way.

It is useful to remember that although Isabel had given lectures about appropriate précis conventions *before* students wrote the précis peer critique, only the lectures and handouts given *after* the critique and workshop made sense to Josiah and Paul. They apparently needed a reason for listening to her directions, which they did not have before they made a failed précis attempt. Additionally, on an affective level, they seemed to need to "commiserate" with their peers—to be assured that they weren't alone in their confusion—before they were able to use Isabel's instructions productively.

DISCUSSION AND IMPLICATIONS

Although my sample was too small to enable generalization from the results, what I saw suggests that different activities enacted within different social relations may have radically different affordances for learning, despite the fact that on the face of it they are aimed at developing the same kind of knowledge. In this case, workshops helped students move toward academic literacies and learn new genre conventions by providing a safe place for students to co-construct genre knowledge in a ZPD, getting help from more able peers and giving it to less able peers (and, at times, vice versa). For Paul and Josiah, peer-only talk was an essential part of learning new genres in this case, although, on its own, this talk did not help the students fully come to terms with the new genre. The peer-only "lack of authority" conversations, with their commiserating, always preceded conversations in which the students worked out solutions to what they did not know. However, one kind of conversation never occurred without the other. Written peer critiques, on the other hand, helped students by providing a place for them to make knowledge within a new community, but only once they had earned the right to speak about a new genre. The two activities had a symbiotic relationship, wherein one made way for and allowed the other to occur.

Thus, it is not surprising that written peer reviews and oral peer workshops afforded and constrained students' authority in different ways, also. Students had to work in a ZPD for a time, voicing confusion and receiving help from one another, before they were able to make knowledge that provided them with the ability to assert authority in a useful way within their peer critiques and workshops. Authority (in the activity system of this classroom) came through knowledge. Knowledge came from drafting, talking to peers, writing peer critiques, and listening to the instructor. Due to differing power relationships, Isabel had to give students some authority (by allowing them a voice in written peer critiques and workshops) before they could assume it; however, this observation of Paul and Josiah suggests that authority must additionally be *earned* before it can be assumed. The students had to carefully earn their right to speak with authority in written critiques because these were seen and graded by the instructor. The group workshop effort made this possible by providing a place for the students to learn new conventions within a peer-only environment without the threat of evaluation but still within the scaffolding context of the teacher's explanations and activity as well as within a sequencing of assignments and group work that involved teacher design.

In light of the fact that I began this study in order to provide writing teachers with concrete strategies, based in research, to help them teach students new academic genres, it seems essential to end with some concrete implications for teaching stemming from this study.

First, in Isabel's class, the peer critiques of a text were written before the students had an opportunity to participate in a group workshop. The results indicate that this sequencing may, perhaps, be backward—at least when students are being introduced to a genre for the first time. Because the students completely ignored any confusing aspects of a new genre when they wrote peer critiques and they talked at length about their confusion when they arrived in workshop groups, the peer critiques the students wrote might have been even more useful if they had been written *after* students had the opportunity to work through their genre confusion together in the context of a workshop group. In this scenario, students could exchange papers with peers outside of their group after the workshop session and then write a peer critique, utilizing the new information they gained while in the workshop group. However, it is also possible that writing peer critiques before the workshop showed students what they did not know and thus motivated the successful workshops—but at the cost of much frustration.

Second, this study suggests that oral, group peer-response activities and written, individual peer-response activities may be equally important and provide very different affordances when students are gaining new genre knowledge and the authority necessary to talk about, read, and write new genres. Many first-year composition classes utilize only one form of peer-response activity. I suggest that teachers think carefully about utilizing several forms of peer response when introducing new genres and, when doing so, be cautious about discounting what might appear to be "off-task" talk. The students I observed very much needed the time they spent "commiserating," talking about how confused they were about new genres. After they did so, they always turned to a group effort to work through the confusion and were then able to assume authority. But neither of these ever occurred without the other: Students needed to feel assured that they weren't alone in their confusion before they could move toward solving their problems and assuming authority.

A third possible implication for teaching might come as consolation to many teachers: in this study, students managed to gain genre knowledge and earn authority despite what seemed initially to be utter confusion. The précis required students to do things they had not been taught to do in class (attend a graduate-level literature conference without their peers, listen to an oral presentation, and write a summary of an oral text) and forge and utilize an entirely new set of strategies. Although the students' uncharacteristically bad work and outward discouragement and confusion supported Isabel's assessment of this as a "poor" assignment, they still managed to learn several important conventions of a new genre. This is perhaps true more often than we realize: despite our well-intentioned but poorly designed assignments, many of our students still manage to learn what they need to know as they work toward academic literacies as long as they are encouraged to create a productive ZPD where they can co-construct genre knowledge and earn the right to assume authority.

This is connected to a final implication about the *sequencing* of assignments: Even assignments (like the précis assignment) that seem immensely unsatisfactory at the time can be an important piece of growing to genre knowledge and earning authority through apparent chaos and confusion. Scheduling several related genres in sequence, explaining their relationship and providing students the opportunity to assert more authority with each passing assignment could be a useful part of teaching genre knowledge.

CONCLUSION

This descriptive study helps concretely illustrate some of the previous theoretical work regarding how students gain new genre knowledge and assume authority within a new and unfamiliar activity system. My observations here affirm Bazerman's suggestion that authority is a negotiation: Although it may be necessary for the teacher to provide students opportunities to assume authority, students must still earn the right to speak with authority about new genre conventions. The results also reaffirm the sociocognitive notion that students learn by doing: in the case of genre conventions, simply hearing appropriate conventions explained is not enough. Students must write the new genre, be told the conventions, and reaffirm those conventions among themselves, hearing the conventions again, and revising. Thus, instructors might expect to have to explain appropriate conventions to students several times, while simultaneously asking students to practice writing in those genres and providing the opportunity for students to work together.

Finally, this exploratory study suggests that genre knowledge happens slowly, over time, and is "complexly laminated" in ongoing activity (see Prior, 1998): Some students may only be able to describe what the conventions are during the course of a semester while others may develop greater rhetorical awareness and come to understand the sorts of activities that motivate those contextual conventions. Both abilities can be seen as progress on the road toward academic literacies.

ACKNOWLEDGMENTS

I'd like to thank Debra Journet, who first encouraged me to pursue this project and patiently helped me learn the conventions of a new genre. I'd also like to thank David Russell, whose positive, thoughtful, and tireless feedback is unmatched, and Charles Bazerman, whose editorial comments put into words some ideas I had not previously been able to express well.

REFERENCES

Bartholomae, D. (1985). Inventing the university. In M. Rose (Ed.), *When a writer can't write* (pp. 134-165). New York: Guilford.

Bazerman, C. (1988). *Shaping written knowledge: The genre and activity of the experimental article in sciences* (pp. 291-317). Madison: University of Wisconsin Press.

Bazerman, C. (1994). The life of genre, the life in the classroom. In A. Freedman & P. Medway (Eds.), *Learning & teaching genre* (pp. 19-26). London: Taylor and Francis.

Berkenkotter, C., & Huckin, T. (1993). Rethinking genre from a sociocognitive perspective. *Written Communication, 10*, 475-507.

Berkenkotter, C., Huckin, T., & Ackerman, J. (1988). Conversations, conventions, and the writer. *Research in the Teaching of English, 22*, 9-44.

Berlin, J. (1987). *Rhetoric and reality: Writing instruction in American colleges, 1900-1985*. Carbondale: Southern Illinois University Press

Bizzell, P. (1982). Cognition, convention, and certainty: What we need to know about writing. *Pre/Text, 3*, 213-243.

Brissland, J. (1980). Peer evaluation method promotes sharper writing. *Journalism Educator, 34*, 17-19.

Bruffee, K. (1973). Collaborative learning: Some practice models. *College English 34*, 634-643.

Butler, S. (1981). *The bridge to real writing: Teaching Editing Skills*. ERIC No. ED 228 639.

Delpit, L. (1995). *Other people's children: Cultural conflict in the classroom*. New York: New Press.

Dias, P., Freedman, A., Medway, P., & Pare, A. (1999). *Worlds apart: Acting and writing in academic workplace contexts*. Mahwah, NJ: Erlbaum.

Forman, E., & Cazden, C. (1985). Exploring Vygotskian perspectives in education: The cognitive value of peer interaction. In J. Wertsch (Ed.), *Culture, communication, and cognition: Vygotskian perspectives* (pp. 323-347). New York: Cambridge University Press.

Gebhardt, R. (1980). Teamwork and feedback: Broadening the base of college writing. *College English, 42*, 69-74.

Gere, A., & Abbott R. (1985). Talking about writing: The language of writing groups. *Research in the Teaching of English, 19*, 362-385.

Gieryn, T. (1983). Boundary work and the demarcation of science from non-science. *American Sociological Review, 48*, 781-795.

Geisler, C. (1990). The artful conversation: Characterizing the development of advanced literacies. In R. Beach & S. Hynds (Eds.), *Developing discourse practices in adolescence and adulthood* (pp. 93-109). Norwood, NJ: Ablex.

Gracian, B. (1992). *The wisdom of Baltasar Gracian: A practical manual for good and perilous times* (J.L. Kaye, ed.). New York: Pocket Books.

Haas, C. (1994). Learning to read biology: One student's rhetorical development in college. *Written Communication, 11*, 43-84.

Harris, J. (1989). The idea of community in the study of writing. *College Composition and Communication, 40,* 11-22.

Herrington, A., & Cadman, D. (1991). Peer review and revising in an anthropology course: Lessons for learning. *College Composition and Communication, 42,* 184-200.

Holt, M. (1992) The value of written peer criticism. *College Composition and Communication, 43,* 384-392.

Hughes, J. (1991). It really works: Encouraging revision using peer writing tutors. *English Journal, 80,* 41-41.

James, D. (1981). Peer teaching in the writing classroom. *English Journal, 70,* 48-49.

Lagana, J.R. (1973). *The development, implementation, and evaluation of a model for teaching composition which utilizes individualized learning and peer grouping.* Unpublished dissertation, University of Pittsburgh, Pittsburgh, PA.

Lamberg, W. (1980). Self-provided and peer-provided feedback. *College Composition and Communication, 31,* 63-69.

Lincoln, Y.S., & Guba, E.G. (1985). *Naturalistic inquiry.* Beverly Hills, CA: Sage.

Marcus, H. (1984). The writing center: Peer tutoring in a supportive setting. *English Journal, 73,* 66-67.

McCarthy, L.P., & Fishman, S.M. (1991). Boundary conversations: Conflicting ways of knowing in philosophy and interdisciplinary research. *Research in the Teaching of English, 25,* 419-468.

Merriam, S.B. (1998). *Qualitative research and case study applications in education.* San Francisco: Jossey-Bass.

Miller, C. (1984). Genre as social action. *Quarterly Journal of Speech, 70,* 151-167.

Prior, P. (1998). *Writing/disciplinarity: A sociohistoric account of literate activity in the academy.* Mahwah, NJ: Erlbaum.

Russell, D. (1997). Rethinking genre in school and society: An activity theory analysis. *Written Communication, 14,* 504-554.

Sager, C. (1973). Improving the quality of writing composition through pupil use of rating scale. ERIC No. ED 089 304.

Vygotsky, L.S. (1978). *Mind in society: The development of higher psychological processes.* Cambridge, MA: Harvard University Press.

6

MEANING AND DEVELOPMENT OF ACADEMIC LITERACY IN A SECOND LANGUAGE

Ilona Leki
University of Tennessee

As English continues to expand into a global language (Kachru, 1992; Pennycook, 1994), English learners worldwide experience pressure to develop literacy in English, often a high level of academic literacy. Yet, book titles such as *The Violence of Literacy* (Stuckey, 1991) and references to literacy as genocidal (Purcell-Gates, 1998) point to a growing recognition that literacy is neither innocent nor unproblematic. The potential negative consequences of enforced literacy described by these writers hold ethical implications for those of us involved in English literacy development and require us to examine the issues raised by second- (or third- or fourth-) language literacy and to become more fully aware of the complexity of the enterprise. This complexity entails differing conceptions of the meaning and role of literacy across cultures. It is my hope that such a cross-cultural approach to thinking about literacy will help to engender sympathy and respect for learners of English as an additional language by promoting a better understanding of the task they face in acquiring English academic literacy.

Even from the perspective only of native language literacy (Street, 1995), it is clear that literacy, certainly including academic literacy, is not a single, uniform, unitary skill and that literacy can be properly understood only from the perspective of a social context and not as the possession or personal cognitive ability of a single individual. If literacy is neither a unitary skill nor a personal possession independent of context, then what it means to be academically literate necessarily varies from one culture to the next. Being academically literate in Chinese, for example, means, among other things, having knowledge of thousands of characters and enough familiarity with the works of writers of antiquity to be able to quote them without hesitation in certain contexts. This concept of academic literacy is not the same for English. Attempting to move across cultures and languages into new literacies, academic or otherwise, complicates literacy acquisition qualitatively.

This chapter examines four of the complicating issues raised by the development of academic literacy in English as a second language (ESL): correctness, range, identity, and discourse community values.

CORRECTNESS

When I first started teaching, the grammar and vocabulary idiosyncrasies of second language (L2) writers were actually called "illiteracies." In other words, if L2 English learners made grammar and vocabulary errors, no matter how competent they were in their own languages, they were, for some, illiterate. These days most trained teachers of L2 academic literacy think of the language variances of L2 writers either as interlanguage forms (Selinker, 1972; i.e., intermediary grammars that are systematic and rule-governed but exhibit features unlike target language features) or as a type of *contact variety* of English, a term that comes from studies of pidgins and creoles and refers to mediating language forms that develop when people who do not speak each other's languages attempt to communicate.

Whatever such forms are called, questions of correctness do arise, if only in terms of whether or not the contact language forms are comprehensible to the members of an academically literate community. These issues of correctness arise not just in terms of producing text but also in interpreting text. How "correct" does a reading have to be to qualify as an instantiation of academic literacy in an L2? Peirce and Stein (1995) recount a striking case of conflicting instantiations of English academic literacy. A group of Black South African high school students whose first language (L1) was not English were asked to participate in piloting a text to be used in an English language proficiency test for university admissions. The text was based on a newspaper story about a group of 80 monkeys, four of whom were shot in the effort to stop their wild rampage against a home in Durban, where they attacked a boy, two policemen, and the house itself. (The monkeys had apparently become enraged at the entrapment of a mother monkey and her baby.) As one of the White, L1 English authors explained, she and her colleagues took the text to be "a simple factual report" about this incident with monkeys in Durban. The Black high school students doing the pilot test, however, regarded the text as racist, one of them interpreting the passage as being "about Black people, who are the 'monkeys' 'on the rampage' in White people's homes" (p. 56). Another said "It's about who owns the land—the monkeys think the land belongs to them but the Whites think they own the land" (p. 56). Although the text was withdrawn as a test item, these students, who hoped eventually to be admitted to the university, were obviously not participants in the same interpretive community as the White test makers. Had the piloting not occurred, the students' "misinterpretation" may well have been read as a simple lack of L2 English academic literacy.

But the issue of correct interpretation can arise at the most basic level. For example, in responding to one student's text written under some time constraints in a composition class, I wrote something like "It's too bad you didn't have more time to finish." He was mortified because as he understood it, I was telling him his paper was bad, "too bad." When issues of correctness and comprehensibility arise, the question becomes, how correct does something have to be to be comprehensible? How distant and unlikely can an interpretive frame be and still qualify as a literate reading in L2? How closely does the reading and writing of an L2 English learner have to match that of other members of an L1 English literate culture, including in terms of grammatical accuracy, and what are the consequences when the mismatch leads to misunderstanding?

RANGE

Range of literate abilities is also a very important issue for L2 English students. Normally, we would probably associate academic literacy with the ability to use and produce texts in a fairly wide range of general academic contexts. This is the meaning of academic literacy that undergirds the undergraduate general education curriculum. But with L2 learners once again we may need a different perspective. For example, one of the participants (Yang) in a research project of mine majored in nursing. Although she was trained as a physician and practiced medicine in the People's Republic of China, when she came to the United States, she was in her middle 30s and had not really studied English beyond high school. She had a great deal of difficulty making herself understood orally and produced contact variety writing. In fact, the first report she wrote for a nursing class was simply returned to her as unacceptable because of the problems her professor noted in language. Yang's general extemporaneous written work never really got much better in the three years of her nursing program, but she eventually graduated with a solid B average because all of her exams in the nursing program were multiple choice; whenever she had to write a paper she always made use of the writing center and of her husband's and her young adolescent daughter's better command of grammar and vocabulary to screen the paper before she turned it in; and much of the writing required of her at the university was in the form of nursing care plans that are written in symbols and abbreviations as incomprehensible to most English users as a foreign language. In sum, the range of her academic literacy was quite narrow although I believe no one would challenge its depth within her field of expertise. Nevertheless, her L2 academic literacy, one that is so narrow and so dependent, again pushes at the margins of what it means to have L2 academic literacy.

IDENTITY ISSUES

Issues of identity arise to some degree in any language learning situation, but the poignancy of the issues are seen most clearly through the example of Fan Shen (1989), whose frequently quoted article appeared in *College Composition and Communication*. As Shen explained, he was a Chinese graduate student studying American literature and having trouble with his writing. His professor told him to stop worrying about being so academic in his writing and to just be himself. That advice made Shen realize that he could not in fact be himself in English because when he was himself, he was Chinese, and when his real Chinese self wrote something, it was not what his American professors were looking for. In order to write what they expected of him, he had to create and pretend to be a different self, an English-speaking self, one that did not mind arrogantly writing in the first person, one who put himself forward as having himself thought up these ideas he wrote and defended, rather than his Chinese self who did not write in the first person and whose native rhetoric required him to look to the authority of other writers and credit them with the ideas he wrote about. He had to pretend to be self-confident and assertive instead of circumspect, tentative, and suggestive as he really was. He managed, but only by becoming someone else, by creating an alter ego, a bold self-centered English speaking person. Asking that someone create an alter ego is quite a lot to ask in the name of English academic literacy development. Why was it not possible for Shen to remain a Chinese person in his English writing?

Shen was a graduate student and possibly a visa student. That is, enough of his emotional and intellectual development had already taken place in Chinese so that he was able to resist the English assault against his Chinese self productively. The tension between identity and the development of L2 academic literacy presents an even more problematic and painful set of issues for younger students, particularly those who come to the United States as permanent residents. First, Cognitive Academic Language Proficiency (CALP), a concept proposed by Cummins (1979), develops somewhat independently from what Cummins called Basic Interpersonal Communicative Skills (BICS). In other words, although permanent resident students may be quite capable of handling their real-world communicative needs, including every day reading and writing needs, that proficiency is of a different nature from the kinds of proficiency needed to succeed in academically oriented tasks. CALP takes a relatively long time to develop, long enough so that permanent resident students entering English medium high schools may in fact get to graduation before having developed academic proficiency in English (Collier, 1987). Bosher (1998) further suggests that this situation is exacerbated for refugee students, whose education may be interrupted by stays in refugee camps en route to permanent residences; to complicate matters, these students may not be academically literate in their first language (Fu, 1995; for a less academic perspective on these issues, see also Fadiman, 1997).

When permanent resident students enter college, we sometimes witness the sad and frustrating result of the educational system's response to these students, who communicate well in the everyday world but whose academic literacy is less well developed. In moving and eye-opening research on L2 students' experiences in the transition between high school and college, Harklau (2000) explored the situation of a small group of permanent resident students whose identities were in effect constructed for them by their teachers and classmates in high school, identities that they embraced. The four whom Harklau studied were considered top students in their high schools because they always did their homework as required, they tried hard academically and seemed to think education was important and teachers were to be respected, and they behaved well in class, so un-like native U.S. students with their disregard for schooling, as their teachers said. These L2 students' teachers in high school praised them to the domestic students as models, pointing out how they obviously valued education despite their language "handicaps." With their first semester in college, however, their identities were reconstructed, not as model students, but first and foremost as ESL students, as students who had to be separated out from the other graduates of U.S. high schools because their proficiency in English (presumably in writing) was judged to be insufficient to allow them to take mainstream freshman writing classes. This reinterpretation of their identities was an embarrassment and a humiliation for these students, who had up to this point been taking all their high school classes with the U.S. students; they dressed like them, liked the same entertainments, lived like U.S. teenagers, and had been praised for their efforts in high school despite their language problems. They had become fully invested in their English-speaking identities. Now, after all this time succeeding in English, they were redefined, in the name of academic literacy, as failures in English, not primarily as model students but as ESL students.

ACADEMIC DISCOURSE COMMUNITY VALUES

At least in part, the development of academic literacy entails sharing the values of an academic discourse community, including subscribing to its expressed or tacit assumptions about what it means to be academically literate, that is, what it means to be one of the members of the literacy club, as Smith (1988) said. The academic discourse community in this U.S. culture currently values, among other things, critical thinking, developing "voice," and avoiding plagiarism. It might be useful to examine these values by first looking at different conceptions of what academic literacy means and how it is acquired in different cultures in order to make the point that beliefs about and attitudes toward literacy themselves form a part of literacy and that the acquisition of academic literacy in an L2 can be impeded by clashing culture-bound, often implicitly held values. The point of such an examination is to problematize these values as local and historical rather than universal and eternal. This critique then is intended to underscore the status of L1 English academic values as contingent and so to work against the colonizing of other literacies and concomitant devaluation of the literacy knowledge and practices of L2 English learners.

Although the research exists (see, e.g., Street, 1993), we in the United States have not focused much on research on cross-cultural academic literacy besides the large volume of work on contrastive rhetoric, which is fairly limited in scope, dealing mainly with patterns of text structure, not with values, beliefs, attitudes toward, or development of academic literacy (see also, Carson, 1992). One possible insight from contrastive rhetoric that moves beyond organizational issues appears in the often cited, although perhaps somewhat controversial, work by Hinds (1987) on Reader- and Writer-Responsible text. From his analyses of texts in Japanese and English, Hinds concluded that in some cultures, such as the United States, the burden of communication falls on the writer. That is, it is the writer's responsibility to make the meaning of a text as transparent as possible for the reader by explicitly explaining what the main point of the text is, how the text is divided, how various parts of the text are related to each other. On the other hand, other cultures prefer Reader-Responsible writing. In this case, it is the reader's responsibility to read between the lines, to intuit the meaning the writer only hints at, to see through disparate parts of the text to their underlying unity. If in fact such cultural preferences exist, it is easy to see why a highly literate reader and writer from a Reader-Responsible academic culture would have some difficulty seeing the value of and thus being willing to take on the habits and preferences of someone from a Writer-Responsible culture, and vice versa. In other words, if Hinds' studies hold up, U.S. reader/writers might find Japanese writing diffuse, suggestive, but unclear; Japanese reader/writers might find U.S. writing lockstep, simplistic, overly specified.

In addition to studying texts across cultures in an attempt to understand the nature of academic literacy, we might look cross-culturally at literacy training. In describing literacy training and practices in Korea, Lee and Scarcella (1992) noted that in grammar school Korean children are encouraged to keep daily journals that are collected once a week though not graded or corrected, that children are regularly asked to write to commemorate special occasions, and that many urban Korean families with children subscribe to special daily newspapers for children that report world, national, and local news, among other things. As adults, Koreans particularly appreciate poetry and short fiction. In fact, Lee and Scarcella reported that Koreans are, amazingly, accustomed to constructing poems on the spot. They refer to an article in the *Los Angeles Times* from 1988 that described a radio talk show host in Korea going out onto the street and randomly asking people to construct poems to express their opinions on the then current government corruption scandal.

However, although the Korean "person on the street" reported on in the article seems able and willing to create poetry, essay writing is not taught in schools and so not practiced much, with the general public apparently feeling, according to these authors, that only experts in a subject area are qualified to write essays on that topic. They also report the comments of a Korean university student who claims that the really good Korean writers spend a great deal of time planning what they will write, gathering their thoughts, and so once an essay is written, writers are unlikely to be inclined to spend time revising it. By contrast, the U.S. literate community seems to hold strong beliefs about the value of revising. Ability and willingness to revise practically define U.S. notions of expertise in writing.

Moving to China for a glimpse of other ways with words, we learn from Kohn (1992) something about reading instruction in the PRC. In Chinese reading classes, children are taught to read slowly and be sure they know each word before moving on; to reread difficult sentences until the meaning is clear; to look up definitions of all unknown words in a dictionary. As Kohn points out, this list of dos and don'ts is almost exactly the opposite of what current reading instruction theory recommends in this country, particularly in the instruction of L2 reading, where learners are encouraged to read fast to get the gist; use background knowledge to guess meaning; focus on main ideas, not details; and guess the meanings of unknown words instead of looking them up right away.

Clearly, attitudes and beliefs about academic literacy and literacy acquisition differ across cultures. With these differences as a backdrop, we might now turn to some of the values and beliefs that undergird academic literacy practices in this culture. One of the currently most pervasive and highly prized stances before text in this culture is that required for critical thinking. Critical thinking appears to mean approaching text with a combination of skepticism and analysis. It also appears to be taken for granted that critical thinking represents a universal good, and it is sometimes argued that for students from countries that value rote memorization in education (with all the negative connotations this term indexes), critical thinking is a skill or attitude that is especially important to teach to L2 students, suggesting that they in particular, because of their educational backgrounds, lack the ability to take such an approach. It is also only recently that writing researchers are finally beginning to examine critical thinking with a bit of critical distance.

Atkinson (1997) links the notion of critical thinking with the glorification of individualism, standing alone against the crowd or against the received wisdom of a particular text. He points out that not all countries have this obsession with the power and importance of the individual above the group that undergirds current notions of critical thinking, and so we should be clear that this notion of critical thinking is culture bound, preferred by some academically literate communities as a way of approaching text at this particular time. It is neither a universal value nor an expression of the universal good. Atkinson's analysis is important for those of us who deal with students who come from cultures where the proper approach to a text is not a critical approach, from cultures that encourage a less individualistic stance before text. His discussion reminds us of the arrogance of believing that, because at this moment in time we feel that a critical approach works well for us, we must require it of every student that comes our way, not as an option but as the only appropriate form of intellectual engagement.

But perhaps more important to remember is that, although the U.S. academic discourse community currently finds the critical thinking approach to text useful and other cultures may find this approach to text less interesting, useful, or appropriate for whatever reason, not adopting a critical thinking stance before a text in an educational context cannot be equated with an inability to think critically. It would in fact be ludicrous to make such an assumption. After all, what culture, what part of the world does not at one time or another witness the political unrest and/or protest that can be one of the consequences of thinking critically, analytically, skeptically? Certainly, L2 English students can and do think critically, without our help, and very often their critical thinking is directed at the United States, at what we do here in general and at what we do in our classes in particular. Those who despair that these students are not critical enough need to have more conversations with them. But approaching a text, especially certain kinds of texts, with a primary view to finding fault with it may simply not be an appropriate stance to take before a text, at least not certain texts and perhaps not in an initial encounter. What might those certain texts be? They might easily be religious texts, but they might well also be academic texts in academic settings, especially on subjects the students do not know much about, and most especially on subjects related to a culture that is not their own (see, e.g., Johns, 1991).

Like critical thinking, another value associated in this culture with academic literacy and taught in writing classes, although mentioned only rarely in disciplinary courses across the curriculum, is the development of an authorial voice. An apparent goal of writing classes in this culture is the development of a sense of individual difference: to set oneself apart from the others, to be unlike other writers, to let individual voices stand out and be heard. Such a stance is open to the criticism, in a post-structuralist context, that it emphasizes to students the discredited notion of the unified, autonomous subjectivity, posits the notion as natural and universal rather than constructed and determined, and thus casts as unnatural anyone for whom such an emphasis on individualism is not automatic.

In addition to reemphasizing our heavy bias toward individualism, the notion of voice appears to be associated, at least to some degree, with a willingness to self-disclose and herein lies another potential problem for L2 writing development. On one hand, not all cultures encourage young people to self-disclose in classrooms, to talk about their personal experiences and opinions; that simply is not what school is for. And on the other hand, in other educational systems, that kind of self-disclosure may in fact be considered very appropriate but exclusively for school children, not for adults at a university, who would be expected to be able to exercise self-control and to find ways to self-disclose among their family and friends, not in a classroom.

In other words, while English writing teachers value voice in student writing, it too must be considered contingent, valued in a particular time and place, but not an essential component of academic literacy and so perhaps not worth hammering on too much in L2 reading/writing classes. (For further discussion of voice in L2 writing, see the special issue on voice in the *Journal of Second Language Writing*, Belcher & Hirvela, 2001.)

And finally, plagiarism. Although critical thinking and voice are relative newcomers to the list of qualities that writers are currently being encouraged to exhibit, the nearly absolute requirement to avoid plagiarism has been around much longer. But not forever. Strictures against plagiarism are neither universal nor ahistorical; they appear to have begun in the English-speaking world during the Renaissance and for specific historical reasons. Pennycook (1996) traces the history of plagiarism in the West and helps us to put into perspective this currently greatest of literacy sins. The reason it is important to see plagiarism as a notion limited to a particular time and place is to blunt the hysteria with which accusations of plagiarism are surrounded. Blunting this hysteria is especially important when dealing with L2 students for at least three reasons. First, in many cultures citing someone else's work without saying who the source is marks the writer as particularly steeped in literate culture. It is a sign of respect toward the reader as well, indicating the writer's belief that the reader is too literate to require a source reference.

The second reason not to exaggerate the importance of plagiarism is related to culturally dependent notions of what it is to learn. For example, in an incident at my school, a group of Malaysian students came to see me in despair that their history teacher was giving them Fs on a recent exam because he was accusing them of plagiarism. As they adamantly maintained, they had not plagiarized. They had simply done what good students do; they had memorized portions of the textbook. During the exam they wrote exactly the correct answer, taken from the textbook word for word, from memory, not copied from the book, which is what they understood we meant here by plagiarism. They had learned the material by heart, which to them meant, really learned it. Clearly, their view of learning clashed with the view the professor had. He had faith in the idea that only if you can more or less say something in your own words can you claim to have learned it. I leave open the question of how well "your own words" are able to accurately retain the meaning of what you might be trying to learn. In any case, this teacher did not want these students to use the textbook author's words.

But the third reason to view plagiarism with a bit more distance is that in a sense L2 students are always using others' words. How can they not? Because of a limited linguistic repertoire in their L2, they may simply have no other way available to them to restate what they just read. They may not be able to tell if an attempted paraphrase in fact paraphrases an original text. Or having limited options themselves, they may find the original captures for them the one best way to say something. As one student said, "If you have a . . . text in perfect English, that's exactly . . . what you should say and this is the best way. Then [because you don't want to plagiarize] you have to find another way. This is funny. . . . So you have to change it and then it gets worse. Kind of sad" (Leki & Carson, 1997, p. 59). This is not to say that L2 English learners do not need to be aware of the great store this culture puts in "using your own words," only that plagiarism elicits emotional reactions from teachers and perhaps others that are entirely out of proportion to the event, and L2 literacy teachers need to be aware of our own deep enculturation on the topic.

To set the beliefs and practices of these different discourse communities in contrast, then, we find some cultures where reading instruction recommends careful focus on detail to understand text and others where the focus is on global approaches to help understand a text; some where poetry is part of every day life but expressing personal opinion in essays is left to experts in the subject area and others where essay writing, developing individual voice, and expressing personal opinion constitute the quintessence of knowing how to write; some that value implicitness above overexplaining, others that consider implicitness to be vague, maybe even deceitful, and value straightforward, clearly explicit approaches instead.

But how much do these differences matter? Could we not just recognize that there are differences and move on? To try to answer these questions, it might be useful to look at the experience of one more L2 learner, highly literate in her L1, English, and very motivated to develop L2 literacy. Bell (1995) describes her attempt to learn Chinese and explains how implicit clashing assumptions about literacy on her part and on the part of her Chinese tutor led to frustration and feelings of failure. Bell began studying written Chinese at the same time as she began oral Chinese. She felt she progressed well in oral Chinese but began to feel increasingly miserable about what she perceived as her lack of progress in written Chinese. Her Chinese writing tutor would introduce one character at a time, showing how the strokes are made and in what order and Bell would then be asked to practice, practice, practice that same character.

But Cindy, her tutor, was never satisfied; her feedback was consistently that the characters lacked balance and that Bell needed to concentrate more, feedback that became increasingly irritating and incomprehensible to Bell as the months went on and she was still practicing the same characters over and over. She finally came to realize that what was getting in her way were certain basic assumptions she had about learning, deeply held convictions that had made of her all her life an efficient and accomplished learner in her own culture. She examines two particularly striking clashes of assumptions. First, Bell assumed that the characters she was learning could more or less be split into their forms and their content, that her goal was to be able to recognize and generally reproduce a character, and that she could clean up the niceties of reproducing the forms perfectly later. That is, as long as the characters were recognizable for what they were, superficial issues like neatness and attractiveness could be worried about later. But for Cindy, the Chinese tutor, appearance was essential; form was inextricably linked to content; presentation, not just ideas, was crucial. There was no first sloppy draft and then going back to clean it up; in Cindy's view, for Bell to develop the mental discipline to succeed (i.e., to become literate), each character needed to be perfect each time.

The second area in which Bell's and Cindy's assumptions conflicted had to do with learning style. Bell had become a successful academic through her engaged, questioning, active learning style. When she tried to use the same style with Cindy in learning to write Chinese, Cindy told her that "the way to learn is to receive. . . . You do a lot of observing and then you think about it" (p. 698). Cindy is clearly not talking about passive, rote learning; you do a lot of observing and then you think about it, she says. But it is possible that the attitude toward learning that Cindy expresses here may be interpreted in U.S. culture as passive, unquestioning, unengaged, and the people, say Chinese, who use this style and believe in this way of learning (and for good reason because they have probably become academically successful using it), these people may well be viewed in U.S. culture as not thinking critically, not developing personal voice, maybe likely to plagiarize by wanting to copy text word for word. As we see in Bell's example, it is difficult to understand cross-cultural literacies without first examining the assumptions of our own L1 literacy and then being willing to challenge or suspend the values tied to it.

The question of academic discourse communities finally presents itself to L2 literacy teachers in two forms. First, if beliefs and attitudes about L1 literacy and about the acquisition of L1 literacy inform approaches and attitudes toward L2 literacy acquisition, L2 literacy teachers need to do more to understand the kinds of literacy expectations and attitudes students bring with them from their families and their home cultures and to build on those expectations. Remaining ignorant of other cultures' approaches to literacy may cause us to misunderstand our students' actions and motivations and to misinterpret the causes of obstacles they may be experiencing in acquiring L2 literacy.

Second, L2 reading/writing teachers need to think long and hard about our own academic discourse community. What is it? Specifically, what community do we belong to? As we introduce L2 students to academic literacy, whose discourse community are we representing to them? In the course of doing research on professors' expectations about writing across disciplines, I learned that in our College of Agriculture, before turning in papers to their professors, students are asked to run a computer check of the length of each of the sentences in their reports. The computers there are programmed to flag any sentences longer than 21 words. I was stunned to learn this. In my L2 writing classes I encouraged students to try to combine short sentences into longer ones, telling them, as I believe, that in English we tend to value embedding at the sentence level; complex sentences lend an air of maturity to writing. Apparently, however, this belief is not shared in the discourse community of the College of Agriculture. There, longer sentences are discouraged as more likely to be confusing than short sentences. Whose discourse community was I representing in what I was teaching my students, my L2 English students who are in college to study engineering, business, agriculture, computer science, math, biology? Clearly, I was representing the English department's discourse community to my students as the very holder of the meaning of what it is to be literate—the English department, the academic discourse community that is the most likely to assign essays to write rather than reports, the one that values personal disclosure to develop a writer's voice, the one that encourages, even requires, students to express personal opinions on topics they may know very little about, the one literacy community that my L2 English students are the very least likely to want to join. I would argue that it is important to keep reminding ourselves that different communities value different aspects of reading and writing, and English department literacy values are not universal and do not define literacy in general. This knowledge, however, puts L2 reading/writing teachers in the odd and conflicted situation of trying to introduce L2 English students to literacy communities we ourselves do not belong to and of belonging to a community they have no reason to be introduced to.

In view of the place of English in the world today and the role it sometimes plays in both empowering and dramatically constraining the lives and futures of people from different L1 backgrounds, I feel an interrogation of the characteristics of L1 English literacy and its place among the other literacies in the world is a task that L1 English literates are morally and ethically obliged to undertake. Given how complex literacy issues in second, third, or fourth languages can become, perhaps the only reasonable stance to take, at least initially, is one of modest flexibility and willingness to learn from others, one in which "You do a lot of observing and then you think about it."

REFERENCES

Atkinson, D. (1997). A critical approach to critical thinking in TESOL. *TESOL Quarterly, 31*, 71-94.

Belcher, D., & Hirvela, A. (Eds.). (2001). *Journal of Second Language Writing, 10* [Special issue on Voice in L2 Writing].

Bell, J. (1995). The relationship between L1 and L2 literacy: Some complicating factors. *TESOL Quarterly, 29*, 687-704.

Bosher, S. (1998). The composing process of three Southeast Asian writers at the post-secondary level. *Journal of Second Language Writing, 7*, 205-241.

Carson, J. (1992). Becoming biliterate: First language influences. *Journal of Second Language Writing, 1*, 37-60.

Collier, V. (1987). Age and acquisition of second language for academic purposes. *TESOL Quarterly, 21*, 617-641.

Cummins, J. (1979). Linguistic interdependence and the educational development of bilingual children. *Review of Education Research, 49*, 222-251.

Fadiman, A. (1997). *The spirit catches you and you fall down.* New York: Farrar, Straus & Giroux.

Fu, D. (1995). *My trouble is my English.* Portsmouth, NH: Boynton/Cook.

Harklau, L. (2000). From "good kids" to the "worst": Representation of English language learners across educational settings. *TESOL Quarterly, 34*, 35-67.

Hinds, J. (1987). Reader vs. writer responsibility: A new typology. In U. Connor & R. Kaplan (Eds.), *Writing across languages: Analysis of L2 text* (pp. 141-152). Reading, MS: Addison-Wesley.

Johns, A.M. (1991). Interpreting an English competency examination: The frustrations of an ESL science student. *Written Communication, 8*, 379-401.

Kachru, B. (1992). *The other tongue: English across cultures.* Urbana: University of Illinois Press.

Kohn, J. (1992). Literacy strategies for Chinese university learners. In F. Dubin & N. Kuhlman (Eds.), *Cross-culture literacy: Global perspectives on reading and writing* (pp. 113-125). Englewood Cliffs, NJ: Prentice-Hall.

Lee, C., & Scarcella, R. (1992). Building upon Korean writing practices: Genres, values, and beliefs. In F. Dubin & N. Kuhlman (Eds.), *Cross-culture literacy: Global perspectives on reading and writing* (pp. 143-161). Englewood Cliffs, NJ: Prentice-Hall.

Leki, I., & Carson, J. (1997). "Completely different worlds": EAP and the writing experiences of ESL students in university courses. *TESOL Quarterly, 31*, 39-69.

Peirce, B., & Stein, P. (1995). Why the "Monkeys passage" bombed: Tests, genres, and teaching. *Harvard Educational Review, 65*, 50-65.

Pennycook, A. (1994). *The cultural politics of English as an international language.* New York: Longman.

Pennycook, A. (1996). Borrowing others' words: Text, ownership, memory, and plagiarism. *TESOL Quarterly, 30*, 201-230.

Purcell-Gates, V. (1998, October). *Literacy at home and beyond.* Paper presented at Watson Conference on Rhetoric and Composition, Louisville, KY.

Selinker, L. (1972). Interlanguage. *International Review of Applied Linguistics, 10*, 209-231.

Shen, F. (1989). The classroom and the wider culture: Identity as a key to learning English composition. *College Composition and Communication, 40*, 459-466.

Smith, F. (1988). *Joining the literacy club.* Princeton, NJ: Princeton University Press.

Street, B. (Ed.). (1993). *Cross-cultural approaches to literacy.* New York: Cambridge.

Street, B. (1995). *Social literacies: Critical approaches to literacy in development, ethnography and education.* New York: Longman.

Stuckey, J. (1991). *The violence of literacy.* Portsmouth, NH: Boynton/Cook.

7

ENHANCING LARGE-GROUP LITERATURE DISCUSSIONS

Richard Beach
University of Minnesota
Sharon Eddleston
Armstrong High School, Robbinsdale, Minnesota
Raymond Philippot
St. Cloud State University

Much of the recent work on classroom discussion of literature has focused on small-group or book club group exchanges (Alvermann, Young, & Green, 1997; Eeds & Wells, 1989; Marshall, Smagorinsky, & Smith, 1995; McMahon, Raphael, Goatley, & Pardo, 1997). One of the obvious advantages of small-group rather than large-group discussions is that more students can share and elaborate on their responses than in large-group discussions (Almasi, 1995). Students are often less intimidated by the more intimate setting of a small-group discussion than in having to respond before an entire group. And, in small-group discussions, students are less likely to be directed by teacher questions, allowing them to formulate their own preferred directions for responses (O'Flahavan, Erting, Marks, Mintz, & Wiencek, 1992).

At the same time, there are some advantages to large-group discussions. Students may be exposed to a wider variety of different responses and perspectives that can enhance the depth of composite interpretations than in a small-group discussion. And, teachers may assume the role of facilitating the discussion, particularly in terms of drawing reluctant participants into the discussion.

Unfortunately, teachers often dominate large-group discussions, posing recitation questions in a ritual-like drama designed as no more than reading checks (Marshall, et al., 1995). Based on their analyses of large-group literature discussions in high school classrooms, Marshall et al. (1995) noted:

> We seldom saw evidence that students were moving much beyond answering their teachers' questions (however carefully those questions may have been framed) or that they were engaging with the literature on a personal level. Their responses tended to be brief and unelaborated, their questions relatively few. Both individually and as a group, they frequently cooperated with the teacher in organizing and sustaining an examination of the text, but the direction and context of that examination were usually in the teacher's control. The student's role was to help develop an interpretation, rarely to construct or defend an interpretation of their own. (p. 56)

In contrast to these teacher-controlled discussions, Freire (1970) articulated an alternative conception of the teacher's role in promoting dialogic exchange in the classroom:

> Through dialogue, the teacher-of-the-students and the students-of-the-teacher cease to exist and a new term emerges: teacher-students with student-teacher. The teacher is no longer merely the one-who-teaches, but one who is himself taught in dialogue with the students, who in turn while being taught also teach. They become jointly responsible for a process in which all grow. (p. 67)

Freire's dialogic exchange can serve as a literacy tool for fostering shared interpretation and critical inquiry in the classroom. Because we were interested in what specific aspects of classroom discussion fosters this dialogic exchange, we conducted a study of two large-group literature discussions in high school classrooms based on some of the aspects identified in previous research on classroom discussion.

STUDENTS' ENGAGEMENT IN "SHARED THINKING"

Central to the collaborative exploration of responses is the extent to which students are willing to engage in what Rogoff and Toma (1997) described as "shared thinking" in which students mutually explore their interpretations of a text. In discussions, students ideally "construct coherent beliefs" by "reasoning together rather than against one another" (Smithson & Diaz, 1996, p. 255). Constructing coherent beliefs includes students verifying their tentative hypotheses, hunches, or "passing theories" (Davidson, 1984; Kent, 1993) through shared thinking (Rogoff & Toma, 1997). According to Davidson's correspondence theory of truth, validity of interpretation depends on the extent to which students' beliefs match with or correspond to the other beliefs in the discussion, a process of triangulation (Kent, 1993). Triangulation requires that students recognize the differences between their own and others' beliefs, or what Bakhtin (1981) defined as *addressivity*—the idea that "we must recognize the otherness of the other—the other's deviation, difference, and variation from us" (Kent, 1993, p. 123). Students are more likely to publicly share their tentative passing theories or hunches if they know that others will provide some reciprocal response that verifies or challenges those hunches. Drawing on Davidson's principle of charity, in which participants are open to entertaining their own and others' "passing theories," however tentative, Porter (2001) posited the need for teachers to adopt a "pedagogy of charity" (p. 574) that assumes that students are capable of mutually formulating and testing out their own passing theories in the classroom.

To study the process of students' engagement in shared thinking, we conducted a research study of two of Sharon's 11th- and 12th-grade contemporary American literature classes students in a midwestern suburban high school (see also Eddleston, 1998). Although each class consisted of 24 students, somewhat lower than classes in many schools with class enrollments over 30, these groups may still be considered relatively "large." The purpose of the study was to identify those features of Sharon's class that served to foster effective discussion practices. Over the period of a 14-week semester, students discussed *The Bean Trees*, *Donald Duk*, *Yellow Raft in Blue Water*, *The Great Gatsby*, *Fences*, *The Piano Player*, and *The Crucible*. All discussions were taped and transcribed. Investigators kept fieldnotes of and reflections on their observations of the discussions. Individual students were also interviewed about their perceptions of the discussions.

Throughout the semester, the teacher, Sharon, modeled various inquiry strategies for responding to texts (for a description of these inquiry strategies, see Beach & Myers, 2001; Short & Hartse, 1996; see also the Inquiry Web Page at the University of Illinois: http://www.inquiry.uiuc.edu).

These strategies included the following:

- Posing questions or hypotheses about concerns, dilemmas, and issues associated with experiences with a text.
- Relating these concerns, dilemmas, or issues to specific, relevant aspects of a text world and their own real-world experiences.

- Generating hypotheses to explain or interpret characters' and students' concerns, dilemmas, or issues.
- Critiquing beliefs or ideologies shaping perceptions of these concerns, dilemmas, or issues.

This modeling also provided students with a metalinguistic framework for talking about and reflecting on discussion strategies. In their research on classroom discussions, Almasi, O'Flahavan, and Poonam (2001) found that even fourth graders devoted a considerable amount of time to meta-talk about their own purposes and strategies in discussions, although excessive use of such meta-talk can impair productive discussions.

In contrast to teachers who lead discussions according to a predetermined set of questions designed to script the direction of the discussion, Sharon assumed that students would shape the direction of the discussion. She was therefore open to student responses that differed from her own expectations. As Nystrand (1997) noted:

> When teachers ask authentic questions and engage their students in substantive conversations, they must be prepared to move with an unfolding discussion that they will not always be able to anticipate fully before class begins and that often cannot be repeated from class to class; for any given class, they will not always be able to anticipate all aspects of the text they may need to discuss. (pp. 106-107)

Based on extensive analysis of many classroom discussions, Nystrand (1999) found that only about 15% of instruction in more than 100 middle and high school classes involved the use of what he described as *authentic questions*—questions with no predetermined answers or attention to following up on students' answers. In his research on how teachers initiate dialogic interaction, Nystrand found that

> dialogic shifts are rare, occurring in less than 7% of all instructional episodes observed. The most striking finding is the virtual absence of dialogic shifts among low track classes: only 2 dialogic shifts in the 197 instructional episodes we observed, no doubt a result of emphasis on skill development and test questions about prior reading. Quite simply, lower track students have little opportunity for engaged discussions. This is particularly important in light of our findings that dialogic classroom discourse increases student achievement. (p. 2)

In addition to modeling inquiry strategies, Sharon adopted a range of different roles in the discussions: facilitator, participant, promoter of diverse perspectives, linker to real-world experiences, and instructor of response strategies.

Facilitator

As discussion facilitator, Sharon consistently invited students to join in the discussion. She prompted students to further extend their responses with questions such as, "Would you please elaborate on your response?" She encouraged reluctant participants to share their responses. She also avoided praising or evaluating students' responses, moves that only serve to reify the teacher's role as dictating the direction of the discussion. And, she reminded students about discussion norms regarding monopolizing the discussion, put-downs, and interrupting.

Participant

Sharon also assumed the role of participant in the discussion by contributing her own responses, a shift designed to de-emphasize her role as discussion leader. In reflecting on this shift in roles, Sharon noted the difficulty of sharing responses to a text she had read many times while her students were responding to the text for the first time. Rabinowitz (1991) noted that because teachers are often responding on the basis of multiple re-readings of a text, they tend to emphasize retrospective interpretations of overall thematic patterns, responding according to what he defined as "rules of coherence." In contrast, students who are reading the text for the first time are often concerned with what he described "rules of configuration," readings having to do with understanding events or predicting outcomes. Sharon therefore attempted to assume the stance of a first-time reader, who is concerned with understanding or interpreting events.

Promoter of Diverse Perspectives

Sharon believed that students are more likely to extend or develop discussions when they disagreed with each other or expressed divergent, alternative perspectives. She therefore perceived her role as promoting diverse perspectives through encouraging a range of different interpretations. For example, in responding to August Wilson's play, *Fences*, students were asked to place the main character, Troy, on a scale from 1 to 10 representing their approval or disapproval of the character's actions as a relatively controlling father and husband. Some students were sympathetic toward Troy given his previous experience with racism in his work and on the baseball field, his support for his family, and the fact that he overcame an abusive childhood. Other students judged him in a more negative light, objecting to his drinking, his jail sentence for manslaughter, his treatment of his wife, and his affair with another woman. In sharing these alternative perspectives of Troy, the students challenged each other's beliefs, requiring them to further explore their interpretations of his actions.

Linker to Lived-World Experiences

Sharon also encouraged students to connect their responses to texts to their own lived-world experiences. In some cases, she modeled her own connections evoked by texts. In doing so, she attempted to show students the value of elaborating on their connections in order to use them to further illuminate the text (Beach & Phinney, 1998). For example, in discussing houses in *The Great Gatsby*, one student asked, "Why is there a little house in among all those mansions?" Sharon provided her own explanation by sharing perceptions of neighborhoods in the Twin City, Minnesota area:

> Well, do you even go around Lake Calhoun and Lake Minnetonka? Go out here on Medicine Lake, and you see that. Some things just got there first, and then the neighborhood gets more upscale, and then they're still left.

Instructor of Response and Inquiry Strategies

Sharon also assumed the role of modeling particular types of response and inquiry strategies (Beach & Myers, 2001). She would detect certain teachable moments in the discussion when she interjected definitions of relevant literary response concepts or strategies. For example, when students were confused about the point of view in the novel, *Donald Duk*, by Frank Chin about a Chinese-American male adolescent living in San Francisco, she noted:

> That's called third-person limited. When you're in the mind of one character. We don't get into Arnold's [another character] mind. It's only when Arnold says something that we know what he's thinking. So this is all sort of stream-of-conscienceness through Donald's point of view. That's called third-person limited. If we were to get into the minds of many characters, then it would be third-person omniscient. This is third person limited. And he is a pretty confused, right?

USE OF WRITING TO INITIATE DISCUSSIONS

Sharon also used various types of informal writing to help students formulate responses, questions, or hypotheses. Individual students then volunteered to initiate discussions by reading aloud their writing to the group. The different types of writing included the following:

1. *Shortwrites.* These were written in the beginning of the class about students' responses to a text or a question about their reading. For example, prior to a discussion of the last act of *The Crucible*, students were asked to "explain the difficult decision John Proctor makes at the end of this play. Explain why he makes this decision and where you think he made the right decision." Students differed in how they viewed Proctor's decision to die at the end of the play as well as his justification for his decision, differences that led to a lively exchange about the value of standing up for one's principles.
2. *Journals.* These were writings in which students recorded their responses during their own private reading of the texts. Prior to discussions, students were frequently asked to review their journals to note particular topics they wanted to discuss in the class. Students also kept their journals open on their desks so that they could refer to them throughout the discussions.
3. *Inquiry Papers.* Individual students were assigned inquiry papers to formulate issues, questions, or hypotheses about a particular text and then address those questions and hypotheses (Beach & Myers, 2001). Sharon modeled specific inquiry processes involved in this writing. Students wrote their questions on the board and the class discussed each question before reading the writers' papers distributed to all students. For example, in the inquiry papers on *Donald Duk*, students questioned why Donald burned his model plane early in the story; why he was able to dream historical dreams about events he knew nothing about; why Chin wrote in a particular style; why did the author include so many references to food in the story; and why did the book end so abruptly.
4. *Oral Essays.* Oral essays are those in which small groups of students, working collaboratively and led by a student moderator, presented to the entire class their discussion of topics selected from a fish bowl the day prior to the discussion. For example, in discussing two August Wilson plays, group members discussed

topics of the characters' development, racism, music, the use of the supernatural, symbols, and gender issues. Their group discussion, which occurred twice during the semester, was used in lieu of written exams. Because students received a group grade, they had to work collaboratively in preparing extensive notes for their presentations. To earn the group grade, each member had to make at least two significant contributions to the discussion.

5. *Written Essays* based on the group discussions of the different texts. Not only did students use writing to prepare for discussion, but they also used their discussion to prepare for writing essay interpretations of the texts.
6. *Written Self-Assessment of Discussions.* One aspect of inquiry is the ability to step back and reflect on one's hypotheses or interpretations. However, as Langer (1995) found, high school students often have difficulty stepping out of and objectifying their experiences with texts in order to assess the validity of their interpretations. (For strategies on using response stances in leading discussions, see Langer & Close, 2001). To help students learn to reflect on their discussion responses, for six discussions during the semester, Sharon asked students to complete written self-assessments of their own discussion abilities based on a rubric. This rubric (see the Appendix) formulates five levels constituting the degree of student participation, formulation and development of response, attention to other students' responses, facilitation of mutual exploration of responses with other students, and nonverbal aspects of participation.

On the rubric form, students highlighted those statements that reflected their own roles in discussions. They then commented on their discussion abilities and noted those discussion skills in which they needed more work. Prior to the next discussion, Sharon then displayed transparencies of frequent students' comments, and the students discussed approaches to improving their discussions. The information on the transparencies provided students with feedback on changes in their individual and group participation. The students recognized that they were not only improving in their responses to literature but that they were also learning how to engage in discussions with others as a valuable social skill.

FRAMING DISCUSSIONS TO FOSTER DEVELOPMENT OF INTERPRETATIONS

In our analysis of the transcripts, we found that effective discussions often contained instances of what we define as *extended stretches*—sustained series of turns by different students with a consistent focus on the same topic or issue. Because students maintained a focus on the same topic in these extended stretches, they mutually explored a topic or issue in some depth, generating some substantive insights into that topic or issue.

We then compared these extended stretches with shorter or nonextended stretches in which one or two students discussed a topic in a short series of turns, but then the group moved to another topic. (We achieved a high level of agreement as to what constituted an extended versus nonextended stretch and the features of the extended stretches.)

One of the features most likely to distinguish the extended versus nonextended stretches was how the stretches were initially framed (Beach & Phinney, 1998). Linguists describe *frames* as meta-messages or meta-narratives that define a particular type of activity participants are engaged in—debating positions, comparing judgments, connecting texts to other texts, and so on, or the type of activity portrayed in a text (Auer & di Luzio, 1992; Duranti & Goodwin, 1992). Teachers often frame discussions using questions to imply that students need to generate an interpretation acceptable to the teacher. Students know that the teacher is framing the discussion as "read my mind." For example, in responding to *The Great Gatsby*, a teacher might ask, "What do your believe was Gatsby's primary motivation in buying West Egg," resulting in students' regurgitating the teacher's lecture notes about Gatsby's desire to impress Daisy. Drawing on Bakhtin (1981), we characterize these types of frames as "monologic" in that they seek a definitive, singular response, with little or no exploration of alternative perspectives.

We found that extended stretches were more likely to be framed by dialogic (Bakhtin, 1981) frames that invited alternative, conflicting perspectives, resulting in disagreements around alternative interpretations. In reading aloud their writing to begin the discussions, students would typically frame "extended stretches" in terms of questions, concerns, issues, tentative beliefs, or "passing theories" (Kent, 1993). By framing their interpretations as tentative, they are implying the need for further verification—agreements or disagreements—from their peers (Porter, 2001; Smithson & Dias, 1996). For example, in describing key scenes in *Gatsby,* students offer some tentative perceptions of characters in the novel:

Nicole: I don't know, it's not exactly a scene, but I think that Daisy and Jordan, they might might be a little bit of a stereotype, or, I don't know. Fitzgerald's maybe making fun of the ways of the 20s, a little bit. You know, especially like upper class ladies, maybe. Because Miss Baker is complaining how she's all stiff from lying on her couch all evening and what else? And just Daisy's . . . when she says, you know, he's [Tom] reading these books with all these long words in them.

Maggie: I think that what you're saying is the he's [Fitzgerald] is kind of mocking the woman.

Nicole: Yeah, totally mocking her. They're all interested in secrets and gossip and stuff.

Sarah: Well, maybe the 20s just don't allow them any other role other than being beautiful fools. Maybe in the 20s that's about all a woman can hope to be. Of course, Jordan's the exception, there, as the professional golfer. But, Daisy doesn't seem to have developed too far, does she?

Kyle: Well, when she talks to Nick there seems to be more to her.

By framing this stretch in a highly tentative manner as passing theory (Kent, 1993), Nicole invited further discussion of her hunch that Fitzgerald's female characters are one-dimensional personalities. The students also adopted relatively tentative, exploratory stances as marked by such words as "I don't know," "maybe," "might," and "seem." And, they posed questions to themselves and each other. In discussing the topic of the stereotypical portrayal of female characters, these students adopt different perspectives. Nicole and Maggie focused on Fitzgerald's own attitude toward females, whereas Sarah adopted an historical perspective, arguing that women in the 1920s may have had little choice but to adopt limited roles. Kyle then complicated the argument by noting that Daisy seems more complex in her relationships with Nick.

These framing processes were further illustrated in another extended stretch that focused on the role of Nick, the narrator of *The Great Gatsby* (Beach & Myers, 2001). The students perceived Nick as engaged in the activity of observing and participating in characters' lives. Most of the students believed that, as an observer, Nick should refrain from asserting his opinions. A smaller, vocal group of students argued a counter position—that he has a moral obligation to openly challenge the other characters. This debate also leads them to a discussion around the issue of discretion in asserting opinions in real-world contexts. The discussion begins with a student, Berke, reading aloud his writing about Nick:

1. Berke: I think that this Nick guy is the most perfect guy in this book because he has no, I don't know, he respects everybody to a certain extent. I thought, in this chapter, to describe what kind of guy he is, like in the end, he goes home. He supposedly sees Gatsby like fifty yards away in his yard. And he's like, should I go talk to him? He's like, no, no. He just lets the guy be alone with his thoughts, you know. He doesn't want to bother him. I mean, that's just a respectable gentleman. I know if I see somebody, and nobody lives around me really, you know, and there's somebody in my yard, I'm going to approach him late at night, you know, what are you doing? This guy, I don't know, he's just...yeah, he's just the kind of guy anybody could talk to and he keeps his own opinions in his head and his actions so far haven't shown much to what he really is. I think he's just a perfect gentleman. That's what I feel.

In this initial frame, Berke adopted a somewhat tentative, exploratory stance about Nick's role as evident by the repetition of "I don't know." He is publicly testing out his hypothesis that Nick is a "perfect gentleman" defined in terms of not intruding in Gatsby's private life. He assumed a "dialogic," "double-voiced" (Bakhtin, 1981) stance by mimicking his version of Nick's own voice: "should I go talk to him? He's like, no, no." And, he contrasted his own propensity to interrogate a late-night intruder with those of Nick.

2. Kyle: I think . . .
3. Tom: Keeping your opinions to yourself is not a good quality . . .
4. Teacher: Tom, just a minute. You interrupted Kyle.
5. Tom: That's my opinion, see? [laughter]
6. Teacher: Let's let Kyle speak for a minute.
7. Kyle: What Berke was saying stems back to, on page 4, ". . . he was going to become that most limited of all specialists, the well-rounded man," and then he says that it's more successfully looked at from a single window, after all. Which I tend to agree with, but the well-rounded man. . . . I think that definitely characterizes Nick and he didn't, maybe he's just kind of soaking things up rather than giving his opinions. Like about the book, and I think that's a very important part of his character.
8. Sarah: That makes sense.

9. Tom: I'll say what I was saying again, in case anyone didn't catch it. I interrupted . . . [laughter]. I don't think keeping your opinions to yourself is a good quality at all [laughter].
10. Teacher: Now why doesn't that surprise us? [laughter]
11. Sarah: It's not necessarily a good quality . . . it's true to Nick's character, though . . .
12. Tom: . . . yeah. But he was saying that was like a good thing, and I don't think that's a good thing.

In this exchange, the students debated the value of Nick's role as a narrator/observer. Tom argued that the failure to assert opinions is "not a good quality" (turn 3). Kyle countered that Nick is a "well-rounded man" who is "soaking things up rather than giving his opinions" (turn 7). Contrary to the other students' stance, Tom posited the value of asserting opinions. In stating that ["keeping your opinions to yourself"] is "not necessarily a good quality . . . it's true to Nick's character, though . . .," Sarah examined Nick's role as narrator within the literary world of the novel.

As the discussion unfolded, the students discussed the problem of defining issues by "closed minded" "specialists" who may not perceive larger moral implications of their acts. Tom argued that without open critiques of slavery, "there would still be slavery." Kyle then discussed the pros and cons of adopting a specialist's perspective, noting that although specialists are "blind to a lot of stuff," they are often "extraordinary." Sarah then posited the value of the "single window" perspective as preferable to the perspective of a "watered-down person" who lacks integrity. John argued that the extent to which people should be assertive "depends on the situation you're in," a framing of the argument to which Tom disagreed. Kyle then returned to Tom's analogy to the need to challenge slavery by positing the value of being "stubborn in some way with their beliefs." Kyle perceived all of this as "a paradox," a summary reflection on the complexity of the competing perspectives.

The group then concluded their discussion by reflecting on the value of openly confronting others as opposed to reserving judgment and not challenging others. Matt noted that, "if everyone agreed on one subject, on one certain point, it wouldn't be worth discussing." John then asked, "Why should you always go out of your way to make arguments with someone?" Tom countered that "you learn a lot from arguing," to which John responded, "but you don't have to go out of your way. I mean, to be the devil's advocate is cool sometimes, but not always." Stephanie responded by noting that "if you believe it, it's not going out of your way." Berke then retorted that "if you go out of your way, a lot of times you're going too far and you're going to look obnoxious and give a bad representation of yourself." Michelle then connected the discussion back to Nick, arguing that if he were talking to the other characters, "he would have given his ideas and information, but I don't think he felt that it was a time to share his information and get an argument going with someone he didn't really know very well."

In this extended stretch, some students argued that the act of asserting opinions has negative social consequences, whereas others argued that people are morally obligated to assert their own beliefs. These students sustained a shared focus on this topic by perceiving their positions as tentative passing theories open to further interrogation and verification, respectfully disagreeing with each other, and citing examples from the text and their own experiences to bolster their positions.

These results suggest that several phenomena precipitate sustained, extended focus on topics or issues: sharing informal writing, initial framing of stretches in terms of issues or problematic aspects, productive student disagreements based on competing stances, and the opportunity to share and verify tentative passing theories.

LOW- VERSUS HIGH-LEVEL DISCUSSION PARTICIPANTS

One of the challenges of large-group discussions is that a large number of students do not participate. They either choose not to participate or, given time constraints, do not have the opportunity to participate. As part of our study, we interviewed low- versus high-level participants regarding their perceptions of the discussions and reasons for their level of participation.

Low-Level Participants

Low-level participants were reluctant to express their own responses for a number of different reasons. They assumed that they needed to formulate—and subsequently articulate—definitive interpretations of the texts under discussion. Although high-level participants were willing to throw out tentative "passing theories" (Kent, 1993), low-level participants believed that their interpretations needed to be "correct"; they were fearful of being perceived as "wrong." As one student noted, "I wonder if I'm saying the right thing; or whether I am wrong." Other students had difficulty publicly sharing a response that had not been fully explicated prior to sharing that response. As one student noted, "I haven't ever been behind in the reading. Sometimes I guess what it is. When I'm trying to formulate a thought, I'm thinking I could say this and this and this, but I just don't know how to say it." Many low-level participants were accustomed to literature instructors telling them the "correct" interpretations; formulating their own interpretations was a novel, risky experience. Low-level participants also assumed that what they had to say was redundant with others' responses. Laurie, for instance, stated, "Well, I usually have something to say, but then, like somebody will change the subject or somebody will speak out, you know, and then the moment just passes, or they say the same thing that I was going to say." Justin offered a similar sentiment: "Lots of times someone else will grab onto that thought [I was considering] and say it before I even get a chance to say anything."

Low-level participants also perceived their roles in terms of being observers or listeners who are concerned with how others perceived their ideas. They described themselves as shy, or at least reluctant to speak in class. They also noted how they often did not participate in other, more traditional, classroom settings that did not involve large-group discussions. Therefore, they preferred to remain on the periphery of the discussion. As one student stated, "I'm usually very quiet in class, actually. I don't raise my hand or anything because I don't like to draw attention to myself, I guess. I don't like to talk at all." Another student claimed, "I just kind of watch what's going on. It's not that I didn't feel anything about the books, but it is mostly that I'm uncomfortable [talking in large groups]."

Finally, low-level participants observed that more talkative peers monopolized or dominated the discussions, so that any attempt they made to speak was seen as being thwarted. However, our own analysis of discussion transcripts did not always indicate that just a few members dominated the discussion. Although some of the most active discussants did speak several times more often than their more quiet counterparts, Sharon repeatedly reinforced a no-monopolizing agenda. If certain individuals were thought to be too vocal, they were asked to limit their comments so others could share ideas.

High-Level Participants

Interviews with high-level participants revealed that they were comfortable expressing their opinions in front of the group. As one student noted, "I have no problem expressing what I think. I'm also used to speaking in front of others." As students grew more accustomed to the class, their comfort level increased: "The more we did this, the more comfortable it became."

High-level participants also relished the opportunity to share different perspectives on their experiences with texts. In a focus-group reflection, three of these students described the process of exploring different perspectives:

Matt: When you read a book, you only get a one-sided opinion, and when you talk with other people you get other ideas and maybe you get different feelings for the characters. I think when you read a book you form your own opinions about each character, and in class discussions people poke holes in that. It makes you re-examine what you've thought and take a look at things differently.

Kyle: I agree. It's just the whole concept of listening to everybody else. There have been things said that I wouldn't have even thought about, and it does away with the paradigm of the individual reader and opens it up.

Sarah: It's easy not to pick up little things when you read. When everybody else is throwing things in, you get a much better understanding, a better grasp of what you're reading. We're all each other's teachers. What Michele said yesterday made me want to re-look at the way I was reading the book [Yellow Raft in Blue Water] and looking at the characters. The conversations you have change the way you look at the novel.

These students also enjoyed engaging in disagreements and debate. As one student noted, "I love tension, and I love saying what I think and then hearing what they think, and if I don't agree with that, that really sparks stuff." These students were also eager to challenge their peers. One of them commented that, "if someone brought up a point I disagree with, I tend to speak right away."

Underlying these high-level participants' attitudes toward discussion is the fact that they perceived the value of reading literature as stimulating their thinking, which, in turn, led them to want to share their responses with the group. As one student noted: "If you read a lot, it starts helping with your writing and understanding, and being able to voice your opinions and formulate thoughts. The more you read and the more you challenge yourself, the better you might be able to talk."

These differences between low- and high-level participants suggest the need for teachers to assume a role in facilitating more student involvement. As did Sharon, teachers could do the following:

- Explicitly teach students the discussion skills of turn-taking, agreeing and disagreeing, and acknowledging diverse responses.
- Convey a clear rationale for using a large-group discussion format, particularly in terms of helping students learn to present their ideas to their peers.
- Elicit student input in determining rules for guiding discussions.
- Use informal writing techniques to help low-level participants formulate their ideas in writing prior to discussions.

- Employ e-mail listservs or Web-based chatrooms—contexts that may reduce intimidation of low-level participants due to nonverbal factors operating in classrooms.
- Work with low-level participants on an individual basis regarding their perceptions of their roles in discussions, particularly in terms of their assumptions about the value and perceived redundancy of their responses. By assuring students they have insights to contribute to the betterment of the class, and that others may benefit from their contributions, low-level participants may slowly mature into confident, active discussants.

STUDENT PERCEPTIONS OF THE OVERALL VALUE OF THE COURSE

At the end of the course, students were asked to complete a survey in which they rated reactions to statements regarding their perceptions of the course on a scale of 1 to 10; they also wrote comments about each statement. The results are presented in Fig. 7.1.

Sixty-one percent of the students indicated that the course had been "quite valuable." When asked to compare the approach of using discussions to approaches employed in other literature courses, 70% of students indicated that they learn "far more" through this approach than in other courses. Students commented that the course helped them learned to engage in inquiry through posing and exploring questions, public inquiry that then shaped their private reading. One student commented that the discussions "help me understand the books a lot better because people have questions that I have questions about too, so I get answers for those questions. And it helps me see the books from a different point of view."

Students also noted that having to share their responses created a social onus to not only read the books, but also to read them carefully in order to formulate responses to share with the group. One student compared her experience of reading texts simply to complete worksheet answers as opposed to reading to share in the discussion:

> The discussion makes me look at the book more closely than I would if I knew that we weren't going to discuss it. Usually in the past we've just done papers on the books or worked on packets of questions so I would just read it enough so I'd be able to write a few paragraphs or answer the questions in the packet.

1. This semester we have spent much of our time in a circle talking about the literature we have read. On a scale from 1 to 10, how valuable have these whole-class discussions of literature been for you?

2. The whole-class discussions of literature represent an alternative method for studying literature. Indicate how successful this approach has been for you, as a student of literature, compared to approaches employed in previous literature courses.

3. On a scale from 1 to 10, how comfortable were you in this setting?

4. If you were free to set a literature course in a way that would best suit you as a learner, how would you put it together?

5. Is discussion an important part of other high school courses you have?

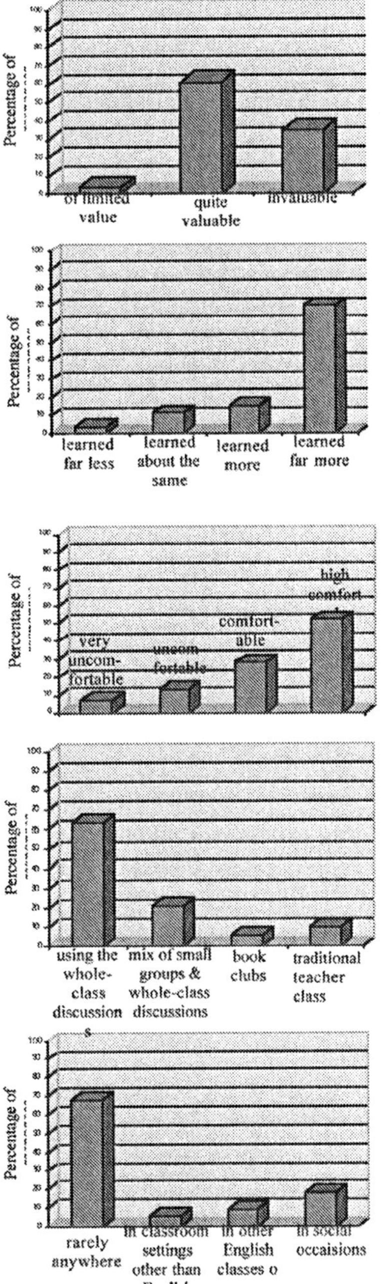

Fig. 7.1. Students' Perceptions of Discussions

Students pointed to journaling while reading as particularly helpful in preparing them for discussions. In the discussions, students could readily refer back to their written record of their responses. As one student noted: "It helps to write down my opinions so I remember them better, and I don't have to look back so much." And, formulating questions in their journals for potential sharing in the discussion focused their attention on aspects of the text they did not understand. As one student explained: "Usually in my journal I try to think of certain questions that I can ask the group. You could say with a careful reading that you wouldn't have as many questions because you understand it more, but I almost think that reading carefully has led me to ask more questions."

Consistent with our findings that low-level participants are often not comfortable in this setting, 20% of the students indicated that they were either *very uncomfortable* or *uncomfortable* in the course. However, 28% indicated that they were *comfortable*, and 52%, that they were *very comfortable*, suggesting that many students had little difficulty adjusting to the course. Some students associated their level of comfort with the lack of a predictable structure. As a student noted, "I just like the fact that you can come in and if something is bothering you, you have questions, you can throw it out, and it can be discussed." The majority of students, therefore, perceived the discussion as an inviting forum in which they could display their competence to their peers just as they might in an art class or in athletics (Czikszentmihalyi & Larson, 1984).

When asked how they would structure literature classes, most students (64%) indicated that they would make use of whole-class discussions, whereas 21% would employ a mixture of small- and large-group discussions. Only 10% would employ a "teacher-led" class. Contrary to the investigators' expectations as well as research indicating the benefits of small-group discussions (Almasi, 1995; McMahon et al., 1997), a number of students pointed to a lack of accountability operating in small group discussions:

> Usually for small groups, you tend to choose your own groups. You don't even talk about the subject, you make stuff up, or nobody really knows each other, or they're nervous to talk about it. In the large group, even though people don't talk that much, it's better—I mean, we've got the teacher. Like small groups, they're just a little too unstructured. I don't think they work well at all. Usually in a small group I'll sit back. I feel like I don't have to do anything, the other person does the writing, so I don't get too involved.

And, another student commented that "I think in the large group you're more on task. You have to talk or else just sit there. You can't talk to your friends and goof off." On the other hand, students who were uncomfortable in large groups preferred the small groups. As one of these students noted, "in small groups, you get to talk more, but you get less opinions because there's less people, whereas in class discussion everybody has different views."

Sixty-eight percent of the students reported that they had few opportunities to engage in classroom discussions outside this course. Only 9% engaged in such discussions in other English classes, and only 18% engaged in such discussions in social studies classes. As one student reported: "I guess this is the only class where we have to really talk." And, "I've noticed that every once in a while in social studies, we'll just talk. We've only done that maybe once or twice this year." This suggests that students spend much of their time in school listening to teacher-talk, affording them little opportunity to actively acquire inquiry practices through participation. All this points to the need to engage students in inquiry-based discussion across the curriculum so that they perceive their entire school, rather than a few, isolated classes, as active construction sites for developing knowledge.

CONCLUSION

In summary, the large-group literature discussions in this study served to foster inquiry about literature due to the teacher's use of a number of teaching techniques. The teacher consistently modeled, encouraged, and evaluated students on their uses of inquiry strategies. She created an environment in which students were comfortable and willing to share tentative, exploratory interpretations with each other. She employed various prewriting activities to help students prepare for discussions. And, she encouraged low-level participants to become more actively engaged in the discussion.

We are not arguing that large-group discussions are necessarily superior to small-group discussions. For many students, particularly for low-level participants, small-group discussions provide a more intimate, less intimidating setting in which to share their responses. Moreover, in small groups, students have more time to articulate their responses than in large group discussions. A useful alternative is for students to begin the class with small-group or paired discussions, which then lead into and prepare them for sharing in large-group discussions. Knowing that they will need to contribute something to the large-group discussion often enhances the accountability of the small-group discussions.

Regardless of group size, students need to adopt a tentative, exploratory stance that contributes to the more successful discussions in this study. In doing so, they are mutually engaged in using the discussion as a tool for testing out and verifying responses. The classroom then becomes a site for constructivist, critical exploration of literary interpretations.

REFERENCES

Almasi, J. (1995). The nature of fourth-graders' sociocognitive conflicts in peer-led and teacher-led discussions of literature. *Reading Research Quarterly, 30*, 314-351.

Almasi, J., O'Flahavan, J., & Poonam, A. (2001). A comparative analysis of student and teacher development in more and less proficient discussions of literature. *Reading Research Quarterly, 36*(2), 96-120.

Alvermann, D., Young, J., & Green, C. (1997). *Adolescents' negotiations of out-of-school reading discussions.* Athens, GA: National Reading Research Center.

Auer, P., & di Luzio, A. (1992). *The contextualization of language.* Amsterdam: Benjamins.

Bakhtin, M. M. (1981). *The dialogic imagination* (C. Emerson & M. Holquist, Trans.). Austin: University of Texas Press.

Beach, R., & Myers, J. (2001). *Inquiry-based English instruction: Engaging students in life and literature.* New York: Teachers College Press.

Beach, R., & Phinney, M. (1998). Framing literary text worlds through real-world social negotiatons. *Linguistics and Education, 9*(2), 159-198.

Czikszentmihalyi, M., & Larson, R. (1984). *Being adolescent: Conflict and growth in the teenage years.* New York: Basic Books.

Davidson, D. (1984). *Inquiries into truth and interpretation.* New York: Clarendon Press.

Duranti, A., & Goodwin, C. (Eds.). (1992). *Rethinking context: Language as an interactive phenomenon.* New York: Cambridge University Press.

Eddleston, S. (1998). *Whole-class discussions of literature: What students and their teachers say in and about them.* Unpublished doctoral dissertation, University of Minnesota, Minneapolis.

Eeds, M., & Wells, D. (1989). Grand conversations: An exploration of meaning construction in literature study groups. *Research in the Teaching of English, 23*, 4-29.

Freire, P. (1970). *Pedagogy of the oppressed.* New York: Continuum.

Kent, T. (1993). *Paralogic rhetoric.* London: Associated University Press.

Langer, J. (1995). *Envisioning literature.* New York: Teachers College Press.

Langer, J., & Close, E. (2001). *Improving literary understanding through classroom conversation.* Albany, NY: National Research Center on English Learning & Achievement.

Marshall, J., Smagorinsky, P., & Smith, M. (1995). *The language of interpretation: Patterns of discourse in discussions of literature.* Urbana, IL: National Council of Teachers of English.

McMahon, S., Raphael, T., Goatley, V., & Pardo, L. (1997). *The book club connection: Literacy learning and classroom talk.* New York: Teachers College Press.

Nystrand, M. (1997). *Opening dialogue: Understanding the dynamics of language and learning in the English classroom.* New York: Teachers College Press.

Nystrand, M. (1999). The contexts of learning: Foundations of academic achievement. *English Update: A Newsletter from the Center on English Learning and Achievement, 2*, 8.

O'Flahavan, J., Erting, L., Marks, T., Mintz, A., & Wiencek, B. (1992, December). *At the intersection of mind and society: Synthesis of research on small group discussion about text from a sociocultural perspective.* Paper presented at the meeting of the National Reading Conference, San Antonio, TX.

Porter, K. (2001). A pedagogy of charity: Donald Davidson and the student-negotiated classroom. *College Composition & Communication, 52*(4), 574-611.

Rabinowitz, P. (1991, February). *A thousand times and never alike: Re-reading for class.* Paper presented at the meeting of the NCTE Assembly on Research Conference, Chicago.

Rogoff, B., & Toma, C. (1997). Shared thinking: Community and institutional variations. *Discourse Processes, 23*, 471-497.

Short, K., & Harste, J. (1996). *Creating classrooms for authors and inquirers.* Portsmouth, NH: Heinemann.

Smithson, J., & Dias, F. (1996). Arguing for a collective voice: Collaborative strategies in problem-oriented conversation. *Text, 16*(2), 251-268.

APPENDIX

Levels of Inquiry Discussion

5

This discussant accepts responsibility for making meaning out of literature. He or she consistently demonstrates a careful reading of the text and makes insightful comments that significantly contribute to our understanding of a reading. The discussant refers to specifics from the class text and compares and contrasts that text to related texts, personal experiences, and social and cultural issues. A respectful listener who avoids monopolizing the conversation, he or she sometimes pulls together and reflects on ideas that have surfaced in the inquiry discussions and may also ask relevant follow-up questions, thereby pulling other students into the discussion.

4

Although speaking less frequently than the discussant described in Level 5, this discussant shows growth in the willingness to express responses. He or she has the ability to explain ideas clearly and to connect those ideas to others being discussed. This discussant may clarify a specific point being discussed or elaborate on specific examples from the text. Body language and eye contact also indicate a substantial involvement in the discussion.

3

Speaking occasionally, this discussant may primarily respond on a personal level to the text ("I liked it," "I didn't . . ."), perhaps supplying some textual evidence for this point of view. This discussant's remarks may be insightful but they tend to be brief. Or, this discussant may speak often but say little that adds significantly to the understanding of a text, and may, in fact, primarily repeat what others have already said or be difficult to follow.

2

This class member says little. This discussant's few remarks may be inaccurate, unclear, or too brief to be helpful. Little textual support is offered; there is little evidence that this student has read the text carefully or at all. Or, this student may belittle other speakers' remarks, monopolize the conversation, interrupt other speakers, ignore their remarks when speaking, or talk to those seated nearby rather than to the whole group.

1

This student says nothing and appears uninterested in the class discussions, according to his or her body language. Or, this student may appear interested in the discussion, but, for whatever reason, does not join in it.

8

LITERACY AND LEARNING IN CONTEXT

Biology Students in the Classroom and the Lab

Marty Patton
University of Missouri–Columbia
Ed Nagelhout
Indiana University–Purdue University Indianapolis

A PROBLEM IN ACADEMIC LITERACY: WHEN FACTS ARE DIVORCED FROM RHETORICAL PROCESSES

Shaw (1941) once quipped that "all professions are conspiracies against the laity" (p. 116).[1] Shaw's comment anticipates some recent scholarship that suggests that one particular profession, the professoriate, is especially guilty of withholding important information from students in order to secure its expertise and their dependency. It is as if an ancient proverb has been reversed: Students are given plenty of fish but no fishing poles; students are presented with the outcome of research practices, the so-called "facts," but are often denied insight into the rhetorical practices—including judgment-making, contingent reasoning, and persuasion—that create the facts. In *Academic Literacy and the Nature of Expertise: Reading, Writing, and Knowing in Academic Philosophy*, Geisler (1994) argued that a majority of undergraduates in philosophy are taught content but not the rhetorical practices that produce it. She further extended the claim to any discipline in which students are given "access to the domain content of expertise as decontextualized facts divorced from rhetorical processes" (p. xiii). This arhetorical method of education, Geisler maintained, creates a general public with a "crippled cultural practice capable of the knowledge consumption . . . but a practice incapable of cultural production on its own" (p. xiii). Similarly, Winsor argued in *Writing Like an Engineer: A Rhetorical Education* that "professional ideology teaches developing engineers to deny the rhetorical nature of their work at the same time as professional practice and experience teach those same developing engineers to write strategically" (p. vii). Both of these scholars call for reform.[2]

THE CALL FOR REFORM IN BIOLOGY

The call for reform rests on a large body of literature in science education, in science studies, and "writing-in-the-disciplines." It has been argued widely that literacy is best understood not only as the understanding and recall of facts and concepts, but also as the meta-understanding of the historically contingent human practices that lead to the creation and codification of facts, a meta-understanding that might be considered rhetorical (Bazerman, 1988; Fahnestock, 1986; Geisler, 1994; Haas, 1994; Lemke, 1990; MacDonald, 1994; Mitman, Mergendoller, Marchman, & Packer, 1987; National Academy of Sciences, 1989; Phelps, 1988; Selzer, 1993; Walvoord & McCarthy, 1990; Young & Fulwiler, 1986).

We are sympathetic to the assumptions that meta-understanding is a necessary component of literacy and that it is all too frequently understated in the science curriculum. However, we doubt that the "problem" results, as Shaw's aphorism seems to imply, from conspiratorial intentions on the part of most faculty. We further doubt that the situation is something that can be "reformed," if "reform" means that we can significantly overcome this problem. To better understand what reform might entail, we examine two classroom settings and a graduate–mentor relationship in which the faculty did do the things we might expect of a reform movement in biology: The faculty tried to show scientific argument, tried to show "science in the making," tried to get students to talk back to and question the text, and tried through guided participation, to help students become producers and not simply consumers of science. In short, these biologists exposed their students to the rhetorical underbelly of science, however much they might disdain the term *rhetoric*. By describing their constructive efforts and exploring the difficulties that some of their students nonetheless continued to have, we hope to deepen an understanding of the complexities at stake in "reforming" science education.

THE LIMITS OF REFORM: THE LIMITS OF ONE-WAY CHANGE

If reform is analogous in some ways to evolution, as we are inclined to believe, then Levins and Lewontin's (1985) discussion of evolution in *The Dialectical Biologist* may be instructive. In evolutionary terms, the interpenetration of organism and environment is complex and multidimensional; evolution is not a matter of one-way adaptation of an organism to a stable environment. That is, Levins and Lewontin insisted that there is an interpenetration of parts and wholes such that each is constituted and changed by the other and evolves in consequence of its mutual relationships. Moreover, what behaviors become adaptive are not fixed for all time. For example, oxygen is very toxic for most constituents of cells, and early organisms presumably evolved in the absence of oxygen. Some unicellular organisms remain obligate anerobes. However, as oxygen was a byproduct of early bacterial photosynthesis and the concentration of oxygen in the atmosphere gradually rose, what was first impossible (life in oxygen) not only became possible, but eventually became necessary, as oxygen-using organisms eventually became predominant in most environments. As this example suggests, no environment can be understood as a fixed surrounding to which organisms adapt; rather, the activities of the organisms help set the stage for their own evolution.

The dialectical viewpoint, then, rejects one-way explanations of cause and effect. To apply the dialectical view to composition, we could say that the development of writing ability is not a matter of one-way adaptation to fixed conventions or one-way adaptation to fixed ideals or expectations of the faculty. Writing conventions, expectations, and so forth do matter, but not in a vacuum of many other ever-changing factors. One corollary is that the individual writer is neither absolute creator of nor absolute victim of the language he or she uses. On one hand, no student writes independently of a set of pre-existing language conventions and, on the other hand, those pre-existing language conventions do not overshadow all acts of imagination or individuality. Another corollary is that all attempts at revision and reform are not necessarily profitable (and are not equally profitable for all members), just as all responses to the environment are not necessarily adaptive. Conversely, some responses, initially nonadaptive may later become necessary. In the evolution of any genre what might have first been ineffective may later become not only effective, but—for given periods of time—necessary.

Admittedly, Levins and Lewontin provided a long-term perspective of change and did not directly reveal anything about change in the short term, especially change in the teaching of writing in one biology class in one semester. Implicitly, however, they reminded us that there is no easy fix, and we do our students a disservice if we create the impression that revision is a matter of one-way adaptation to a fixed idea of genre, just as we do our colleagues a disservice if we suggest that educational reform is a matter of one-way adaptation of a few particular teaching methods. Moreover, Levins and Lewontin implicitly cautioned against confusing cause and effect: Just because students struggle to develop a rhetorical awareness does not necessarily mean that their struggle is caused by ineffective teaching and that it can be overcome by different teaching methods.

Levins and Lewontin's (1985) interactive view of evolution parallels scholarship that derives from the social thinking of Vygotsky (1962), who argued that our biologically determined intellectual abilities give way at a young age to culturally determined abilities that emerge in the process of using them. By having to adapt to the possibilities that different tools present to us, we are intellectually stretched in different ways. In a sense, every tool becomes a potential heuristic. Perhaps our most important intellectual tool, language, is one that not only has generative heuristic value but also permits culturally or socially derived ideas to become internalized. That is, language is a tool that can restructure thinking or, in Vygotsky's (1962) own words, "The system of signs restructures the whole psychological process" (p. 35). Other tools, however, including different material technologies, also provide opportunities for intellectual adaptation in novel ways. Eisenstein (1979) claimed that the invention of the printing press invited new forms of intelligence, just as Postman (1982) and others claim that the imagistic electronic medium might also affect the ways in which we think. Other material technologies, including the introduction within the recent past of DNA sequencing, Southern blotting, and polymerase chain reaction (PCR), provide new problems in biology and new ways of thinking about old ones.

This interactive, dynamic view of organism, tool, and environment is shared as well by activity theorists such as Charles Bazerman, Carol Berkenkotter, Paul Prior, and David Russell, who also draw on the thinking of Vygotsky (see in particular the 1997 special issue of *Mind, Culture, and Activity*). Activity theory describes the complex interaction among subjects, objects, and tools, and considers in addition the various modes of production, consumption, rules of exchange, and distribution in which activity occurs. Certain behaviors might indeed ripple through an entire activity system, but any notion of "educational reform" would, from this perspective, need to take into account many elements of a given activity system. Furthermore, any notion of "educational reform" would need to be considered tentative and responsive to local conditions.

Neither Levins, Lewontin, nor most of the scholars just cited would argue that reform is impossible. Indeed, most of those cited here have argued against repressive ideologies and practices and have favored practices based on broad participation. Nonetheless, Levins and Lewontin's dialectical view of evolution and activity theorists' views of academic systems suggest that reform, if it comes, is not a matter of one-way adaptation or a simple, generalizable fix.

MEASURED REFORM IN THREE ENVIRONMENTS

However much we resist thinking of reform as a fixed set of practices that, once enacted, will ensure certain outcomes, we do observe local practices that illustrate some of what a "reform movement" in biology education could entail. Although the particular practices of these biologists need to be understood in the context of their local classes, their own departments, and their own universities, their practices may generalize to some degree across a broad spectrum of activity systems. That is, we are willing to risk some qualified generalizations as long as we also consider their limitations.

We describe two classroom settings and a graduate–mentor relationship. The editorial "we" in the text is used to avoid awkward pronoun changes; however, "we" both did not observe all three environments. Marty Patton observed the genetics class in the winter of 1994 and the cell biology class in the fall of 1997. Ed Nagelhout observed the graduate–mentor over a two-semester period in 1994. In each instance, the author sat in on all class or mentoring meetings, interviewed students multiple times, interviewed the professor multiple times, and read working drafts of writing produced for the class or the student's thesis. We have changed the names of students (but not of the MU faculty), and we both have thoroughly discussed each other's observations. Our independent naturalistic studies follow methods described by Lincoln and Guba (1985) in *Naturalistic Inquiry* and Walvoord and McCarthy (1990) in *Thinking and Writing in College: A Naturalistic Study of Students in Four Disciplines.*

INTEGRATING FACTS AND RHETORICAL PROCESSES

We call particular attention to three issues: First, the biology professors we are about to describe are among the best we know, partly because of their efforts (by degree) to expose students to the rhetorical practices of judgment-making, contingent reasoning, and persuading, what others have called "knowledge production" or "science in the making." Second, nonetheless, some of their students continue to struggle, and, when that is the case, the problem is rarely a matter of "professional conspiracy." Rather, we trace the problem to the inherent limits of "reform." Finally, the most powerful teaching seems to occur not when students are simply exposed to "rhetorical practices," but when students are simultaneously exposed to rhetorical practices and to domain knowledge. It is as if the most naïve science students maintain very separate threads for "rhetorical writing" (involving decision making, contingent reasoning, and persuasion) and for "domain writing" (involving reporting of facts). The most sophisticated science students, however, wind these separate threads around each other so that "rhetorical writing" is at every twist and turn constrained by "domain writing." The most powerful writing opportunities we observed, then, provide students with two threads: an open-ended problem demanding contingent reasoning, and a body of information that will constrain each line of reasoning. The students' job is then to twist those threads together to produce well-informed arguments. To provide students with just one thread, to ask science students to make judgments about open-ended problems without the constraints of domain knowledge, may be irresponsible. Or in the words of the doctor who, in G. B. Shaw's play, branded his own profession a conspiracy, to put a tube of serum in the wrong hands is "murder: simple murder" (p. 116).

DR. MIRIAM GOLOMB'S OPEN-ENDED, EVIDENCE-BASED GENETICS ASSIGNMENTS

In the mid-1980s, Golomb was the first in her department to offer a designated writing-intensive course, "Genetics and Society," a lower-level course open to non-majors as well as to majors. In the 15 years since she first offered the course as writing-intensive, Golomb has continued to carry the bulk of her department's responsibility to offer writing-intensive courses for biology majors, and the composition of her class has evolved from an even mixture of majors and non-majors to mostly graduating seniors enrolled with mixed motives. Most of her students express interest in genetics, but some students simply need to meet a university writing requirement. Other biologists, including Dr. Tobias Baskin, whom we discuss momentarily, have come forward in recent years, but in 1994 Golomb was one of only two biology professors in her department to offer a writing-intensive course.

Her students are required to write short essays called *microthemes* (see Bean, Drenk, & Lee, 1982) on a variety of topics. Ideally, as Fahnestock (1986) suggested in "Accommodating Science: The Rhetorical Life of Scientific Facts," students in upper division courses should receive "extensive practice in addressing different audiences, specialist and non-specialist," so that they will "experience the problems, moral as well as technical, of accommodating information for different genres, audiences, and purposes" (p. 294). Golomb does include a mix of genres: She assigns some ethical papers, a critical review, and some arguments based on data interpretation or technical literature. Critical to the design of each assignment is the coupling of the opportunity to think in open-ended ways about unsolved problems and the need to constrain reasoning with discipline-specific "right/wrong" knowledge. Golomb's difficult problems invited her students to "repopulate" their lecture notes and textbook theories with "new intentions" and are intended to be manageable by non-majors as well as majors. Yet, even in this progressive classroom where most students thrive and the professor's good reputation is well established, we observed a few individuals in the winter of 1994 who did not flourish. In some cases, students may have had insufficient domain knowledge, which led us to revise our understanding of the relationship between domain and rhetorical knowledge. In other cases, students may have had sufficient domain knowledge but insufficient English proficiency, further complicating their ability to demonstrate a meta-understanding of the discipline (see, for example, Silva et al., 1997).

To illustrate both progressive teaching practices and the problems some students nonetheless encountered, we focus on the second microtheme for the semester of 1994. This assignment presented students with some anomalous research findings, given what was then known about both cancer and the role of cyclins in the cell cycle. Specifically, students were to suggest an explanation for the correlation between cyclin D1 overproduction and human cancer: Why did the mutant allele act dominant on the cellular level? Why did artificially induced overexpression of cyclin D1 not make tissue culture cells cancerous?

A few of the other 1994 microthemes were less constrained by factual information, but we would argue that the cyclin D1 microtheme, which did ask students to think through an argument within the constraints of domain content, pushed students to think in ways that the ethical arguments did not. The ethics assignments were valuable—one assignment asked students to evaluate the ethics of conducting human growth hormone trials on children; another asked students to evaluate the ethics of funding controversial research on the "genetic basis" of crime. The ethics assignments exposed the interface between science and society, between experimental research and the politics of funding, and so forth, and we would encourage Dr. Golomb to continue assigning such papers. They were "rhetorical" in the added sense that they were persuasive papers unconstrained by much technical evidence. In some ways, however, they allowed undergraduates to naively maintain the idea that "opinion" papers and "scientific" papers are unrelated. In contrast, the cyclin D1 paper asked students to think rhetorically in more sophisticated ways, within the constraints of the discipline.

A look at the difficulties experienced by one highly articulate nonmajor, Kim, helps illustrate some of the complexities attending reform. Kim, now a successful law student, had demonstrated in other writing for other courses great versatility; distinct awareness of audience, purpose, and evidence; and a definite willingness to question assumptions, warrants, and cultural biases.[3] She did not entertain an overly positivistic view of science and felt extremely comfortable with assignments that explicitly called for making social–science connections. She was painfully conscious, however, that she lacked the background information that would enable her to constrain an argument, to know why to develop it this way instead of that way. Kim protested in an early interview:

> I read Catherine's and Jill's and Kari's papers, and they were very good. . . . I just felt horrible because I was just using layman's terms to describe a lot of scientific things, and I felt really, I don't know, I felt shut out. That's the word, and it was very hard for me to write. (Interview 2)

Dr. Golomb did provide background information in the lecture and in the assignment itself, but it would be impossible for her to provide all of the possible background knowledge that might be needed to constrain certain lines of reasoning. Even the reading that was provided could be misunderstood without broad familiarity with other scientific literature.

The primary method for acquiring scientific literacy, of course, is reading, and nonscience majors in particular had great difficulties with reading. That difficulty is somewhat discipline-specific and in science traces in part to the constraints on technical terms and the demand for large-scale coherence (and what linguists call the *lexicogrammar of science*[4]). Terms must be understood in relation to other parts of a sentence, in relation to other parts of the text, and in relation to an enormous body of accepted scientific knowledge—and then questioned. Often the third element, understanding the relation between a term and something outside the text (but within the enormous body of accepted scientific knowledge), is the Achilles' heel for nonscience majors. Without the constraints imposed by prior reading (specifically, the constraints imposed by other parts of interlocking definitions), the chance of misunderstanding any scientific text is increased. For example, Kim misunderstood the central problem in one microtheme because she did not realize that the technical meaning of the word "infection" is not pathological. A rich background of scientific knowledge provides the matrix not only for reading, but also for appropriately relating one idea to another in writing. Kim was keenly aware of her deficiency.

Even when all five members of Kim's group orally shared the same information, they returned to their individual rooms and connected in writing the "bits" of shared information in different ways, reasoning with different sets of tacit constraints. When Kim's group met again to review their drafts, Kim felt a need to apologize: "I'm not a biology major, and there's a lot I didn't understand." As Catherine and Jill listened to Kim's draft, they were able to recognize and affirm the potential reasonableness of everything that Kim argued, but they were also able to identify specific wrong turns in the pathway of her thinking. For example, Kim had not realized how many cyclins there are and she had taken the textbook diagram far more literally than did Catherine and Jill, who considered it overly simplistic and somewhat misleading. Consequently, Kim lacked the information that would have delimited one branch of reasoning and opened another. There was no constraining thread around her major argumentative thread.

This is evident not only on the essay level, but also on the sentence level, as suggested in a separate study based on Halliday and Hasan's theory of cohesion (see Patton & Lance, 1997, for details). The content words in Kim's first three sentences have few references, whether full synonyms or partially related terms, and stand alone without the constraints of other technical terms. That is, words like "cancer," "scientists," "cure," and "cyclin D1's overproduction" don't hook back to other words in previous sentences. In contrast, the content words in Jill's first three sentences have multiple references and relationships with each other. For example, "cell division," is related to "mitosis," and "grow and repair damaged tissue," phrases that are then set in tension with "potentially harmful cell division," "unregulated cell division," "damage," "cancer," and "cyclins that initiate cell division." Noticeable in Jill's lexicogrammar is that each term is constrained by multiple references, some of which are synonyms, some antonyms, some hypernyms, some hyponyms. On the surface, Kim had much of the same content, but multiple relationships were not explicitly established in and among content words.

Kim did struggle, for she devoted as many as twenty hours to some microthemes. To a lesser degree, other students in the class struggled too. However, while it would be simpler, it would not be better if Kim never had to struggle with information-based rhetorical thinking.

DR. TOBIAS BASKINS' PEER-REVIEWED JOURNALS

Although we applaud Golomb's use of well-designed microthemes, we do not suggest that microthemes are a panacea, as Baskin discovered in 1996.

Having hypothesized that his students might think more critically (or rhetorically) if they wrote weekly microthemes, Baskin eliminated the usual exams and organized his cell biology course around weekly microthemes—to avoid the typical "cram, exam, and forget" format. To test his hypothesis, he gave a final exam, expecting students to ace it. "The mean was 36 out of 100," he reported, "falsifying my hypothesis in a spectacular manner." From his trial run, he concluded that students actually require the discipline of exams throughout the semester to "force them to memorize" the information.

Baskin was ready to put exams back in the curriculum but was still searching for a way to integrate writing in the course when he heard George Gopen present a workshop on peer-reviewed journals in the summer of 1997. Although Gopen's concept of peer-reviewed journals might not strike most compositionists as particularly unusual, Gopen spoke to Baskin with unusual authority and Baskin shortly adopted Gopen's program. In fact, when Baskin first learned that Gopen would be the featured speaker at the faculty workshop, he exclaimed, "Holy semi-colon! I read Gopen's article in *American Scientist* . . . and it changed my life." Gopen and Swan's 1990 article "The Science of Scientific Writing" summarized reader-based editing principles and prepared Baskin for the significance of reader-based student writing in the form of peer-reviewed journals.

Gopen described a journaling sequence that, like his editing program, is based on the assumption that writers are more careful when they think about the reading processes of their audiences, live audiences in particular. Because Gopen believes that a live audience of one's peers is best, his peer-reviewed journal program encourages students to question, probe, and explain course material to each other. According to his plan, on a given Wednesday, each student submits four copies of a two-paged journal entry responding to the text. Three copies are distributed to peers and one copy is given to the professor. On the following Monday, each student must write a two-page response to each of the three students. Students, then, are writing six pages each Monday, two pages each Wednesday, and well over 100 pages each semester. The professor, in turn, has 2,000 to 4,000 thousand pages of writing. After hearing Gopen blame dull writing on students' natural inclination to produce "demonstration writing" for the teacher rather than real communication for their peers, Baskin decided to give Gopen's peer-reviewed journals a try in his cell biology class. Several weeks into the class he commented that, "Today at the end of class, I gathered in 240 pages of student writing and at the prospect of reading all of this work, I was eager. My response, in contrast to the customary despair, convinces me that this style of assignment is good."

We applaud Baskin for recognizing that different methods of assessment are appropriate for different kinds of learning. Microthemes, for example, have been found to be particularly valuable when professors want to hold students accountable for exploring particular focused questions, perhaps questions that students could not formulate in the language and conventions of the discipline. Microthemes can be modified to serve many different learning purposes but rarely can be counted on to measure breadth of understanding or questioning of problem areas. Given that cell biology is a coverage course and a prerequisite for many other courses in the biology curriculum, Baskin found that a combination of exams and journals best suited his goals. From our perspective, the journals not only permitted Baskin to assess a broad base of material and to manage his time, they permitted students to "talk back" to the "autonomous text"—only to discover that the text is not as autonomous as they might have once thought. By "talking back" to it and to each other, they developed skills in "rhetorical reading" as much as in writing.

It should be noted, however, that Baskin is rarely the only professor to teach cell biology in a given semester, and his counterparts typically teach in a traditional lecture/exam format. Students are aware of different professors' strategies, compare notes, and steer each other into this or that section. Many biology majors are pre-med and are extremely grade-point- and MCAT-conscious, and these students can be harsh critics of policies they suspect might leave them ill-prepared for the competitive world of test-takers. What do they care about "rhetorical reading"? Although Baskin is not afraid of criticism, it is not as if he is an individual teaching independently of a competitive culture. His department is not much different from biology departments elsewhere or from other departments at the University of Missouri; risks taken for teaching are seldom well rewarded. Fortunately, Baskin's 1997 cell biology students scored well on their final exams. Furthermore, students made such comments as, "Overall, I think I learned most of the material simply by doing the journals and responses. . . . The responses force me to reread the material and to think about the material in order to answer the questions raised by members of my group." Others judged the journaling by comparing it to other writing-intensive courses: "I must admit it was not as difficult as I had imagined it would be, but it was still pretty time consuming. Of the classes I have taken that required writing, by far this has been my favorite."

But did the journaling work? One student commented at the end of the semester, "It seems like I have been writing journals and responses my entire life. . . ," which might suggest that journaling has been used throughout the curriculum. However, as far as we could tell, few students had ever journaled in a science class, and fewer yet had been encouraged to develop questions. Of interest to us was the degree to which identifying trouble spots in the text triggered a chain of questions, which in turn led to a questioning of the autonomous text and of the absoluteness of scientific facts.[5] Unlike journaling in some classes, effective journaling in cell biology required students to integrate open-ended questioning with the constraints of other factual information in the text. The least effective journals presented large chunks of summary serving no obvious purpose (the summary wasn't in response to a question, wasn't used as evidence for tentative claims), unrelated metacomments serving no obvious purpose ("I don't understand something" type comments weren't linked to questions or observations), and free association or humor having little to do with course content. The most successful journals, on the other hand, demonstrated scientific thinking even if a personal, reflective style was used: The metacomments (expressing awe, confusion) led to curiosity and placeholder questions, and placeholder questions were followed by a mixture of textual paraphrase (which focused and delimited the general question), inferences, tentative hypotheses, more textual evidence, elimination of possible answers, and more and more refined questions.

> *General wonder/amazement*
> It never ceases to amaze me when I think about what tremendously efficient seemingly perfect cycles that exist and function to govern our entire universe. [Some text summary used in support]
> *Particular wonder/amazement*
> I have always thought the process of photosynthesis by plants coupled with the respiration of other organisms was a fascinating cycle. [Some text/general knowledge summary used in support, plus a value judgment about the importance of protecting the environment to maintain symbiotic relationships]
> **Summary/gap*
> One thing that really caught my attention in this reading was that it is believed that the first cells on earth were not able to conduct photosynthetic or respiratory processes.
> *General statement of curiosity/question*
> This makes me wonder how these primitive cells were able to function.
> *Second-tier focused question*
> What was their source of energy?
> *Third-tier focused question*
> What causes evolution to eventually favor a symbiotic relationship between photosynthetic organisms and aerobic organisms? [The following selective summary isn't yet used to address the questions; rather, it leans into new ones, such as why it took billions of years for photosynthetic processes to build up sufficient O2 to sustain aerobic processes.]

Although the process of journaling moved students in the direction of more sophisticated rhetorical reading, the product of journaling might have resulted in occasional ill-formed questions. Does evolution favor a symbiotic relationship between photosynthetic organisms and aerobic organisms? A more knowledgeable mentor might question the underlying assumption in the third-tier question and might then push the student to pose testable hypotheses. That is, although all students probably derived some benefit from writing about their reading, we suspect that those advanced students who were already on the "edge of their competency" needed more advanced mentoring, needed to be moved farther along in what Vygotsky would call their zones of proximal development. The questioning in their peer-reviewed journals may not have pushed beyond questioning of established knowledge to hypothesizing about unsolved problems and weighing of alternative hypotheses. Although the most advanced students served as ideal mentors for their peers, they perhaps needed not only more feedback from the professor but different kinds of problems. All of this is to say that it is difficult to think of reform without thinking of particular audiences; the most powerful strategies for stimulating thinking in some students may not be powerful for others.

The literature on the value of journaling is voluminous. Much of the literature about "writing-to-learn" in biology is anecdotal, however, and several critical reviews find it lacking. Moore (1993) responds to his title question, "Does Writing About Science Improve Learning About Science?" by claiming that "merely writing about biology does not necessarily ensure that students learn about biology" (p. 214). He further cites studies by Whimbey and Jenkins (1987) and Linden and Whimbey (1990), who argue that "unguided writing about a subject does not appreciably improve students' writing skills or their understanding of the subject" (p. 214). In a critical review of writing-to-learn in science, Rivard conceded that "writing can enhance science learning" (p. 978) under specified conditions, but argued that "a number of issues must be addressed before the research base that supports writing-to-learn becomes widely accepted by science educators" (p. 975). Scientists accustomed to experimental research with controlled independent variables may have unrealistic expectations of writing research, but they are entirely justified in holding us accountable for our claims. Our claims are probably not wrong as much as they are radically unqualified.

THE DISSERTATION PROSPECTUS AND THE COMMITTEE REPORT

One response to the need for guided writing in the sciences is the use of context-specific documents that have meaning for both undergraduate and graduate students. Moore implicitly asks us to consider what kinds of writing situations do stimulate learning. While he decried writing for the sake of writing, he affirmed the value of providing undergraduates with guided writing-to-learn assignments, and he would probably vouch for the importance of mentoring graduates in the higher stakes production of documents. In graduate education, there are certainly documents created by graduate students that are important to them and to their education. Two such documents are the prospectus and the committee report. Although these documents are written for the graduate students' dissertation committees, they assist their professional development by requiring them to show their thinking about their own research and argue for the value of their scientific work in terms of the larger disciplinary community with professionals in the field other than their major professor.

Part of what heightens the learning process when writing a prospectus may be that graduate students are not only writing about open-ended problems, they're having to prove to members of the larger disciplinary community that the problems are open-ended and warrant research. Likewise, graduate students are not only constraining the research problem with evidence, some of which has never before been available. When do preliminary results become accepted as fact? At what point will their committee members, as representatives of the larger professional community, be persuaded that certain observations can be construed as facts? A graduate student, in writing a prospectus and the subsequent committee reports, must tighten both the thread of his or her major argument as well as the constraining thread of emerging evidence.

In the prospectus, graduate students prove that they can establish a research project, and in the committee reports they show that their work is adequately progressing or that they have reconfigured the project based on their current findings. Both of these documents provide opportunities for graduate students to write a professional document in language appropriate for scientific readers and to situate their work within the debate of the larger community. The strength of this rhetorical situation is that the professional, scientific readers are a local committee—led by the student's major professor—known to the graduate students and who are willing to provide guidance and insight for the dissertation project. Ideally, in answering the call to reform, the major professor and dissertation committee will also provide guidance and insight into the rhetorical nature of scientific writing.

In the two labs that we studied, the prospectus represented the first time that each graduate student's own professional research and thinking were scrutinized by reviewers outside the confines of the lab. This is a very important moment in their graduate education, and the major professor who approaches the construction of this document as a formal publication introduces graduate students to the necessary rigor for successful publishing. The committee reports in these labs were offered as updates, written for the dissertation committee, and described the graduate student's research progress over the previous year, along with the prospects for completing the dissertation. These two documents are considered both routine and complex. For the documents situate these graduate student writers firmly in a specific knowledge domain within biological studies while demanding that the writers think rhetorically about their writing practices. In other words, the goals of the documents were straightforward, but the delivery needed to display how the graduate student's research was aligned with current thinking in the field and also how the research would potentially establish new insights, a goal very much like any professional publication. Writing science to learn in this situation means facing the rhetorical complexity of science writing. In other words, in constructing these documents, these graduate students were assisted by their major professors in realizing that their approach to writing should be open to adaptation away from the fixed conventions so often associated with scientists' writing.

Interestingly, the graduate students who participated in this study were trained to think of document construction in terms of the introduction, materials and methods, results, analysis, and discussion format of scientific research articles. For most of them, this outline provided a straightforward approach to writing, a set of fixed conventions that they could seemingly transfer to all rhetorical situations. On the surface, the prospectuses designed by these graduate students did show constructions similar to these conventions; however, a closer examination revealed that each varied the document in terms of his or her particular situation. These modifications presented the best evidence of the kinds of rhetorical mentoring necessary for these students to best understand the difficulties they will face in their future writing, and their major professors encouraged them to think of these local writing situations as variable, a clear corollary with Levins and Lewontin's (1985) dialectical adaptation.

Although the prospectus was locally distributed and used as a local examination of a graduate student's ability and potential, one of the major professors described the prospectus as written like a grant, a kind of writing that attended to disciplinary values for good science and featured many of the same requirements for good writing outlined by scientific journals. In this respect, the prospectus was designed as primary evidence for determining the graduate student's maturity of scientific thinking. The other major professor who participated in our study saw the prospectus as the beginning of a process when graduate students started thinking independently. At this point, the graduate students have to come to grips with what they are doing, to begin to think on their own, and then, in oral fashion, answer to a committee. If the prospectus acted as written proof of the state of the graduate student's thinking, then the committee functioned as reviewers to accept, reject, or accept with revisions the future work proposed in the prospectus.

One graduate student, Jeffrey, wrote a prospectus that was 14 pages long and was accepted without revisions by his dissertation committee. An examination of his prospectus showed that its construction was based on the first three items in the research article format—introduction, materials and methods, and results—in order to meet the prospectus requirements. Jeffrey's introduction and background and significance sections attempted to describe his overall understanding of the issue, and his specific objectives section delineated the intersections of his project with the field. Finally, by combining methods and preliminary results, he illustrated the quality of his research methods by incorporating his initial findings into the discussion and illustrating their significance. This persuasive move argued for the validity of his methodology by providing examples of his preliminary results and indicated specifically how these results might be situated in the larger disciplinary debate. Jeffrey's prospectus was a representative sample of the most common construction for the prospectus. Another graduate student, Kelly, explained that she designed her prospectus "along the lines of an article in the *Journal of Virology*." Thus, Jeffrey and Kelly were both advised to organize their prospectuses in ways familiar to their readers, to construct arguments based on their understanding of scientific logic, and to use language they perceived as appropriate in this rhetorical situation.

A third graduate student, Seth, wrote a prospectus that was 13 pages long, but the technical section was quite long and written in 10-point type. In this respect, an examination of Seth's prospectus revealed less of a similarity to the research article format, unless the technical section acted more as an addendum, which might be credible considering the overt change in type size. For Seth, the specific aims section came before the background and significance section. This allowed Seth to discuss the current thinking in the field in terms of his project. Jeffrey, who placed the background section before the objectives section, appeared to discuss his project in terms of the current thinking in the field. One reason Seth might have taken this approach was that he was arguing in his prospectus for the use of a number of new and innovative research techniques, which might account for the long technical section at the end of the prospectus as well. Thus, an assessment of Seth's rhetorical situation showed a need for a slight variation on the construction of his prospectus; however, his arguments and use of language consistently presented his understanding of acceptable scientific discourse. All the prospectuses that we examined were successful documents that portrayed these graduate students as novice scientists who had thought about their topics in depth, understood the nature of the debates, and had quality plans for performing the necessary research and providing new insights for the field.

The graduate students' committee reports were written annually, and their value can be viewed in two respects: (a) the committee reports served as opportunities for interaction between the graduate students and their dissertation committee, opportunities that allowed the graduate students to inform and update the committee, as well as for the committee to provide feedback and direction for future work; and (b) the committee reports acted as written records to chart progress and potential for attaining the PhD. As a written record, the committee reports could potentially be used as evidence for discontinuing funding or terminating a graduate student's education, a kind of panoptic power wielded by the department over the graduate students. Although none of the graduate students acknowledged this contingency, the potential remained.

Each year on the anniversary of a graduate student's prospectus defense, the department sends a memo requiring the student to submit a committee progress report to all members of the committee by a specified date. From a departmental perspective, this memo might have implied a commitment to graduate students making progress and graduating in a timely manner. All of the graduate students who participated in this study described the committee reports as a routine procedure, nothing to worry about, but they all wrote multiple drafts and sought feedback from their major professors before distributing the final draft of the report to the rest of their dissertation committee.

Seth's committee report was constructed to reflect the past, present, and future. In this way, Seth was able to show the progression of his thinking from the inception of his project to its current state. The initial findings section helped to re-establish the basis for the project in the minds of the committee members. The research progress section showed the kind of work that Seth had been doing over the past year, setting up a relationship between his past work and his current thinking. Finally, Seth outlined his future work and the kinds of rethinking he had done about his project. Based on the difficulty of the new methods that Seth was attempting, he reconfigured his research proposal and argued for a slightly different approach to the dissertation project. In Seth's case, this committee report allowed him to reevaluate his dissertation for his committee and make the completion of the research project a more focused proposition and attainable in the very near future.

Kelly's committee report exhibited a different approach than Seth's, but the committee report sought to accomplish many of the same objectives. Like Seth, Kelly reiterated the basis for her research in the introduction to reacquaint her committee with her project. But since her project was progressing adequately along lines similar to those described in her prospectus, the second and third sections concentrated on the primary research that she had completed during the previous year. The final section explained the directions that her research was taking her and the prospects for staying on track with her dissertation progress. Kelly's approach was the most common construction for the committee report. The primary goal in writing the committee reports was to reestablish the context of the dissertation project, describe the research and findings from the previous year, and assess future work and goals.

For these graduate students, writing these local documents represented an important step in their professional development. Admittedly, these documents were not submitted for publication, but they certainly asked the graduate students to wind the separate threads of domain writing and rhetorical writing to create effective documents in each situation, considering that these documents were subjected to intense intellectual scrutiny by their local readers. Therefore, these moments of independent thinking—of rhetorical understanding—forced the graduate students to see beyond the fixed conventions of the scientific article. And although each used these conventions as a point of departure, each also adapted both the scientific writing style and the scientific document itself to achieve success. As such, these local documents provided these graduate student writers with insights into the kinds of language appropriate for publication and helped them better understand that they were not hindered by the language of science nor were they completely free to use language outside the boundaries of scientific practice.

CONCLUSION

The reform that we are suggesting, finally, is one that is driven from behind, not from ahead. We resist the notion that there are fixed teaching ideals toward which we are all inching along; rather we embrace a more Darwinian view of change that is driven from the back end. As new opportunities appear, as new tools are available, as new problems arise, teachers, students, and institutions all need to make some adaptations without losing sight of some of the more stable, highly conserved elements of the discipline. As compositionists, we might support constructive adaptation by nurturing in our colleagues a healthy self-consciousness and ongoing questioning, a self-consciousness and questioning that the biologists who participated in these studies already bring to their teaching and learning. At the same time, we need to appreciate the good teaching that is already being done and the idea that some of the hard work of learning isn't a "problem" that will ever "go away," including the hard work of developing both rhetorical insight and a subtle understanding of the content of the discipline.

ENDNOTES

1. Shaw "quips" this only through the voice of a character in a play. The character is indicting his own profession as well as others.
2. Geisler (1993) explicitly called for reform in pages 250-255 of *Academic Literacy*, although she did acknowledge numerous barriers to reform and is wary of being oversimplistic. Winsor (1996) implies the need for reform by repeatedly referring to impediments in the educational process for engineers (see, e.g., p. 8).
3. Patton collected from Kim not only all of her genetics drafts but also papers done for Kim's non-science classes.
4. "Lexicogrammar," as defined by Halliday and Martin (1993), is the "wording as a whole" (p. 8) and in science is characterized by many nominal groups and classes. As a new lexicon developed in science, so did new grammatical patterns. The dense nominal groups typical of science writing pack into a given sentence more propositions and make reading more difficult.
5. The journals were coded via an inductively-modified protocol adapted from one developed by Charney for another purpose:

Coding Scheme for Analysis of Peer-Reviewed Journals

1 **Free-standing personal opinion or observation** (not explicitly used as support for some other claim)

2 **Rehearsal** (working and reworking received ideas)
- 2.1 Definition
- 2.2 Summary (initially detached from any claim on the student's part)
- 2.3 Restatement/paraphrase of definition or summary
- 2.4 Testing of summarized idea against background knowledge
- 2.5 Revision of definition or summarized material (paraphrase with a twist)
- 2.6 Inductively arrived-at conclusion

3 **Metacomment** (comments upon the topic or self)
- 3.1 Reaction to text/comment/topic (I like, don't like . . .)
- 3.2 Reaction to/assessment of self (I'm confused about)

3.3 Heading within another comment (. . . , I feel, is . . .)
3.4 Statement of uncertainty or explicit recognition of a gap

4. **Discovery**
   4.1 Placeholder question or general what-if statement
   4.2 Specific question or specific what-if statement
   4.3 Second-tier question
   4.4 Third- or fourth-tier question
   4.5 Tentative response to self-posed question
   4.6 Request for feedback
   4.7 Inductively arrived-at conclusion (as a result of Q/A dialogue)

5 **Claim & Justification**
   5.1 Claim (more or less the student's claim—might overlap with 2.6 or 4.7)
   5.2 Reason
   5.3 Evidence
   5.31 Anecdotal/personal experience
   5.32 Recollection
   5.33 Quote from class notes
   5.34 Quote from the text
   5.35 Quote from the expert in text
   5.36 Quote based in theory
   5.37 Indirect evidence: comparison, synthesis

REFERENCES

Bazerman, C. (1997). Discursively structured activities. *Mind, Culture, and Activity: An International Journal, 4*(4), 296-308.

Bazerman, C. (1989). *The informed writer: Using sources in the disciplines.* Boston, MA: Houghton Mifflin.

Bazerman, C. (1988). *Shaping written knowledge: The genre and activity of the experimental article in science.* Madison: University of Wisconsin Press.

Bean, J., Drenk, D., & Lee, F. D. (1982). Microtheme strategies for developing cognitive skills. *New Directions for Teaching and Learning: Teaching Writing in All Disciplines*, No. 12. San Francisco, CA: Jossey-Bass.

Eisenstein, E. (1979.) *The printing press as an agent of change* (2 vols.). Cambridge: Cambridge University Press.

Fahnestock, J. (1986). Accommodating science: The rhetorical life of scientific facts. *Written Communication, 3*, 275-296.

Geisler, C. (1994). *Academic literacy and the nature of expertise: Reading, writing, and knowing in academic philosophy.* Hillsdale, NJ: Erlbaum.

Gopen, G. D., & Swan, J. (1990). The science of scientific writing. *American Scientist, 78*, 550-558.

Haas, C. (1994). Learning to read biology: One student's rhetorical development in college. *Written Communication, 11*, 43-84.

Halliday, M.A.K., & Martin, J.R. (1993). *Writing science: Literacy and discursive power*. Pittsburgh, PA: University of Pittsburgh Press.

Lemke, J.L. (1990). *Talking science: Language, learning, and values*. Norwood, NJ: Ablex.

Levins, R., & Lewontin, R. (1985). *The dialectical biologist*. Cambridge, MA: Harvard University Press.

Lincoln, Y., & Guba, E. (1985). *Naturalistic inquiry*. Beverly Hills, CA: Sage.

MacDonald, S.P. (1994). *Professional academic writing in the humanities and social sciences*. Carbondale: Southern Illinois University Press.

Mitman, A.L., Mergendoller, J.R., Marchman, V.A., & Packer, M.J. (1987). Instruction addressing the components of scientific literacy and its relation to student outcomes. *American Educational Research Journal, 24*, 611-633.

Moore, R. (1993). Does writing about science improve learning about science? *Journal of College Science Teaching, 22*(4), 212-217.

National Academy of Sciences. (1989). *On being a scientist*. Washington, DC: Author.

Patton, M., & Lance, D. (1997). Sequential chains of connections: A linguistic analysis of written expository discourse. In X. Li, L. López, & T. Stroile (Eds.), *Papers from the 1997 Mid-America Linguistics Conference*. Columbia, MO: Linguistics Area Program.

Phelps, L. W. (1988). *Composition as a human science: Contributions to the self-understanding of a discipline*. New York: Oxford.

Postman, N. (1982). *The disappearance of childhood*. New York: Delacorte Press.

Rivard, L. P. (1994). A review of writing to learn in science: Implications for practice and research. *Journal of Research in Science Teaching. 31*(9), 969-983.

Selzer, J. (1993) *Understanding scientific prose*. Madison: University of Wisconsin Press.

Shaw, G. B. (1941). *The doctor's dilemma*. Baltimore, MD: Penguin.

Silva, T., Leki, I., & Carson, J. (1997). Broadening the perspective of mainstream composition studies: Some thoughts from the disciplinary margins. *Written Communication, 14*, 398-428.

Vygotsky, L. S. (1962). *Thought and language*. Cambridge, MA: MIT Press.

Walvoord, B., & McCarthy, L. (1990). *Thinking and writing in college: A naturalistic study of students in four disciplines*. Urbana, IL: National Council of Teachers of English.

Winsor, D. (1996). *Writing like an engineer: A rhetorical education*. Mahwah, NJ: Erlbaum.

Young, A., & Fulwiler, T. (1986). *Writing across the disciplines: Research into practice*. Portsmouth, NJ: Boynton Cook/Heinemann.

III

LITERACY AND TECHNOLOGY

9

THE LITERACY OF ELECTRONIC PEER RESPONSE

Terry Tannacito
Frostburg State University

Recently, I introduced my professional writing students to the procedure we would follow for our first peer-response workshop. I explained that, because our classes are held in a computer classroom, they should bring in their drafts on disk. We would load them in Word and use its "track changes while editing" tool to conduct our peer responses electronically. I added that, after they revised their workshop drafts, they could send me a later draft as an e-mail attachment, and I, too, would respond to their drafts electronically. My students' reactions showed that they were not only comfortable with but also enthusiastic about electronic response. Later, a colleague came into my office as I was responding electronically to one of the many drafts sent to me, and he asked me to show him how electronic response works. After I had shared with him the process and some of the products, I thought he was impressed with the quality of the interaction. Then, he surprised me with a question, "Okay, Terry, I think I understand *how* to implement the process in my classes. But can you tell me *why* I should implement it?"

My first thought was to repeat the words of Van der Geest and Remmers (1994), who described one of the few published classroom studies of electronic peer response in "The Computer as Means of Communication for Peer-Review Groups." The conclusion of their early study, using a computer program that was the prototype of the one I later used in my own, was that, although it seemed to involve more problems than profits, we, nevertheless, should conduct peer-response groups electronically. I practically knew their words, almost the direct opposite of my colleague's, by heart: "With increasing pace, people *are* using networks to collaborate on writing tasks. The central question then should become *how* writers can collaborate optimally in such a writing environment rather than *why* they should do so" (p. 249). My second thought was that my colleague simply would not find this an acceptable response, and I'm not sure I do either. Besides, I had a better one. My own recent research, conducted with a refined program at a later time, had given me a much more encouraging conclusion. I found, "Electronic peer-response groups offer great potential to benefit both the process and products of most students' writing" (Tannacito, 1998, p. v). I realized then, as I shared my thoughts with my colleague, and I realize now, as I share them with a wider audience, that more explanation is needed to make a claim such as this one credible, and I hope to provide it here.

ELECTRONIC LITERACY AND ELECTRONIC PEER RESPONSE

As a professional writing teacher, I seem to spend more time every day on electronic communication in general and electronic response in particular—even when I am not working in an environment with a formal electronic-response program in place. Both my business writing and technical writing texts emphasize the importance of electronic communication, and my technology-oriented students quickly grasp the benefits of communicating with me and with one another electronically. They see it as an opportunity to share entire documents without the constraints of time and space, and they see the benefits to them in future courses and future careers of gaining electronic communication skills now. Our meeting in a computer classroom greatly facilitates their immersion into this new medium of communication, and they immerse themselves without hesitation.

Electronic communication is undeniably becoming increasingly common in academic and professional life, but it is only in the past decade that literacy scholars have begun to examine the ways this new technology affects literacy (Costanzo, 1994; Haas, 1998; Selfe, 1989; Tuman, 1992). I find it fascinating that, as the discussion over the relationship between orality and literacy continues, electronic literacy is taking center stage with its unique hybridization of features from both. Although all the details of its linguistic and rhetorical nature are still being explored, it is becoming clear that electronic literacy does have a distinctive nature, and it is also becoming clear that electronic literacy changes not only the communication but also the communicator. It is quite possible that what I call *electronic literacy* will be recognized by scholars in the early 21st century not only as different from print literacy but also as a new literacy of its own. I believe that electronic peer response is one of the most important and least explored forms of electronic literacy, and it is on this form that I have focused my own research.

Any history on the literacy of electronic peer response, because it is so new and unexplored, necessarily draws on the history of the two practices from which it is derived. Simply explained, peer-response groups are communities of students who work collaboratively to improve one another's writing, and electronic peer-response groups do most of this collaborative work via electronic communication of one type or another. Viewed from the larger perspective of composition studies, both of these practices are relatively new. A review of the literature on composition theory shows strong support over only the past 30 years for peer-response groups (Gere, 1987) and over only the past 10 years for electronic communication (Spitzer, 1989).

One interesting feature of peer-response groups and electronic communication is that both are pedagogical applications that exemplify the ideas of Vygotsky (1978) and the social view of writing he inspired. Composition scholars now agree that peer-response groups are inherently social, and most agree that each individual within a group composed of students with varying abilities can serve, in some way, as a more capable peer to help the other peers reach their potential (Bruffee, 1984; Ede & Lunsford, 1985; Gere, 1987). Computers and writing scholars agree that electronic communication is also inherently social, and they have been advocating this view in mainstream composition studies (Barber & Kemp, 1990; Burns, 1992; Flores, 1990; Hawisher, 1992; Holdstein, 1990; Miller, 1991; Moran, 1992; Selfe & Meyer, 1991; Taylor, 1992; Wright, 1992). For example, Spitzer (1990), one of the early proponents of computer conferencing, claimed, "Computers, which were once thought to promote isolation, may in fact prove to be of greatest help in creating cooperative learning environments" (p. 59). Theoretically, adding the socially oriented electronic environment to the already socially oriented peer-response groups would have a dramatically positive impact on the social construction of meaning.

Despite this theoretical potential, there has been very little research on electronic peer response, and the research that has been completed is problematic. The problem with this research is that it has the same limitations as research on peer response in general: It focuses only on the social construction, or process, and excludes the meaning, or products, of the electronic peer response. In "Some Difficulties with Collaborative Learning," Smit (1994) said, of all the studies of peer-response groups, "Few of them analyze the effects of collaborative pedagogy on writing per se." He explained, "They demonstrate that students improve such things as feeling good about the class, having better attitudes about writing, having an increased ability to interact in small groups and participate in discussion, and being able to critically analyze the writing of others" (p. 77).

In the very few studies that exist on this interactive pedagogical application of electronic peer-response groups, the trend described by Smit continues. Langston and Batson (1990) provided one of the foundational articles with "The Social Shifts Invited by Working Collaboratively on Computer Networks: The ENFI Project." As their pilot study's most significant conclusion, they said: "We found indications that groups working on-line will show a more evenly distributed interactive pattern than face-to-face groups" (p. 146). Mabrito (1991) analyzed "Electronic Mail as a Vehicle for Peer Response," and he also observed affective benefits in the process. He said, "For the high-apprehensive writers in this study, e-mail peer groups provided a productive and apparently non-threatening forum for sharing their writing with other students and responding to other students' texts" (p. 529). Selfe (1992) confirmed both findings in "Computer-Based Conversations and the Changing Nature of Collaboration." She noted, "On-line conferences seem to offer alternative spaces for academic student involvement because they offer different conversational power structures than those characterizing collaboration in the form of a traditional classroom setting" (p. 149), and "On-line collaborative forums do indeed present group members with a reduced-risk environment" (p. 162). All three of these articles have two things in common: They conclude that electronic peer response is a worthwhile practice, and they conclude this based on affective gains made by students using it. In other words, students enjoy the process of electronic peer response and, therefore, enjoy writing.

MY STUDY OF ELECTRONIC PEER RESPONSE

I was impressed with the affective gains researchers discovered students made with electronic peer response. After all, any writing teacher is happy when students enjoy the process of writing and want to write. However, with this practice or any other, I have never been convinced that affective gains are sufficient justification for utilization in the writing classroom. After all, the primary purpose of peer response is to improve the writing. Because my own experience convinced me electronic peer response did, I wanted to examine the effects of electronic peer response on not only the process but also the products. In a composition class taught by a colleague I call "Sandy," I conducted 16 case studies of electronic peer-response groups using the program *CommonSpace*. My goal was to answer one general research question: How does electronic peer response affect the social construction of meaning in the writing of composition students in terms of both process and products?

The theory behind the results of my research showed me that, although there are problems with this pedagogical application as with any other, electronic peer response improves the process and the products of most students' writing. Although the growing prevalence of electronic peer response in academic and professional contexts was a motivating reason for me to use it, this is a much more significant one. I organized my findings according to each of my seven research subquestions, and here I am going to share details on the four that are most enlightening about the literacy of electronic peer response: two on the process and two on the products. Because I cannot possibly provide illustrative data from all my cases, I selected my examples from a group I considered a typical case. I call this group "John's group," and I call its members "John," "Kim," and "Trish."

FINDINGS ON THE PROCESS OF RESPONSE

The Students Liked Using the Computers for Electronic Peer-Response Groups

My statement of findings in response to this question may seem overly simplistic, but it also is very true. My data, and I had more extensive data on this finding than on any other, showed three primary reasons that the students liked the electronic peer-response groups: they liked computers more than writing; they liked responding electronically rather than face-to-face; and they liked having the written record, provided by the electronic response, from which to revise.

The first reason students liked the electronic peer-response groups was that they liked computers more than writing. This preference was established early in a questionnaire given on the first night of class in which the students showed a clear preference for computers over writing and, even without knowing much about them, for electronic peer-response groups over traditional ones. By the end of the semester, positive feelings toward both writing and computers had increased, but the preferences were the same: 46% expressed positive feelings toward writing, and 85% expressed positive feelings toward computers. Although these numbers clearly support my claim that most of the students were more comfortable with computers than with writing, the strongest evidence was in the words of the students themselves. At the beginning of the semester, John shared this: "Not yet comfortable with writing. I would like to become proficient in writing to help attain my goals." Yet, when discussing computers, he reversed his position: "Very comfortable using them. I make use of computers every day and learn something new about them every day." John showed his clear preference for computers over writing by sending me his early informant e-mail messages not in text but in sound attachments in his best *Mission Impossible* voice and complete with self-destruct pronouncements at the end. I remembered Faigley (1992) saying, in *Fragments of Rationality: Postmodernity and the Subject of Composition*; "These [electronic communication] programs have spread quickly across campuses in large part because students are enthusiastic about using them" (p. 168), and John's words and actions made sense.

An even stronger reason students liked the electronic peer-response groups was that they liked responding electronically rather than face-to-face. Kim's comment to her teacher in a mid-semester conference showed the advantage to the writer: "I think I'm getting more honest feedback from my peers in the electronic response because [John] and [Trish] aren't afraid of hurting my feelings by telling me what I need to change." She explained that she let them know during the oral component that she wanted and needed their help, and then they gave it to her in the electronic component. She thought for a moment and then added, "Maybe if we didn't have the electronic part, they would tell me the same things orally, but somehow I doubt it." Trish approached her preference for electronic response from the other perspective, that of the responder. She stated emphatically, "I greatly prefer giving my responses electronically," and the first reason she gave was social: "[John], [Kim], and I are friends now. Even though I know that they trust and want my responses to their essays, it is much easier for me to write my responses in the electronic component than to provide them all orally because I don't feel as if I'm hurting their feelings." In "Computer-Based Conversations and the Changing Nature of Collaboration," Selfe (1992) provided a great explanation from our perspective of Kim's and Trish's concerns about hurt feelings in peer response. "Those of us who have found our own face-to-face critique sessions with certain colleagues difficult, alienating, patronizing, or falsely encouraging know just how powerful such social constraints can be" (p. 161). Yet Trish's reasons for preferring electronic peer response did not stop with the social; other reasons she gave were academic: "I think I provide much better responses electronically rather than orally. The room is silent, and I can look at the essay closely and take a moment to decide how to phrase my suggestion so it will be most helpful. I just can't do this when we're all talking in the oral part." And, this comment leads to the final and most significant reason.

As strong as these reasons were, the strongest reason students liked using the computers for electronic peer-response groups was that they found it helpful to have a written record, provided by the electronic response, from which to revise. Supporting statements given for this preference ranged from the simple to the complex. John wrote, on one of his writing-process cover sheets, "I depend on the printout when I revise. If I didn't have it in front of me, I would forget half of what was said about my essay." Of course, students could take notes to help them remember, but that is not the simple solution it seems to be. Trish explained why the electronically written responses were better than her own notes could ever be. "After a brief time when our thoughts are clear, we can read again our peers' comments, in their exact words, not the words that we have written from a verbal evaluation. Sometimes what people say and what we hear are two different things." All the students, at one time or another, made it clear that they looked at the electronic responses as they were revising their essays, but Trish was one of several who went down the list of comments and addressed each one methodically in her revision. She explained her process to me: "When I went to revise my essays, I took out the printout of my peers' comments and wrote my own remarks about what feedback I was going to use and what I wasn't going to." After I asked her for more information about her responses to her peers' responses, she shared with me her annotated response document for the fourth essay. It looked like a dialogue journal between her and a friend. Even though she was annotating only for herself, she wrote responses to her peers' comments, such as "OK" to a suggestion she was going to follow and "I do" in rebuttal to one she did not feel would be an improvement. She even included a smiley face after one of her responses as if anticipating yet another response from her peer responder. Although her discussion is about traditional peer response, Holt (1992) would understand this positive reaction. In "The Value of Written Peer Criticism," she argued for including a written component to peer response because peer responders put more thought into a written response, and writers have a thoughtful written response from which to revise. In "Electronic Mail as a Vehicle for Peer Response: Conversations of High- and Low-Apprehensive Writers," Mabrito (1991) reinforced this with an explicit reference to electronically written peer responses: "Previous research in electronic communication has indicated that participants in computer conferences retain more information from these conferences than they do from face-to-face meetings because people generally retain more from reading than listening" (p. 528). John and Trish certainly did not know about this earlier research, but their comments clearly not only reinforce but also expand on it. Like Kim, they considered the written records provided by the electronic peer response invaluable.

The Students Felt They Built Extremely Close and Supportive Communities in Their Electronic Peer-Response Groups

In addition to or perhaps because of the reasons already given in the findings for the first question, the students liked using the computers for electronic peer-response groups because of the extremely close and supportive communities they built within those groups. Sandy had made building community a priority from the first night of class, and this resulted in a strongly positive sense of community. She greeted students and put them at ease as they entered, confused over why a writing class was being taught in a computer classroom. She told a joke that got the students laughing, she asked them questions about their writing backgrounds, and she asked them how they were feeling about the writing/computer combination. Finally, she had them share some information about themselves: first in writing and then in small-group discussion. During that class and in subsequent classes, Sandy took a few minutes to conduct community-building activities and began to use small-group work for class activities. By the time the first peer-response workshop was conducted during the third class session, the sense of community was firmly established. Sandy's classroom was a pleasant and comfortable place to be.

The students made comments about the impressive sense of community within both the whole class and the various groups throughout the semester. However, some of the most concrete examples were on the concluding questionnaire in which I asked an explicit question about the subject. In response to the question, "Tell me about the sense of community you do or do not have in your electronic peer-response group," 62% expressed a totally positive view on this subject.

The members of John's group felt that working in the electronic peer-response groups encouraged a comfort with their peers that made them both enjoy class more and help each other more with their writing. John told me, "I had never thought about having a community in a writing class, but [Kim], [Trish], and I have a close one. It has helped me enjoy class and improve my writing." Kim added, "I had a great sense of community with my group. We laughed and had a great time together. They helped me a lot as far as writing; they gave me a lot of good information and great hints." And Trish was the most enthusiastic of all.

> Our peer group has an overwhelming sense of community. We can joke with each other, and this makes it easier to share our writing with each other as well. I looked forward to our peer-group sessions because I knew I would enjoy the company of my peers. And I also knew they would be serious when we needed to get our work done.

Trish had been making unsolicited comments to this effect all semester. Her e-mails to me about the electronic peer-response group workshops frequently opened and closed with comments about community. Her e-mail after the fourth workshop is a good example of this:

> Peer group tonight was fun and constructive as usual [Kim], [John], and I have become very good friends, and I don't think it would have happened if we were not in the same peer group all semester.
>
> I have really enjoyed the time we spent in peer group this semester. Not only did I receive valuable information that helped me improve my writing, but I made some great friends as well.
>
> I am going to try attaching the journal entry I wrote about our peer group. Let me know if you can get it to open. See you Monday night!

The journal she attached, written for an unrelated class assignment, exhibits the sense of community, evident in all groups but especially strong in John's group, better than any other source. She entitled it "What Makes Me Laugh."

> A lot of things make me laugh, especially people. My friends in my peer group for English 101 are two people who have the ability to make me laugh until my cheeks hurt. Their names are [Kim] and [John], and they are so funny. When the three of us get together, it is hard to believe we accomplish anything because our laughing can be heard throughout the classroom. I have a lot of fun in our peer-group sessions, and I think it is great. We are serious when we are sharing our essay and opinions, but lighten the mood with a joke or comment that makes it so easy to do so. I realize that school is a place to be serious, but sometimes it is beneficial to share a good laugh or two. Or in our case a hundred. We make a great team, and I am thankful to be a part of it. I will never forget them and how much fun we had together in English 101.

Clearly relevant to the dynamics of John, Kim, and Trish are the words of Handa (1990), who edited the first primary work on the role of community in computer environments in her collection, *Computers and Community*. In her closing essay, "Politics, Ideology, and the Isolated Composer or Why We Need Community in the Writing Classroom," Handa explained the importance of this sense of community and the opportunity to and importance of developing it in the computer classroom. Handa argued that computers can promote isolation or collaboration; they can promote the teacher's authority or the students' authority. It is, therefore, critical that a sense of community be developed. She claimed, "An instructor aware of the politics of pedagogy can use the computer as a medium for communication and interaction, a tool fostering democratic patterns of exchange, and a tool including those traditionally excluded at the margins of discourse" (p. 183). Many other scholars have since agreed with the importance of the teacher using the power of electronic communication and collaboration to achieve community and empower the students. Sandy, although new to the computer environment, was an experienced and talented teacher who intuitively understood and implemented this practice, and her students were clearly empowered by it.

FINDINGS ON THE PRODUCTS OF RESPONSE

The Students Gave Compliments and Made Suggestions in Their Electronic Peer-Response Groups

The first component of the products of response that I examined was the actual comments the students made to one another in the electronic peer-response groups. Because I felt that it was very important to do a careful analysis of the types of comments made, I completed a complex coding process for each comment and created tables summarizing comments by types. The members of John's group averaged 16 comments in each response, making a total of 284 comments to one another in three workshops. Of these, 36% were compliments, and 64% were suggestions. The primary purpose of the compliments seemed to be to affirm the writers, and I attributed their unexpectedly large numbers to the positive feelings described in the findings on process. The primary purpose of the suggestions seemed to be to improve the essays, and, therefore, they were generally the types of comments expected from a peer-response session.

After completing this basic coding of comments as one of these two main types, I moved on to code them in other meaningful ways. First, I divided the compliments and suggestions according to scope as either global or local. This yielded the following results:

Total compliments	36%
Global compliments	36%
Local compliments	64%
Total suggestions	64%
Global suggestions	10%
Local suggestions	90%

Second, I coded them according to focus by using an analytical set of criteria that are fairly typical in writing evaluation and used by the portfolio evaluators who, eventually, would assign grades to the work of the students participating in the study. This yielded the following results:

Content	45%
Organization	12%
Style	27%
Grammar/punctuation/mechanics	13%
All	3%

Now what is the significance of this coding by scope and focus? To me, the primary significance is that there was a great variety of comments—a fact that proves wrong a frequently cited limitation of peer-response groups in general and Sandy's concern about electronic peer-response groups in particular. In terms of scope, the students made both global and local comments, and they seemed to distribute them in ways that were most effective. For example, they made significantly more global, or general, comments in their compliments, and these seemed to provide a foundation of trust that made the students more comfortable accepting one another's suggestions. They made significantly more local, or specific, comments in their suggestions, and these provided concrete guidance for revision. In terms of focus, the students surprised Sandy with their comments on higher order concerns, such as content. The electronic peer-response program being used included a linking feature that enabled students to highlight a specific part of the writer's essay and provide a comment that was clearly linked to that particular part. Sandy was sure that this would exacerbate a tendency she believed already existed for students to make most local comments about lower order concerns such as grammar/punctuation/mechanics. This definitely, however, was not the case. The students were not editing one another's essays. They were providing substantive comments, primarily in the area of content, that were truly meant to improve one another's essays in significant ways.

As an illustration of the types of comments the students made to one another, here are comments John and Kim made to Trish on Essay 4. Trish was the strongest peer responder in terms of both quantity and quality, so comments from her would be more impressive. However, her peers' responses to her essay are more representative, so they are the ones I share. In their responses to this essay, John made 5 compliments and 11 suggestions, and Kim made 13 compliments and 13 suggestions. Table 9.1 provides these comments, categorized into the 16 major types.

Although representative, these are not the only comments John and Kim made to Trish in this workshop. I must admit that I am especially partial to John's compliment, "This makes it sound like you know what you're talking about," and Kim's compliment, "Good point, [Trish]. You go, girl!"

The students in John's group certainly appeared not to face the misdirection described by Newkirk (1984) in "Direction and Misdirection in Peer Response"; there seemed to be no conflict between their sense of effective writing and the teacher's sense. I attributed this to Sandy's relatively extensive modeling for and guiding of the students. As Zhu (1995) pointed out in the results of his study on the "Effects of Training for Peer Response on Students' Comments and Interaction," training is the key to avoiding misdirection. He said, "When teachers trained students to assist one another

Table 9.1. Examples of John's and Kim's Comments to Trish on Essay 4

	Compliments	Suggestions
Global content	Well-rounded and very good supporting details	You have three good paragraphs with really good supporting data.
Global organization	Paragraphs 2 and 3 have great topic sentences!	Are these reasons in the best order?
Global style	Good way of putting in those arguments	Check word choice.
Global grammar/ punctuation/mechanics	None	None
Local content	Good supporting detail. Fits well.	I think your introduction needs a little work. Maybe you need to develop the lead-in a little more.
Local organization	Good topic sentence! Very strong.	Doesn't really show ordering plan. Use better transitions.
Local style	Nicely put.	Species?
Local grammar/ punctuation/mechanics	None	No comma in these.

in classroom peer-response sessions, students indeed assisted one another much more effectively" (p. 520). Sandy provided a great deal of training, and that seems to have helped create the similarity between the teacher's and peers' senses of effective writing, and, therefore, the overall helpfulness of the comments they made in the electronic peer-response workshop. However, the extent of this helpfulness became even more apparent as I analyzed further.

The Revisions the Students Made in Their Essays Were Closely Associated with the Suggestions Their Peers Made in the Electronic Peer-Response Workshops, and all the Peer-Suggested Revisions Were Effective

The second component of the products of response that I examined was the revisions the students made in response to their peers' responses, and my findings here were the most unexpected and dramatic of all. I was amazed at the extent to which the students used their peers' suggestions when they revised, and I was even more amazed when I discovered that there was not a single peer-suggested revision that was not effective in improving the essay in which it was made.

I analyzed the relationship between the responders' suggestions and the writers' revisions from two perspectives: (a) the percentage of peer suggestions that were followed and (b) the percentage of revisions that were peer-suggested. Both of these analyses, in different ways, show the power of the peer suggestion on the writer. I expected the second number to be consistently lower than the first because I assumed that writers would follow some of their peers' suggestions but also would make quite a few other revisions on their own. I was surprised at both how similar and how high both percentages were.

In order to see the trends from Workshops 2–4, I combined the data from those individual tables into a summary table. To simplify that data, I created Table 9.2, which provides product-average percentages showing both methods of determining the relationship between peer suggestions and revisions. It was very interesting to me that, although they varied within workshops and among writers, the overall percentages across the three workshops were almost exactly the same for the two different methods of analysis.

In summary, more than three quarters of the peer suggestions resulted in revisions (79%), and more than three quarters of the revisions were peer-suggested (83%): a very strong association between the responders' suggestions and the writers' revisions. In order to understand better why this

Table 9.2.Relationship between Suggestions and Revisions in Workshops 2–4

Writer	Percentage of Peer-Suggested Revisions	Percentage of Revisions Peer-Suggested
John	89%	91%
Kim	83%	98%
Trish	66%	61%
Total	79%	83%

association was so strong, I returned to a close examination of the data and discovered further evidence of the interrelationship between the process and products of response. Because of the comfort with the electronic peer-response process, the students frequently solicited comments about matters with which they were struggling and, therefore, were very interested in revising based on those suggestions.

For example, in Workshop 3, Kim told the group she was missing a thesis and needed help constructing one that accurately controlled her entire essay. She told them, "Up here in the introduction, I don't tell what the whole story is about." Then, after the three of them collaboratively constructed a tentative thesis, Kim said, "I need a title to go with my new thesis." Of course, during the electronic component, both John and Trish made a reminder comment about Kim's need to revise her thesis and title as the three of them had discussed. And, of course, both of these comments resulted in and were categorized as having resulted in revisions. The important point here is that Kim was very involved in the process of negotiating suggestions that would help her with issues she saw a need for during her drafting, and her use of her peers' suggestions just indicated that she considered the negotiation successful. John, during the oral response in Workshop 4, asked for help with grammar/punctuation/mechanics. This resulted in 10 of the 40 suggestions, an unusually high proportion, being made to him in that area, and it resulted in all 10 of them being addressed in his revision. This sort of negotiation, or social construction of meaning, occurred many other times with other writers and in other workshops.

This great success in terms of suggestions resulting in revisions raises a potentially problematic issue that I felt compelled to explore. If the majority of the students' revisions are the result of their peers' suggestions, have the students lost authority over or ownership of their own texts? Berkenkotter (1984) raised this issue in "Student Writers and Their Sense of Authority over Texts." She described her surprise at learning that "out of their transactions with their readers some students would assert their proprietary rights over their texts while others would gain—or lose—a sense of authority" (p. 313). Berkenkotter made it clear that she believes in using peer-response groups; however, she added, "These responses hinge on a number of subtle emotional and intellectual factors. We need to learn more about these factors and about the process through which writers gain a sense of authority over their texts" (p. 318). Spigelman (1998) returned to this issue in her more recent "Habits of Mind: Historical Configurations of Textual Ownership in Peer Writing Groups," but her different perspective reflects the different context in which students are currently writing, responding, and revising. Spigelman described the "newer communal view of textual ownership" and attributed this primarily to the way electronic communication blurs the lines between public and private intellectual property. She described how "software packages that provide for interactive conferencing allow students to actively collaborate in—that is, help to write—each other's papers" (p. 237). Spigelman recommended that teachers explore with students the "irredeemably dialectical" phenomenon of textual ownership, which is especially evident in productive peer-response groups. She suggested that students take into consideration the suggestions of their peers and offer justification for their doing so. In summary, it seems that in today's climate of collaboration, which is both encouraged and exacerbated by electronic communication, a sense of authority or ownership is simply not perceived as narrowly as it was even 15 years ago. John, Kim, and Trish were doing exactly what they were asked to do: responding to one another's writing and responding to those responses through their revisions.

I had decided to determine the effectiveness of peer suggestions because experiences of my own and comments of critics both indicated that, sometimes, in traditional peer-response groups, students make peer-suggested revisions that are ineffective in improving their essays. When I realized that the majority of the peer suggestions were being followed in revisions and the majority of the revisions were peer-suggested, I knew that the answer to this research question was even more important than I had thought it would be, and I refined my data analysis to address it thoroughly. My analysis procedure involved a computerized comparison of rough and revised drafts that isolated all the revisions. Sandy and I met to review several of these comparison documents and discuss what we would code as effective, neutral, and ineffective revisions in any of the four evaluative areas: content, organization, style, and grammar/punctuation/mechanics. For example, in the area of content, we considered the providing of more vivid detail on a relevant topic effective, but we considered digression to an irrelevant topic ineffective. In the area of grammar/punctuation/mechanics, the distinction was more obvious because we considered a change that corrected an existing error effective but considered the creation of a previously nonexistent error ineffective. After Sandy and I had refined our coding process, we reviewed all the revisions in all the essays responded to within John's group, and we were both amazed to discover that, according to both our individual coding processes, 100% of the peer-suggested revisions in John's group were effective. There was not a single peer-suggested revision that did not have a positive effect on the essay in which it was made.

This finding clearly merits further thought and examination. Obviously, this was not a quantitative, comparative study, so I would not even venture to assign causation for this finding. However, I can provide my best guess about the circumstances that led to such effective suggestions, and my guess is that it was a combination of the benefits of both the process and products of electronic response discussed earlier and the interrelationship between the two. I believe the process added to the effectiveness of the suggestions and resulting revisions because the students liked using the computers for their electronic response, and they established a sense of community with their peers in the groups. In summary, they cared about one another. I believe the products added to the effectiveness of the suggestions and resulting revisions because of the written/electronic rather then oral-traditional nature of the suggestion-making medium. With the ease of commenting provided by the electronic environment and the time for thinking provided by the written medium, they made more effective suggestions that, therefore, resulted in more effective revisions. In summary, they responded better. To me, this seemed to be a clear case of socially constructed meaning that was very beneficial to the writers.

CONCLUSION

The four findings I described were not, as mentioned at the beginning of the previous section, my only findings in this study There were three others: (a) both the quantity and quality of the comments and revisions improved with each workshop; (b) the types of comments and revisions differed across electronic peer-response groups; and (c) although her comfort level improved over time, using electronic peer-response groups was stressful for the teacher. Although I do not develop them here since they are not as critical to the understanding of the literacy of electronic peer response as were the other four findings, the seven findings provided a clear answer to my original research question. How does electronic peer response affect the social construction of meaning in the writing of composition students in terms of both process and products? In terms of first process and then products, the following is the answer.

The students liked using the computers in electronic peer-response groups because they liked computers more than they liked writing, and they found electronic response more comfortable, more helpful, or both. Therefore, they were more committed to and effective in the peer-response activity than they would have been with traditional peer response. Furthermore, the social interaction that occurred in the electronic peer-response groups led to a strong sense of community, which not only made the students feel good about themselves, their peers, and the peer-response process, but also helped the students improve their writing. The comments the students made to one another in their electronic peer-response groups were clearly effective. The responders made many comments to one another, with a ratio of approximately one compliment to every two suggestions, and they concentrated their suggestions on the higher order concerns, which writing teachers consider most important. Furthermore, there was a totally positive association between peer suggestions and effective revisions. The writers took the responders' suggestions seriously, and more than three quarters of their revisions were directly related to peer suggestions. Finally and most significant, all these peer-suggested revisions improved the essays in which they were made. This answer to my research question leads to one clear recommendation: Electronic peer-response groups offer great potential to benefit both the process and products of most students' writing, and teachers interested in those goals should strongly consider their use.

I believe that the literacy of electronic peer response is an increasingly important literacy because both the process (or social construction) and the products (or meaning) of it are such critical components and are so intricately interrelated. Electronic peer response is an interactive pedagogical application, and one could say it is an interactive literacy. Increasingly, both students and scholars participating in both academic and professional activities are using electronic media for communication in general and for peer response in particular, and I am convinced this trend will continue. If we are to understand the multiple literacies of the 21st century, we need to include the important literacy of electronic peer response in our exploration.

REFERENCES

Barker, T.T., & Kemp, F.O. (1990). Network theory: A postmodern pedagogy for the writing classroom. In C. Handa (Ed.), *Computers and community: Teaching composition in the twenty-first century* (pp. 1–27). Portsmouth, NH: Boyton/Cook.

Berkenkotter, C. (1984). Student writers and their sense of authority over texts. *College Composition and Communication, 35*, 312–319.

Bruffee, K.A. (1984). Collaborative learning and the conversation of mankind. *College English, 46*, 635–652.

Burns, H. (1992). Teaching composition in tomorrow's multimedia, multinetworked classrooms. In G.E. Hawisher & P. LeBlanc (Eds.), *Re-imagining computers and composition: Teaching and research in the virtual age* (pp. 115-130). Portsmouth, NH: Boynton/Cook.

Costanzo, W. (1994). Reading, writing, and thinking in an age of electronic literacy. In C. Selfe & S. Hilligoss (Eds.), *Literacy and computers: The complications of teaching and learning with technology* (pp. 11–21). New York: Modern Language Association.

Ede, L., & Lunsford, A. (1985). Let them write—together. *English Quarterly, 18*, 119–127.

Faigley, L. (1992). *Fragments of rationality: Postmodernity and the subject of composition*. Pittsburgh, PA: University of Pittsburgh Press.

Flores, M. J. (1990). Computer conferencing: Composing a feminist community of writers. In C. Handa (Ed.), *Computers and community: Teaching composition in the twenty-first century* (pp. 106–117). Portsmouth, NH: Boyton/Cook.

Gere, A. R. (1987). *Writing groups: History, theory, and implications*. Carbondale: Southern Illinois University Press.

Haas, C. H. (1996). *Writing technology: Studies on the materiality of literacy*. Mahway, NJ: Erlbaum.

Handa, C. (1990). Politics, ideology, and the strange, slow death of the isolated computer or why we need community in the writing classroom. In C. Handa (Ed.), *Computers and community: Teaching composition in the twenty-first century* (pp. 160–184). Portsmouth, NH: Boynton/Cook.

Hawisher, G. E. (1992). Electronic meetings of the minds: Research, electronic conferences, and composition studies. In G. E. Hawisher & P. LeBlanc (Eds.), *Re-imagining computers and composition: Teaching and research in the virtual age* (pp. 81–101). Portsmouth, NH: Boynton/Cook.

Holdstein, D. H. (1990). A theory of one's own? An introduction to theoretical and critical contexts for composition and computers. In D. H. Holdstein & C.L. Selfe (Eds.), *Computers and writing: Theory, research, practice* (pp. 31–39). New York: Modern Language Association.

Holt, M. (1992). The value of written peer criticism. *College Composition and Communication, 43*, 384–392.

Langston, M. D., & Batson, T. W. (1990). The social shifts invited by working collaborating on computer networks: The ENFI project. In C. Handa (Ed.), *Computers and community: Teaching composition in the twenty-first century* (pp. 140–159). Portsmouth, NH: Boynton/Cook.

Marbrito, M. (1991). Electronic mail as a vehicle for peer response: Conversations of high- and low-apprehensive writers. *Written Communication, 8*, 509–532.

Miller, M. M. (1991). Electronic conferencing in the networked classroom. *College Teaching, 39*(4), 136–139.

Moran, C. (1992). Computers and the writing classroom: A look to the future. In G. E. Hawisher & P. LeBlanc (Eds.), *Re-imagining computers and composition:*

Teaching and research in the virtual age (pp. 7–23). Portsmouth, NH: Boynton/Cook.

Newkirk, T. (1984). Direction and misdirection in peer response. *College Composition and Communication, 35*, 301-311.

Selfe, C. L. (1989). Redefining literacy: The multilayered grammars of computers. In G. E. Hawisher & C. L. Selfe (Eds.), *Critical perspectives on computers and composition instruction* (pp. 3-15). New York: Teachers College Press.

Selfe, C. L. (1992). Computer-based conversations and the changing nature of collaboration. In J. Forman (Ed.), *New visions of collaborative writing* (pp. 147-169). Portsmouth, NH: Boynton/Cook.

Selfe, C. L., & Meyer, P. R. (1991). Testing claims for on-line conferencing. *Written Communication, 8*, 163-192.

Smit, D. W. (1994). Some difficulties with collaborative learning. In G. A. Olson & D. I. Dobrin (Eds.), *Composition theory for the postmodern classroom* (pp. 70-81). Albany: State University of New York Press.

Spigelman, C. (1998). Habits of mind: Historical configurations of textual ownership in peer writing groups. *College Composition and Communication, 49*, 234-255.

Spitzer, M. (1989). Computer conferencing: An emerging technology. In G. E. Hawisher & C. L. Selfe (Eds.), *Critical perspectives on computers and composition instruction* (pp. 187-200). New York: Teachers College Press.

Spitzer, M. (1990). Local and global networking: Implications for the future. In D.H. Holdstein & C. L. Selfe (Eds.), *Critical perspectives on computers and composition instruction* (pp. 58-70). New York: Modern Language Association.

Tannacito, T. (1998). Electronic peer-response groups: Case studies of computer-mediated communication in a composition class (Doctoral dissertation, Indiana University of Pennsylvania). *Dissertation Abstracts International* (UMI No. AAT9912826).

Taylor, P. (1992). Social epistemic rhetoric and chaotic discourse. In G. E. Hawisher & P. LeBlanc (Eds.), *Re-imagining computers and composition: Teaching and research in the virtual age* (pp. 131-148). Portsmouth, NH: Boynton/Cook.

Tuman, M. (1992). *Word perfect: Literacy in the computer age*. Pittsburgh, PA: University of Pittsburgh Press.

Van der Geest, T., & Remmers, T. (1994). The computer as means of communication for peer-review groups. *Computers and Composition, 11*(3), 237-250.

Vygotsky, L. (1978). *Mind in society: The development of higher psychological processes* (M. Cole, V. John-Steiner, S. Scribner, & E. Souberman, eds.). Cambridge, MA: Harvard University Press.

Wright, W. W., Jr. (1992). Breaking down barriers: High schools and computer conferencing. In G.E. Hawisher & P. LeBlanc (Eds.), *Re-imagining computers and composition: Teaching and research in the virtual age* (pp. 102-114). Portsmouth, NH: Boynton/Cook.

Zhu, W. (1995). Effects of training for peer response on students' comments and interaction. *Written Communication*, 492-528.

10

TOWARD A THEORY OF ONLINE COLLABORATION

Ellen Schendel
Grand Valley State University
Michael Neal
Clemson University
Cecilia Hartley
Writerspace.com

Although extensive research has examined *collaboration*[1] within composition studies, and research into online spaces increases, there is relatively little written about the intersection of these two literacy practices. Studying this intersection is important because by studying multiple literacy practices at work together, we increase our opportunities to learn more about each practice. And, as writers collaborate online more frequently, it is important to consider our field's assumptions about collaboration and computer-mediated communication (CMC), and how these practices expand options available to writers. In what ways does CMC support and/or undercut collaboration? In what ways are CMC and collaboration different activities? Do computers change collaborative processes? Do online technologies require us to rethink our theories about collaborative literacy and literacy education?

In this chapter, we examine CMC and collaboration as separate but intertwined and interdependent technologies, and we explore the theoretical implications of the convergence of these two technologies. We examine composition studies' dominant discourses about CMC and collaboration to show how they overlap, and we point to research that still needs to be done in joining these two areas. We then propose theoretical assertions based on our own experiences in collaborating online that we believe warrant investigation as our field studies online collaboration in the 21st century.

THE RELATIONSHIP BETWEEN CMC AND COLLABORATION

Early in our field's use of networked computers, scholars stressed a connection between social construction—and by extension, collaboration—and the use of computers for networked communication among students (Barker & Kemp, 1990; Bruce, Peyton, & Batson, 1993; Cooper & Selfe, 1990; Eldred & Hawisher, 1995; Handa, 1990; Kinkead, 1987; Shriner & Rice, 1989). Scholars believed that racial, class, and gender cues were muted if not invisible online, and students who were too intimidated to speak out in the traditional classroom could express themselves without fear of being ignored or having their views rejected simply because they did not belong to a group that traditionally claims authority in our culture and classrooms.

Such a utopian view of computer-mediated conversation was later critiqued by many of the same scholars who had ushered it in. In 1990 and 1991, Hawisher and Selfe published a number of articles as well as a special issue of *Computers and Composition* focused on the "rhetoric of technology" that had developed around the use of CMC in composition. They defined this "rhetoric of technology" as one that characterized technological change as inherently beneficial. They called for rigorous research that would lay new theoretical groundwork for computer-mediated instruction, and scholars such as Takayoshi (1994), Janangelo (1991), and Herring (1993) began exploring issues of gender and power and the ways these issues play themselves out on computer networks as students discuss issues and collaborate together, finding that lack of visual cues does not stop students from recognizing diversity online—through verbal cues or question/response. Regardless of the utopian or critical views CMC advocates have taken over the years, however, the variable of implicit collaboration has remained intact.

Although much CMC scholarship assumes engagement with collaboration, the reverse is not true; scholarship about collaboration does not always assume that collaborators are engaged in online technologies nor consider how such interactions might affect collaborative processes. Furthermore, articles that discuss *both* computers and collaboration often do so not in terms of co-authorship—collaboratively writing an article, for instance—but rather in a broader sense: people coming together via online technologies to make knowledge together through chat, e-mail, bulletin board postings, and Web site construction.

In "Computer-Based Conversations and The Changing Nature of Collaboration," Selfe (1992) discussed the ways research about online discourse supports collaboration. She argued that "characteristics of electronic collaboration, in contrast to the characteristics of face-to-face exchanges, may allow group members to experiment more freely with exploring differences in individual approaches to problems, writing tasks, and issues" (p. 147). Selfe examined the asynchronous discourse of Megabyte U as an online collaborative site for academics and found that (a) participants were not interrupted in mid-thought, as they might be in face-to-face conversations; (b) online collaboration as a whole was different than face-to-face collaboration, for women wrote longer messages and all participants took pains to be more polite than they might through face-to-face discourse; and (c) the fact that Megabyte U allowed participants to use pseudonyms might have altered the way that people responded to one another, freeing people up to say what they thought without feeling implicated by differences in gender, race, ethnicity, or class. These conversations produced knowledge, but they were not necessarily tightly focused on co-authorship (although Selfe pointed out that participants did write articles that came out of these exchanges at Megabyte U). Selfe's article is valuable for the way it demonstrates how online technologies facilitate and even assume collaborative knowledge-making. However, by not exploring the ways collaboration shapes CMC, it implies the reverse does not take place.

Spooner and Yancey's (1996, 1998, 1999) articles about collaboration seem also to suggest that technology shapes collaboration—not just the process, but also the products. Spooner and Yancey (1999) composed online—a process that they contended generates a different sort of discourse than writing without computers would—to produce what they term the *new essay*. In "A Single Good Mind," Yancey and Spooner (1998) claimed that the form the article takes—an e-mail dialogue/exchange—is representative of the process they went through in constructing the document, arguing that "to expose the gears and pulleys does in fact represent the collaborative process" (p. 61). That is, instead of producing a seamless document in which Yancey and Spooner speak consistently from the perspective of a collaborative "we," they choose to present their ideas as a dialogue that indicates not only where they reach agreement, but also highlights moments of dissension.

But an issue that remains unaddressed in Yancey and Spooner's work is the role that technology played in their collaborative processes and their construction of a multivocal document. Yancey and Spooner presented their article as a model of collaborative writing, one that shows the messy process of its construction as well as the carefully thought-through content of collaborative arguments. What is left unarticulated and unclear in these articles is the extent to which Spooner and Yancey see technology as fostering a particular kind of collaboration, and to what end.

In "Petals on a Wet Black Bough," Spooner and Yancey (Vielstimmig, 1999) began to answer such questions, using Kirsch's (1997) opinion piece, "Multi-Vocal Texts and Interpretive Responsibility," as a springboard from which to address how the processes of collaboration are represented in collaborative writing. Kirsch's argument centers on a discussion of how literacy experiences—for writers and readers—change when constructing and reading multivocal texts, and how these changes are happening amid a field of professionals who increasingly want to view their work as contributing to a larger community (one outside of academe). Kirsch stressed caution in our construction of multivocal, alternatively written texts, arguing that they are not yet adequately theorized, and we do not yet know the practical consequences of presenting our work to ourselves and others in this way. Spooner and Yancey acknowledged Kirsch's need for caution in choosing a nontraditional way to represent collaborative texts, noting that experimental visual forms can create interpretive problems for readers, potentially creating a text that has meaning only for its writers. Ultimately, however, they continue to stress in this article the importance of representing collaborative processes visually, here arguing that readers should develop new interpretive strategies for engaging such texts.

What we suggest is a consideration of the implications of presenting collaborative work in formats that demonstrate or represent technology. Crafting articles to capture the shape of online discourse when they are in fact *representations* of online discourse makes assumptions about technology that visual cues alone do not flesh out. And constructing representations of technology in the way that Spooner and Yancey (1998) do attributes a particular "aesthetic of difference" to technology that we ourselves create. When choosing how to represent the role technology plays in what/how we write, we should also study that role to examine the opportunities and limitations technologies offer, the ways we contribute to the outcomes of technological discourse, and the relationship between technology and the shape our writing takes. However, we must also interrogate the representation itself, to determine what it can and cannot reveal about the processes of collaboration.

POINTS OF INTEREST TO CONSIDER IN EXAMINING THE RELATIONSHIP OF CMC TO COLLABORATION

In responding to a preliminary draft of Yancey and Spooner's (1998) "A Single Good Mind," Harris asked, "What is important to collaboration and collaborators—the process or the representation of that process?" (cited in Yancey & Spooner, 1998, p. 53). We write this chapter with Harris' question in mind, and we consciously choose to represent our collaboration in what some readers may see as a monologic manner. There are no obvious breaks between speakers, none of the visual cues that would indicate when one of us has taken over the keyboard, no direct evidence of the moments when ideas clash or theoretical stances differ. And yet this chapter, we hope, speaks directly to how our processes of collaboration shape and are shaped by the media in which we choose to communicate. Although Spooner and Yancey used the structure of their articles to show us their collaborative process, we want to make the connections between collaboration and CMC more explicit, drawing on our own experiences in collaborating online to propose a series of statements or axioms that we believe warrant further examination as our field continues to study the intersection of online discourse and collaboration.

A brief background of our own experiences as collaborators is necessary at this point. Approximately a year and a half before writing this chapter, the three of us worked together to construct a three-tiered online site, including a student chat room, a bulletin board, and a URL electronic research library, that we designed for the explicit purpose of student use in first-year composition classes.[2] As we constructed these online spaces, we came to understand that our collaborative processes might well lead to a productive article about how composition teachers who, like us, were not particularly knowledgeable about computer scripting, could construct electronic sites by using coding languages such as Perl. We saw value in teachers designing such sites themselves, for teachers would benefit from theorizing the sites they designed, and they could consistently represent their approaches to language and language learning in the design of the sites rather than relying upon mass-produced programs.

Our own reflections as we created the site became the subject of "*Writing* (Online) *Spaces*: Ideology, Technology, and Pedagogy" (Hartley, Schendel, & Neal, 1999). Even as we wrote that article, we realized that our co-authorship provided another setting for examination. We soon found that the process of composing the article online—using the chatroom and the project bulletin board we constructed for our students—allowed us the opportunity to re-examine the values that had motivated us to construct the electronic site in the first place. We realized that the ways that we had defined the spaces were steeped in unexamined assumptions that we had about collaboration and online discourse. When designing the site, we had a clear vision of the way our students might collaborate in each space. We, therefore, defined the chatroom as a space for conversation and idea-generating, the bulletin board for posting drafts of papers, and the URL library for sharing online research. The ways that we understood online collaboration to work provided a frame of reference in our construction of these spaces, but their existence also limited the sorts of spaces we could imagine constructing.

These axioms, then, are the result of our thinking and reflection about collaboration and online discourse that resulted from the construction of "Writing Spaces" and the co-authorship of an academic article about that site.

Axiom 1: *Face-to-face collaboration and online collaboration are different activities requiring different literacy practices.*

Collaboration is not a single act. By extension, we feel it necessary to state explicitly that not all collaborative acts are the same. We believe that it is important for us to clearly state the obvious precisely because mediums through which collaboration, particularly co-authorship, takes place have been transparent in so much of the scholarship which interrogates collaboration. If we cannot assume that the medium in which collaboration takes place has no effect on collaborative processes, we cannot assume that collaborating online and offline are conducted in the same manner or produce the same outcomes. For instance, in our earlier article we collaborated in a number of ways: We generated ideas together; we read and discussed published texts; we solicited and received feedback from trusted colleagues; we wrote parts of the article individually and then fused them together; and we wrote sections of the article together online (via e-mail, chat, and bulletin board posts) and face to face, sitting over a pad of paper or in front of a computer together. And we engaged in these different forms of collaboration for various reasons and to different ends.

Although collaboration can exist in a multitude of forms, we see three distinct and significant differences between face-to-face and online collaboration: (a) online collaboration allows the process to occur over a length of time and space; (b) online collaboration relies on print literacies, and as a result (c) online collaboration generates artifacts of the collaborative process. These characteristics of online collaboration lead us to theorize it differently than we would face-to-face collaboration. In terms of our own collaborative efforts, because the chat space supports electronic discourse in real time, we often found ourselves utilizing that technology for organizational meetings instead of meeting face to face because Ellen lived 1-1/2 hours away from Cecilia and Michael. What we came to value about the chat space is that it preserves our conversations—much like a taperecorder would—and so we were able to mine from those conversations more effectively than we would have with sketchy notes or memories of what was said in a face-to-face meeting.

Because online and offline collaboration are different activities, and because online collaboration itself is not monolithic, taking place instead in various forms and formats, producing very different kinds of outcomes, it is problematic to assume that collaboration can be discussed or theorized without taking into account the many forms in which it can occur and acknowledging the physical and theoretical implications of each type of collaboration.

Axiom 2: *Collaboration and online discourse are both technologies. Therefore, when we engage in online collaboration, we are engaging in two technologies simultaneously.*

When scholars in our field addresses technologies, they look at how they replicate and shape cultural values (Ede & Lunsford, 1990; Haas, 1996; Selfe & Selfe, 1994; Trimbur, 1989), unequal participation (Herreman, 1988; Ede & Lunsford, 1990; Whitworth, 1988), and silencing/marginalization (Ede & Lunsford, 1990; Selfe, 1992). Technologies are not merely laden with the values of the culture in which they are produced and/or used, but because they are ideologically imbued, they continue to replicate certain social values even as they challenge and expand our literacy practices. For example, although online discourse challenges the way compositionists understand classroom conversation, writing, and even genre (Cooper & Selfe, 1990; Faigley, 1992; Feenberg, 1991; Kiesler, Siegel, & McGuire, 1984), it may not challenge traditional conceptions of gender, class, and ethnicity (Regan, 1993; Selfe & Selfe, 1994). Therefore, although CMC may change our literal communication practices, those changes in the ways we engage one another do not necessarily challenge what we think about who is empowered, who is silenced, and to what ends. For these reasons, computers and composition scholars have called for teachers and researchers to examine our uses of technology critically, always mindful of the ways that technology may not just replicate social injustices, but even blind us to that replication (Hawisher & Selfe, 1991; Selfe & Selfe, 1994).

Technology, in this view, is a culturally situated event rather than a value-free tool. Technologies are not merely means by which humans realize a task; rather, in acting with technologies, we engage with values, ways of thinking, ways of creating meaning, and material effects. Therefore, we can potentially change social values and worldviews when we use technologies. In his discussion of assessment as technology, for example, Madaus (1994) wrote the following:

> Technology gives people the power and will to create new possibilities, allowing for increased choices, opportunities, and freedom. However,

> although the benefits of technology are enormous, technology simultaneously creates problems, opens new ways to make big mistakes, alters institutions in unanticipated negative ways, and impacts negatively on certain populations. (p. 78)

That is, technology is not inherently benevolent, despite the fact that the dominant discourse our culture generates about technology represents it as always improving our culture (Barton).[3] Computers and composition scholarship has already addressed the ways that technology both increases opportunity and creates new problems. Janangelo's (1991) "Technopower and Technoppression," for example, directly deals with this issue, describing how technology allows colleagues to monitor each other, teachers to unethically monitor student activities, and students to anonymously but publicly harass others in classroom online activities.

Because technologies are shaped by culture and in turn shape culture, technologies are unstable, always in a state of flux and renegotiation. Moreover, technologies exist as interactions; the particular use of a technology and the outcomes of that use determine the value of that technology. Because "technology" in this view does not necessarily denote a piece of machinery, but rather suggests the use of cultural practices with underlying shared values (Madaus, 1994), we view collaboration as yet another technology. In this view, collaborative acts are culturally situated interactions that produce results particular to the ways that participants engage with the technology. Collaboration is at once a tool—a means to an end—and a sociocultural product: We collaborate in order to produce an essay or a project, but collaboration itself becomes a social interaction with values and goals determined by a community of people with similar goals. Further, collaboration culminates in the production of material products that are valued, to differing degrees, by the cultures for which they are produced. As Ede and Lunsford (1990), and Spooner and Yancey (1996, 1998, 1999) pointed out, collaborative texts are often "worth" less to tenure committees and university deans than single-authored works. And yet we often value co-authored texts in our writing classrooms.

Axiom 3: *Processes of collaboration shape technology even as technology shapes collaborative processes.*

The ways that computer technologies shape online collaboration are fairly overt—advances in computer technologies such as the development of local area networks (LAN) and the world wide web (WWW) affect the scope of the audience available for collaboration as well as open new venues for collaboration over time and space. The availability and forms of computer-based communication technologies have in a very real sense shaped the ways in which we have been able to participate in and think about online collaboration. However, even as computer technologies facilitate online communication, they can limit the potential for collaboration. Network connection speed, the availability of networked computers, the need to type all communication, the text-based nature of the communication, among other elements, each has the potential to constrain collaborative processes as they slow down or otherwise impede communication.

Although the influence of computer technologies on collaboration is fairly overt, envisioning ways in which collaboration enables and limits computer technologies may not be as immediately apparent. Yet, collaboration does indeed influence CMC, for our assumptions about collaboration often dictate our uses and constructions of computer technologies. For example, as teachers have begun to value collaboration in a first-year writing class, they have also begun to request and use computer technologies that do such things as allow students to electronically post papers for peer review, communicate with one another electronically about essays or topics, and communicate with the instructor outside classroom walls. As the demand for collaborative communication technologies increase, publishing companies are investing more resources into developing software to meet these needs.[4] In fact, many companies have worked directly with teachers in developing software to fit the needs of the writing classroom. Thus, the ways that teachers envision and use collaboration in the classroom and communicate those needs with others can directly shape the construction of collaborative technologies. As we continue to theorize about and imagine new possibilities for online collaboration, the computer technologies will no doubt be developed to meet those needs; however, inasmuch as we do not seek to imagine new ways to communicate and collaborate, we risk being passive recipients of communication technologies rather than having a voice in their evolution and development.

An analysis of the social systems in which online collaboration operates helps us to understand better the ways in which computer and collaborative technologies mutually influence one another. The people who interact online to create knowledge are central to the system—either those actively engaged in current communication or those who have participated previously by publishing online. The ways in which people contribute to and the technologies they use to participate in the system largely influence the work that can be accomplished collaboratively. In our case, the computer technologies we used—the chatroom, electronic bulletin board, and e-mail—both allowed for and constrained our collaborative efforts to learn Perl, create our site, and write our first co-authored article.

In our cooperative efforts, we created three specific tools for online communication, and they reflect the same concern—that the computer technologies both provide the means for and restrict collaboration. Because we were familiar with Web communication, we saw the potential of these tools for use in a first-year writing class. These existing Web tools enabled us to envision what online collaboration could look like in our classes. However, at the same time these pre-existing tools may actually have limited the ways that we envisioned collaboration happening online. We communicated the individual "purposes" of each of these spaces to our students, expecting them to use the spaces for particular functions. In this way, the same tools that facilitated online collaboration for our students may have also channeled it in one specific direction—potentially limiting interactions that would continue to shape new ideas about CMC and about collaboration.

Even as we note how computer and collaborative technologies enabled and constrained our composing processes, an outcome of online collaboration that we find useful are the records that were preserved from our online collaboration. The multiple products of our online collaboration took a variety of forms including the drafts of our article that were posted on the electronic bulletin board and the ideas for the article as they were formed online, such as the organizational structure of the article. Although the value of "productive conflict" is one aspect or function of collaboration (Burnett, 1993), the ways that CMC mediated or even highlighted that conflict ultimately, for us, made the "productive conflict" even more productive. Burnett's (1993) "Decision-Making During the Collaborative Planning of Co-authors" argues that

> the collaborative process is beneficial in large part because of the alternatives collaborators generate and their willingness to critically examine these alternatives. In other words, they defer, and in some cases even actively resist, consensus in order to explore alternatives, and they value explicit disagreement that helps them focus on potential problems. (p. 133)

Conflict can actually make collaboration more productive, and online technology highlighted that fact for us. The slower pace of conversation at the bulletin board allowed us to preserve conflict, and use that conflict productively by highlighting it rather than masking it. The collaborative space of the bulletin board allowed our differences to be heard, as we all had equal access to these collaborative turfs. The bulletin board also allowed our differences to be preserved, as the conflict was archived indefinitely within that collaborative space. We found that as we shifted from idea-generating to drafting the structure for the article to writing sections of the article, we could mine the conflicts we had and the consensus or dissensus we eventually came to for use in the article we produced. As such, we can see what Spooner and Yancey say to be true: technologies that foster communication allow us to construct discourse which represents the multiple voices that make up a text whether or not we choose not to represent those voices though an alternatively stylized text. How the processes of collaboration affect our texts leads directly to our fourth and final point:

Axiom 4: *Online collaboration produces artifacts that can be used for systematic analysis and theory building.*

Although Spooner and Yancey (1996, 1998, 1999) contributed greatly to our understanding of online collaboration by presenting to readers a visual representation of their process, we want to suggest here another form of inquiry into the shape of collaborative writing. An important and often overlooked byproduct of online collaboration—the artifacts produced by online discourse—give us insight into the process of collaborating and interacting online.

As Kuutti (1996) noted in her discussion of activity systems:

> An activity always contains various artifacts (e.g., instruments, signs, procedures, machines, methods, laws, forms of work organization). An essential feature of these artifacts is that they have a mediating role. . . . Artifacts themselves have been created and transformed during the development of the activity itself and carry with them a particular culture-a historical residue of that development. (p. 26)

And the artifacts for online collaboration are particularly evident and important for our study. Whether they be saved e-mail messages, electronic essays posted to a bulletin board, dialogue about the organizational structure of an essay in an archived chat site, or a link to a relevant site saved to a URL library, the artifacts of online collaboration exist tangibly, in ways that may not be true of other types of collaboration.

We see immense value in collaborators having access to the artifacts of their own collaboration as they work to co-author text. Some benefits include the ability to preserve and analyze dissent and conflict in order to enrich and complicate the text being constructed or the ability to systematically observe and analyze the artifacts as data for research into collaboration and online communication.

Finally, the artifacts that are produced by online collaboration are records of the multivocality and dialogic nature of our collaboration. The artifacts created by our online collaboration for both this article and our first reveal for us the complicated and multivocal nature of our collaborative processes. As writers and researchers, we are able to draw from those artifacts for a history of our collaboration in ways that truly represent the multivocality of the texts we have created, some of which we have presented here.

IMPLICATIONS FOR COLLABORATION IN THE 21ST CENTURY

The intersection of collaboration and CMC is central to our field's understanding of literacy practices in the 21st century, and for several reasons. First, online collaboration is a hyper-literate practice—a process of interaction that is conducted through and preserved by writing. As such, online collaboration affords us the opportunity to view "frozen moments" within collaboration, allowing us to see how individual voices come together to build communities, grapple with and negotiate power differentials, and construct end products that are constrained by or expand generic boundaries. Second, online collaboration is increasingly a common way for people to work together, and as such, it is a literacy practice that warrants further exploration as our field continues to expand to study literacy practices outside the academy. And finally, studying the relationship between electronic literacies and collaboration can help us to imagine new ways of interacting with one another, challenging us to construct not just new theories and practices for the teaching of writing, but also new technologies to help us realize those theories and practices.

ENDNOTES

1. *Collaboration* can mean many things. On the one hand, it can mean conversation among people with similar interests; on the other, it can denote people working together toward a common goal. However, we want to point out that much of what we have come to understand about collaboration comes from our working to co-author this and another article online. Co-authoring is just one form of collaboration, but to us it is a particularly palatable sort of collaboration to study further because it is hyper-literate. Because the collaborative process happens online, it relies upon and is preserved through print-based literacies.
2. We wanted to construct a site that archived our students' conversations and writing processes so that they could continue to use the ideas and preliminary writing they generated there throughout the term, and so that they could reflect on their writing processes and see how their writing and ideas contributed to and were influenced by classwide conversations. In short, we wanted students to benefit from working at a site that archived their collaborations with each other.

3. For example, our culture increasingly discusses the need for more and better technology in schools, as if increasing the number of computers per classroom will automatically improve education and make students better citizens.
4. Note the emergence of software programs designed for and marketed to writing programs, such as Daedalus, Interchange, and Textra Connect.

REFERENCES

Barker, T. T., & Kemp, F.O. (1990). Network theory: A postmodern pedagogy for the writing classroom. In C. Handa (Ed.), *Computers and community: Teaching composition in the twenty-first century* (pp. 1-27). Portsmouth, NH: Boynton/Cook Heinemann.

Bruce, B., Peyton, J. K., & Batson, T. (Eds.). (1993). *Network-based classrooms: Promises and realities*. Cambridge, MA: Cambridge University Press.

Burnett, R. (1993). Decision-making during the collaborative planning of coauthors. In A. M. Penrose, B. M. Sitko, & L. Flower (Eds.), *Hearing ourselves think: Cognitive research in the college writing classroom* (pp. 125-46). New York: Oxford University Press.

Cooper, M., & Selfe, C. L. (1990). Computer conferences and learning: Authority, resistance, and internally persuasive discourse. *College English, 52*, 847-869.

Ede, L., & Lunsford, A. (1990). *Singular texts/plural authors: Perspectives on collaborative writing*. Carbondale: Southern Illinois University Press.

Eldred, J. C., & Hawisher, G. E. (1995). Researching electronic networks. *Written Communication, 12*, 330-359.

Faigley, L. (1992). *Fragments of rationality: Postmodernity and the subject of composition*. Pittsburgh: University of Pittsburgh Press.

Feenberg, A. (1991). *Critical theory of technology*. New York: Oxford University Press.

Haas, C. (1996). *Writing technology: Studies on the materiality of literacy*. Mahwah, NJ: Erlbaum.

Handa, C. (1990). Politics, ideology, and the strange, slow death of the isolated composer; Or, why we need community in the writing classroom. In C. Handa (Ed.), *Computers & community: Teaching composition in the twenty-first century* (pp. 160-184). Portsmouth: Boynton/Cook.

Hartley C. A., Schendel, E. E., & Neal, M. R. (1999). Writing (online) spaces: Ideology, technology, and pedagogy. *Computers and Composition: An International Journal for Teachers of Writing, 16*, 359-370.

Hawisher, G. E., & Selfe, C. L. (Eds). (1990). *Computers and Composition: An International Journal for Teachers of Writing, 7* [Special issue].

Hawisher, G. E., & Selfe, C. L. (1991). The rhetoric of technology and the electronic writing class. *College Composition and Communication, 42*, 55-65.

Herreman, D. (1988). None of us is as smart as all of us. In NCTE Committee on Classroom Practices in Teaching English (Ed.), *Focus on collaborative learning: Classroom practices in teaching English* (pp. 5-12). Urbana: NCTE.

Herring, S. (1993). Gender and democracy in computer-mediated communication. *Electronic Journal of Communication, 3*, 1-16.

Janangelo, J. (1991). Technopower and technoppression: Some abuses of power and control in computer-assisted writing environments. *Computers and Composition: An International Journal for Teachers of Writing, 9*, 47-64.

Kiesler, S., Siegel, J., & McGuire, T. W. (1984). Social psychological aspects of computer-mediated communication. *American Psychologist, 39*, 1123-1134.

Kinkead, J. (1987). Computer conversations: E-mail and writing instruction. *College Composition and Communication, 38*, 337-341.

Kirsch, G. (1997). Multi-vocal texts and interpretive responsibility. *College English, 59*, 191-202.

Kuutti, K. (1996). Activity theory as a potential framework for human-computer interaction research. In B. A. Nardi (Ed.), *Context and consciousness: Activity theory and human-computer interaction* (p. 17-44). Cambridge, MA: MIT Press.

Madaus, G. (1994). A technological and historical consideration of equity issues associated with proposals to change the nation's testing policy. *Harvard Educational Review, 64*(1), 76-95.

Regan, A. (1993). "Type normal like the rest of us": Writing, power, and homophobia in the networked composition classroom. *Computers and Composition: An International Journal for Teachers of Writing, 10*(4), 11-23.

Selfe, C. L. (1992). Computer-based conversations and the changing nature of collaboration. In J. Forman (Ed.), *New visions of collaborative writing* (pp. 147-169). Portsmouth, NH: Boynton/Cook.

Selfe, C. L., & Selfe, R. J. (1994). The politics of the interface: Power and its exercise in electronic contact zones. *College Composition and Communication, 45*, 480-504.

Shriner, D. K., & Rice, W. C. (1989). Computer conferencing and collaborative learning: A discourse community. *College Composition and Communication, 40*, 472-478.

Spooner, M., & Yancey, K.B. (1996). Postings on a genre of email. *College Composition and Communication, 47*, 252-278.

Takayoshi, P. (1994). Building new networks from the old: Women's experiences with electronic communications. *Computers and Composition: An International Journal for Teachers of Writing, 11*, 21-36.

Trimbur, J. (1989). Consensus and difference in collaborative learning. *College English, 51*(6), 602-616.

Vielstimmig, M. (1999). Petals on a wet black bough: Textuality, collaboration, and the new essay. In G. E. Hawisher & C. L. Selfe (Eds.), *Passions, pedagogies, and 21st century technologies* (pp. 89-114). Logan: Utah State University Press.

Whitworth, R. (1988). Collaborative learning and other disasters. In NCTE Committee on Classroom Practices in Teaching English (Ed.), *Focus on collaborative learning: Classroom practices in teaching English* (pp. 13-20). Urbana, IL: NCTE.

Yancey, K. B., & Spooner, M. (1998). A single good mind: Collaboration, cooperation and the writing self. *College Composition and Communication, 49*, 45-62.

11

THE VISUAL VERBAL RHETORIC OF A WEB SITE

MarineLINK as Imagetext Delivery System

John W. Ramey
Coastal Carolina University

The electronic writing space is a hybrid form of discourse that mixes visual elements with verbal text. The result of this hybridity can be thought of as an *imagetext*, a confluence of images, icons, and words that intermingle to produce what Mitchell (1994) called an "inextricable weaving together of representation and discourse, the imbrication of the visual and verbal experience" (p. 83). In order to unpack the elements of the electronic imagetext, a hybrid vocabulary may be necessary. Principles of layout and design based on Gestalt theory that are currently employed by technical writing scholars and teachers like Bernhardt (1993), Kramer and Bernhardt (1996), and Kostelnick and Roberts (1998), although valid in some areas, especially print-based documents, seem inadequate to the task of truly understanding the complex rhetorical negotiations of an electronic imagetext. The same may be said of the online Web page evaluation criteria of Alexander and Tate (1998) at Widener.edu or the print-based principles of Black (1997) as outlined in his *Web Pages That Work*.

I suggest that some of our most ancient rhetorical concepts can better illuminate the structure of our newest form of discourse. In this chapter, I demonstrate this theory by employing the services of the classical rhetorical notions of ethos, logos, pathos, *kairos,* and the two least discussed canons, *memoria* and delivery, as interpretive tools to examine the U.S. Marine Corps' Web site, *MarineLINK*, an example of a complex, electronic imagetext delivery system.

When dealing with electronic writing spaces, it is important to keep in mind their transitory nature; they are impermanent, mutable structures existing in the volatile, ethereal realms of cyberspace. They lack the state of relative permanence that one takes for granted when discussing print-bound texts. Although the site as a whole is basically the same, the homepage or welcome page of *MarineLINK* has changed considerably since I first began this study. One might argue that a study based on a text that no longer exists is irrelevant. I suggest, however, that a study based on a missing or altered text serves as an archaeological site of knowledge, placing forever the gone cyber-structure in the permanent archives of the bound historical record.

The visual structure of the earlier home page gestured toward a textual world governed by a unique confluence of image and word, a network of interdependencies launched by imagetext icons. The present homepage (at this writing) is far less compelling and more "traditional"—a central photograph of the famous World War II statue in Arlington National Cemetery commemorating the raising of the flag at Iwo Jima surrounded by verbal, text-based links in the form of underlined words and phrases (see Fig. 11.1).

The links on the old homepage, however, are quite different; they take the form of imagetexts and are displayed on the page as a circular grouping of iconic portraits (see Fig. 11.2). When a mouse is positioned on any one of these miniature portraits, the image disappears and text "appears," as if the image has been rolled up on a shade. I can only speculate why this change in the splash page occurred. The old page is far more sophisticated and rhetorically complex as a delivery system for the site. But Web sites, by their natures, are changeable. Perhaps a new

Fig. 11.1. Central image on new homepage.

Fig. 11.2. Old homepage with imagetext portrait icons.

Webmaster-Sargeant felt that the whimsical rhetoric of the old page needed revamping. Perhaps there are other, more subtle purposes, linked to positive propaganda for the initiation of another military intervention—no major military conflicts were afoot in 1997, but in 1999 the Balkan conflict involving Yugoslavia and Kosovo was a major military and political obsession. America's stepped-up military involvement is represented by the jingoistic, memory-inducing icon of the famous Iwo Jima memorial that recalls the Marine Corps' finest hour. Whatever the reasons for the change, I focus my examination and analysis on the older, more sophisticated version because it presents a richer field to till, more complicated use of imagetexts as rhetorical structuring devices.

Beneath the icon of the soldier are the words "Information Page," containing the main logos- and ethos-building links of the site, a history of and rationale for the existence of the Marine Corps. Beneath the child in the Marine dress cap appear the words "Family and Friends," a pathos-building link. Beneath the marching Marines are "Public Events and The Commandant's Page," an important link filled with logos, ethos, pathos, *memoria,* and *kairos,* the ancient Greek notion of timeliness or appropriateness. And beneath the chopper-and-flag icon are the words: "M.E.U.S. Marine Expeditionary Units," another link to the ethos and logos of the Marine Corps.

These portrait icons as imagetexts, then, act as the delivery system of the hypersite, taking the reader/viewer to a variety of places within the intricate web of *MarineLINK*. Delivery, the fifth of the five classical canons, like memory, is not discussed much in modern rhetoric. Based on oratory, delivery is concerned with the manner in which a rhetor delivers the speech—vocal pitch, tone, volume, body language, and gesture—the amplitude and emphasis of the discourse-event. The hypertextual network that begins with the imagetext icons on the Welcome or Splash Page can be viewed as the delivery mechanism of the rhetoric of *MarineLINK*. Within discussions of electronic writing spaces, delivery takes on a new meaning as a configuration system of pixels and bits arranged to deliver text, image, and in some cases, video, animation, and sound.

Now, in an age of electronically *delivered* texts, this ancient, oral canon, which had faded in importance with the increased emphasis on writing, takes on new significance. Delivery is now concerned not with an oratorical and theatrical "treading the boards," but the striking of keyboards and the manipulating of central processing units have become part and parcel of the delivery system of imagetexts. Bolter (1993), in a discussion of hypertextual spaces and the canons of rhetoric, pointed out that "hypertext as a new mode of delivery redefines the other canons . . . hypertext brings together the canons of delivery and arrangement, in the sense that the arrangement of a hypertext, the order in which the topics appear on the reader's screen, is determined in the act of delivery" (p. 100).

More and more, writing is taking place within these hypertextually negotiated or delivered, electronic environments. Texts are now delivered through a graphical (i.e., imagetextual, icon-based) user interface. Iconically situated e-mail has rapidly taken over the function of the purely text-based memo or letter, and Web writing is becoming a commonplace. E-mail is a hybrid discourse that partakes of the oral as well as the textual. So a canon that was used in an oral form is resurrected in a hybrid discourse that employs oral features. E-mail must be delivered in order to exist.

Web writing too, which is visual as well as verbal, is a form of writing that must be delivered from the architecture of personal computers via the delivery system of HTML through modems and fiber-optic lines of communication. The visual and verbal structures of Web sites are delivered potentially to millions of reader/viewers all across the world. The world becomes the platform, the stage, if you will, where delivery is performed, where the tone and voice and visual gesture of texts are enacted through the delivery-system mechanics of computers and html-encoded texts.

If one were to click on the imagetext icon of the boy in the cap (see Fig. 11.3), the image would "roll up" like a shade, and the text, "Friends and Family," would appear. Another click, and one enters the Friends and

Family page. Pathos, the appeal to the emotions, is displayed most clearly within the links and nodes of this sector of the site. The image-text icon of the little boy wearing the oversized Marine Dress Cap standing in front of a Marine (his father? his "commandant"?) in dress blues, is an obvious pathetic gesture, and the Friends and Family page reads like a church bulletin full of concern for the children and spouses of the Marine Corps Family.

Fig. 11.3. The friends and family link.

In the link called "Marine Kids Speak Up," one notices an overt gesture toward a politically correct openness, a gesture that is concerned with the civil rights of Marine Corps children. A striking example of this gesture is a letter written by "Jennifer," a teenage member of the USMC Family, and advertised as "an ode to Marine Corps Air Station, Tustin, California." Describing "the life of a military teen at MCAS Tustin," Jennifer waxes poetic about West Coast life "from the snowy mountain tops to the sunny beaches." Jennifer describes a typical year:

> When school starts, so do busy weekends and full minds. Our first Adventure of the season is the Halloween celebration at Knott's Berry Farm. The amusement park takes on the atmosphere of a haunted house. Finally the first semester of school ends and we start our winter break. We head up to Big Bear or Mammoth mountain for a weekend of playing in the snow. Up on top of the mountain we go snow boarding, skiing and tubing. We usually return home with bruised bodies but happy souls. Our next opportunity for a get away is during spring break. We head off to Magic Mountain for some of the fastest and tallest rollercoaster rides. We are also located within minutes of Disneyland, where you can go back to the fantasy of your childhood. Let us not forgot [*sic*] Universal Studio were [sic] you can return to your favorite movie.

It is difficult not to notice that everything described in Jennifer's effusive paean to Marine Corps life exists *outside* of Tustin Air Station; Disneyland, Knott's Berry Farm, the beaches, Magic Mountain, Universal Studio are all exotic locales far removed from the day-to-day reality of a military air base. In fact, Jennifer's "ode" to Marine Corps Air Station Tustin is a narrative of escape from the close confines of the military base with its regimented lifestyle. Ironically, the places Jennifer and her friends escape to are themselves highly structured and regimented forms of leisure. Athletic activities and outdoor sports like "jogging, biking or playing racket ball" dominate Jennifer's list of things to do.

The same picture is painted in the imagetext structure of the teenage chat site, "Military Teens on the Move" (see Fig. 11.4). Ghostly, larger-than-life images of teens engaged in a variety of sports are spread out across a flat horizon while, in the foreground, the painted lines of a paved highway diminish into a perspectival vanishing point. Here, one of the more obvious drawbacks to growing up in the military, the constant moving from place to place with a concomitant rupturing of relationships, is re-visioned, propagandized into an ethereal, emotional world of smiles, thrills, and wholesome, shared activities like biking, skating, and karate. Pathos dramatically informs the subtext of this link's visual and verbal structure by its appeal to some fundamental, emotional needs of most teenagers—a sense of belonging to a community of one's peers and a sense of security within that community through shared activities. "Yes, Marine teen, you may be constantly on the move," the imagetext seems to say, "but look at what new adventures wait for you down the road."

"SpouseNet," another chatroom and bulletin board link from the pathos-building "Friends and Family" page, positively drips with attempts to create a sense of community and well-being among spouses of Marine personnel (see Fig. 11.5). The happy little "dancing" musical notes, and the steaming hot cartoon cups of coffee are strong, emotional images that reinforce the promise held out in the message of the text "Where Military

Fig. 11.4. Military teens. Larger than life figures on a horizon above a lonely road.

Fig. 11.5. Old version of "SpouseNet."

Spouses Can March to Their Own Tunes." Recently, the splash page for SpouseNet has been changed to reflect a more serious, but no less emotional tone. Instead of the carefree chats over cups of coffee that the "old" image-text implies—a pathos reflecting a peace-time sensibility—the new page reflects a serious concern for Marine pilots over a vast, mountainous no-man's land (see Fig. 11.6). Developments in Iraq and Yugoslavia that have

Fig. 11.6. The new version of "SpouseNet."

put Marine pilots in harm's way are, perhaps, behind the decision to replace the easy-going, "pacifistic," emotional tone of an imagetext depiction of military spouses dancing to their own tunes with the emotional tone of patriotic support, apprehension, and concern for loved ones flying missions above Serbia, Kosovo, and the Iraqui "no-fly zone."

Having examined how pathos operates within the visual/verbal structure of *MarineLINK*, I now examine logos. How can an electronically (re)conceived notion of logos help us to examine the complex ideology of Web sites like *MarineLINK*? Logos is a complicated concept. In its most basic form it denotes "the word," or speech, and is perhaps most commonly associated with Aristotle's appeal to reason. And, as Kennedy (1963) noted, logos "may be used abstractly to indicate the meaning behind a word or expression or the power of thought and organization or the rational principle of the universe" (p. 8).

Within the pages of *MarineLINK*, especially within the information page and the Commandant's page, we are continually presented with logos as a Strategic Concept. Logos operates as rationale, as proof, as a dynamic, persuasive force. The "Information For and About Marines" link, accessed formerly by clicking on the imagetext portrait icon of the soldier-in-field-cap (see Fig. 11.1), spells out the rational *raison d'etre* of the Corps. In a series of imagetexts, the logos and the ethos of the Corps is dramatically spelled out. Ethos is inseparably intertwined with the logical rationale for the Corps' existence. The Information link maintains that "ultimately, our ethos springs from our reason for being—our 'strategic concept'. . . if a Service does not have a clearly defined 'reason for being' it will forfeit its place in national defense, its claim to increasingly scarce resources, and ultimately its own special identity." According to *MarineLINK*, the Corps' "reason for being," its "special identity," its logos-as-ethos, was mandated by law, by the second session of the 82nd Congress in 1952 (see Fig. 11.7). On a field of military colors and ribbons, with simulated brass uniform buttons as bullets, the imagetext reproduced in Fig. 11.8 spells out the Marine Corps' logos, its rational argument for its own existence, its Strategic Concept. And that politically mandated Strategic Concept can be summed up in one word—"ready." Readiness could be seen here as a warlike *kairos*, a timeliness, an appropriate and timely military response. So, in a rhetorically hyper-real way, the Marine Corps' ethos springs from its logos, its rationale, its reason for being, which in turn is driven by its military *kairos*, "*readiness*," its "strategic concept." Beneath this imagetext, at the end of an explanatory paragraph, appear these words: "And it is from this Strategic Concept that springs our institutional ethos—an ethos marked by five unique attributes that distinguish the Corp from the other Services." These five attributes: "Combined Arms in Three Dimensions," "Every Marine a

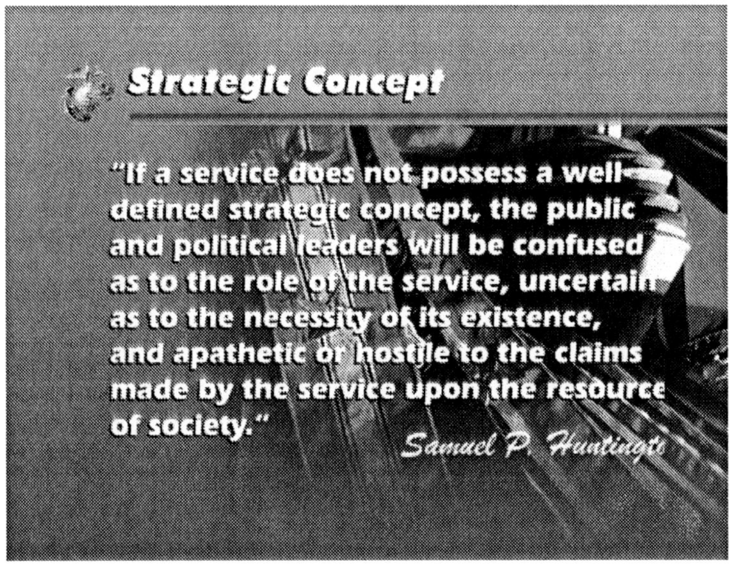

Fig. 11.7. A strategic concept: The Corps' logos as ethos.

Rifleman," "Task Oriented," "Soldiers of the Sea," and "Most Ready when Nation is Least Ready" spell out the Marine Corps' ethos, its logos, and its special brand of military *kairos*.

The 26 pages of imagetexts with accompanying verbal elaborations that make up the Information link are an extended argument, an argument that seeks to present convincing verbal/visual evidence and a logical rationale for the existence and maintenance of a strong Marine Corps. One important part of this argument is an economic one, a "more bang-for-the-buck" rationale. Page after page is devoted to showing in word and image how the Marine Corps, unlike the other services, deliver the best value for the least cost. One page stresses the notion that, no matter what his or her specialty, every Marine is a rifleman. Another page stresses the fact that the Marine Corps has the lowest officer to enlisted man ratio of any of the services. A second, and no less important part of the Corps' logical argument, seems to be a constant appeal to the Corps' uniqueness, to its special or privileged position as a small but elite force able to strike from the land, the sea, and the air. This attitude bears a striking resemblance to the one cultivated some 2,000 years ago by the Praetorian Guard of the Roman military complex, a "*corps d'élite* . . . who formed the escort troops of the commander-in-chief" (Charlesworth, 1967, p. 24). It is no small wonder, then, that

Marines in Dress Blues are always highly visible at official White House functions and that the celebrated Marine Corp Band calls itself "The President's Own." There are striking parallels, and parallels that are consciously drawn by the Corps itself, between the Marine Corps and the Legions of Imperial Rome. The last page of the Information link consciously refers to this attitude when its author states in summary "your Marine Corps remains America's Legion—forward, capable, and cost effective."

The function of logos within the pages of *MarineLINK* becomes even clearer if we expand Aristotle's notion of logos to include Isocrates's prior notion as a dynamic relevance, as a powerful function in society. By logos, Isocrates meant "the art of political discourse on important subjects" (Kennedy, 1994, p. 43). One of the more striking imagetexts within *MarineLINK* is an attempt to visually portray one aspect of the Marine Corps' 21st century warfighting strategy, Operation Sea Dragon (see Fig. 11.8). This rather frightening imagetext portraying the Marine Corps' warfare strategy for the new millennium shows Isocrates's notion of logos as political discourse on powerful and important subjects. It also illustrates the rhetorical principle of *kairos,* the notion of timeliness, or "the right moment," by the visual and verbal metaphor of the Dragon of Change. The Corps "rides the dragon" into the 21st century to deliver the power of its logos, its forceful discourse, to any future enemy of America. The text beneath the imagetext reproduced in Fig. 11.8 maintains that

Fig. 11.8. The Corps "Rides the Dragon" into the 21st century.

> Sea Dragon is the Marine Corps' name for the laboratory's open ended process for rapid military innovation. It is a play off the old Chinese saying that "change is a dragon." If you choose to ignore it, it will sneak up and eat you. If you try to control the dragon and it is too strong, it will knock you down and eat you. But if you ride the dragon, you can avoid his lethal powers, and even prosper. We intend to "ride the dragon of change" into the 21st Century, both to continue to take advantage of the opportunities it brings, and to be prepared to respond to and prevail over whatever threats may arise. The nation demands nothing less from its force in *readiness.*

Interestingly, ethos and pathos are also intertwined in this complex imagetext. As we have seen, the Marine Corps maintains that its institutional ethos is its "strategic concept" and this concept is captured by the one word: *readiness.* The imagetext also evokes an emotional response in the viewers/readers, appealing variously to their fear for the future, or to their patriotic pride in the efficacy of America's Armed Services. *Kairos,* the notion of timeliness, or "the right moment" is also invoked by the metaphor of the Dragon of Change.

Memoria, or memory, the fourth and least discussed canon of classical rhetoric, was called the "treasure house of invention" by the anonymous author of the 1st century BC *Rhetorica ad Herennium.* Cicero repeats this description in his influential *De Oratore*, and amplifies on it by identifying memory as a form of writing, likening it to an inscription upon a wax tablet. Both texts tell the apocryphal tale of the invention of a unique and highly visual way of accessing the memory. The system of memory based on visual structures, *loci,* or places in the mind modeled after concrete, physical places, is attributed to Simonides of Ceos, a travelling Greek poet-for-hire. One evening, while entertaining a large group of dinner guests at a wealthy man's house, he was called away from his recitation because there were two gentlemen at the door who wanted to see him. While he was outside, the roof of the banquet hall collapsed, crushing all the merry-makers and mangling their bodies beyond recognition. The distraught widows, sons, and daughters pleaded with Simonides to help them identify their loved ones. So he reconstructed in his mind's eye the names and faces of those at the feast based on their physical seating at the table. This led him to create and elaborate a system of memory retrieval based on physical structures, or *loci* placed in the mind. *Topoi,* or topics would be associated with the *loci* and all the rhetor had to do to retrieve memories or *topoi* was to summon up the *loci* or structure in the mind. Cicero and Quintilian both employed and wrote about this visual mnemonic system, and Renaissance scholars like Giulio Camillo invented elaborate, visually encoded Theatres of Memory based on architectural structures (see Yates, 1966).

In the architecture of a computer's operating system there also exist *loci,* physical places where encoded memories in the form of bits and bytes are stored and constantly await retrieval. (Of course, it has become a commonplace now—with the influence of human factors and cognitive psychology studies—to link and liken the processes of the brain with the parallel-distributed processing systems of computers.) These *loci,* these spaces in the architecture of the computer, the Random Accessed Memory (RAM) and Read Only Memory (ROM) are accessed now through visual icons that exist as *memory delivery systems* in the graphical user interface. As I process these words and design this space, my eye looks up to a series of icons at the top of my screen. A picture of a clip board reminds me that I can access something that I had highlighted earlier, an image perhaps, or a word. An icon that represents a pair of shears invites me to cut this sentence. Or the next. Clicking on a paint roller will search the memory of this system and allow me to access an entire palette of colors. An iconic rendering of a 3.5" diskette invites me to save my text to another physical space in the architecture of this visually oriented structure for designing imagetexts.

But memory, as the ancients conceived it, and as we use it, is certainly more complicated than a system for information retrieval. It also involves "the ability to recall issues, ideas, concepts, and feelings," and includes "psychology and interior discourse," as well as the "ability to form and reform constructions" (Welch, 1990, p. 169). Within electronic writing spaces, *memoria* can be thought of in terms of a computer's storage and retrieval system, its ROM and its RAM. The hypertextual and graphical writing spaces of Web environments like *MarineLINK* act as replacements for the memory system outlined in the *Rhetorica ad Herennium*. This more complicated notion of memory can be seen to operate on at least three levels within the rhetoric of *MarineLINK*:

1. As part of the delivery system, mimicking electronically the *Ars memoriae* of the ancients. The past glories of the Corps in World War I, World War II, Korea, Vietnam, and Desert Storm are presented as iconic imagetext *loci* in the Marine Corps' Theatre of Memory.
2. *Memoria* acts as a psychological device that invokes the glorious past of memorable acts of bravery in battle—Iwo Jima, Belleau Wood, 1775—through visual and verbal invocations. In these images of marine heroics from 1775 to Desert Storm, *memoria* is configured as the psychological foundation of the Corps.
3. *Memoria* acts as a rhetorical device that reconfigures the present in terms of the past. This rhetorical move is especially evident in the Commandant's speeches where the memory of the legions of

> Imperial Rome are, quite explicitly, melded to the image of the Marine Corps.

If we examine the imagetexts as *loci* depicted in Fig. 11.9, we can clearly see the first two levels in action. The image of the Marine in his original 1775 uniform recalls the Marine Corps' role in the War for Independence, and also serves to summon up the patriotic jingoism associated with the founding of the United States itself. Smaller imagetexts elaborate on the glorious battles that the Corps has fought throughout its history to preserve America's freedom: doughboys fighting hand to hand in the trenches of World War I; the bloody, island-hopping fighting in the Pacific Theatre during World War II—what some have called the Corps' "finest hour" (Lawliss, 1988, p. 45); the brutal, anti-Communist police action in Korea; the morass that was Vietnam; and finally the punitive action against Iraq. These memories are summoned up in each case, not by the official name of the war or military action, but by a stereotypical photograph labeled with a phrase and a date. "Belleau Wood 1918" beneath an image of Marine riflemen with fixed bayonets, "Inchon 1950," "Chu Lai 1965," all become linked in the Memory Theatre of the Corps to the glorious and patriotic legacy of the Revolutionary War of 1775. Memories of the massacre at My Lai, or the bombing of Hiroshima, or the thousands of brutal atrocities that accompany war are buried beneath the imagetext icons that evoke glory and honor in simple phrases like "Guadalcanal 1942," and "Desert Storm 1991."

Fig. 11.9. Ars Memoriae and the corps—imagetexts as loci.

In M*arineLINK*, memory also acts as a device to reconfigure the past as part of the present so that a strong Marine Corps will be part of America's future. This rhetorical gesture is most evident within the speeches found in the Commandant's Page. One of the major obsessions in many of Commandant Charles Krulak's speeches deals with the following question: What will happen to the American Way of Life if our fighting forces, particularly the Marine Corps, are not constantly kept in a state of vigilance and preparedness? Krulak's speech, whatever the occasion, or whomever he is addressing, the National Press Club, Conoco Oil's senior management team, the Center for Naval Analysis, always tells the same tale, with slight variations, of the destruction of 3 Roman Legions led by Quinctilius Varus in 9 AD by German barbarians in the Teutoberg Forest. It is a cautionary tale about preparedness—remember the Corps' institutional ethos, readiness—and about underestimating the power and cunning of one's enemies. In this speech, the past is raised up as a parable to point the way to the future. In fact, one version of the speech is entitled "The Past Is Prologue." The most striking features of Krulak's narrative are the implicit parallels he draws between America and Imperial Rome, and the Marine Corps and the Legions of Rome.

Before examining Krulak's speech as sites of memory, ethos, pathos, and *kairos*, I point out that these parallels do not exist merely in the Commandant's imagination. America was founded on the principles and structures of Rome. Washington, Jefferson, and Adams were neo-classicists who were, like most educated late 18th-century Americans and Europeans, heavily influenced by classical architecture, philosophy, history, and rhetoric. Every gentleman's education included Latin and Greek. It is, then, no small wonder that our system of government with its Senate and Senators was directly modeled on Rome. We borrowed their architecture and we borrowed their visual symbols and icons. The American Eagle is actually the Eagle of Imperial Rome. The fasces, the ancient icon of Roman law and official authority symbolized by an ax head surrounded by a bundle of rods, adorns the walls of the House and Senate chambers. And, like imperial Rome, whose Legions were the mightiest military force in the world, America since World War II has maintained a shaky *Pax Americanus* by periodically sending in the Marines or threatening to do so. At this writing, America's winged legions deliver death from above nightly over the mountainous terrain of what the Romans called Pannonia and Dalmatia. Krulak's speech, without much variation, begins in this way:

> In 9 AD, a Roman Proconsul by the name of Qunctilius Varus led three Roman legions across the German border to bring recalcitrant barbarian tribes under control. This was the second time in three years that he had

> crossed that same border. Three years prior—Varus and his legions put down a similar uprising—decimating the Germans—sending over 20,000 prisoners—men, women, and children—back to Rome as slaves. . . . The Romans expected that this outing would be no different than previous ones. On a hot August morning, a confident Varus was in the vanguard of his legions as they approached the Teutoberg Forest near what is today the city of Minden, Germany. In front of each legion—on a staff—was the famous gold eagle that signified the power of Rome. Later that morning the two forces joined in battle—and as the sun was going down Varus found himself fighting a desperate rear-guard action as he tried to bring what remained of his force back across the German border. As he retreated back towards the border he could be seen with his head down muttering . . . "Ne Cras, Ne Cras"—Not like Yesterday. . . . And, it wasn't like yesterday.

The barbarians had learned from the past; they had, as Krulak notes, "watched CNN." For on that hot August day they lured the Roman heavy cavalry into the marshes and their archers into a dense forest. In 3 days, the Germans wore down the Romans and finally destroyed all three legions. "At the end of the battle," Krulak relates, "Varus' head sat upon a warpike in a German camp surrounded by those three gold eagles."

In the Commandant's allegorical fable, his cautionary tale for the future set in the classical past, America is clearly Imperial Rome at her height, her most powerful, and the Marine Corps are the first rank of the Imperial Legions. Yet, the mightiest military force in the world is destroyed by the asymmetrical guerrilla strategies of a technologically inferior band of barbarians. The parallel with the American War machine mired down in the jungles of Vietnam is striking and clearly drawn. The mighty warriors of the Empire drawn into the dense forest and picked off by the Viet Cong. Even the paranoid, jowly, unshaven Richard Nixon in the later years of the war can be seen in the allegorical role of a distraught and deranged Augustus:

> Upon hearing the news of Varus' defeat, Caesar Augustus suffered a nervous breakdown. So greatly affected was Augustus that for several months he cut neither his hair not his beard, and sometimes he would dash his head against a door, crying Quinctilius Varus, give me back my legions.

Krulak generally ends his cautionary tales with a plea for greater attention to the Marine Corps' institutional ethos, a call for preparedness and readiness. Krulak-as-visionary prophesies a future in which, much like Imperial Rome, we are always in a state of war somewhere in the Empire.

> This is the landscape upon which the 21st Century battle will be fought. It will be an asymmetrical battlefield. Much like the Germanic tribes, our enemies will not allow us to fight the Son of Desert Storm, but will try to draw us into the stepchild of Chechnya. In one moment in time, our service members will be feeding and clothing displaced refugees—in the next moment they will be holding two warring tribes apart . . . and, finally, they will be fighting a highly lethal mid-intensity battle—all on the same day. We can make the same mistakes as Quinctilius Varus and ignore the implications of change . . . or we can learn from history and prepare now for the inevitable battles to come.

Proconsul Krulak, of course, needs to think this way. It is what he is paid for; it is his duty as the Commandant of America's elite Praetorian Guard, the U.S. Marine Corps.

The familiar Marine Corps Emblem operates as an ubiquitous leitmotif throughout the Marine Corps' Web site. As a visual text, the Emblem works as a memory and delivery device, linking pages together and threading its way throughout the structure of the docuverse of *MarineLINK* (see Fig. 11.10). The Eagle with its wings spread out—aggressively and protectively—over the world is, of course, simultaneously the American Eagle and the Imperial Eagle of Rome, and as such it is intricately bound up in *memoria* as a locating device for memories of the glories of the past, both ancient and modern, of Caesar, of Cicero, of Washington, of Lincoln, of Eisenhower, and yes, even of Nixon. The ancient symbol of war and freedom perching atop the world seems to say: Let us not forget. And if we heed General Krulak's warning and remember the past as prologue, if we are always mindful of our ethos which springs from a kairos-driven logos, then the Imperial Legions of the 21st century will have dominion over the air, symbolized by the eagle, over the sea, symbolized by the anchor, and over the land, symbolized by the globe-shaped map of the world.

Fig. 11.10. The Marine Corp emblem as signifier of the Imperial Legions of the 21st century.

This rhetorical analysis of *MarineLINK* set out to demonstrate that the fundamental classical rhetorical concepts—the neglected canons of memory and delivery, the notion of *kairos,* and Aristotle's *entechnoi,* ethos, logos, and pathos—travel remarkably well from one techno-cultural milieu to another. These concepts have successfully migrated in the past from oral discourse to writing, from manual chirographic inscription to the printing press, and now from print-bound media to screen-based, hypermediated, electronic writing spaces like *MarineLINK.* As we have seen, these rhetorical concepts still serve to illuminate practice, to deconstruct technique, and to model processes.

Students of composition who wish to create more effective documents in imagetextual environments, and teachers of composition who wish to help their students create these kinds of text, can both profit from examining the dynamics of classical rhetorical principles as they operate in electronic writing spaces. Studying models helps students internalize principles and structures. It is reasonable, then, to assume that studying models of analysis similar to the *MarineLINK* reading can enhance the learning processes of writing students engaged in electronic discourse.

Examining the rhetorical dynamics of images and texts in Web writing can be an important first step in the successful creation of image-texts and imagetextual documents for the World Wide Web and other electronically and hypertextually mediated writings. A refashioned or renegotiated vision of what classical rhetoric is and does in these types of compositions can be useful to students and teachers not only as invention or heuristic strategies, but also as hermeneutic devices. Welch (1990) pointed out that "[t]he unusual adaptability of classical rhetoric and its preoccupation with producing discourse and not merely analyzing it after someone has produced it, makes it one of the most powerful discourse systems that we have" (p. 164), and that "classical rhetoric can readily address any situation partly because it focuses not only on critical stances toward discourse that already exist, but because it presents elaborate theories for the production of discourse as well" (p. 5).

Some of the principles from classical rhetoric, then, and, in particular, a refashioned, or a re-mediated notion of these principles, can lead to a greater understanding of how images and words operate in electronic writing spaces. A greater understanding of these operations can, in turn, lead to more successful Web writing. This examination of *MarineLINK* demonstrates that some of our most ancient rhetorical notions, far from being tired and worn-out concepts, are now more relevant than ever when discussing or unpacking our newest form of literacy, electronically mediated writing spaces. Corbett (1990) noted that, "[u]ndoubtedly there will be a 'new rhetoric' for the twenty-first century, a rhetoric that will be more comprehensive than any that has been devised so far. . . . But in that new rhetoric there will be noticeable residues of classical rhetoric" (p. viii). His statement seems now to be prescient. The ancient Greeks, and later the Romans, who systematized the principles of effective persuasion looked deeply into the human psyche and pinpointed ways to effectively move the minds and hearts of men and women through discourse. Like Euclidean geometry, whose fundamental structure has withstood the test of time, the rhetorical principles of ethos, logos, and pathos, the canons of memory and delivery, and the notion of *kairos* provide structural and analytical tools for creating and understanding texts. Applying them to our newest form of inscription, the electronic writing space, can afford us greater insight into the ways that this visual–verbal discourse system operates to achieve its goals of persuasion and communication.

REFERENCES

Alexander, J., & Tate, M. (1998). Checklist for a personal home page [online]. Available: http://www.science.widener.edu/~withers/perspg.htm.

Black, R., with Elder, S. (1997). *Web sites that work*. San Jose: Adobe Press.

Bernhardt, S.A. (1993). The shape of text to come: The texture of print on screens. *College Composition and Communication, 44*, 151-175.

Bolter, J.D. (1993). Hypertext and the rhetorical canons. In J. F. Reynolds (Ed.), *Rhetorical memory and delivery: Classical concepts for contemporary composition and communication* (pp. 97-111). Hillsdale, NJ: Erlbaum.

Charlesworth, M.P. (1967). *The Roman empire*. London: Oxford University Press.

Corbett, E.P.J. (1990). *Classical rhetoric for the modern student* (3rd ed.). New York: Oxford University Press.

Kennedy, G.A. (1963). *The art of persuasion in Greece*. Princeton, NJ: Princeton University Press.

Kennedy, G.A. (1994). *A new history of classical rhetoric*. Princeton, NJ: Princeton University Press.

Kostelnick, C., & Roberts, D.D. (1998). *Designing visual language*. Boston: Allyn & Bacon.

Kramer, R., & Bernhardt, S.A. (1996). Teaching text design. *Technical Communication Quarterly, 5*, 35-60.

Lawliss, C. (1988). *The Marine book: A portrait of America's military elite*. New York: Thames & Hudson.

MarineLINK. The United States Marine Corps' official Web site [online]. Available: http://www/usmc.mil/.

Mitchell, W.J.T. (1994). *Picture theory: Essays on verbal and visual representation*. Chicago: The University of Chicago Press.

Welch, K.E. (1990). *The contemporary reception of classical rhetoric: Appropriations of ancient discourse*. Hillsdale, NJ: Erlbaum.

Yates, F. A. (1966). *The art of memory*. Chicago: The University of Chicago Press.

12

LEARNING FROM FATTY BEAR

Calling Forth Gender in Interactive Children's Multimedia Software

Anne Frances Wysocki
Michigan Technological University

My question: A child—a girl—sitting down, her face shining with light from a screen, a computer screen—a computer game. Into what shapes is that light carving her? Into what sense of self is that light calling her?

It is not uncommon now to note—or bemoan, or celebrate—the shift in the ratio of word to image that computer screens have brought to the texts with which many children now grow up.[1] Nor is it uncommon to note the play of identities that computer screens and software seem to make possible.[2] This chapter takes its motivation from the amount and kind of interactive software being developed for children (at the time of this writing, "Barbie, Fashion Designer" was the most highly selling piece of children's software package[3]), and considers some of the visual skills, understandings, and practices—the literacies—we need to develop if we are to work with and teach thoughtfully the relations between the visual and identity that are taking shape on computer screens for children, for us all. My work here shows me that to be literate in the 21st century—to be literate, that is, in the strong sense used throughout this volume—requires that the attentions we give to the use, structures, and articulations of alphabetic texts within cultures be extended to texts that may (as in the case of the text I analyze here) have few visible words in them.

In this chapter, I apply feminist/psychoanalytic film theory to computer-based interactive multimedia[4]—in particular, to "Fatty Bear's Birthday Surprise," a game for 3- to 7-year old children. I use film theory as an opening into multimedia first for an obvious reason, that film and multimedia are both matters of screens and spectators. But, in addition, feminist film theory that takes its grounding in psychoanalysis makes its criticisms of film based not only on how the "content" of a film (the narrative and/or the relationships between the variously gendered characters) reproduces the gendered structures of domination and exploitation we encounter socially, but also on how the "form" of a film (how a spectator is positioned relative to the screen) reproduces those structures. Much of the work of such theorists has been about how we might find strategies for making and viewing films so that the domination and exploitation of women are countered; I hope that such considerations will help me find strategies for constructing—and for helping people in my classes construct—multimedia projects that likewise do not work simply to keep the eyes of women, and of girls, fixed onto a limited, rigid set of possibilities for what women are and do.

In this chapter, through applying two schema feminist film theorists use for understanding and critiquing film—identification and the gaze—to "Fatty Bear's Birthday Surprise," I initially find some room for hope, some space in which girls are not required to play this game through a predefined set of actions and attitudes labeled "girl," some space in which gender is backgrounded. But by examining the particular visual space through which that backgrounding is made possible, by considering the use of a "home" as the place where the software is visually situated, I argue that the backgrounding is for a purpose, a purpose inseparable from the construction of gender in our time and place.

FIRST: FATTY BEAR'S BIRTHDAY SURPRISE

"Fatty Bear's Birthday Surprise" is published by Humongous Entertainment, a company co-founded in 1992 by a woman who has expressed concern for developing children's software attentive to presentations of gender (Fryer, 1997). Humongous Entertainment has become a successful developer of children's multimedia, called by *Newsweek* "the Disney of children's software," and in March 1997 the company announced that it would develop "original television, motion picture, and home video pro-

Fig. 12.1. The opening screen to "Fatty Bear's Birthday Surprise."

gramming based on its family of original characters" ("Humongous Entertainment Fast Facts," 1998). The commercial success of Humongous shows that the software the company makes—all of which works similarly to "Fatty Bear's Birthday Surprise"—is appealing to parents, who seem to buy the software for their sons and daughters equally: In a positive review from *WIRED* magazine, for example, Nancy Kalow (1993) noted that "I've noticed that both boys and girls love to play 'Fatty Bear,'" and I have observed such equal attraction among the children I have seen play this game. The structures of "Fatty Bear's Birthday Surprise," then, allow parents to feel—and children to show in their playing—that the game does not tilt toward supporting or attracting one gender or the other; part of my analysis here is to determine why. In what follows, I describe the structure of the game[5] in order to consider what feminist film theory can help me understand about this gender unspecificity.

Printed on the box in which "Fatty Bear's Birthday Surprise" comes is a description of the game:

> Ever wonder if your stuffed animals come to life while you sleep?
>
> With Kayla's birthday only hours away, Fatty Bear and the other toys are planning a surprise party. Matilda Rabbit will help with the cake,

> while Gretchen works on the decorations. Sound easy? It would be except a pesky puppy keeps taking things you need, and a game of lawn bowling is always hard to resist . . .
>
> Fatty Bear's Birthday Surprise is an adventure game designed especially for children. Children enhance problem-solving skills while happily exploring Fatty Bear's world; the goals vary in response to your child's actions. So what are you waiting for? Morning's almost here, and a bear can only do so much alone.

The opening sequence of the game starts with the image of a two-story house, isolated on the screen with no indication of the neighborhood around it; people in my multimedia classes assume that the house is in a middle-class suburb, built sometime within the last 20 years. On screen, the opening sequence uses a dissolve to move from the house into an upstairs bedroom, where Kayla, a girl with brown skin, is in bed, holding her teddy bear. Kayla's father puts his head around the door to say goodnight and to discuss their plans for tomorrow's birthday party for Kayla.

The father closes the door, Kayla immediately falls asleep, and the teddy bear comes to life, to become Fatty Bear, a round, nearly human-sized (according to the scale established by Kayla and her father) cartoon-type character. Fatty Bear turns to face the screen, to address directly whoever is

Fig. 12.2. End of the opening sequence: Kayla says goodnight to Fatty Bear the stuffed animal.

playing the game on the other side of the monitor from him. He tells the player that he needs help preparing a birthday cake for Kayla and decorating her room: He gives some instructions for searching the house to find the cake's ingredients and the letters for her birthday sign . . . and then control of the game's action is turned over to the player.[6]

The player can now click various objects on screen—doors, windows—to move through the house and search for the cake's ingredients (which can be stored, until they are all found, in a set of pockets that appear at the bottom of the screen once Fatty Bear has finished his directions). In the different rooms of the house, the player finds not only the cake's ingredients but also objects that animate in response to a mouse click: an aquarium that noisily drains or a toy rabbit with ears like helicopter propellors. There are also situations for further interaction, such as a lawn bowling game, where children perform simple math operations, or a piano where children can (see Fig. 12.3) play the musical scores of childhood tunes or where they can play or record their own music.

As a player moves through the house, Fatty Bear offers encouragement and occasional hints about where to look for the cake ingredients. Players can move outside the house (e.g., where the bowling game is), but most outside activities are visually circumscribed by a wooden fence; if the fence is not present, as when a player faces the front of the house, there is

Fig. 12.3. The player piano.

no indication of other houses in the neighborhood: Kayla's house and garage fill the screen, and clicking to the side of the screen, which in the logic of this game's navigation would turn a player's view toward what else is in the neighborhood, yields no action.

THEORY: ONE KIND OF FILMIC IDENTIFICATION

Feminist film theory has been concerned with understanding and undoing the domination and exploitation of women as it is supported and continued by the structures of film. Early feminist considerations of film argued this could be achieved if filmmakers resisted showing people acting within the traditional roles of passive femininity and active masculinity; for example, Artel and Wengraf (1978) argued that films should show "girls and women, boys and men with non-stereotyped behavior and attitudes; independent, intelligent women; adventurous, resourceful girls; men who are nurturing; boys who are not afraid to show their vulnerability" (p. 9). Artel and Wengraf's argument depends on film always working such that spectators learn who they are by identifying with characters on screen. To lose oneself into another in this way is pleasurable, other film theorists have noted, but is pleasure at a cost; Silverman (1996) argued, for example, that:

> the pleasure of identifying with a fictional character always turns on the spectator's rediscovery of his or her preordained place within gender, class, and race. [This] identification . . . is frequently equated with interpellation into the dominant fiction. (p. 85)

This process of identification, then, asks us to learn our ways of behavior from those we see on screen—which means, then, that we learn (in some part) how to be women from the women we see on screen and feel ourselves to be for the time of our watching—obviously a problem if the women we tend to see on screen are always and ever passive, dumb, beautiful, hysterical, impossibly thin, unempowered . . . we all know the list.

"Fatty Bear's Birthday Surprise" is not free of such female characters on screen,[7] and neither is it free of male characters whose roles are equally stereotyped: the words from the game's packaging speak of Matilda Rabbit and Gretchen (a Dutch-girl doll), female characters who are respectively responsible for baking the birthday cake and arranging the birthday decorations, and Fatty Bear is the male "master of ceremonies," giving shape and direction to the game. Although the makers of the game have made efforts to break some traditional gender stereotypes—they have given the father the role of putting Kayla to bed (and they have also worked against how race is frequently handled in such games, by making Kayla and her father dark-skinned)—the appearance of and roles of characters like Matilda and Gretchen must contribute in some way to girls and boys taking away different senses of what is appropriate for them. Nonetheless, I argue that the power of this kind of identification is weakened in this game, for two reasons.

First, although I refer to the cartoon figures in the game as characters, they are nothing like characters in a Hollywood-style narrative film: Some of the game's characters—many of the stuffed animals in Kayla's room, for example—exist only to be clicked by a player in order to yield an animation that adds nothing to the progression of the game, and even Kayla, her father, and Fatty Bear appear more as devices for setting the stage for the game rather than as protagonists whose actions determine the outcome of the game. Also, for the most part, the screens of the game are characterless as a player moves through them: The game is played in a house whose inhabitants are mostly sleeping, hidden away in their beds. Kayla and her father, for example, appear only twice, first in the opening of the game and then—if a player decides to try to find all the cake ingredients and is successful—at the end. Fatty Bear appears in the opening sequence but then he appears intermittently afterwards, to offer help as a player tries to find the cake ingredients. There are, then, no characters—male or female—to whom the game's players can attach themselves for any length of time.

Second, even were this game to contain characters who acted more like characters in a narrative film, a player's identification with such characters on screen would still be difficult: A player enters this game as him or her "self" and so is busied with making choices about what happens in the game rather than with imagining him or herself as being Matilda or Gretchen. The player is not a spectator but rather makes choices about what to click and when and even how to play. The player can choose to work at finding the cake ingredients or can simply move around the house and yard, clicking to see what happens. I have watched 6-year-old children ignore the problem-solving aspects of the game, instead clicking the aquarium over and over—and over—to see it spill (and then refill), or playing giddily with the piano. No game characters materialize to tell children that the cake must be built or that their behavior is in anyway inappropriate; instead, the player makes choices based on who she or he already is, relative to what the game offers.

Although there are aspects of the game that do, as I mentioned earlier, encourage players to see females as helpful, good in the kitchen, and attentive to decoration, players of the game are not asked to play as boys or as girls: The game does not address them by gender, does not change depending on their gender, and does not offer different games for boys or girls. There is then, I think, the potential for children to experiment, to have some moments to play without gender in general—or their own particular gender—being foregrounded.

But before I sound as though I am arguing that children should be raised on a diet of such multimedia, let me step into an argument that could make this kind of multimedia sound like a feminist parent's worst nightmare.

THEORY: ANOTHER, PRIMARY, IDENTIFICATION

For various reasons, the argument made by writers like Artel and Wengraf—that making more films with positive female characters would be enough to change how women come to see themselves through film watching—came under criticism for being too simple, for missing deeper running structures of film. Other feminist critics pointed to the work of Metz (1982), for example, who argued that film spectators identified with more than just the characters on screen:

> When I say that "I see" the film, I mean thereby a unique mixture of two contrary currents: the film is what I receive, and it is also what I release, since it does not pre-exist my entering the auditorium and I only need close my eyes to suppress it. Releasing it, I am the projector, receiving it, I am the screen; in both these figures together, I am the camera, which points and yet records. (p. 51)

Metz thus proposed that, when we watch a film, we identify not only with the characters on screen but also, prior to identifying with what is on screen, with the camera and projector. As another writer explained,

> Metz defines primary cinematic identification as the spectator's identification with the act of looking itself. He called the spectator "all-perceiving" and says it is s/he who literally makes the film happen. For this reason, "the spectator identifies with himself, with himself as a pure act of perception;" without the spectator, the film cannot exist. This type of identification is considered primary because it is what makes all secondary identifications with characters and events on the screen possible. This process, both perceptual (the viewer sees the object) and unconscious (the viewer participates in a fantasmatic or imaginary way), is at once constructed and directed by the look of the camera and its stand-in, the projector. From a look that seems to proceed from the back of the head (from the projector at the back of the

> theater)—"precisely where fantasy locates the 'focus' of all vision"—the spectator is given that illusory capacity to be everywhere at once. (Flitterman-Lewis, 1992, pp. 213-214)

Secondary identification is thus what I discussed in the preceding section, when a spectator gets caught up in the particularities of a film narrative from the perspective of one of the characters in the narrative, but what Metz called primary identification, according to some feminist theorists, is what fundamentally supports the positive sense of maleness of films—and erases the possibility of any female position relative to a film screen.

In "Visual Pleasure and Narrative Cinema," an article that one writer called "one of the most frequently cited essays in all fields of contemporary humanistic studies" (Olin, 1996, p. 211), Mulvey (1989b) argued that the identificatory structures of film don't exist solely for the pleasures of individual viewers, but that, rather, in traditional Hollywood cinema, they support and prolong polarized male and female ways of being in the world. For Mulvey, women in film are to be looked at for the pleasure of the male—for the male in the film and in the audience:

> As the spectator identifies with the main male protagonist, he projects his look on to that of his like, his screen surrogate, so that the power of the male protagonist as he controls events coincides with the active power of the erotic look, both giving a satisfying sense of omnipotence. (p. 20)

Mulvey argued that women in film serve only to help men deal with the fear that grounds the psychoanalysis I have been discussing, the fear of castration: Women are there either to be investigated as the reminder of the threat of not having a penis and then devalued and so made unthreatening, or women are there to be fetishized, made into something bigger than life, something big enough to fill in for what is missing.

Mulvey's article is meant to construct strategies for filmmakers to pursue in order to help film spectators work their way out of fixed gender roles of positive masculinity and negative femininity—but Mulvey's observations keep her from simply recommending more positive images of women; instead, Mulvey argued that male fantasies of overcoming castration can only be pleasurably satisfied if viewers are allowed to settle into their fantasies, to forget the temporal and material conditions of their watching:

> There are three different looks associated with the cinema: that of the camera as it records the pro-filmic event, that of the audience as it watches the final product, and that of the characters at each other within

> the screen illusion. The conventions of narrative film deny the first two and subordinate them to the third, the conscious aim being always to eliminate intrusive camera presence and prevent a distancing awareness in the audience. (p. 25)

For Mulvey, viewers can only lose themselves—and any questioning they might do of the gendering presented in the film—if they are never aware of their primary identification with the camera, of how they have been positioned within the filmic structures that encourage their fantasies:

> the mass of mainstream film, and the conventions within which it has unconsciously evolved, portray a hermetically sealed world which unwinds magically, indifferent to the presence of the audience, producing a sense of separation and playing on their voyeuristic fantasy. . . . Although the film is really being shown, is there to be seen, conditions of screening and narrative conventions give the spectator an illusion of looking in on a private world. (p. 17)

Mulvey thus argued for filmmakers to construct films in which these conditions are made visible by the film, in which spectators are prevented from losing themselves pleasurably into identification with the characters on screen by being prevented from losing themselves pleasurably into identification with the camera/projector that makes the secondary identification possible.

BUT . . .

But "Fatty Bear's Birthday Surprise" and other multimedia games structured like it do not adhere to Mulvey's call for self-consciously structuralist filmmaking; instead, their structures would seem to reinforce exactly the kind of primary identification Mulvey described—and to reinforce that identification even more strongly than film can do. "Fatty Bear's Birthday Surprise" depends precisely on a player's view being aligned with the images projected onto the computer screen (even if the projection no longer comes from the back of the player's head, as it does in film): What is on the screen has been designed to appear as though it were a three-dimensional space into which the player happened to walk. The intention of this game is precisely to do what I quoted Mulvey describing earlier: the player, moving through the house of Kayla and her father, is given exactly the "illusion of looking in on a private world." But, in this game, what is on screen is not "indifferent to the presence of the audience": instead, what happens on screen happens because a player takes actions that change what is on screen. Because she is both aligned with the camera and at the same time making the game proceed at her will, anyone playing this game is asked doubly to identify with the action and power—and hence maleness—Mulvey described in the first quotation of this section. The possibility of gender being backgrounded—of children being allowed to play this game without being asked to play within the bounds of some definition of male- or female-ness, as I described previously—is thus, following Mulvey, overshadowed by a more primary set of the game's structuring conditions.

For Mulvey, there is no way out of the maleness of primary identification. In her "Afterthoughts on 'Visual Pleasure and Narrative Cinema'" (Mulvey, 1989a) she speaks of how in the original article (Mulvey, 1989b) she had addressed only what going-to-narrative-films does for males, but in this later article she speaks of how a woman might "find herself secretly, unconsciously almost, enjoying the freedom of action and control over the diegetic world that identification with a hero provides" (p. 29); for Mulvey, then, the woman finds herself also caught in an "oscillation" between a pleasurable memory of an earlier held position of strength and action (a "phallic" stage, according to Mulvey's reading of Freud, that all children, male or female, undergo) and the requirements of passivity that patriarchal society imposes on adult females. For Mulvey, there is nothing in traditional narrative film that speaks directly to women; all the structures and events are there to support unencumbered masculinity and to confound femininity—and this then would seem to be doubly the case for multimedia structured like "Fatty Bear's Birthday Surprise." If I accept Mulvey's argument, then my analysis of "Fatty Bear's Birthday Surprise" only serves to remind us how new technologies can be put to old purposes: the actions encouraged in a female player by this piece of multimedia are actions that either support the phallic stage of a girl playing the game, encouraging her to develop a sense of self that will only frustrate her later, or—if she is older when she plays the game—will only cause what Mulvey (1989a), at the end of the second article, referred to as "the female spectator's fantasy of masculinization at cross-purposes with itself, restless in its transvestite clothes" (p. 37).

But Mulvey's argument, and my preliminary conclusions about its applications to multimedia, depend on two, related, considerations that have been called into question by later feminist theory: first, Mulvey takes action as only and ever being male, and thus, secondarily, she accepts that the camera (and, by extension, the computer screen) can only look upon the world from a masculine position. Given the further critiques of these positions, there is still room for me to argue that multimedia games structured like "Fatty Bear's Birthday Surprise" offer potential respite from children being interpellated into either positive male or negative female subject positions.

In "Rethinking Women's Cinema: Aesthetics and Feminist Theory," de Lauretis addressed both of Mulvey's considerations. De Lauretis argued that a position such as Mulvey's "was couched in the terms of a traditional notion of art" and hence in "the theoretical paradigm of a subject-object dialectic" (pp. 128-130). De Lauretis speaks instead of how over time feminism

> has conceived a new social subject, women: as speakers, writers, readers, spectators, users, and makers of cultural forms, shapers of cultural processes. The project of women's cinema, therefore, is no longer that of destroying or disrupting man-centered vision by representing its blind spots, its gaps, or its repressed. The effort and challenge are how to effect another vision: to construct other objects and subjects of vision, and to formulate the conditions of representability of another social subject. (pp. 134-135)

In addition, de Lauretis analyzed two particular films, *Jeanne Dielman* and *Born in Flames*, to argue that their visual strategies—such as the camera staying fixed at a certain height in *Jeanne Dielman* and staying within the space of Jeanne Dielman's apartment—allow female spectators to be addressed in other ways than Mulvey posited:

> These films do not put me in the place of the female spectator, do not assign me a role, a self-image, a positionality in language or desire. Instead, they make a place for what I will call me, knowing that I don't know it, and give "me" space to try to know, to see, to understand. Put another way, by addressing me as a woman, they do not bind me or appoint me as Woman. (p. 142)

And, finally, for de Lauretis, (again because of their visual strategies) these films make possible a "dis-appointment of spectator and text," that is

> the disappointment of not finding oneself, not finding oneself "interpellated" or solicited by the film, whose images and discourses project back to the viewer a space of heterogeneity, differences and fragmented coherences that just do not add up to one individual viewer or one spectator-subject, bourgeois or otherwise. (p. 143)

If, then, we move away from Mulvey's notion of subjectivity, so that we no longer strive to see ourselves as unified individuals who can be encompassed within the larger cultural notion of Woman—that is, if we resist the definition of Woman as being simply a list of characteristics that are the negatives of the positive list that have been used to define Man—then so too can the camera be used to display a position that is other than strictly male. If, as de Lauretis argues, we see film (or multimedia) as "a social technology," then these technologies can be used in various ways to raise questions about how subjects are—and can resist being—gendered as specifically as they are by (for example) traditional narrative film.

I do not argue here that "Fatty Bear's Birthday Surprise" is somehow *Born in Flames* for 3- to 7-year olds or that it would be *Jeanne Dielman* if there were a murder in the kitchen alongside the cake-baking. Nor do I argue that "Fatty Bear's Birthday Surprise" has been made by people steeped in structuralist film theory, or—as the characters of Matilda or Gretchen show—by people much familiar with feminist theory. But if, as de Lauretis argued, the main position with which a player identifies, the position that makes things happen, doesn't always have to be male, then that position can be fluid: the position from which a player looks into this game does not necessarily force a player into "the place of the female spectator," and does not strictly assign to a player "a role, a self-image, a positionality in language or desire." Again, I am not saying that this game presents its young players with any of the complexity of possible subjectivities as do the films discussed by de Lauretis, but the structures of this particular game do show that a player is not required to align with some fixed and stable gender position in order to play.

I do not want to imply that the possible backgrounding of gender in this game is inevitable in multimedia designed for children: an easy argument against such a position is to note that the title of a highly popular piece of children's multimedia is "Barbie Fashion Designer"—"Design party dresses, career outfits, vacation clothes, trendy outfits, wedding gowns, and even something special for a romantic date with Ken. It's up to your imagination!" a catalogue blurb reads—which is a game that, even without further description, we would probably be comfortable describing as assigning a fixed gender position to any player. In comparison, "Fatty Bear's Birthday Surprise"—as limited as it is in its awareness (for example) of how the genders of Matilda and Gretchen and Fatty Bear might affect children—still offers space for its players to experience their own actions outside the restrictions of "this is what a girl does" or "this is what a boy does."

THE GAZE

Part of what I think makes possible the gender backgrounding I have been arguing for in "Fatty Bear's Birthday Surprise" is that the house in which the game takes place is empty—except for sleeping people and dancing stuffed animals. There are no gendered characters on screen for the length of the game to support the structures of primary identification. Only Fatty Bear is on screen to address players; no adult asks them what they are doing digging through a strange house at night. The game could be structured so that players were asked their names when they started playing, and then the game's characters could later address players by name—but it is not technologically easy now to create a one-player game that could interact any more "personally" with a player. And so the game has been designed to take place in a house where players interact with no people: for a player to interact with people would require in the interaction—if the interaction were not to seem silly or false—an amount of quirkiness, unpredictability, and complexity that is both devilish and expensive to program. Within the empty house of "Fatty Bear's Birthday Surprise," then, there is no one to address a player by name or call attention to her gender; there is no one calling attention to her race or age or style of dress or the time she takes to solve the problem of the cake, or even whether she solves the problem.

This is not to say, however, that a child can approach this game to play as though she were just anyone. In the previous two sections of this chapter, I have discussed aspects of feminist film theory that consider how spectators are shaped by being asked to identify with screen and camera; in this penultimate section, I pull in a different perspective—that of "the gaze"—which asks us to consider a spectator not as he or she looks onto a screen but rather how the spectator is seen as though the screen were looking back at him or her.[8] It is a perspective that makes the house of Fatty Bear feel much less empty and much less open.

Both Silverman (1996)—in *The Threshold of the Visible World*—and Jay (1993)—in *Downcast Eyes: The Denigration of Vision in Twentieth-Century French Thought*—developed arguments about "the gaze" as Lacan discussed it. Although Jay gave a fuller background for Lacan's analysis as coming out of and responding to work by Merleau-Ponty and Callois, both Jay and Silverman showed how Lacan's analysis develops centrally out of Sartre's discussion of *le regard*, where someone peeking through a keyhole—so lost into looking that he has no sense of self—hears a sound (footsteps?) and becomes jarred into awareness of himself as an object for the apprehension of someone else. Whereas my writing thus far in this chapter focuses on the action and power of someone looking, Lacanian analysis stresses how "vision . . . may be understood as a conflictual field in which the looker is always a body to be observed" (Jay, 1993, p. 368). As Silverman (1996) put it, "To 'be' is in effect to 'be seen'" (p. 133): in the act of looking, whether at a film or a children's multimedia game, we are ourselves the object of someone else's regard—which, as my description of Sartre's keyhole scenario implies, does not necessarily mean that one has to be seen; instead, one only has to be aware of the presence of others who can and might see her.

Because she is writing specifically about film, Silverman stressed the visual elements of this moment when one becomes aware of *le regard*, but both she and Jay also gave importance to how Lacan's analysis, when in his considerations he develops *le regard* into the gaze, argues against vision as being able to encompass all that there is about our experience of being. The unsatisfiable desire that Lacan understands us to be, the desire to feel that we are unified, full, transcendent (the desire that encourages us not to see the suturing at work in traditional narrative film), leads us to hope (and sometimes believe) that we can immediately comprehend all with our sight or that, in turn, we can be fully and immediately comprehended—fully understood and loved—in the sight of another. There are, however, consequences to this desire to be comprehended by others; as a third writer put it,

> The subject-turned-object sees itself as the other sees it: it internalizes the gaze. Thus the poor self-image and limited sense of one's own possibilities that result when women see themselves as men see them, when minorities see themselves as the majority sees them. (Olin, 1996, p. 215)

But because, as Jay put it, "A lack, after all, is precisely that which cannot be seen; it must exceed the realm of the visual" (pp. 368-369), the gaze—any gaze—cannot be fixed. What Silverman emphasized out of this incompleteness of the visual—diverging from Lacan—is the temporality and materiality of the gaze, and that "acute variations separate one culture and one epoch from another . . . these variations pertain to how the gaze is apprehended; how the world is perceived; and how the subject experiences his or her visibility" (p. 134). Silverman's argument allowed her to speak of how the filmic gaze works in different places and times; I turn her argument about the gaze to a different technology, as I apply this notion from film to develop how multimedia can create spaces for calling forth gender in a player.

In the lectures from which Jay and Silverman derived their respective analyses of Lacan, Lacan diagrammed two triangles in order to describe the workings of the two kinds of sight, of how I see and how I understand myself to be seen (see Fig. 12.4). When the two triangles are overlapped, Silverman argued, what is emphasized is that our relations to others—both when we look and when we are looked at—are always mediated by the "screen." This is not the physical screen of a movie theater, but rather the recognition that (to quote from another article by Silverman, 1994):

> What must be demonstrated over and over again is that all subjects, male or female, rely for their identity upon the repertoire of culturally available images and upon a gaze that, radically exceeding the libidinally vulnerable look, is not theirs to deploy. (p. 295)

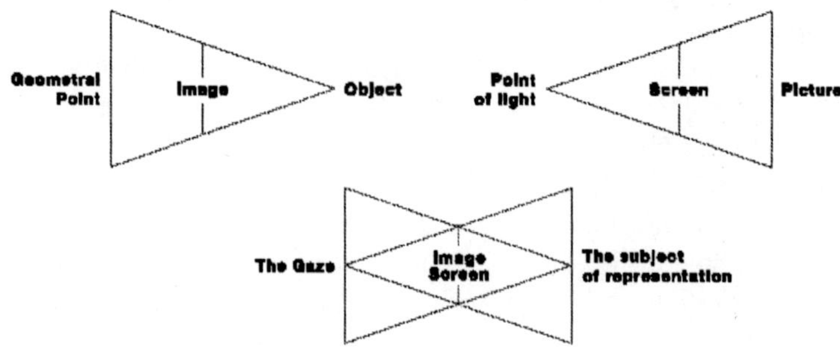

Fig. 12.4. The Lacanian Field of Vision (Silverman, *Threshold*, 132)

That is, for Silverman, when one is seen by others, one is always seen through a set of possibilities—tied to race, gender, class, and so on—that belong to a particular time and place: one can control neither being seen nor the set of possibilities through which one is seen.

To turn away from the sublimity of Lacan and back to Fatty Bear, there is this: Although I have argued that the identificatory structures of multimedia games like Fatty Bear can allow issues of gender to be quieted for someone playing the game, other matters are foregrounded. If I take the setting of Fatty Bear to be, in effect, the screen through which a player is "seen" by those who made the game—as a screen that projects culturally available ways of being onto the player, ways of being that the player must accept (consciously or no) in order to play—then there are in this game "culturally available images" that we might find problematic; some of these appear in what follows, observations made in a Daedalus Interchange discussion [all spellings intact] by members of a multimedia class I taught:

> (CW) One thing that just occurred to me, though, was that ["Fatty Bear's Birthday Surprise"] teaches kids how to function in a Western lifestyle, with all the modern conveniences—answering machine, garage door opener, washer, dryer, etc . . .
>
> (MR) I think that Fatty Bear teaches kids how to be, not quite politically correct, but at least polite and courteous. Fatty Bear doesn't ever swear or anything when he falls down the laundry shoot, or get angry when the dog pops the balloons, he just politely goes on, like little kids should. Just blow up some more balloons, and life is fine.
>
> (LS) Faty Bear is awfully careful in his word choice, it seems. I can't recall exactly what he says when he talks, but he is very precise, and it was usually correct English, too.

> (MS) I think that if a child is brought up in a certain environment where certain things are in certain places or orders, then [Fatty Bear] affects the way we think about the way things should be in order. For example, at my house we have the garbage under the sink. One of the things I have noticed is that most people keep their garbage under the sink. Probably, because it is cleaner and convenient. I will probably do the same. I think Fatty Bear just reinforces that order we see every day.

The on-screen actions of Fatty Bear and the arrangements of the game, then, tell players that they are expected to know how a Western house works (along with all its gadgets) and that things in the house are to be stored in certain ways; they tell players that, in this house, the players are seen as people who values order, politeness, and proper English. But the players are also seen by the game as people who will not question the utter normality of a single-family house, a house having both mother and father (who are sleeping together quietly in the same bed when a player enters their bedroom, where—in their closet—the player will find necessary objects for completing the game), a house having a car, a garden, and a separate bedroom full of stuffed animals for the daughter.

So, although Fatty Bear may allow a child to forget her gender for her length of play, the game is able to reinforce other aspects of the child's life—including those aspects that are tightly bound with gender, such as the life of the household, the relations we have with others in that household, and the shape of the house itself. The division of our houses into particular rooms with particular functions, for example, develops out of, allows for, and encourages our senses of who we are and the relations we have with others—as Wigley (1992) in "Untitled: The Housing of Gender" describes, based on his reading of Alberti's 15th-century text on architecture:

> While one of the first signs of the growing desire for privacy for the individual, such that "a privacy within the house developed beyond the privacy of the house," was the separation of the bedrooms that Alberti prescribes, which established a masculine space, this space is not completely private, since women can enter it, albeit only when allowed. The first truly private space was the man's study, a small locked room off his bedroom which no one else ever enters, an intellectual space beyond that of sexuality. (p. 347)

So although the house of Fatty Bear may not contain the same kind of overtly gendered spaces implied by Wigley—mother in the kitchen, father in the study—the contemporary middle-class room arrangements of Fatty Bear's home, and the contemporary middle-class people who live in that home, are nonetheless impossible without the earlier kinds of spaces Wigley described. For Young (1997),

> Home is a concept and desire that expresses a bounded and secure identity. Home is where a person can be "herself"; one is "at home" when she feels that she is with others who understand her in her particularity. The longing for home is just this longing for a settled, safe, affirmative, and bounded identity. Thus home is often a metaphor for mutually affirming, exclusive community defined by gender, class, or race. (p. 157)

Although Fatty Bear's game may background gender for a child who plays, the gaze that the empty house fixes upon the child helps the child acquire a sense of individual, bounded self. Bourdieu writes that:

> inhabited space—and above all the house—is the principal locus for the objectification of the generative schemes [of a culture]; and, through the intermediary of the divisions and hierarchies it sets up between things, persons, and practices, this tangible classifying system continuously inculcates and reinforces the taxonomic principles underlying all the arbitrary provisions of this culture. (p. 89)

If this is true for us, then "Fatty Bear's Birthday Surprise" may allow a child time for playing free from some gender constraints, but only because the game's space is foregrounded, enabled to do the groundwork—the creation of the child's sense of self and relationships with others—that is preliminary to and inseparable from the sense of gender being placed on her as she grows.

CONCLUSION

Despite the place where this argument has taken me—a place that seems to deny the possibility of some not rigidly gender-bound spaces in which children can play—I am not without hope for the possibilities of such spaces. My analysis of the structures of identification in first-person multimedia does argue that, "Barbie Fashion Designer" notwithstanding, such spaces might be possible because of how the structures of multimedia differ from film—but such spaces are possible only if those making multimedia are careful about the embodiment of those spaces on screen.

It is not enough that players aren't faced with rigidly constructed male or female characters on screen, or that the structures and actions of the game do not ask them to play—or to look—as girls or as boys: if the visual space in which the game takes place is a cultural ground for the development of gender—and race and class and sexual orientation—then the other potentially freeing aspects of the game are mitigated, at best. What my analysis here shows me is that I must better question—and encourage people in my classes to question—where we situate those who use the multimedia we make if we hope to encourage young women to understand themselves as something other than the negative of the binary whose positive term is *man.* What my analysis here shows me is that the visual skills and understandings and relations—the literacies—we need for working on computer screens must consider not only the workings of color and typefaces and visual arrangement and images but also how the specifically visual spaces we make and work within on computer screen are neither neutral nor empty but do themselves ground our other self-constructions. We need to question how we have learned to see and be seen.

ENDNOTES

1. For those who bemoan, see Birkerts (1994) or Sanders (1995). For a celebration, see Lanham (1993). For various other statements on the increase in images, tied to our development and use of computers, see Bolter (1998) or Kress and van Leeuwen (1996).
2. For hopeful, enthusiastic tellings of the possibilities of new media and identity, see Stone (1995) or Maso (1996). For more cautioned accountings, see Tamblyn (1997), Slane (1997), or Milthorp (1996).
3. Of this multimedia piece, Pearce (1997) said, "On the heels of a dwindling CD-ROM market, the smash hit of the 1996 Christmas season was a title that was not only designed to appeal to girls, but was designed to appeal exclusively to girls. It outsold every other game that year and as of this writing in the summer of 1997, is about to hit the one million mark *within its first year of release.* This is an almost unheard of success in the hit-and-miss CD-ROM market" (p. 206).
4. I stress here that my work in this chapter is not intended to be a full-blown discursis on film theory. Those of you who are well-settled in feminist/psychoanalytic film theory will note that my analyses here are broad and preliminary—as befits my intentions of finding initial points of alignment between film and multimedia where film theory offers developed critiques and suggests directions for action.

   I also do not wish to imply with this chapter that film theory aligns in some perfect way to multimedia: instead, in what follows, I mark points of difference that I think need establishing.
5. I cannot expect the piece of multimedia I discuss here to stand in for all other multimedia, multimedia aimed at adults or intended to help a child learn to cook or an apprentice fix airplanes or a student learn about the development of the atom bomb. But neither is "Fatty Bear's Birthday Surprise" monolithic: there are many other pieces of multimedia that share what I am describing to to be the main structures of this particular piece; in addition to what I will mention below, there are "Chop Suey" and "Smarty," multimedia designed

for girls in which players wander through and play within the houses and buildings of a town, or "P.A.W.S," in which children look into the screen as though they were a puppy exploring the yard of a home, or "The Dark Eye," multimedia for adults in which players move through a house to experience Poe's poetry interactively, or "Herbie Hanock Presents Living Jazz," where players wander through New Orleans to enter bars and churches to learn about jazz, or "Versailles 1685," where the inside of the palace provides the structure in which players can figure out who is conspiring against the king.

"Fatty Bear's Birthday Surprise" is what I call "first-person" multimedia, where a player sees what is on the computer screen as though it were the plane of her eyesight as she moved through the scenes of the action. There are other ways of divvying up and categorizing what is produced for interactivity on computer screens. Joyce (1995), for example, in his much-cited article "Siren Shapes," made a distinction between exploratory and constructive hypertexts—a distinction that Guyer (1996), a hypertext writer, later described in her piece "Along the Estuary" in these terms: exploratory hypertexts are those where you simply choose a path for walking through and constructive are those where you add to and make changes (p. 159). In *Designing Multimedia Environments for Children: Computers, Creativity, and Kids,* Druin and Solomon said about how to categorize multimedia: "we look at computer environments and their cultures within this framework: Expressive Medium—where the child is in control of the computer—and Interactive Textbook—where the computer is in control of the child" (p. 8).

For my purposes here, I turn from these other categories to speak of how "Fatty Bear' Birthday Surprise," like many other multimedia pieces, puts someone playing the game into a first-person perspective, as though the player were somehow in the game. This kind of multimedia is often constructed using 3D modeling and rendering software, which adheres to the rules of visual perspective: models are set up geometrically, and then captured by "cameras" that have been placed to make two-dimensional scenes out of different areas of the model. These resulting scenes are meant to appear as "lifelike" (i.e., as through-the-lens-of-a-camera) as possible; examples of such multimedia include the "best-selling computer game of all time" "Myst" (Carroll, 1997, p. 127), "Cosmic Osmo" (an early computer game by the makers of "Myst"), "The Residents' Bad Day on the Midway," or "Doom"—the only one of these intended for children is "Cosmic Osmo". "Fatty Bear's Birthday Surprise" was not created with such software—its scenes were created in a 2D painting program—but its appearance on screen is still intended to have a spatial depth given by perspective.

In addition, the spaces of such games are "closed" in some way, so that no attention is called to the fiction of the game and its rules: players are intended to feel that they are within a complete and full space, a world where the rules of the game make full and exclusive sense. "Myst," for example, takes place on an island: when a player "looks" out over the water, fog obscures the horizon, so that a player is visually discouraged from thoughts about how this game is un-real and constructed. "The Residents' Bad Day on the Midway" takes place within a fenced-in carnival, where it is impossible to go outside the fence, and "Doom" takes place in the halls and passageways of an underground bunker-space, where the object is for a player to kill his way to the outside and so to the end of the game and freedom.

But it is not only the simulation of "real" space that is meant to make a player of such a multimedia game feel that the computer screen aligns with her eyes: she is also—to a certain extent—the controller of the action that takes place within her plane of sight. The creators of the multimedia have set up a series of screens, and animations or sounds on those screens, through which a player moves—but the order of movement or of animations is determined by choices the player makes. It is, finally, as though she were "inside" the screen, as much a character or actor in the game as any image on screen—hence, "first-person multimedia."

(I do not address here that this first-person structure, which is inseparable from what I argue in this chapter, separates computer-based multimedia from film in some way that others would perceive as fundamental. For example, of films that are shot to give the same sort of experience to a viewer as I describe here for "first-person" multimedia, Zizek (1992) gave three examples, saying that, "Each of these three films is an artificial, overstrained formal experiment, but from where does the undeniable impression of failure derive? . . . [I]t is as if the author decided to renounce one of the key constituents of the 'normal' sound film (montage, objective shot, voice) for the sake of purely formal experiment" (p. 43). Obviously, the success of multimedia pieces like "Myst" argue against this structure being at all bothersome—or even much remarked—by those using computer-based multimedia.)

6. I move away here from film theory by moving away from "spectator" when I discuss computer-based multimedia. "Spectator" is the generally preferred theoretic term for anyone watching a film or television, but, as Crary (1990) argued,

> Spectator . . . carries specific connotations . . . of one who is a passive onlooker at a spectacle, as at an art gallery or theater. (p. 5)

For the reasons of his particular analysis of the construction of vision in the nineteenth century, Crary uses "observer" instead of "spectator" to describe someone, anyone, looking, anywhere at any time. For my purposes here, regarding computer-based multimedia, I am, for reasons similar to Crary's critique of the passivity of "spectator," turning from that word; I will instead use "player."

I could turn to "user," the term most frequently employed for someone working with a computer-based text; this name comes out of the early days of computers, when the focus was on computers as functional devices: the conversations were about how people use computers to achieve specific ends, and so, for example, the term "user interface" developed. In recent books about computer-based multimedia, "user" is simply used, without discussion of why it is more appropriate than anything else: the term shows up in books highlighting the visual design of multimedia, or highlighting how to develop a commercially viable product, or highlighting how to design multimedia for children. (See, e.g., the unexamined use of "user" in Donnelly, 1996, in Olsen, 1997, or Druin and Solomon, 1996.) Occasionally, someone will argue for the term, as Aarseth (1997) did: although the bulk of Aarseth's discussion is of what most people would call hypertexts—that is, computer-based texts where words are given more visual emphasis than images (or words + images)—his discussion does include wordless, image-based computer games, which he nonetheless discusses as "texts":

> Since most of the texts and textual practices discussed in this study differ much from "normal" texts and from each other, especially in terms of their operational use, I dispense with the figure of the reader and instead bring in the user, a much less predisposed character, at least in literary theory. . . . The user is allowed a wider range of behavior and roles across the field of media, from the observing member of a theater audience to the subcreator of a game world. This distinction is both practical and ideological; it keeps the established terms free from conceptual distortion, and it signals that to apply the term reader to a different kind of media practice is an act of appropriation that should at the very least be discussed in advance. Finally, the political connotations of the word user are conveniently ambivalent, suggesting both active participation and dependency, a figure under the influence of some kind of pleasure-giving system. (pp. 173-174)

For me, however, unlike for Aarseth, *user* is not an active term, but instead carries too much of two connotations, first that of the dependency Aarseth mentions, of passive and deadening injection or inhalation of pleasure, and then that of a mechanical world view, in which people are simply what is necessary for a mechanical process to complete itself. If what I hope to be an outcome of my considerations here is the possibility of structuring multimedia so that its "users" can understand themselves to have some say in how they are represented as subjects, I want other terms for describing them (and me).

For the kind of multimedia I discuss, *player* seems appropriate: the piece of multimedia I discuss is, after all, marketed as a game for children, and it is "interactive," in the sense that a child engaged in the game must continually make choices about what actions to take, actions that both keep the game moving and that affect the outcome of the game. *Player* does also carry with it the notion of a play, of drama and roles, of trying actions and behaviors without being stuck to them. My concern with *player* is that it implies perhaps too active a relationship between a child and the processes of subject-shaping I discuss here; this is an issue I hold in abeyance, for future considerations.

7. In what I write about "Fatty Bear's Birthday Surprise," I talk about film screens and computer screens as though they were interchangeable. Although we do sit in different physical relations to the two different screens, and the two kinds of screens have their images projected onto them differently, I am

nonetheless going to speak here—with the exception of my changing from "spectator" to "player" when I change from talking about film to talking about "Fatty Bear's Birthday Surprise"—as though people experience both screens and both projection processes similarly.

Some might argue that sitting in front of computer is more like sitting in front of a television than a film in a theater: after all, a computer monitor is essentially a TV screen in its mechanical and electronic functioning (some monitors are interchangeable for computer or TV use: WebTV is based precisely on this interchangeability), and computers can be found in the same rooms of a home as the TV set; it might therefore seem more reasonable for me here to be using TV theory rather than film to be talking about computer-based multimedia. But when theorists contrast television watching to film watching, I find that the relationships they argue viewers establish with computer screens are closer to those of film than television screens.

Friedberg (1993), for example, argued that whereas with a film (at least in the days prior to VCRs) we are immobile, in a large darkened room, watching "projected luminous images" that are framed on a large screen surface and that we cannot change, TV is itself a light source that we watch—on its small screen—while moving about freely in our homes, under many different lighting conditions and with the remote control in our hands. Flitterman-Lewis (1992) pointed to film requiring "sustained and concentrated" attention from a spectator in contrast to how television "merely requires the glance of the viewer" (p. 217); in addition, she argued that film, through editing, is capable of presenting "an illusory, fictive continuity," whereas, with television, "it is never a question of 'creating' a coherent space, of concealing the activity of an organizing principle outside the text, because the spectator is never moved through space. . . . The quality of viewer involvement [with TV] is one of continual, momentary, and constant visual repositioning" (p. 224). Finally, in the same collection from which the Flitterman-Lewis piece comes, Allen (1992) pointed out how TV, unlike cinema, "must fit into the social world of the family," and is "social rather than self-absorbing" (p. 12).

So even though computer monitors can be discussed as technically equivalent to television monitors, they are differently experienced and put to use. We do not "watch" computer games with a remote control in our hands: computer games call for the same kind of sustained and concentrated attentions as film narratives (at least when we watch the narratives in theaters)—and we generally sit closer to computer monitors than we do to television screens, so that when we are in front of a monitor our field of vision can be as filled as it is when we are in front of a cinema screen—and thus the games call forth, I believe, more of the self-absorption that Allen mentions. Although computer-games can be played by more than one person at a time, across networks, that does not make them any less self-absorbing or more social: there is still, generally, one person per computer monitor, and there is little difference between playing other people or playing the computer—the effort in such games is most often still to win for oneself (which often requires killing off the others), no matter who the opponent. And while "Fatty Bear's Birthday Surprise" is not a game with winners or losers, I still would argue that it is capable of pulling players into the same sort of self-absorption and sense of fictive continuity as the to-death games, or as narrative film. I have seen two children play "Fatty Bear's Birthday Surprise" together at the same monitor, but most often only one person plays at a time—and, as I have described above, the efforts of the game-makers have been to pull the players into feeling that they are in the "real" space of the game—even in their use of simulated cameras. First-person multimedia games work to create a sense of closed and coherent spaces, as the writers I quoted here argued that film does.

So, even though the screens of films and computers are very different objects, and have their images projected onto them differently, I have been arguing that the intentions of those who make narrative films and those who make computer games—and hence their uses of their differing apparatuses—are similar. For these reasons, I will not change my use of "screen" and "camera" when I shift from talking about film to talking about computer-based multimedia.

8. I examine a particular conception of the "gaze" here, as developed primarily by Silverman in her later work, and I am not going to address the question of suture in film, as (theorists argue) spectators are placed into a film through strategies such as shot/reverse shot, with the spectator filling in for the character who is temporarily offscreen. For other perspectives and for discussion of "suture," see Doane (1987), Williams (1984), or Silverman's (1983) earlier work in *The Subject of Semiotics.*

REFERENCES

Aarseth, E. J. (1997). *Cybertext: Perspectives on ergodic literature.* Baltimore, MD: Johns Hopkins University Press.

Allen, R. (1992). Introduction to the second edition: More talk about TV. In R. C. Allen (Ed.), *Channels of discourse, reassembled* (pp. 1-30). Chapel Hill: University of North Carolina Press.

Artel, L., & Wengraf, S. (1990). Positive images: Screening women's films. In P. Erens (Ed.), *Issues in feminist film criticism* (pp. 9-12). Bloomington: Indiana University Press

Barbie Fashion Designer [CD-ROM]. (1996). Mattel Media.

Birkerts, S. (1994). *The Gutenberg elegies: The fate of reading in an electronic age.* New York: Fawcett Columbine.

Bolter, J. D. (1998). Hypertext and the question of visual literacy. In D. Reinking, L.D. Labbo, & R.D. Kieffer (Eds.), *The handbook of literacy and technology: Transformation in a post-typographic world* (pp. 3-14). Mahwah, NJ: Erlbaum.

Bourdieu, P. (1977). *Outline of a theory of practice.* Cambridge: Cambridge University Press.

Carroll, J. (1997, September). (D)Riven. *WIRED, 5*(9), 170-181.

Chop Suey [CD-ROM]. (1995). Magnet Interactive Studios, Inc.

Cosmic Osmo [CD-ROM]. (1989). Cyan, Inc.

Crary, J. (1990). *Techniques of the observer: On vision and modernity in the nineteenth century.* Cambridge, MA: MIT Press.

The Dark Eye [CD-ROM]. (1995). Inscape.

de Lauretis, T. (1987). Rethinking women's cinema: Aesthetics and feminist theory. In *Technologies of gender: Essays on theory, film, and fiction* (pp. 127-148). Bloomington: Indiana University Press.

Doane, M.A. (1987). *The desire to desire.* Bloomington: Indiana University Press.

Donnelly, D. (1996). *In your face: The best of interactive interface design.* Rockport, MA: Rockport.

Doom [Computer software]. (1994-1996). GT Interactive.

Druin, A., & Solomon, C. (1996). *Designing multimedia environments for children.* New York: Wiley.

Fatty Bear's Birthday Surprise [CD-ROM]. (1993). Humongous Entertainment.

Flitterman-Lewis, S. (1992). Psychoanalysis, film, and television. In R.C. Allen (Ed.), *Channels of discourse, reassembled* (pp. 203-256). Chapel Hill: University of North Carolina Press.

Friedberg, A. (1993) *Window shopping: Cinema and the postmodern.* Berkeley: University of California Press.

Fryer, B. (1997). Shelley Day: Kids' software wizard. [Women to Watch interview]. Retrieved June 2, 1997 from the World Wide Web: http://more.women.com/work/profile/more/970602.profile.html.

Guyer, C. (1996). Along the estuary. In S. Birkerts (Ed.), *Tolstoy's dictaphone: Technology and the muse* (pp. 157-164). St. Paul: Graywolf Press.

Herbie Hancock Presents Living Jazz [CD-ROM]. (1996). Graphix Zone, Inc.: Hancock and Joe Productions, Inc.

Humongous Entertainment Fast Facts. (1998). Retrieved January 24, 1998 from the World Wide Web: http://www.humongous.com/about/pr/more/corp.html.

Jay, M. (1993). *Downcast eyes: The denigration of vision in twentieth-century French thought.* Berkeley: University of California Press.

Joyce, M. (1995). *Of two minds: Hypertext pedagogy and poetics* (pp. 39-60). Ann Arbor: The University of Michigan Press.

Kalow, N. (1993, December). A cure for Barney addiction. *WIRED, 1*(6), 111.

Kress, G., & van Leeuwen, T. (1996). *Reading images: The grammar of visual design.* London: Routledge.

Lanham, R. (1993). *The electronic word: Democracy, technology, and the arts.* Chicago: University of Chicago Press.

Maso, C. (1996). Rupture, verge, and precipice/Precipice, verge, and hurt not. In S. Birkerts (Ed.), *Tolstoy's dictaphone: Technology and the muse* (pp. 50-72). St. Paul: Graywolf Press.

Metz, C. (1982). *The imaginary signifier: Psychoanalysis and the cinema* (C. Britton, A. Williams, B. Brewster, & A. Guzzetti, Trans.). Bloomington: Indiana University Press.

Milthorp, R. (1996). Fascination, masculinity, and cyberspace. In M.A. Moser & D. MacLeod (Eds.), *Immersed in technology: Art and virtual environments* (pp. 129-150). Cambridge, MA: MIT Press.

Mulvey, L. (1989a). *Visual and other pleasures* (pp. 29-36). Bloomington: Indiana University Press.

Mulvey, L. (1989b). *Visual pleasure and narrative cinema.* In *Visual and other pleasures* (pp. 14-26). Bloomington: Indiana University Press.

Myst [CD-ROM]. (1993). Cyan, Inc.

Olin, M. (1996). Gaze. In R. S. Nelson & R. Shiff (Eds.), *Critical terms for art history* (pp. 208–219). Chicago: University of Chicago Press.

Olsen, G. (1997). *Getting started in multimedia.* Cincinnati: North Light Books.

Pearce, C. (1997). *The interactive book: A guide to the interactive revolution.* Indianapolis: Macmillan Technical.

The Residents' Bad Day at the Midway [CD-ROM]. (1995). Inscape.

Sanders, B. (1995). *A is for ox: The collapse of literacy and the rise of violence in an electronic age.* New York: Vintage.

Silverman, K. (1983). *The subject of semiotics.* New York: Oxford University Press.

Silverman, K. (1994). Fassbinder and Lacan: A reconsideration of gaze, look, and image. In N. Bryson, M.A. Holly, & K. Moxey (Eds.), *Visual culture: Images and interpretations* (pp. 272-301). Middletown, CT: Wesleyan University Press.

Silverman, K. (1996). *The threshold of the visible world.* New York: Routledge.

Slane, A. (1997). Romancing the system: Women, narrative film, and the sexuality of computers. In J. Terry & M. Calvert (Eds.), *Processed lives: Gender and technology in everyday life* (pp. 71-79). London: Routledge.

Smarty [CD-ROM]. (1996). Tom Nicholson Associates, Inc.

Stone, A. R. (1995). *The war of desire and technology at the close of the mechanical age.* Cambridge: MIT Press.

Tamblyn, C. (1997). Remote control: The electronic transference. In J. Terry & M. Calvert (Eds.), *Processed lives: Gender and technology in everyday life* (pp. 41-46). London: Routledge.

Versailles 1685: Intrigue at the Court of Louis XIV [CD-ROM]. (1996). Réunion des Musées Nationaux; Canal+Multimedia; Cryo Interactive Entertainment.

Wigley, M. (1992). Untitled: The housing of gender. In B. Colomina (Ed.), *Sexuality & space* (pp. 327-389). New York: Princeton Architectural Press.

Williams, L. (1984). When the woman looks. In M.A. Doane, P. Mellencamp, & L. Williams (Eds.), *Re-vision: Essays in feminist film criticism* (pp. 83-99). Frederick, MD: University Publications of America.

Young, I. M. (1997). *Intersecting voices: Dilemmas of gender, political philosophy, and policy.* Princeton: Princeton University Press.

Zizek, S. (1992). *Looking wry: An introduction to Jacques Lacan through popular culture.* Cambridge: MIT Press.

13

PROFESSIONAL LITERACY

Representing Teaching as Discursive Practice in Multimedia

Lucretia E. Penny Pence
University of New Mexico

We face an important and interesting problem in the 21st century. As we navigate the rapid changes in an increasingly diverse and global society, we cannot always predict what counts as knowledge in different situations and at different times. Even so, we talk about knowledge in fairly concrete terms. For example, in education we refer to a "body" of knowledge and subject "matter." We talk about what students should "know" and "be able to do." Our use of language separates knowing and doing; and in many teaching methodologies, we imagine that students need to know a great deal of information before they can apply it—knowing is a prerequisite for doing. We talk about a "subject area" knowledge, as if a discipline were a place, and to know that place we need to "cover" curriculum. Knowledge is "measured" on standardized tests in quantifiable bits. And those bits have come to represent knowledge. Knowing is doing well on the tests. We expect teachers to have knowledge and to give it to their students so that they can pass the tests. In the popular media, the metaphor of knowledge as stuff is perpetuated by survey after survey of the facts that people don't know and surrounded by the rhetoric of educational failure.

This concrete metaphor for knowing and its separation from doing has had profound effects on the profession of teaching. Professional knowledge is separate from what it is that teachers do. Even the National Board for Professional Teaching Standards (NBTPS) frames its five propositions as "what teachers should know and be able to do" (NBPTS, 1991). And we test beginning teachers on their general, subject, and pedagogical knowledges, as if they are separate, quantifiable entities. Theory, which is articulation of beliefs about knowing and practice are represented as discrete entities and are often positioned in opposition to each other. We, as a profession, need a metaphor for professional knowledge and ability that better represents the interplay between knowing and doing and that accommodates change and cultural difference. Teaching and learning to be a teacher are fluid and dynamic, requiring a metaphor that more accurately portrays its complexity.

A more useful way to think of knowledge might be to consider the development of knowledge as the development of *literacies.* In this chapter, I explore the implications of shifting our metaphor for knowing away from the concrete and quantifiable toward consideration of professional knowledge and ability as a form of literacy—an ever-evolving literacy—rather than a fixed knowledge base. Then I present a way of representing teaching as literacy in a multimedia CD-ROM.

KNOWLEDGE AND ABILITY AS LITERACY

I begin with a definition of *literacy.* Gee (1989a) defined *literacy* as mastery of, or fluency in, sets of social practices or discourses. *Discourses,* he posited, are "saying (writing)-doing-being-valuing-believing combinations" (p. 6) that are shared by particular communities. Discourses are identity kits that ensure acceptance and participation in particular social situations. Children begin their social lives by acquiring the intimate discourse of the home, what Gee (1989a) termed a *primary discourse*. Then, as they move into the world, they acquire or learn various secondary discourses—the social practices acceptable, for example, in the communities of school, profession, workplace, or even a bar or sporting event. In other words, literacy goes beyond just being able to read and write; it means being able to read (listen, view) and write (say) something to or do something with someone for some purpose in a way that will display understanding of the beliefs and values of a particular community. He argued that there are only novices and experts within discourses, that those who do not achieve fluency will remain outsiders.

Hence, in the world of teaching, expertise is more closely aligned with the development of a professional identity within the professional discourse of teaching than with the accumulation of knowledge and skills (Britzman, 1994). And professional identity is developed through participation in the discourse; whereas those more expert make their participation observable and support and scaffold the novice's emerging participation (Lave, 1988; Lave & Wenger, 1991; Wenger, 1990). You cannot teach literacy; you can only invite others to participate with you, to take on the role of teacher and approximate the habits of mind, action, and communication indicative of that identity (Schön, 1985).

Conceptualizing professional knowledge as a kind of literacy also provides a way out of the knowing and doing dichotomy. Gee distinguished between Discourses (with a capital D) and discourses (with a small d). Discourses represent the universe of thought, action, and communication; whereas discourses represent differing perspectives within that universe. Discourses and discourses are represented within *texts* (Ricoeur, 1991), which are connected segments of language (signs and action) that make sense. Standards, outcomes, lesson plans, assignments, and segments of classroom interaction are texts that are representative of the various discourses within the larger Discourse of teaching. Texts may differ in the beliefs they communicate, reflecting their positions within competing ideologies within the larger Discourse. A way to think of the difference between discourse and Discourse lies within the following oversimplification: The larger Discourse of teaching is concerned with how people learn, yet there are many competing discourses that differ in their beliefs about children, the nature of learning, and what to do in classrooms. For example, participants in the Discourse of teaching are all concerned with helping students learn how to read. However, views on what reading is and the best ways of achieving that goal differ widely, depending on the particular discourse (e.g., whole language, phonics, genre studies) and the identity position of a particular teacher.

These various professional discourses are represented in the texts used within a profession (Delandshere & Petrosky, 1994), and, given Gee's definition of literacy, it could be argued that the development of professional knowledge is the development of the ability to interpret and create these texts. In other words, professional expertise is professional literacy (Pence, 1996). Using this more dynamic metaphor allows the world of professional education to become a world of composing and interpreting the world (Freire, 1990), using the lenses of a particular profession. Knowing and doing, theory and practice, become interwoven, rather than separate, in the identity of the professional. The work of novices becomes text to be interpreted, rather than products to be measured.

This viewpoint provided explanatory power for some of the characteristics of novice teachers. Acquisition takes place without formal teaching, at the subconscious level through contact with models and a process of trial and error. On the other hand, learning that occurs through explanation and analysis is usually guided by a teacher and results in more conscious knowledge. People who acquire a Discourse are usually better performers within that Discourse, but they have less ability to stand outside their performance to explain or analyze. Those who *learn* a discourse are not usually as strong in performance but have more metaknowledge about what they are doing. He advocated for opportunities for both acquisition and learning and for providing novices with enough strategies to allow them to successfully participate in the new communities in which they are being asked to participate. If novices are not provided with sufficient strategies, they will rely on often inappropriate practices from their primary Discourse, a related secondary Discourse, or a stereotypical version of the Discourse in question.

In teaching, perhaps more than in any other profession, novices come with strong existing models acquired over their sixteen years or so of schooling. In Gee's terms, they have subconsciously *acquired* their model for teaching. Apprenticeships with more experienced members of the profession can allow novices to perform well as teachers within the novices' existing models. In our rapidly changing society, however, the Discourse of teaching is not a unified or static entity. There are discourses within and around the Discourse of teaching that may differ from the one(s) they experienced as students; thus, the process of becoming a teacher relies more heavily on *learning* than on subconscious acquisition. One such discourse is that of constructivism (Howe & Berv, 2000).

In constructivist teacher education, novices most often need to radically revise their existing models in their coursework and field experience. Novice teachers read methods books and professional literature; they write and receive feedback on their own lesson plans; they review and discuss their own and others' teaching; they interact with students; and they analyze and interpret student performance. But revision of a model takes time, and currently, most post-baccalaureate teacher education programs are just a little over a year in duration. As writers know, revision is an arduous process of re-seeing and rethinking, and novice teachers have just one year to revise 16 years of acquisition.

Given this short preparation period, novices, who are often uncomfortable or tentative in their new identities, revert to their acquired models for teaching, rather than use their learned model. Thus, the most powerful influence on novice teachers' teaching is how they were taught (Fieman-Nemser & Remillard, 1996). One example from my own experience as an English teacher educator illustrates my point. Our secondary English program operates within a response to literature paradigm (Beach, 1993; Rosenblatt, 1991). We teach our students to assess student reading of literature through written responses, discussion, and observation. Nowhere in our program do we instruct novice teachers in the construction and administration of quizzes; yet, almost invariably, when novices enter student teaching, they produce and administer numerous quizzes on the literature students are reading. Because our program offers them only a few months of experience using less familiar assessment strategies, novices, as Gee's theory predicts, fall back on their acquired Discourse when they enter the high stress situation of their first few months of teaching.

PROPOSITIONS, CASES, AND STRATEGIES

The literacy metaphor for professional education can extend our view of how we develop professional knowledge. Categories of teacher knowledge can be framed as types of texts to be generated and interpreted and interrogated for the ideologies of the discourses that they represent. For example, Shulman (1986) contended that teacher knowledge takes on three different forms: propositional knowledge, case knowledge, and strategic knowledge. Propositional knowledge, he argued, is represented in explicit statements of principles, maxims based on practical experience, or normative statements. These may be derived from disciplined empirical or philosophical inquiry, from practical experience, or from moral or ethical reasoning. Propositions are economical in form, containing and simplifying a great deal of complexity. Case knowledge is a repertoire of specific examples of teaching that serve to illustrate or represent theory, principles or maxims, norms or values. Strategic knowledge is developed through the dialectic of the general with the particular, the propositional with specific cases. Strategic knowledge extends understanding beyond principles to the wisdom of practice. Texts that represent these forms of knowledge are evident in the profession of teaching, and their construction and interpretation are foundational to professional development.

Currently, within the professional Discourse of teaching, we have been preoccupied with the articulation of standards—lists of what teachers should know and be able to do. These standards are propositional in nature. They encapsulate the essence of what it means to teach in a few statements. They are principles or maxims articulated by members of the profession, based on their understanding of theory and research and their own experience as practitioners. Standards are meant to reflect a shared vision of the profession and to provide a means of ensuring quality teachers for all students. For example, the NBPTS (1991) articulates five core propositions of exemplary practice; and the Interstate New Teacher and Support

Consortium (INTASC, 1992) represents standards for novice knowledge, skill, and dispositions in 10 principles (see Appendices A and B). These texts are meant to represent the skeleton of what novice teachers need to learn.

Standards and other propositional texts represent discourse practices common to the Discourse of teaching. Teachers read educational theories and review state competencies. They read methods books and articles that give advice on what to do. They craft curriculum and standards for student performance; they interpret standards and curriculum when they write lesson plans and interact with students. If we consider teacher preparation as the development of professional literacy, what becomes important is not that novices simply comprehend all of these texts (which would be impossible) but that they know how to transact with and compose these kinds of texts in ways that empower them as professionals. This shift in metaphors has subtle implications for how propositional texts are dealt with in teacher education. For example, if we were working with the concrete knowledge and ability metaphor, we would distribute standards for student performance to our novice teachers and explain to them that these are their goals as teachers. Then once they were familiar with the standards, we would proceed to help them learn how to teach to the standards.

However, if we look at standards as representations of a discourse practice, the way we introduce standards changes. For example, my colleagues and I at the University of New Mexico begin our methods courses for secondary teachers by having them articulate their understanding of the field in which they will be teaching—what big ideas they think their students will need to learn. This activity mirrors the process of articulating standards and invites them into a discourse practice that is common in teaching. Only after they have engaged in this process themselves are they introduced to the standards for student performance in their discipline, and we note the similarity of the processes. The next step is that the novice teachers review those standards in light of the different social and historical perspectives, interrogating what the standards imply about the nature of their discipline, students, and teaching. Novices still become familiar with the standards, but they also understand the role teachers and the current sociocultural context play in creating those standards.

A second category of texts in the Discourse of teaching, which corresponds to Shulman's category of case knowledge, includes cases of teaching. Cases are specific moments of teaching, narratives of specific instances in which principled knowledge are played out in practice. Cases are used extensively in business, medicine, law, and sometimes in education (Merseth, 1991). Novice's reflections on their own and others' teaching can also be considered cases. Following Shulman's (1986) theory, teachers develop strategic knowledge by moving back and forth between principled knowledge and specific cases, each case adding to a teacher's repertoire of strategies. Through this process of negotiation among sometimes dissonant principles and cases, teachers develop their abilities to teach. The job of teacher education, then, is to help novices learn the propositions of the field, fleshing out and interrogating that skeletal knowledge through their own and others' examples of practice.

This correspondence between types of professional knowledge and professional texts is an effective frame for teacher education, if we consider how readers make meaning with text. In reading theory, Rosenblatt (1978) made a distinction between efferent and aesthetic reading. Efferent reading has as its purpose to carry away information. Aesthetic reading engages readers in experiencing events, feelings, images, and characters represented in a text. Although both types of reading occur almost simultaneously in any one reading event, readers most often adopt one of these stances as their primary stance when reading particular kinds of texts. Texts like research articles, business memos, and methods books often signal primarily efferent reading; while a novel, poem, or movie most often signals an aesthetic reading. In Gee's (1989b) terms, an efferent reading experience may support literacy *learning;* while an aesthetic experience would more likely support literacy *acquisition.* In other words, the imaginative living through of a narrative may provide novices with vicarious experiences that allow them to develop performance expertise through the taking on of teacherly roles.

Cases present teaching as a complex, socially situated practice (Harrington & Garrison, 1992; Kagan, 1993; Merseth, 1991). These texts are story-like in nature. They are tales from one's own practice or from another's; they are found in informal teacher conversation or are formally crafted. They may be illustrated with artifacts of instruction, like assignments, lesson plans, handouts, videotape of interaction, and student work. Cases tell stories, carve out moments of practice, and frame them as texts for the self and others. Their form invites readers to enter into a story world (Langer, 1992), to identify with characters, to experience events, and to respond emotionally. More formal cases are usually framed with questions that ask the audience to consider salient issues related to those stories. Transaction with such cases allows novice teachers to engage in trying on the ways of thinking, discussing, and writing that are valued in the profession—to enter into the "discourse of practice" (Lampert, 1999).

Again, it is important to note that Discourse is not static. Rather it is ever-evolving and needs to be presented to novice teachers as such. If schooling is to meet the demands of the increasingly fast pace of societal change, teaching must be presented to novices as a dynamic process that is both responsive to cultural difference and an agent for social justice, not as a set of fixed best practices. The tension for teacher-educators lies between needing to provide novices with enough strategies to begin their participation in the professional community and helping novices to understand the sociocultural complexities of the profession.

One of these complexities arises from the fact that teaching takes place among the Discourses of the community and home. Novice teachers need to be aware of, respect, and adapt to the dissonance their students may experience as they move among home, community, and school contexts. How these contexts are represented in their teacher preparation can have profound effects on how novice teachers understand and relate to diversity in their classrooms (Tatto, 1996). Novice teachers need to understand teacherly Discourse in juxtaposition with other related Discourses to develop an understanding of knowledge as constructed and relational—to better understand that their students already participate in discourses outside the school, that they are not unknowing or illiterate. Conceptualizing knowledge as situational is fundamental to constructivist teaching (Richardson, 1999), that is, teaching that capitalizes on and foregrounds how people make meaning from the texts around them. It is teaching that invites participation in disciplinary Discourse, with the associated role-taking and approximation of expert interpreting and composing within the genres of that discipline (Bakhtin, 1986).

MULTIMEDIA CASES

To facilitate the entry of novice teachers into a professional Discourse of constructivist teaching, we need a new genre of texts that will (a) promote acquisition through immersion in teacherly discourse practices, (b) juxtapose professional Discourse with family and community Discourses, and (c) allow novice teachers to develop strategic knowledge through transacting both aesthetically and efferently with both propositional texts and cases. Until recently, it would have been impossible to conceive of such all-encompassing texts, but with the recent developments in technology, it is now possible to better represent the complexities of teaching in immersive, interactive, multimedia texts.

To illustrate, I turn to a two-volume CD-ROM program, entitled *Circles of Support: Teaching and Learning in Multicultural Settings* (NMTLC, 2000).[1] My colleagues and I developed this program in conjunction with the New Mexico Teacher Learning Community (NMTLC),[2] a partnership between a university teacher preparation program and a culturally diverse, rural school district. The purpose of the partnership was to explore new ways for preparing teachers for work with students who come from a range of cultural and linguistic backgrounds. The first volume, "Teacher Education," presents the institutional model for the partnership, excerpts from key partnership activities, and extensive community background. The second volume, "Site Visits," presents cases of teaching and learning derived from actual practice in the district. Both volumes grew out of a qualitative inquiry into the experiences of those who participated in the partnership and our desire to not only report results but also create texts that can be used in constructivist teacher preparation. I focus primarily on "Site Visits" as such a text.

THE INTERFACE

Johnson (1997) argued that computer interfaces reflect and affect our culture. They reflect our culture by relying on culturally familiar metaphors to aid users. For example, the trash can or recycling bin icon on the computer screen provides a place metaphor for files one wishes to discard. Yet, at the same time, the nature of the interface also has the power to transform perceptions. Johnson pointed out that the development of the Apple interface and the Internet shifted our notion of the computer as a tool to viewing it as space—a place to store information, a virtual world to explore, an environment in which we can interact and create. Following a theory of cyberspace narrative proposed by Murray (1997), we used the metaphor of the visit to establish "a border between the virtual world and ordinary life because a visit involves explicit limits on both time and space" (p. 106). Users are able to virtually visit not just classrooms but the inner thinking of teachers and the larger ideological context in which those classrooms operate.

When novice teachers enter into "Site Visits," they metaphorically go to the classrooms of real teachers and students in a real community. They visit with the teacher, teacher educators, students, and community members. They can access research and theory into topics related to what is happening in the classroom, and they are asked to assume the role of colleague—to look at things with a teacherly eye, to discuss pertinent issues, and to analyze student work. It is the interface that brings all of this together and organizes a user's experience. And it is this particular interface that can serve as a visual metaphor for the complex professional Discourse of teaching—a Gestalt (Korthagen & Kessels, 1999) that unites both theory and practice.

An interface like that of *Circles* requires us to shift away from our linear, print-based notion of propositional and narrative, theoretical and practical, texts toward a more mosaic notion of how aspects of the

Discourse of teaching fit together (Gaggi, 1998). In a mosaic, images are created through the juxtaposition of smaller images—the cracks between the pieces contribute to the overall effect. The goal is not to erase and smooth out difference; rather, the shape and contour of the fissures between ideas become part of the larger part of the representation. The interface is the mortar that connects and organizes the themes, categories, narratives, and descriptions that come together as theory in practice. As difficult as it is to describe, in the medium of print, the overall effect of the interface, I now use the parts of the "Site Visits" interface (see Fig. 13.1) to organize a discussion of how it can serve as a visual representation of professional literacy for the field of teaching.

Main Screen: Classroom Interaction

Because the classroom is where the Discourses of the school, community, and family all come together, we placed videotape of classroom interaction in the largest central position on the computer screen. These classroom segments provide the central narratives around which all other aspects of teaching revolve. To create these narratives, we asked mentor and preservice teachers to allow us to videotape their classes as they introduced a new concept or activity. We edited the videotape for key moments that could best represent the segmenting and ordering of each teacher's instruction, striving for segments that were short enough to maintain user interest yet long enough to allow a realistic immersion into classroom life. The resultant video narratives are intended to move beyond description of events toward placing users closer to the activities, allowing them to more fully experience and empathize with the participants (Eisner, 1991). These segments are indexed to the left of the main screen in chronological order, starting with the beginning of the sequence and ending with close-ups of students at work and final products that resulted from the instruction. The index provides the more propositional, skeletal information about the narrative, akin to a list of steps the teacher followed. However, users can enter into the sequence in any order by clicking on any part of the index.

Resources—Teacher Reflection

At anytime while viewing segments of classroom interaction, users can access video of the teacher's reflections related to those segments by clicking on a Resource window where the teacher's face appears (see Resources in Fig. 13.1.). In these reflections, teachers explain their reasoning behind their actions, offer their insights on their students, and evaluate their own

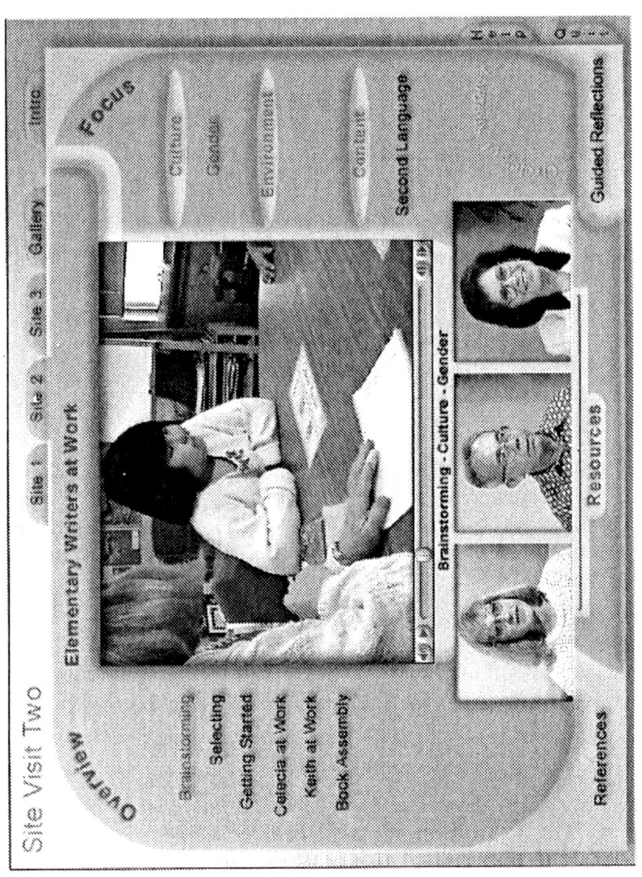
Site Visit Two
Overview
Brainstorming
Selecting
Getting Started
Celecia at Work
Keith at Work
Book Assembly
Elementary Writers at Work
Site 1
Site 2
Site 3
Gallery
Intro
Focus
Culture
Gender
Environment
Content
Second Language
Brainstorming - Culture - Gender
Resources
References
Guided Reflections

Fig. 13.1.

performances. Such reflections invite novice teachers into the personal professional discourse of the teacher, a rare opportunity in an observation situation, given teachers' busy schedules. When we piloted the interface with preservice teachers, they found this feature to be most valuable.

Focus Areas: Culture, Environment, and Content

Three major themes emerged as we analyzed the video texts in light of the discourse of constructivist teaching (Richardson, 1999), including its commitment to diverse learners (Tatto, 1996). These three themes are indexed to the right of the main screen as "Culture," "Environment," and "Content." By clicking on a topic under Culture, the user enters into a discourse about cultural influences on learning—how perceptions of ethnicity, race, class, and gender affect teaching and learning. Topics under Environment engage the user in discourse about how the routines, structure, and management of the classroom affect learning. And topics under Content invite discourse on the kind of knowledge and abilities students will most likely develop as the result of instruction.

Guided Reflections and Focus-Related Resources and References

Users may enter these theme-related discourses at two differing levels. The first level is that of an observer. Clicking on a theme changes the main screen and the Resources at the bottom of the interface. The main window articulates an issue raised by the segment of classroom interaction and asks the user to consider the issue. The Resource windows shift to reveal not only the teacher but also members of the local community and teacher educators who comment on the selected theme. By clicking on these windows, users can watch and listen to multiple perspectives on that issue. In other words, they can observe competing discourses. The second level offers users the opportunity to take on the role and ways of thinking of a teacher. This level is accessed when users click on the Guided Reflection button at the bottom right of the interface. At this point, users are presented with tasks that engage them in analyzing, researching, and discussing the issue and its related classroom moment with colleagues. The tone of the tasks is collegial, and the tasks ask users to position themselves among the discourses represented in the Resources. References to professional publications related to the theme are also available by clicking on the lower left of the interface.

A BRIEF VISIT TO SITE TWO

To better illustrate how the interface works, I take you on an excursion into "Site Visits"—to the extent that such an excursion can be simulated in print. Figure 13.1 is a representation of the interface. Refer to it as we navigate. At the top of the interface are four tabs—Site 1, Site 2, Site 3, and Gallery. By clicking on each of these tabs, you can visit three different classrooms for extended visits and analysis or visit a Gallery of Teaching Moments, briefer visits that act as springboards for discussion. For purposes of this demonstration, we click on "Site 2: Elementary Writers at Work." By clicking on the main screen, a brief montage of pictures introduces us to a first-grade classroom in a Native-American community in northern New Mexico. The teacher and her students are writing books for their classroom library. At any time during or after the introduction, you can click on any classroom segment listed on the left side of the screen (Brainstorming, Selecting, Getting Started, Celecia at Work, Keith at Work, and Publishing). The segments are listed in the order in which they occurred, but you can start anywhere. The teacher and her students begin by brainstorming topics, and then each student selects a topic to write about, starts by drawing pictures as a first draft, and later adds words. You can closely monitor two students, Celecia and Keith, as they work. You can finish your visit by viewing the process for publishing the final draft of the books.

We begin our short visit by clicking on the first segment, "Brainstorming." In this segment, the teacher begins by explaining to a small group of students—one girl and two boys—that they are going to write a book and that one of the things that writers do is get "lots and lots of ideas to think about before they begin writing." She begins by asking the students what it is that they like to do. The boys speak up quickly. She asks the boys probing questions about their topics, and they respond enthusiastically and at length about sports, riding horses, chopping wood, and hunting. The teacher takes careful notes about what the boys say.

When the boys are finished, she turns to Celecia, and asks, "So, Celecia, do you ever help your mother cook?" Celecia wrinkles her nose and looks away from the teacher in silence. The boys answer for her, "Tortillas," and then make a joke that she helps her mother cook adobe. Celecia continues to look down, thinking. Finally, she responds that she helps her mother make pottery. The teacher is pleased and writes her idea down.

At any time, we can click on the Resources windows below the main screen where the teacher appears. When we do so, we hear her explain that the students are writing books because so few children's books reflect the experiences of these Pueblo Indian children. We can also hear her explain how working together in small groups like this is consistent with the community culture, how "they help each other out quite naturally." At this point we could continue through other segments, but if we want to more deeply explore this segment and engage in teacherly discourse, we can click on either of the two focus areas in which titles appear. "Gender" appears under the Culture focus area, and "Second Language" appears under content. When we click on "Gender," the main screen highlights a problem that we face in teaching, in this case, "How teachers interact with children can value some children's participation over others." By clicking on the main screen, we can see a smaller portion of the lesson segment that highlights this problem.

At the bottom of the screen under Resources, three perspectives are available—one from the teacher, one from a teacher educator who is also a member of the Pueblo Indian community, and one from another teacher educator. These three perspectives point out the problem of gender bias and issues related to achieving gender equity in the classroom. In the left-hand Resources window, the teacher herself recognizes her biases toward the boys in the segment. She explains,

> What I found myself doing was really responding to these little boys because they were so animated and not really responding very much to the little girl. And I didn't realize that until I saw it on videotape and then realized that she wasn't really participating as much as the boys were, but we did need to get started on the book project, and so I pretty much handed her some choices, and she had to make one.

She had indeed begun the segment by asking an open-ended question of the group, and when the boys responded vigorously, she did devote most of the brainstorming time to probing their ideas further and engaging them in extensive oral rehearsal of their writing. Then, in her effort to include Celecia, as well as to move things along, she hurriedly asked the young girl a less open-ended question. Celecia takes the question as an invitation to share her ideas, but in order to do that, she had to respond outside the parameters of the question.

In the center Resources window, the Pueblo Indian teacher educator points out that people outside a culture cannot always easily determine the complexities of the power relationships between genders. To illustrate his point he states,

> As a matter of face in my culture, women really . . . the traditional Indian law is that the women really own the children and the home and the fields and everything else. Men may be in government roles more so because those distinctions are made. You know, you can play government all you want, but you might find yourself with your possessions out in the yard one morning and see how far you go.

And in the right-hand Resources window, another teacher educator raises yet another issue related to gender. She comments,

> Part of the problem is . . . you know on *Star Trek* . . . are you familiar with that prime directive thing, you know where they visit other worlds and they are never supposed to mess around with the cultural . . . or whatever's going on . . . interfere? When you work with diverse cultural groups and one element of that group, women, for example, is oppressed, and you see it, that's one of those issues. How far do you go with that? Again what you are doing is that you are imposing your cultural values of our culture right now on this other group. An when the gender roles are so clearly defined as they are in lots of minority groups, how far can you go to say, "How can you put up with this and why should you do this?" If you know that a community is suppressing women for the purposes of maintaining something that isn't fair, it's just like anything else.

Hence, the three perspectives under Resources open up space for users to consider the complexities of achieving gender equity in schools and what it means to value the participation of both boys and girls equally.

A dialogic space (Bakhtin, 1986) is open, but novice teachers may need guidance and information in order to position themselves in relationship to these gently competing discourses. By clicking on Guided Reflection, at the bottom right of the interface, the main window fills with recommendations for exploring aspects of teaching suggested by the Overview segment. The first part of each Guided Reflection states the intent of the task—what kinds of teacherly thinking it promotes. Then it anchors the task in the classroom interaction, Resources, and/or References. Step-by-step guidelines provide frames for analysis of the classroom interaction and issues to consider in discussion. In some instances the Guided Reflection finishes with teacher tips.

> The Guided Reflection that focuses on gender begins by stating its purpose: Achieving equity for children in classrooms is an important goal for teachers. Sometimes, however, during our interactions with students, we unconsciously value some students' participation over others. This Guided Reflection will help you to develop ways to monitor your interaction with students to see the extent to which you encourage all learners.

Users are referred to the teacher's comments as a starting point and then told to review the Brainstorming segment, noting questions, length and numbers of turns taken by the teacher and students, and body language. Next, users are provided with a set of questions that focus them on differences between the treatment of boys and girls in the segment, based on the data they have collected. This Guided Reflection ends with a set of recommendations (Teaching Tips) for dealing with classroom discourse to ensure equity, including advice on the effects of silence in the classroom, engaging students in active listening, and videotaping one's own teaching. At this point, we end our visit, but we could spend many more hours (at least 8, not including time to complete Guided Reflections or to consult References) exploring this space. It is now time to step outside and reflect on the implications of representing professional knowledge and experience as Discourse and the role that multimedia technologies might play in that representation.

LIVING THROUGH AND CARRYING AWAY

The capabilities of CD-ROM afforded us the opportunity to present cases that enable novice teachers to vicariously live through extended classroom experiences, while at the same time enabling them to carry away information related to the issues raised by those experiences (Rosenblatt, 1978). Juxtaposition of narratives opens up space for "multiple meaningful interpretations" (Murray, 1997) and provides novices with "opportunities to see the context specificity of the teaching and learning process and to begin to 'think like teachers'" (Harrington & Garrison, 1992, p. 717). In *Circles,* thinking like a teacher means positioning oneself among the discourses represented—pedagogical, curricular, scholarly, community, parental, and student discourses. It means creating one's identity within the larger Discourse of teaching.

"Site Visits" facilitates this identity creation through immersing users in authentic classroom interaction and surrounding that interaction with differing perspectives. The interface provides flexible meta-information (Johnson, 1997) about the classroom image. The Focus Areas, Resources, References, and Guided Reflections (see Fig. 13.1) help users make sense of classroom action; they are filters on information that may greatly exceed novice teachers' capacities to process it (Johnson, 1997). The interface acts as a "good guide" (Eisner, 1991) through the images and information, allowing users to deepen and broaden their experience and to try on the perspectives of constructivist teaching. The guide allows different points of entry and levels of understanding, ranging from a brief overview of classroom experience to careful instructions for analysis and discussion.

In a computer-generated environment, agency is "the satisfying power to take meaningful action and see the results of our decisions and choices" (Murray 1992, p. 126). The sense of agency created by the *Circles* interface increases immersion in an environment of dialogue and decision making. Rather than following a linear narrative, users have choice; they can move within the environment, creating their own paths through the mosaic of discourses. Such visits allow novices to become familiar with the culture (Lave & Wenger, 1991) or Discourse (Gee, 1989a) of teachers. More specifically, thinking and discussion evoked by these visits allow users to engage in the discourse of constructivist teaching.

As explained earlier, the interface—how these visits are framed and indexed—have the potential to shape our cultural perceptions of teaching (Johnson, 1997). For me, this shaping is one of the most important aspects of the *Circles of Support* site visits. Constructivist theory is implicitly presented through our selection of cases, yet it is also questioned through the presentation of multiple perspectives. Teaching strategies are presented, but they are presented in light of theory, community, values, and student learning. And, users are encouraged to develop their own perspectives through role-taking and dialogue. In visual, oral, and print texts, the *Circles* interface integrates both the propositions and cases of the Discourse of teaching. Cases are embedded in an interface that can organize the memory structures in which novices retain these and future cases effectively (Edelson, 1998). How the cases are framed and indexed can determine which examples are applicable to new situations and enable retrieval of examples that might be helpful. Although *Circles* has only a bank of three site visits, I think the structure of the interface shows great promise for the development and organization of a discourse-based teacher preparation program.

The interface can serve to organize additional visits—multimedia or not—by indexing cases both pedagogically and thematically, situating cases within a framework of propositions indicative of the larger Discourse. For example, as explained earlier, Site Visit 2 encompasses a writing-for-publication cycle in a first-grade classroom. This narrative sequence is indexed chronologically by instructional segment. The titles of these instructional segments serve as a skeletal set of propositions about writing pedagogy, a set of pedagogical phases inherent to writing instruction—exploration of genre (in this case, picture books), supporting the writing process (brainstorming, getting started, drawing, talking), publication, and assessment of student work (Arnberg, 1999). If we had a large bank of such instructional sequences, created by different teachers who teach at different grade levels and in different contexts, we could immerse novices in many variations on the same pedagogical phase. They could, theoretically, develop strategic knowledge that would prepare them for a wider range of contexts and developmental levels than is currently possible. Thematic indexing (culture, environment, and content) provides a different set of propositions. These themes represent what is valued in a particular discourse of teaching—the qualities that constructivist teachers strive for. These values serve as lenses on any classroom event. Again, given a large bank of cases, novices can access different ways that these values are enacted. They could, for example, access numerous examples of dissonance between home and school cultures and how different teachers in different settings have addressed those differences.

I believe the *Circles* model for representing the Discourse of teaching can shape the future of teacher education, both with and without the use of technology. With such an approach apprenticeship into teaching becomes an invitation into a rich professional discourse—with opportunities to move among propositions and cases, to develop more than just strategic knowledge—to develop the "saying (writing)-doing-being-valuing-believing combinations," to develop the identity of teacher (Gee, 1989a, p. 6).

APPENDIX A: NATIONAL BOARD FOR PROFESSIONAL TEACHING STANDARDS

Five Propositions of What Teachers Should Know and Be Able to Do

1. Teachers are committed to students and their learning.
2. Teachers know their subjects and how to teach their subjects to students.
3. Teachers are responsible for managing and monitoring student learning.
4. Teachers think systematically about their practice and learn from experience.
5. Teachers are members of learning communities.

APPENDIX B: INTERSTATE NEW TEACHER ASSESSMENT AND SUPPORT CONSORTIUM

Model Standards for Beginning Teacher Licensing and Development: A Resource for State Dialogue

Principle 1: The teacher understands the central concepts, tools of inquiry, and structures of the discipline(s) he or she teaches and can create learning experiences that make these aspects of subject matter meaningful for students.

Principle 2: The teacher understands how children learn and develop, and can provide learning opportunities that support their intellectual, social, and personal development.

Principle 3: The teacher understands how students differ in their approaches to learning and creates instructional opportunities that are adapted to diverse learners.

Principle 4: The teacher understands and uses a variety of instructional strategies to encourage students' development of critical thinking, problem-solving, and performance skills.

Principle 5: The teacher uses an understanding of individual and group motivation and behavior to create a learning environment that encourages positive social interaction, active engagement in learning, and self-motivation.

Principle 6: The teacher uses knowledge of effective verbal, nonverbal, and media communication techniques to foster active inquiry, collaboration, and supportive interaction in the classroom.

Principle 7: The teacher plans instruction based on knowledge of subject matter, students, the community, and curriculum goals.

Principle 8: The teacher understands and uses formal and informal assessment strategies to evaluate and ensure the continuous intellectual, social, and physical development of the learner.

Principle 9: The teacher is a reflective practitioner who continually evaluates the effects of his or her choices and actions on others (students, parents, and other professionals in the learning community) and who actively seeks out opportunities to grow professionally.

Principle 10: The teacher fosters relationships with school colleagues, parents, and agencies in the larger community to support students' learning and well-being.

ENDNOTES

1. Information on ordering *Circles of Support* can be found at www.mediadesigns.com.
2. I thank the NMTLC for allowing us to document their experiences on CD-ROM. And I give special thanks to Sue Gradisar, Carolyn Wood, and Lori Connors-Tadros for their continuing support and willingness to listen, long after the project is over.

REFERENCES

Arnberg, A. (1999). A study of memoir. *Primary Voices K-6, 8*(1), 13-20.

Bakhtin, M. (1986). The problem of speech genres. In C. Emerson & M. Holquist (Eds.), & V. W. McGee (Trans.), *Speech genres and other late essays* (pp. 60-102). Austin: University of Texas Press.

Beach, R. W. (1993). *A teacher's introduction to reader response theories*. Urbana, IL: National Council of Teachers of English.

Britzman, D. P. (1994). Is there a problem with knowing thyself? Toward a post-structuralist view of teacher identity. In T. Shanahan (Ed.), *Teachers thinking, teachers knowing: Reflections on literacy and language education* (pp. 53-75). Urbana, IL: National Council of Teachers of English.

Delandshere, G., & Petrosky, A. (1994). Capturing teachers' knowledge: Performance assessment a) and post-structuralist epistemology, b) from a post-structuralist perspective, c) and post-structuralism, d) none of the above. *Educational Researcher, 23*(5), 11-18.

Eisner, E. (1991). *The enlightened eye: Qualitative inquiry and the enhancement of educational practice*. New York: Macmillan.

Edelson, D. C. (1998). Learning from stories: An architecture for Socratic case based teaching. In R. Schank (Ed.), *Insider multimedia case based instruction* (pp. 174-198). Mahwah, NJ: Erlbaum.

Fieman-Nemser, S., & Remillard, J. (1996). Perspectives in learning to teach. In F. B. Murray (Ed.), *The teacher educator's handbook: Building a knowledge base for the preparation of teachers* (pp. 63-91). San Francisco, CA: Jossey-Bass.

Freire, P. (1990). *Pedagogy of the oppressed.* New York: Continuum.

Gaggi, S. (1998). *From text to hypertext: Decentering the subject in fiction, film, the visual arts, and electronic media*. Philadelphia: University of Pennsylvania.

Gee, J. P. (1989a). Literacy, discourse, and linguistics. *Journal of Education, 71*(1), 5-17.

Gee, J. P. (1989b). What is literacy? *Journal of Education, 71*(1), 18-25.

Harrington, H. L., & Garrison, J. W. (1992). Cases as shared inquiry: A dialogical model of teacher preparation. *American Educational Research Journal, 20*(4), 715-735.

Howe, K. R., & Berv, J. (2000). Constructing constructivism, epistemological and pedagogical. In D. C. Phillips (Ed.), *Constructivism in education: Opinions and second opinions on controversial issues* (pp. 19-40). Chicago: University of Chicago Press.

Interstate New Teacher Assessment and Support Consortium. (1992). *Model standards for beginning teachers: A resource for state dialogue.* Washington, DC: INTASC

Johnson, S. (1997). *Interface culture: How new technology transforms the way we create and communicate.* San Francisco, CA: Basic Books.

Kagan, D. M. (1993). Contexts for the use of classroom cases. *American Educational Research Journal, 30*(4), 703-723.

Korthagen, F. A. J., & Kessels, J. P. A. (1999). Linking theory and practice: Changing the pedagogy of teacher education. *Educational Researcher, 28*(4), 4-17.

Lampert, M. (1999). Knowing teaching from the inside out: Implications of inquiry in practice for teacher education. In G. A. Griffin & M. Early (Ed.), *The education of teachers: The ninety-eighth yearbook of the national society for the study of education* (Part I, pp. 167-84). Chicago: University of Chicago Press.

Langer, J. A. (1992). Rethinking literature instruction. In J. A. Langer (Ed.), *Literature instruction: A focus on student response* (pp. 35-53). Urbana, IL: National Council of Teachers of English.

Lave, J. (1988). *Cognition in practice: Mind, mathematics and culture in everyday life.* Cambridge: Cambridge University Press.

Lave, J., & Wenger, E. (1991). *Situated cognition: Legitimate peripheral participation.* New York: Cambridge University Press.

Merseth, K. K. (1991). The early history of case-based instruction: Insights for teacher education today. *Journal of Teacher Education, 42*(4), 243-249.

Murray, J. (1997). *Hamlet on the holodeck: The future of narrative in cyberspace.* Cambridge, MA: MIT Press.

National Board for Professional Teaching Standards. (1991). *Toward high and rigorous standards for the teaching profession: Initial policies and perspectives of the National Board for Professional Teaching Standards.* Detroit, MI: NBPTS.

New Mexico Teacher Learning Community. (2000). *Circles of support: Teaching and learning in multicultural settings.* Albuquerque, NM: Mediadesigns.

Pence, L. (1996). *Theoretical orientation as a way of reading performance assessment teachers.* Ann Arbor, MI: UMI Dissertation Services.

Richardson, V. (1999). Teacher education and the construction of meaning. In G. A. Griffin & M. Early (Eds.), *The education of teachers: The ninety-eighth yearbook of the national society for the study of education* (Part I, pp. 145-66). Chicago: University of Chicago Press.

Ricoeur, P. (1991). What is a text? Explanation and understanding. In M. J. Valdéz (Ed.), *A Ricoeur reader: Reflection and imagination* (pp. 43-85). Toronto: University of Toronto Press.

Rosenblatt, L. (1978). *The reader, the text, and the poem.* Carbondale: Southern Illinois University Press.

Rosenblatt, L. (1991). Literary theory. In J. Flood, J. M. Jensen, J. M. Lapp, & J. R. Squire (Eds.), *Handbook of research on teaching the English language arts* (pp. 57-62). New York: Macmillan.

Schön, D. (1985). *The design studio: An exploration of its traditions and potentials.* London: RIBA Publications.

Shulman, L. S. (1986). Those who understand: Knowledge and growth in teaching. *Educational Researcher, 15*(2), 4-14.

Tatto, M. T. (1996). Examining values and beliefs about teaching diverse students: Understanding the challenges for teacher education. *Educational Evaluation and Policy Analysis, 18*(2), 155-180.

Wenger, E. (1990). *Toward a theory of cultural transparency: Elements of a social discourse of the visible and the invisible*. Palo Alto, CA: Institute for Research on Learning.

IV

LITERACY AND OTHER SENSES/CAPACITIES

14

ABC'S AND *AMAZING GRACE*

To Literacy Through Music for College Freshmen

Katherine K. Sohn
Pikeville College

> *When I was a little girl, my Papaw Reed used to sit me in his lap and read music to me. He was a bass singer and sang to me quite often. He often tried to teach me how to read music, and I still can today. I can remember his sitting in his favorite green chair reading the Bible before he would go to bed. Sometimes he and I would sneak off to go down the road, and he would make me write Mamaw a note to tell her where we had gone.*
>
> —*Laurie*

Laurie's literacy narrative recounts this warm encounter with her grandfather whom she credited with teaching her music and hence text. Laurie is one of many freshmen I teach from mostly working-class backgrounds who reside within a 100-mile radius of Pikeville College in eastern Kentucky, in the heart of the coal mining area of central Appalachia.

Having lived in the region since 1975, I have grown to love my adopted home. I bristle with anger at the ridicule my neighbors endure from ignorant people outside the area who caricature and demean them for the way they act and speak, despite the fact that linguists affirm every language system legitimate and rule-governed (Labov, 1972; Trudgill, 1975).

Although they are 98% White, they are often as marginalized as people of color by attitudes that picture them living on the draw (welfare), barefooted, dressed in bib overalls, sipping on a jug of homemade moonshine. Because my students are an "invisible minority" (Obermiller, 1999), academics and others tend to stigmatize them, alienating them further from education.

Among positive central Appalachian values reflected in narratives like Laurie's is a strong family orientation. Families live close to one another up and down hollows, socialize with each other on Sundays and holidays, call or visit throughout the week, and assist one another during family catastrophes. Family members who move away to get jobs in Detroit, Cincinnati, or Columbus, come home regularly and at death are buried in the family burial plot.

This attachment to family bodes well for learning. My students grow up close to their grandparents; some were even raised by them. As their literacy narratives reported, many students spent hours with them singing or playing music either at home or in church. Additionally, some parents and grandparents wrote music, an activity that reinforced literacy for themselves as well as their children. One such student, Jane, talked about her grandfather's legacy to her:

> My grandfather wrote lyrics to songs and set them to music. He could play many instruments including the guitar, banjo, mandolin, and harmonica. He wrote his songs and music down on paper. He made the little worn pockets in his guitar case his portfolio. My grandfather wrote a last will and testament in which he left his instruments to my mother and me. I now possess these compositions which are very dear to me.

This powerful connection of generational teachers by what many would consider barely literate people is a lesson for composition teachers. We have to rid ourselves of prejudice against any literacy that does not emerge from the classroom.

DEFINITIONS

Local literacy theorists (Barton & Hamilton, 1998; Brandt, 1995; Heath, 1983; among others) expand the traditional definition of literacy as academic reading and writing to include cultural practice, craft, expression of religious and moral beliefs, critical reflection and thought, or any symbols that make sense of a person's world. Literacy has social contexts—it is "embedded in practices, beliefs, and values of the culture, so it is always ideological" (Daniell, 1999, p. 398).

Literacy can occur in something as insignificant as a grocery list: Witte (1992) observed how knowledge of menus, of preparation, of the list itself, and of the items in the grocery store contribute to the literacy act. Merrifield, Bingman, Hemphill, and de Marrais (1997) look at local literacy among six Appalachians (and Californians) recommended by social service agencies to see how they manage their lives, especially reading and writing. The authors found that these participants managed reading texts quite well—those who could not read relied on family and friends, memorized things, or took educated guesses. These are the families that my students write about in their literacy narratives.

Purves (1990) and Witte would say that students use music as part of the textual environment that helps them make sense of their world, an ordered set of signs from which they construct meaning. Music is a strong symbol of cultural identity, a way of being connected to a group and separate from others who don't like the same kind of music.

THE ASSIGNMENT: LITERACY NARRATIVES

I came upon the importance of music in students' lives without intending to. In the fall of 1996, I had assigned literacy narratives based on my positive experience with them in my first doctoral class. Knowing I would complete graduate work the following summer, I secured permissions and brought the narratives with me to use in my graduate classes. Reading them the first time was instructive; reading them to do a content analysis was like finding hidden jewels. In addition to Laurie, several other students' literacy histories revealed additional examples of language acquisition facilitated by music. It appears that musical activity with their parents and grandparents supported their literacy development in ways that life without music would not have. Ironically, the original list of questions (see appendix) that was compiled from graduate school lists and Atwell's (1987) reading survey contained no question about music.

Because of my discovery of music's impact, I have added questions to that first assignment related to other forms of literacy including music, art, and mathematics. Instead of a polished essay gleaned from informal notes, I now have them answer questions in journal format that encourages more exploration of issues posed by the questions. At the end of the semester, they do a presentation to the class on some aspect of their literacy that opens up a discussion of literacy's implications in their lives.

These presentations and the journals add to my knowledge about the literacy students bring to the classroom. Hearing about music as part of their multiple literacies opens my mind to their potential and offers a bridge to integrate academic literacy into the configuration (Heath, 1983; Scollon & Scollon, 1981; Scribner & Cole, 1981).

MUSIC AND LANGUAGE: SIMILARITIES AND DIFFERENCES

Because I was curious to observe if any sources beyond my students recognized the connection between music and language, I decided to examine the literature. In psycholinguistics, I came across Jackendoff (1994) who believes that language and music are deeply tied together in our cognitive systems. Just as we have an innate sense of language, Jackendoff believes we also have an innate ability from birth to recognize music without any kind of specific music training, a concept that he called *musical grammar.* This musical grammar lets us know "what counts as order in music, what features of it should be attended to, what makes melodies similar and different, what properly makes a tune end, and so forth" (Serafine, 1988, p. 5). Because some music has words or language, we combine two innate features of our brain.

If Jackendoff's belief is true, then music must be universal. Aitchison (1996), Gardner (1993), and Serafine among others point to its presence among all cultures and its existence for as long as language has existed. Musical instruments dating to the Stone Age have been found. Dowling and Harwood (1986) find among the early tribesmen that singing and music helped to keep a group cohesive and served as a symbol of cultural identity, a concept that continues to this day.

My research also led me to observe that music and language are not the same. Unlike language, music is not necessary for human survival; its main value is aesthetic, the survival of the human spirit. Although music communicates, it conveys meaning in symbols rather than words. It has underdeveloped semantics and incomplete grammaticality; it cannot ask questions and receive answers (Gardner, 1993; Jackendoff, 1994). Persons encounter language mainly through listening; they can encounter music through many other ways: singing, playing instruments, reading music, listening to records, or watching dances (Gardner, 1993). Knowing these differences, I avoid the pitfalls of grouping them together unthinkingly.

MUSIC AND LANGUAGE: DEVELOPMENT

Thinking about how music aided my students in learning literacy, I wondered how music and language paralleled one another during the preschool years. (See Table 14.1 for those parallels.) Parental talk, my students' first music, and language takes place in both categories. Pinker (1994) referred to this talk as "Motherese, the interpretable melodies: a rise and fall contour for approving, a set of sharp, staccato bursts for prohibiting, a rise pattern for directing attention and smooth, low legato murmurs for comforting" (p. 279). Children develop music ability beginning with babbling, and 2-month-olds can follow pitch, loudness, and melodic contour of their mother's songs (Gardner, 1993). Four-month-olds turn their heads to the human voice and match their parents' songs. Authorities claim "that infants are especially predisposed to pick up these aspects of music—far more than they are sensitive to the core properties of speech" (Gardner, 1993, p. 109).

From 6 months to a year, infants vocalize to themselves and imitate what they hear around them, utterances that include rhythm, accent, and pitch (Zimmerman, 1984). They make noises to go with the music, something that mimics some of the rudimentary characteristics of singing (Jalongo & Stamp, 1997). At this point, their babbling contains all the sounds of human speech (Baron, 1992). After 1, children continue to play with words, but they also begin to produce recognizable songs (Dowling & Hardwood, 1980) as they begin to understand more words (Baron, 1992).

Two-year-olds, using their increasing vocabulary of more than 50 words (Baron, 1992), sing spontaneously, repeating words over and over, using adult features of pitch and rhythm in a systematic form (Dowling & Harwood, 1986).

From 2- to 4-years-old, children's music ability parallels their "progress in learning stories [where they] focus on an isolated incident" (Dowling & Harwood, p. 148). As they age, they add more components to stories as they do to their songs. Three-year-olds are able to sing elaborate songs like the "Alphabet Song" correctly, although their pitch may be wandering. My student, Sally, illustrates this principle:

> It [her learning to read and write] started with the A-B-C song when I was three years old. My mom and I always sung songs around the house and especially in the car on road trips. She began teaching me my ABCs when I was about 3 years old and then taught me to put them in a song. I thought it was the coolest song ever. When I finally learned the whole song, I almost drove my family crazy with A,B,C,D,E,F,G, etc.

Table 14.1. Music and Language: Development

Age	Music	Language
Infants:		
From birth	"Motherese"	"Motherese"
2-3 months	Matches pitch and melody of parent's song	Smiles when talked to; cooing
4-5 months	Matches rhythmic structure of parents' songs	Turns head in response to human voice; makes vowel and consonant sounds while cooing
6-8 months	Vocalizes what they hear; gibberish	Changes cooing to babbling that contains all sounds of human speech; repeats syllables
12 months	Produces recognizable songs	Understands a few words; may say a few
Toddlers:		
18-30 months	Sings spontaneously; repeats words over and over; uses adult features of pitch and rhythm	Goes from vocabulary of 50 to several hundred words; moves from two-word to three- to five-word phrases
Pre-school—Primary		
36 months	Able to sing elaborate songs like "ABCs" with wandering pitch; makes up spontaneous songs	Increases words to about 1000
48 months	Knows musical scale	Establishes basic aspects of language
5 years	Knows nursery rhymes; maintains stable key throughout; invents recognizable songs	Elaborates basic aspects of language
6 years	Is at musical peak without further training; singing voice does not improve	Has vocabulary of 14,000; learns new words daily
6-12 years	With training, music and singing skills increase	Continues to develop speech until it's complete

Sources: Pinker (1994); Gardner (1993); Zimmerman (1984); Baron (1992); Jalongo and Stamp (1997) Dowling and Harwood (1986); Davidson (1984).

In addition to these familiar tunes, 3-year-olds make up spontaneous songs as they play. They now have a vocabulary of about 1,000 words (Baron, 1992).

Marty, another student, writes about how music helped her learn to recognize words at this same age:

> I learned how to read from my mamaw [grandmother], who was really my aunt, when I was around two or three. When she sang from her hymn books and followed the words with her finger, I would follow along too, and soon I knew what she was saying and could recognize the words if I saw them in other places.

Child psychologists believe that the most basic aspects of language are developed in children at the age of 4. Advancing their abilities, they know musical scales (Dowling & Harwood, 1986). At 5, children know many nursery rhymes and maintain a stable key throughout. They recognize the symbolic nature of musical stairsteps and invent more recognizable songs. They like to repeat songs over and over until they know them (Jalongo & Stamp, 1997). At 6 and 7, children are at their musical peak, and unless they choose to take music lessons, many stabilize at this point (Davidson, 1984; Dowling & Harwood; Dowling, 1982; Gardner, 1993). In fact, "the singing voices of most adults are not developed much beyond the singing abilities acquired by age six or seven unless they receive voice training" (Scott, cited in Jalongo & Stamp, 1997, p. 78).

Linguistically, 6-year-olds have an extensive 14,000 words in their vocabulary and are learning new words daily. From 6 to 12, they continue to develop speech until it is complete (Baron, 1992). So, although music development seems to stop at age 6 or 7 unless children have further training, language development continues until puberty.

MUSIC AND LANGUAGE: IMPLICATIONS

> My grandfather played an instrumental role in my learning to read. There are several pictures of me wearing huge stereo headphones before I was even old enough to sit up by myself. Even at this early age, I was enjoying classical music. One of my grandfather's favorite compositions is *The Creation* by Franz Joseph Hayden. It is an opera about the Bible's account of the creation of man. The words were originally written in German. But the English translation was printed alongside the German words on the inside of the album's dust cover. So together, we would sit in the floor, listen to the record in sections, read the German lyrics for that section, and then read the English translation.

Mark's story, my favorite among my students, suggests to us again a relationship of music to literacy. Imagine Mark sitting patiently with his grandfather and looking from the German to the English lyrics. Activities like this supplemented print literacy—I read in these literacy narratives countless tales of being read to from children's books but especially the Bible. Music at home was reinforced with music in the church, where children might observe their elders "lining out a song" or "singing the preacher down," much like the "raised hymns" of the Trackton churches in Heath.

Before I read the literacy narratives, I had assumed from my students' poorly written and inadequately organized essays that literacy had not been modeled at home or reinforced in elementary and secondary schools. These literacy narratives challenged my biases by revealing a rich preschool literacy, so I began to wonder what happened to my students between that special time and their freshman year in college. One solution to what might happen in the intervening years is proposed by Fox (1992). He believes that the playful settings that encouraged students' music and its connection with language disappear as the students grow up. As they progress through their schooling, they begin connecting literacy skills to achieving success, so literacy as "play and adventure" becomes literacy as a "chore" (p. 6). Developmentally, children move from play and adventure to more concrete stages. Then later, in the teen years, reading and writing may not be valued by their peers or teens may not have time, so students may lose interest.

Another plausible explanation for students' losing the joy in early learning could be the denigration of students' home language in the classroom. After years of being told that they do not speak correctly, students may lose confidence. Though they are exposed both to standard and nonstandard language throughout their lives, they have teachers who devalue their speech though we know that linguistically all languages are equal.

> When I was in the second grade, my teacher tried to help me to say my words "correctly." She was from the north and lived in a big city, so I thought that her language was the one that needed fixing. I learned the proper way of saying things and felt that I was really smart. I could talk just like my teacher. My grandmother never heard this type of talk, and it was all new to her. When my grandmother heard me say "school," she just about killed me. Of course she said, "So you are tryin' to out grow your britches!" I was playing tug of war with my vocal chords. At school I had to talk like a "city-slicker" (as Granny called me), then at home I had to talk like a "hillbilly" (as my teacher called me). (Tom)

Tom echoes on a local level the dilemma of working-class authors Jennings (1998), Roskelly (1993), and Lynch (1994) who wrote about the mixed identity that comes from being educated and returning to the family. Tom was a "city slicker" to his grandmother who was one of his first teachers, and a "hillbilly" to his teacher. His grandmother's observation that he was growing out of his britches was similar to the other saying I have heard from my students: getting above your raisings. Surely these mixed messages reinforce stereotypes perpetuated from inside and outside. This prejudice against language is as insidious as that based on race and gender.

In addition to working-class students being put down for their language, they are demeaned for class differences. Lucy, one of the case study participants in my dissertation said:

> I was from a low-income family, and they [the teachers] had to teach me. And that's basically the only relationship I had with them. . . . Everyday that I came to school, she [the teacher] would have something to say about my clothing. Everyday. I was in sixth grade. And every time I came to school, she might say, "Well, it looks like Lucy left her skirt at home and wore her shirt." So one day I told her, "Well, if you want me to wear it, buy it for me."

Particularly in Appalachia the promise of literacy has been the promise of spiritual and economic uplifting. Realistically, we know that literacy alone cannot erase poverty. Many working-class people do not see the relevance of education for their families because those promises are usually reserved for the middle and upper class and their children. As literacy professionals, we can welcome these students to our classroom, affirm their voices, offer a way for them to end their silence, and hopefully give them the tools for success in college.

MUSIC AND LANGUAGE: PEDAGOGY

My students have illustrated how music fit into the scenario of their early literacy learning. In elementary school, music assisted teachers in passing along information in a palatable and memorable way. Chants like the ABC song "give a structure for language development. . . . When language and melody are united, the children's creation can be more easily recalled because of the melody" (Conner & McCarthy, 1989). Danny, one of my students, confirmed the connection in his literacy journal:

> I had one inspirational teacher in the second grade that integrated music with our reading and writing. This gave us all an incentive to learn and master what we knew existed in the English language system.

Most musical activities in the classroom cease after elementary school unless students enroll in band or music education or take private lessons. Although students may enjoy listening to their own music at home, they rarely hear it in academic settings. Research confirms that music abilities do not grow after first grade without training. However, listening to music does not stop—in fact it permeates our daily lives.

Perhaps one way to keep music in the curriculum beyond early elementary school is to integrate it as an art form for every subsequent year of school. Music offers students a vehicle to communicate beyond the spoken or written word and aids in developing personal discipline, and social skills, while it "demands that students learn to read, write, and interpret complex symbols" (Koebler, 1992, p. 95).

Knowing that music can assist language learning, many college instructors have introduced music to achieve other pedagogical purposes. In a unit on poetry, students may bring in their favorite song lyrics to read, discuss, and provide models for writing their own poems (Barnett, interview, 1998). To stimulate discussion with his African-American students, Brown (1995) has them bring rap lyrics to class. They take a position on Gangsta' Rap and then write their own rap lyrics, bridging the gap between home and school.

Music might also be used to elicit ideas for writing topics during free-writing. Relaxing as they listen to emotive music, writers can release thoughts they never thought were there to generate story ideas to write about.

None of these activities depends on the musical abilities of students because any one can respond to music. Integrating music into writing classes stimulates students' imaginations, stretching "their minds beyond the literal and rule-governed," and the preventing "the death of imagination . . . provid[ing] expressive, meaningful learning experiences" (Koebler, 1992, pp. 97-98). Acknowledging that music is part of students' and their own lives, that it stimulates and communicates thought, teachers can restore music to the classroom with the hope that students will "reconnect literacy and intimacy, language and play, words and joy" (Fox, 1992, p. 7) to come full circle from preschool to college, from ABCs to *Amazing Grace*.

ACKNOWLEDGMENT

Gratitude goes to my English composition classes for use of their autobiographies in this chapter.

APPENDIX: READING AND WRITING AUTOBIOGRAPHY HANDOUT

Writing Prompts Fall/Spring 1996-7

Examining your reading and writing history will enable you and me to see how reading and writing are defined, learned, and practiced. I think you will be amazed and surprised at your discoveries.

Below are listed some questions, separated into the two categories. You are to use these to reflect on in journal or rough draft entries; sometimes we will do these in class. Then on the designated day in your course outline, you will be expected to come to class with a rough draft of the total document to read to your group; the final draft will be due the following week.

While there is a tendency to write down answers one by one, I ask you to organize your essay by perhaps focusing on the answers to a few questions; as you reflect on the answers, a pattern may emerge that could be the crux of your essay. If you are unsure about how to organize it, ask people in your group; then let me look at your responses if you're still puzzled.

WRITING QUESTIONS

1. What education do your parents and grandparents have?
2. What sort of writing did/do they use? Think of recipes, grocery lists, notes to teachers, letters to the editor of paper, letters to relatives, absolutely any kind of writing.
3. Did/Does your church use writing? Think of bulletins, notices, newsletters, grants.
4. Did/Do you write letters to relatives who live away from here, friends at other colleges?
5. Did/Do you write notes in classes and pass them; do you write love notes to loved ones?
6. What kind of in-class writing did you do in elementary and high school? If you did portfolios in any subject, describe that experience in detail.
7. Have you ever had anything published?
8. Did you ever work on a school newspaper or annual?
9. Who are the significant people who influenced your writing (either good or bad)?
10. Can you list failures and successes as a writer?
11. Why in general do people write?

12. Imagine a world where people didn't write.
13. Describe a good writer/good writing.

READING QUESTIONS

1. Were your parents/grandparents readers (signs, directions, lists, racing forms, recipes, newspapers, astrology signs, magazines)?
2. What is attitude toward reading in your house? (waste of time, good use of time)
3. Did your parents read to you? If so, what were your favorite books?
4. How did you learn to read? (Sesame Street, school, parents, others)
5. What are your attitudes toward reading? Do you like/dislike it? Are you good/average/bad at it? What are strengths/weaknesses as a reader?
6. If you could guess, how many books would you say you owned? Magazines? Newspapers?
7. How many books have you read in the last 12 months?
8. Why do you/other people read?
9. In elementary and secondary school, how much reading did you do?
10. What kind of books do you like to read? Your favorite authors?
11. What people played a significant role in your reading development?
12. Imagine a world without reading.
13. Describe a good reader.
14. How do you use reading in your daily life?

REFERENCES

Aitchison, J. (1996). *The seeds of speech: Language origin and evolution.* Cambridge: Cambridge University Press.

Atwell, N. (1987). *In the middle: Writing and learning with adolescents.* Upper Montclair, NJ: Boynton/Cook.

Baron, R. A. (1992). *Psychology.* Boston: Allyn & Bacon.

Barton, D., & Hamilton, M. (1998). *Local literacies: Reading and writing in one community.* New York: Routledge.

Brandt, D. (1995). Accumulating literacy: Writing and learning to write in the twentieth century. *College English, 57*(6), 649-668.

Brown, S. (1995, March). *Unwrapping rap: A literacy of lived experience.* Paper presented at the 46th annual College Composition and Communication

Conference, Washington, DC. (ERIC Document Reproduction Service No. ED 384 907)

Conner, J., & McCarthy, W.G. (Ed.), (1989). Music and language: Partners in communication. In W. G. McCarthy (Ed.), *Whole language learning for elementary school teachers, children, and parents.* Terre Haute, IN: Curriculum Research and Development Center. (ERIC Document Reproduction Service No. ED 320 103)

Daniell, B. (1999). Narratives of literacy: Connecting composition to culture. *College Composition and Communication, 50*(3), 393-410.

Davidson, L. (1984). Preschool children's tonal knowledge: Antecedents of scale. In J. Boswell (Ed.), *The young children and music: Contemporary principles in child development and music education.* Proceedings of the Music in Early Childhood Conference. (ERIC Document Reproduction Service No. ED 265 949)

Dowling, W. J. (1982). Melodic information processing and its development. In Deutsch (Ed.), *The psychology of music* (pp. 413-429). New York: Academic Press.

Dowling, W. J., & Harwood, D. L. (1986). *Music cognition.* Orlando, FL: Academic Press.

Fox, S. (1992). *Memories of play, dreams of success: Literacy autobiographies of 101 students.* (ERIC Document Reproduction Service No. ED 348 681)

Gardner, H. (1993). *Frames of mind: The theory of multiple intelligences.* New York: HarperCollins.

Heath, S. B. (1983). *Way with words.* Cambridge: Cambridge University Press.

Jackendoff, R. (1994). *Patterns in the mind: Language and human nature.* New York: Basic Books.

Jalongo, M. R., & L. N. Stamp. (1997). *The arts in children's lives: Aesthetic education in early childhood.* Boston: Allyn & Bacon.

Jennings, K. (1998). White like me: A confession on race, religion, and class. *Appalachian Journal,* 150-174.

Koebler, K. A. (1992). Story and song: Integrating music into the literature curriculum. In N. D. Padak et al. (Eds.), *Literacy research and practice: Foundations for the year 2000.* College Reading Association.

Labov, W. (1972). The logic of non-standard English. In *Language in the inner city.* Philadelphia: University of Pennsylvania Press.

Lynch, C. E. (1994). Breaking the Kentucky cycle: A native's struggle with language and identity. *The Central Quarterly, 32*(4), 141-148.

Merrifield, J., Bingman, M. B., Hemphill, D., & deMarrais, K. (1997). *Life at the margins: Literacy, language, and technology in everyday life.* New York: Teachers College Press.

Obermiller, P. (1999). Paving the way. In D. Billings, G. Norman, & K. Ledford (Eds.), *Confronting Appalachian stereotypes* (pp. 251-266). Lexington: University Press of Kentucky.

Pinker, S. (1994). *The language instinct: How the mind creates language.* New York: HarperCollins.

Purves, A. (1990). *The scribal society: An essay on literacy and schooling in the information age*. White Plains, NY: Longman.

Roskelly, H. (1993). Telling tales in school: A redneck daughter in the academy. In M. M. Tokarczyk & E. A. Fay (Eds.), *Working-class women in the academy: Laborers in the knowledge factory* (pp. 292-307). Amherst: University of Massachussetts Press.

Scollon, R., & Scollon, S.W. (1981). *Narrative, literacy, and face in interethnic communication*. Norwood, NJ: Ablex.

Trudgill, P. (1975). *Accent, dialect, and the school*. London: Edward Arnold.

Scribner, S., & Cole, M. (1981). *The psychology of literacy*. Cambridge, MA: Harvard University Press.

Serafine, M. L. (1988). *Music as cognition: The development of thought in sound*. New York: Columbia University Press.

Witte, S. P. (1992). Context, text, intertext: Toward a constructivist semiotic of writing. *Written Communication*, 9(2), 237-308.

Zimmerman, M. (1984). State of the art in early childhood music and research. In J. Boswell (Ed.), *The young children and music: Contemporary principles in child development and music education*. Proceedings of the Music in Early Childhood Conference. (ERIC Document Reproduction Service No. ED 265 949)

15

EMOTIONAL HEGEMONY, CITIZENSHIP, AND POPULAR LITERACIES IN COMPOSITION 1955–1965

Lisa Langstraat
University of Southern Mississippi

> *Given its definition as nature, at least in the West, emotion discourses may be one of the most likely and powerful devices by which domination proceeds. Talk about emotion, is talk about power and its exercise.*
> —Lutz (1988, p. 78)

> *By rethinking the absence of emotion, how emotion shapes how we treat other people and informs our moral assumptions and judgements, I believe we have the potential to radically change our cultural values and violent practices of cruelty and injustice, which are often rooted in unspoken "emotional" investments and unexamined ideological beliefs. In short, what is the effect of affect in the classroom?*
> —Boler (1999, p. xvii)

Because literacy practices are saturated with affective and emotional features,[1] it is baffling that so few compositionists have made explicit attempts to wrangle with and respond to the question, "What is the effect of affect in the classroom?" As Brand (1994) and McLeod (1991) suggested, with the exception of studies in writing apprehension (which too often delimit emotional states as mere interruptions to writing processes), there has been a paucity of research on affect and emotions in composition theory. The emotional realm instead often circulates as a cherished but not rigorously explored version of lore, encased in claims that "the affective usually controls the cognitive, and affective responses have to be dealt with first" (Murray, 1982, p. 53), or suggestions that our students have different "affective styles" of communication which dramatically influence their collaborative efforts (Bleich, 1995). More recently, however, several compositionists have begun the difficult work of articulating the ways in which affective relationships, as sites of power, social control, and transformation, influence literacy learning. For example, in "Dispositions Toward Language: Teacher Constructs of Knowledge and the Ann Arbor Black English Case" Ball and Lardner (1997) suggested that theorizing the emotional tone of classroom interactions is central for creating an anti-racist pedagogy. "By making affect a central issue in theorizing pedagogy," Ball and Lardner contended, teachers can understand the "largely unspoken dimensions of pedagogical experience when, let's say, white teachers in university writing courses attempt to mediate the discourse practices of African American English speaking students" (p. 478). Similarly, Worsham (1993), in "Emotion and Pedagogic Violence" insisted that one of the primary functions of education is

> to organize an emotional world—a world that can be characterized by a distinctive and pervasive mood—and to inculcate patterns of feeling and appreciation appropriate to, for example, gender, race, and class locations, patterns that support the legitimacy of dominant interests. (p. 126)

Dominant pedagogy, Worsham maintained, achieves this effect through colonizing affective identifications; thus, educators must work toward an "affective decolonization" which would not only serve to "reconstitute the emotional life of the individual, but also . . . to restructure the feeling or mood that characterizes an age" (p. 122). This nascent research on affect is particularly important as it emphasizes the sociocultural influences that shape affective identifications. Resisting the impulse to naturalize emotions as those biologically hard-wired, cross-cultural features of human experience is no easy task. But it is vital to historicize affect, to denaturalize the emotional experiences that contour literacy teaching and learning, thereby rethinking the epistemic potential of emotions and their role in our composing theories and pedagogies.

In this chapter I join the efforts of those compositionists who work toward historicizing and theorizing the affective realm in composition studies. My exploration of affect, however, does not focus on developing a classification of specific emotions or affective states, nor do I inquire into the role of emotional variations during writing processes.[2] I am less interested in "the way the mind works"—whether cognition precedes emotion or emotion precedes cognition, for example (see Brand, 1994)—than in how emotion work is configured in relation to the social/educational goals of composition. I discuss emotion culture historically by first presenting the concept of emotional hegemony as a framework through which we can deepen our understanding of the role of affect in composition studies. I then discuss the cultural shifts that led to an American emotional style of cool constraint, an affective stance firmly entrenched by the 1950s, an affective stance that remains in play today. Following that discussion, I examine two reports: NCTE's (1961) *The National Interest and the Teaching of English* and the College Entrance Examination Board's (1965) *Freedom and Discipline in English*. These documents, as reflections of "official" positions on U.S. literacy instruction, illustrate the ways in which a dominant emotional style influenced conceptions of literacy in the period, particularly in light of the intersections of democratic citizenship and popular literacies. Finally, I argue that the hegemonic practices evident in these documents continue to influence contemporary compositionists in significant ways.

THROUGH THE LENS OF EMOTIONAL HEGEMONY

I borrow the term *emotional hegemony* from Jaggar (1992) who used it to describe the processes through which dominant groups struggle to regulate the epistemic potential of emotions, thereby determining which emotional states are valued and can contribute to knowledge-making, and which are othered and mistrusted, in particular contexts. Like any form of hegemony, emotional hegemony is effective insofar as it wins our consent by naturalizing that which is saturated with ideology and power relations. And little is more naturalized in our culture than the emotional realm, which has historically been reduced to the "non-theorizable dimensions of human experience" or considered "synonymous with the 'other side' of culture, order, or the social" (Mercer, 1983, p. 87). Understanding emotional hegemony requires understanding emotions as culturally and socially shaped. As cultural psychologists Kitayama and Marcus (1994) suggested, our emotional constitutions, although certainly afforded by a number of biologically hardwired cognitive processes, are primarily shaped by cultural influences; we learn socially sanctioned "emotion scripts" that develop as "individuals actively, personally, and collectively adapt and adjust to their immediate sociocultural, semiotic environment" (p. 5). Emotion scripts in composition studies, like those in any area of human interaction, engender forms of hegemony that preserve dominant class- and gender-based values, particularly those inherent in conceptions of "citizenship."

Consider, for example, Boler's (1999) claim that the "subterranean disciplining of emotions" was a central aim in all Progressive Movement education policies at the turn of the century (p. 30). Citing the crusade-like policies of the National Committee for Mental-Hygiene (established in 1909), Boler argued that the movement's emphasis on individual pathologies as the root of all social conflicts served to mask the anxiety induced by the vast increase of immigrant populations. The committee conflated moral and physical traits and attempted to "adjust" youth through the techniques of mental hygiene which, through labyrinth structures of shame, demonized difference as the central threat to democracy. Boler's interpretation of the movement's attempts to school emotions corresponds to Miller's (1991) discussion of the shifts in composition policies at the turn of the century. Although Miller only implicitly referred to the emotional hegemony of the mental hygiene movement, she correlated the obsessive emphasis on mechanical and vernacular appropriateness with the 19th century "project of cleanliness" that instituted a pervasive fear of "contamination from the pointedly unwashed masses" (p. 57). The mental hygiene movement thus enforced a form of emotional hegemony that defined democracy and citizenship in light of particular emotional constitutions—those reflecting Anglo-Protestant values of middle-class meritocracy, contained self-expression, and "cleanliness." Although this brief example of the mental hygiene movement is certainly not intended to mark the beginning—or the end—of strategies for schooling emotions, it does illustrate the ways emotional hegemony links the values of dominant cultural institutions to the writing pedagogies serving those institutions.

Processes of emotional hegemony bear on every aspect of our pedagogies and theories—from how we construct our authority in our interactions with students to the very conception of what constitutes "good writing." Therefore, unearthing emotional hegemony is absolutely vital when we consider that one of the central, although often unspoken, goals of all theoretical and pedagogical endeavors is a (re)education of what Grossberg (1992) called "affective alliances"—the affective identifications through which individuals authorize particular ideological formations to have meaning in their lives. Struggling within and against emotional hegemony in our teaching and writing practices is not a question of overcoming cultural emotion scripts to get at an authentic emotional attunement that guides our thoughts and actions. Instead, "denaturalizing" the overly naturalized realm of emotions requires historicizing structures of feeling in relation to the power formations which shape them.

FROM PASSIONATE TO COOL: THE GROWTH OF AN AMERICAN EMOTIONAL STYLE

The mid-1950s was an important period in the redefinition of acceptable emotional styles in U.S. work, family, and school relations. In *American Cool: Constructing a Twentieth-Century Emotional Style*, P. Stearns (1994) chronicled the shift from the Victorian celebration of intense emotion to a 1950s "cool" or constrained emotional style. According to Stearns, Victorians stressed the importance of passion (a word they rarely associated with the sexual realm) as the source of all great deeds in civilized societies. Despite common constructions of Victorian culture as repressed, Stearns' analysis of the etiquette and advice literature of the period illustrates that emotional fervor was not disdained. Instead, Victorians were confident that "dangerous" emotions (such as anger) were integral to social progression, particularly in the areas of politics, business, and religion; the key, of course, was to direct emotional vigor toward a larger good. The "feeling rules"—"the recommended norms by which people are supposed to shape their emotional reactions and react to the expressions of others" (p. 2)—of the late 19th century valued the possibility of experiencing life primarily through intense emotionality. As Pavletich (1998) noted, in Victorian emotion culture "feeling itself became a form of action" (p. 56).[3]

A new mainstream middle class emotional culture, however, emerged from the 1920s onward and was firmly in place by the 1950s. As Stearns (1994) explains, no longer were strong emotions the treasured source of civilization; instead, "emotions became all-or-nothing propositions, a set of impulses that could run a person into the ground" (p. 137). Victorians had expressed confidence that strong emotions could be put to valuable use; by the 1950s, however, most advice literature, particularly as it related to workplace and school, counseled Americans to either avoid situations that might provoke intense emotions or to conceal all evidence of heightened emotionality. As the culture grew suspicious of any intense emotional expression that threatened self-control and reflected antisociability, "American cool," the affective stance of restraint and the containment of emotional expressivity, was born.

Stearns identified several causes for this new emotional style: efforts to homogenize national culture, given the influx of immigrants; new goals for childhood socialization; the standardization of U.S. media; growing distinctions between urban and suburban communities; and shifts in U.S. middle-class identity as divisions between the service-sector population and older entrepreneurial and professional groups became more pronounced. Pavletich (1998) offered additional insight into this shift in emotion culture:

> The retreat to emotional inexpressivity on the part of the dominant classes coincided with two important political movements: serious and potent attempts on the part of middle class women, the working class, and people of color to change the fact of U.S. power dynamics, and the equally serious and potent attempts by the dominant class to homogenize and incorporate U.S. culture. (p. 57)

Pavletich contended that these social changes, firmly in place by the 1950s, particularly influenced White, middle-class male subjectivity: As women and minorities vied for political and economic opportunities, and as corporate economy threatened the autonomy afforded to merchant and small-scale capitalism, "middle class men moved toward an emotion culture that reflected their cultural position: cautious and restrained" (p. 57).

This dominant emotional disposition profoundly influenced philosophies of education: U.S. schools, particularly middle-class schools, embraced a new set of emotional goals as "strong emotion came to be seen as a distraction from, even a deterrent to, educational performance rather than a spur to achievement" (P. Stearns, 1994, p. 255). One of the most significant manifestations of this new emotional style was a massive escalation of average grades from elementary school through postsecondary education. Higher grades, education theorists reasoned, reduced student anxiety and anger, thus providing an affectively neutral learning environment and helping teachers avoid emotional confrontations with students and parents. By the end of the decade, P. Stearns (1994) explained, most middle-class students "seemed not illogically to assume that a friendly personality and controlled emotional behavior largely sufficed to merit good marks" (p. 255). Colleges and universities participated in this new emotional climate by creating dictates against fraternity hazing practices, providing counseling services and student affairs personnel who were responsible for making students feel less emotionally threatened, and developing new course evaluation procedures that encouraged students to comment on the personality attributes of faculty, thus "promoting a sense that traditional aloofness or invocations of fear should be replaced by a more relaxed, at least apparently affable manner" (p. 255).

In this attempt to create an *affectively neutral* educational setting, passionate outbursts of pleasure and passionate expressions of anger were understood as equally damaging. An educational environment free of the distraction of strong emotions, however, merely veiled several of the most pronounced features of 1950s emotional hegemony—features of "American cool" that are sustained in contemporary culture.[4] For example, middle-class emotional style, particularly as it was associated with middle-class masculinity, became the normative emotional style by which other expressions of affect were judged. As Worsham (1993) explained, women, people of color, the working class, and other members of subordinate groups are often considered more emotional and, therefore, less reliable sources of knowledge and power. This perception is, in part, an effect of a second, particularly salient form of emotional hegemony: the privatizing of emotional expression as natural and individually constructed, rather than socially constituted. P. Stearns (1994) noted that by the 1950s, the normative affective style of cool restraint gave rise to "such a significant bias against strong emotional expressions that it was often the emotional individual, not the object of his or her emotion, who was seen as requiring remediation" (p. 230). For example, if a student displayed outrage about standard testing requirements, the cultural and economic sources of that anger were often left unexamined in favor of a privatized explanation—the student's anger could simply be interpreted as an expression of personal inadequacy and a break with the unspoken demands of cool emotional expression.[5]

This affectively "neutral" environment—a cool climate of pleasantries divested of zealous emotional expression—reproduced particular forms of emotional hegemony. When merged with pre-existing social inequities, the demand for a middle-class, masculine form of emotional expression, along with the privatizing of affect, greatly influenced the goals and pedagogies of literacy education. I turn now to two reports, *The National Interest and the Teaching of English* (NCTE, 1961) and *Freedom and Discipline in English* (College Examination Board, 1965), which illustrate how normative American emotional styles were embodied in composition practices from 1955 to 1965.

SCHOOLING EMOTIONS, 1955–1965

Because they represent "official" positions on English studies in the decade of 1955–1965, NCTE's *The National Interest and the Teaching of English: A Report on the Status of the Profession* and The College Examination Board's *Freedom and Discipline in English: Report of the Commission on English* are important to review. Most analyses of the composition practices included in these reports focus on two, interrelated issues: attempts to define the purview of English studies by establishing a "coherent" curriculum, and efforts to counter the increasingly bureaucratic nature of administration at all levels of education through the development of "expressivist" pedagogies that opposed current traditional rhetoric's emphasis on modes of discourse and emphasized the import of students' individual experience and voice in writing practices (see Dolan, 1978; Harris, 1991; Kantor, 1979).[6] In addition to these issues, however, these documents reflect several significant cultural shifts: the redefinition of citizenship, given the Sputnik-inspired national discourse of the era, which competed with the rhetoric of civil rights and other social movements; dramatic developments in and the increased availability of technologies of mass media; the move toward a post-Fordist economy; and a new emphasis on specialization in education and work, an emphasis that contributed to the formation of composition studies as an independent discipline. Each of these issues influence the emotional style of the reports, as well as their recommendations for teachers' perceptions of the appropriate emotion style for English classrooms.

It is important to note that, although *The National Interest* was published in 1961 and *Freedom and Discipline* was published in 1965, I consider these reports the culmination of the affective styles of the decade between 1955 and 1965 because of the government and economic policies that enormously influenced them. In 1954, Congress passed Public Law 531, which set the precedent of federally funded and controlled educational research; by 1958, monies were available through the National Defense Education Act (NDEA) to fund curricular reform projects in an effort to battle Cold War-inspired paranoia about the U.S. education system. Literacy was a key weapon in the defense against communism and the creation of "future citizens of a great democracy" (College Examination Board, 1965, p. viii). English educators, however, received none of the funding granted to science, mathematics, and foreign language in the interest of national defense (Dolan, 1978). When in 1958 the Ford Foundation funded the "Basic Issues" Conference, English teachers involved in NCTE made a concerted effort to tap into the potential of Public Law 531, and the result was the production of *The National Interest.* As Dolan (1978) explained, NCTE distributed *The National Interest* to every Congressman prior to the vote on the 1961 revision of the NDEA, and U.S. Commissioner of Education Sterling McMurrin used *The National Interest* report to convince the Senate that written and oral communication was a matter of national importance. In September 1961, Congress authorized limited funds for the improvement of English instruction. Congress' recognition of the value of English studies in national welfare gave rise to the College Examination Board's report, *Freedom and Discipline.* As Pearson, president of the board, explained, the report was meant to offer "support to the United States Office of Education, and to the educational community generally, in connection with the National Defense Education Act and its recent extension to include English and reading" (cited in Dolan, 1978, p. viii).

Clearly, this history enormously influenced these documents in light of their aims—to legitimize English studies as central to democracy—and their audiences—the Congressmen and other officials who made funding decisions in light of national efforts to battle communism. Faigley (1992) pointed out that "Even at the apex of American confidence during the 1950s and 1960s, there were fears that something had gone terribly wrong, that the dreaded loss of individualism under communism had occurred in the midst of capitalist prosperity" (p. 56). Such fears are certainly suggested in the rather ominous titles of the reports, titles that reflect Cold War rhetoric's penchant to mesh government control with government protection. As *The National Interest* report explained,

> The fate of our democracy now rests on the way we develop our manpower [sic]. And English can, in transmitting the humanistic tradition, help vitalize democracy and, in developing the art and skill of communication, help assure its lasting strength. (p. 30)

Imparting emotional dispositions appropriate for democratic citizenship is a central goal in these reports, saturated as they are with references to the import of emotions in teaching and learning. *The National Interest*, for example, states, "The importance of English—the language and its literature—lies in its hold upon the intellect and the *emotions* of man [*sic*]. The process of becoming articulate and literate are central to man's [*sic*] attainment of full human dignity" (p. 16, italics added). *The Freedom and Discipline* (1965) report echoes this sentiment, arguing that the composition teacher must "recognize what a student is seeking and learn how to make assignments that lead . . . to discoveries of *perception* and *emotion* out of which writing may come" (p. 90, italics added). Moreover, the recommendations for needed research in both reports include specific attention to the affective aspects of language use, illustrated by *The National Interest*'s call for "a study of the *emotional*, psychological, experiential and educational differences between good and poor writers at the high school level" (p. 133, italics added).

That these reports emphasize the role of emotions in literacy learning is hardly surprising. Though often discussed only implicitly, the role of the emotional in defining the purview of composition was—and continues to be—a key issue. The 1966 Dartmouth Seminar, for example, reflected a culmination of concerns about striking the appropriate balance between English curricula that focused on "feelings and responses" and those which concentrated on defining a "concrete subject of study" (Harris, 1991, p. 633). The emotional hegemony evident in *The National Interest* and *Freedom and Discipline* reports is especially significant in light of two, intersecting issues: definitions of appropriate emotional dispositions required for good citizenship in a democracy; and the threat that popular culture posed to democratic education.

"CIVILIZED JOY": AFFECT AND COMPOSING PRACTICES

Borrowing from Whitehead's (1952) *The Aims of Education*, the authors of *Freedom and Discipline* presented "the stage of romantic emotion" as the first step in composition instruction; in this stage the teacher tries to reach students' "inmost interests and real thoughts" by allowing students the freedom to explore their emotional responses and feelings (p. 90). After students have found an outlet for their feelings, they should move to the second stage, "the discipline of form" and the third stage, "the development of style." Such stages of writing—clearly still in vogue in textbooks that begin with personal writing and progress to the presumably more difficult task of argumentative writing—are an effort to school emotions, to ensure that students express romantic emotions then control those emotions through socially sanctioned disciplines of form and style. In this way, the report argues, students come to see composition as a "source of civilized joy and human discipline" (p. 90). The operative phrase here, it seems to me, is *civilized joy*. The assignments that *Freedom and Discipline* promote ultimately channel students' expression of emotions into "civilized" forms in line with appropriate middle-class emotional style. Good writing, both reports suggest, demonstrates feelings only within approved boundaries of affective expression.

In both reports, such affective boundaries are intricately tied to the Arnoldian, humanist tradition in education. For example, identifying various features of a post-Fordist economy—"complex organization, sudden technological changes, the passionate pressure of self-seeking groups, conflicting ideologies, uncertainty about the future, baffling international problems"—as central challenges to democracy, *The National Interest* report asserts that familiarity "with the best that has been known and thought in the past" is the most effective way to equip students for the "increasing complexity of modern life" (p. 17).[7] The *Freedom and Discipline* report echoes this stance. The authors repeatedly discuss the threat of losing sight of tradition and great works: "The humanities most often suffer from having their essence diluted or obscured by what appears to be new" such that "*Macbeth* vies with the writing of thank-you notes for time in the curriculum" (p. 3).

Interesting in these documents is not their emphasis on the Arnoldian tradition of ensuring "intimate contact" with beauty and truth. Such an emphasis is hardly surprising. What I find fascinating is the reports' assumption that such a tradition can impart to students a constant, unchanging emotional disposition. The emotional experience of the good and the beautiful, these reports suggest, is *natural* and, therefore, unaffected by the radically shifting economic and social realities of the period. This perception is consonant with the new emotional style in educational policy, an emotional style that cast any strong affective expression as the exception, rather than the rule, of good teaching practices.

Hence, in their concern with establishing the "correct" emotional constitution necessary for democracy, these reports define the good student as the even-tempered future citizen who, having absorbed the best of literary and rhetorical traditions, *naturally* obtains the superior affective stance of constrained emotional expression. This perception is particularly clear in a rare reference to social upheaval in *The National Interest* report: "Some special pressures have developed to de-emphasize imaginative literature in our classrooms in favor of sociological documentation. We must not starve our students' imagination or intellect in order to fatten their social conscience" (p. 25). Given the social movements prevalent at the time of these documents' publication, it is safe to presume that these "sociological" "special pressures" include civil rights, anti-war, and feminist protests. That the report makes only oblique reference to such important social movements is significant. The distinction drawn between imagination and intellect versus social conscience illustrates a central feature of the emotional hegemony in these documents. Democracy and good citizenship, as *The National Interest* defines them, need not be concerned with "social conscience." By simply acquiring the affective disposition associated with the "higher" emotions of the humanistic literary tradition, democratic principles will emerge. Other affective identifications—rage over social injustice, for instance—are cut out of the picture. The good citizen is the student of the humanist tradition, not the politically aware participant in democratic processes of protest.

The *Freedom and Discipline* report illustrates a similar, unshakable conviction in the unchanging values—and resulting "civilized" affective stance—of the humanist tradition. It does, however, explicitly acknowledge the challenges many English teachers encountered, given the social upheaval so prevalent in the events beyond school doors. The report claims,

> Many among the younger English teachers must now often be disturbed by the inconsistency between the liberalism of their convictions about music, painting and philosophy, and the conservativism and conventionality of the doctrine and taste they may be teaching in English Composition. . . . [I]n our own time the awareness that language operates on a scale of relativity is so widely admitted, in practice even when not in theory, that a teacher of composition must often feel that he [*sic*] has nothing but shifting sands under his [*sic*] feet. (pp. 83-84)

The teacher can firm up the shifting sands, the report contends, by reaffirming the qualities of honesty and morality integral to "conventional" doctrine and taste.

In particular, the report claims, "Like life itself, all writing is concerned with truth"; hence, the bad piece of writing is "*false in feeling*," the result of self-deception (pp. 85-86, italics added). To determine the writers' authenticity of feeling, the report suggests that teachers take the stance of a "*friendly enemy*" who leads the student toward "discoveries of perception and emotion" (p. 90). Like the concept of a "friendly enemy," the report embodies a contradictory position toward the role of emotion in composition: How to mesh the demand for "civilized joy" and "authenticity of feeling" in writing? This contradictory demand for real feeling and cool affective expression is a significant aspect of the emotional hegemony reflected in the report; students should be sincere in their expression of feeling-through-writing, yet that sincere expression should not break the boundaries of socially acceptable (read: civilized) affective presentation.

As the reports conflate democratic citizenship with normative emotional expression, they embody contradictions inherent to emotional hegemonic practices. Perhaps nowhere is the emotional hegemony of these reports more evident than in their discussion of the threat that popular culture posed to the humanist tradition—and the emotional dispositions concomitant with that tradition.

POPULAR CULTURE AND EMOTIONAL APPROPRIATENESS

Because television and other media played an important role in the reproduction of the Cold War ideologies informing the reports' calls for educational reform, and because popular media were ingrained in U.S. leisure activities by 1955,[8] there is no overt rejection of the popular in these documents. Instead, the reports show a predilection to control the popular, to put it in the service of democratic ideals and the emotional dispositions proper to citizenship. The urgency with which these reports address the dangerously persuasive pressures of popular culture reveals the challenge new media presented to humanist conceptions of emotions. That is, many literacy workers, confronted with the rapid development of mass media, assumed that students' capacities to reason were radically curtailed, if not undermined, by the emotionality of popular culture forms.

Both reports share a proclivity to assume that popular culture forms engender a kind of groupthink that undermines U.S. democracy. Taking a rather resigned position on the prevalence and availability of the "both barren and rich" features of popular culture, *The National Interest* report insists that

> Our young people need to be educated in both the dangers and possibilities inherent in the use of these modern media, and inevitably much of this responsibility falls upon the teacher of English, the teacher most concerned about the uses of language and the student's ability to think both critically and imaginatively. (p. 25)

The report makes clear, however, that the dangers of popular culture far exceed its desirable attributes, and the teacher's role is that of comptroller. This perspective is repeated in *Freedom and Discipline*:

> Precisely because the humanities, the study of one's native language and literature among them, are so thoroughly implicated in everyday human activity, they are highly susceptible to immediate and ephemeral influences. The fashion of a time often so overlays them, particularly in their popular forms, that their real nature is all but lost sight of. (p. 3)

Maintaining the "real nature" of language and literature, the *Freedom and Discipline*'s primary goal is to "distinguish between the passing and the permanent, to affirm and describe the nature of English as a subject" (pp. 3-4).

The emotional plays a significant role in distinguishing between the passing (i.e., the emotions inspired by the popular) and the permanent (i.e., the emotions inherent in the humanist tradition). Consider a *Freedom and Discipline* assignment that suggests using a popular artifact in the writing classroom. The authors suggest beginning with a cartoon

> like the now famous one that appeared originally in the *New Yorker* several years back showing a child at the dinner table who, when her mother says, "It's broccoli, dear," replies, "I say it's spinach, and I say to hell with it." [This cartoon] poses the same question as that raised by Juliet's confidence that a rose by any other name would smell as sweet. (p. 94)

Such an appropriation of the popular in the name of "higher goals"—Shakespeare's philosophical inquiry, to be exact—is hardly surprising. But here the popular is stripped of its content precisely because it is stripped of the affective identifications it represents. In this case, amusement, enjoyment of the drawing, or resistance to authority are replaced with the more "elevated"—that is, more emotionally restrained—attunement of the humanistic tradition. The student who interprets the cartoon not in light of Shakespeare's commentary on language and reality, but as, say, evidence of troubled familial relations, would not only be "misreading" the assignment, but would be stepping outside of the boundaries of the appropriate emotional response inherent in this example.

This form of emotional hegemony is evident in the responses *The National Interest* report received from teachers surveyed about the most urgent problems facing English Studies. In a familiar lament, one teacher comments, "Our most crucial need is to develop within our students some ideas more profound than those which they gather from their narrow teenage world. . . . Our graduates are able to write, but they don't have anything to say" (p. 132). The "narrow teenage world" at issue here is, presumably, the world of popular films, music, sports, and television.

Although resistance to the popular in composition studies has been well documented, few have concentrated primarily on the affective aspects of this resistance. *The National Interest* and *Freedom and Discipline* are particularly fruitful sources for such a concentration because they reflect a period of social history in which new technologies blended with new affective styles. The popular culture explosion of the 1950s and 1960s worked in concert with the dominant emphasis on emotional constraint. Popular culture provided "emotions that were far stronger and less alloyed than their audience could allow themselves to experience in the daily routine" (P. Stearns, 1994, p. 277). Because the new emotion culture prevented the expression of emotional intensity among people, popular culture became a site of surrogate emotional expression. According to Stearns, the contrast between the vicarious quest for depth of feeling and the dominant culture's ubiquitous hostility to emotional intensity offered no real contradiction in American culture. "The two movements," he explains, "fed each other, as cathartic cultures have always done" (p. 281).

But a contradiction did—and does—arise in educational discourse of these reports, which assume that emotional experience must be reordered in light of democratic principles—and the affective disposition those principles embody. That contradiction is more than simply a generational clash between staid composition teachers and hip, young students. It is, instead, a contradiction inherent in processes of emotional hegemony, and it is a contradiction that remains with us today.

AN EMOTIONAL HERITAGE

My exploration of the history of emotion styles and their influence on composition instruction is intended to serve two purposes. The first is to denaturalize emotions, to foster an awareness of the ways in which emotions, rather than simply rerouted in changing cultural climates, are reconstituted. The second is to show that emotional hegemony is a ubiquitous and effective strategy for social control, a strategy with ethical and material consequences. The forms of emotional hegemony that I have discussed—especially the penchant to cast emotions as "natural" and unchanging, as well as the privatization of intense emotional response as a reflection of maladjusted individual psyches—continue to shape many composition practices and theories. In particular, this legacy of emotional hegemony has influenced two vexing issues in contemporary writing theory and practices: the continuing lack of a critical vocabulary for articulating the role of emotions in writing theory and pedagogy; and the cultivation of "cool" affective stances, which have evolved into composition practices that too often sever learning from citizenship, classroom writing from public rhetoric.

The first issue—the absence of a critical vocabulary for affect—hobbles our conversations, our attempts to build theories and practices that respond to contemporary emotion culture. Consider, for example, the often virulent "turf wars" between champions of expressivist and social epistemic or cultural studies pedagogies. Their debates are not only highly emotional, but often are grounded in competing conceptions of emotions, politics and ethics—their role in writing processes, in identity formation, and in the comfort and contact zones of writing communities. For example, Hairston (1992), in a now-notorious condemnation of cultural studies approaches to composition (as well as any "leftist" or "postmodern" approach), charged that advocates of critical pedagogy "show open contempt for their students' values, preferences, or interests" (p. 181). Hairston instead proposed a "low-risk" classroom where students' lives are the focus of all writing, where diversity "organically" comes to the fore as students write about their own "unique" experiences. Similarly, Spellmeyer (1996) accused cultural studies pedagogies of fostering the same feeling of lack that one might experience while looking at a Guess Jeans ad: Like the fashion industry, Spellmeyer contended, cultural studies composition promotes alienation from the "true self," and English teachers should, instead, attempt to help students "feel at home in the world" by finding means to "renew emotional coherence" and "search for basic grammars of emotional life" (pp. 910, 911).

The Ebonics-like quandary of *whose* "basic grammars" aside, Spellmeyer's critique, like Hairston's, is informed by the premise that our feelings and emotions are repressed by many cultural formations, and the goal of the writing class should be to bring those *repressed* feelings and emotions to the fore. At issue is the question of students' "private" affective investments, which these critics assume are sacrificed when the "social" and "political" are fronted in the writing classroom. This conflict between proponents of expressionist or "liberal pluralist" pedagogies and those who promote critical or cultural studies pedagogies is thus more than a question of political orientation, of who is left and who is right. It is also a question of how we construct the relations between the public and private, the academic and the personal, and the role of emotions in these relations. When writing pedagogies challenge conceptions of writing as private, individual acts, they concomitantly challenge conceptions of emotions as naturalized, private, individual matters.

When I explain my research interests, many of my colleagues assume that any scholarship on emotions must be associated with full-frontal expressivism—some (perhaps illusory) pedagogical approach in which students' (highly individualized, privately experienced, and rather self-indulgent) feelings are the fodder for every communicative act. Certainly, the emphasis on authentic voice and sincerity in some expressivist rhetorics—an emphasis that echoes *Freedom and Discipline*'s claim that writing "false in feeling" will always be poor writing—can foster an unreflective conception of affect as individual and natural. Yet, despite their concern with historicizing and analyzing cultural artifacts, particularly popular culture texts, many social epistemic pedagogies continue to disdain the affective realm of popular literacy as merely a reflection of what Postman (1985) called "counterfeit emotions"—false, surface emotions that simply camouflage the deeper crisis that is American consumption today (Langstraat, 1996). In fact, social epistemic and cultural studies proponents must take partial responsibility for the often scathing accusations that they disregard students' emotional lives, reduce those emotional lives to mere false consciousness, or inculcate patterns of alienation, rather than agency. Simply bringing into the classroom suppressed or ignored forms of knowledge, such as popular culture or leftist discourses that might spark "pleasure" or "resistance," cannot fully attend to the goals of cultural critique. Following a long tradition of Marxist methods in cultural studies, the emotional—as it is linked to politics and ethics—has been a notoriously difficult topic for cultural critics who often try to explain it as if it were "merely the aura of ideological effects" (Grossberg 1992, p. 79). For example, in a considerate critique of Ira Shor's critical pedagogy, Gorzelsky (2002) contended that, despite its call for experiential learning, it "implies that ideological change is driven by argument-based, rationalist discourse rather than by affective dynamics and experiential shifts" (p. 313). Gorzelsky instead proposed methods of helping students articulate "an alternate, previously inaudible perspective" that draws on both emotional and rational elements (p. 313). Yet our lexicon for articulating the affective in both theory and practice is so limited that finding ways to enact Gorzelsky's proposal remains an awesome challenge.

When composition teachers ask students to write about their experiences and emotional dispositions, we seek to empower students, to offer them an opportunity to gain, through writing, a deeper understanding of themselves and their cultural positions. Yet the institutionalized emotional hegemony that inevitably influences our teaching also influences our response to such "emotional" writing—whether we identify with expressivist or social epistemic pedagogies. Consider, for example, Faigley's (1992) discussion of Axelrod and Cooper's critique of a student essay in the *St. Martin's Guide to Writing.* The essay expresses outrage that her campus paper ran an advertisement recruiting women to pose nude for a magazine. As Faigley (1992) pointed out, Axelrod and Cooper, rather than engaging with the emotional tenor of the essay, criticize the author for using "feminist buzzwords," such as "exploitation," "sexism," and "sex object" (p. 161). The student's anger, her expression of her affective responses to campus issues, is circumscribed by Axelrod and Cooper's assumption that unique expression (i.e., avoiding "cliches") marks good writing. Hence, although many contemporary assignments and assessment standards seem to celebrate the affective features of student writing, they too often respond to that writing and experience within institutional demands for rationality (Faigley, 1992) and normative affective expression of "cool" or reserved emotionality.

It is no surprise, then, that what Edmundson (1997) called "cool consumerism" is often the primary affective modality of college classrooms today. The "civilized joy" called for in *Freedom and Discipline* has evolved into an affective stance of self-containment and blending-in that, as Edmundson (1997) argued, prohibits passionate engagement: "Strong emotional display is forbidden. When conflicts arise, it's generally understood that one of the parties will say something sarcastically propitiating ('whatever' often does it) and slouch away" (p. 41). This cool ethos, a marketing bonanza for the targeted youth of "buy in order to be" consumerism, shapes every aspect of university interaction, and while Edmundson may generalize by glossing over those moments of students' avid participation and lively conversation, I suspect his observations ring true to many of us. Of course, it is not only an ethos of postmodern consumerism which leads to this cool emotional stance. After decades of American cool, students have learned that strong emotional engagement might lead to the very response the student just mentioned received: a demand that the student temper her affective identifications and make them palatable in light of the emotional hegemony that often informs our definitions of good academic discourse.

A lack of engaged classroom interaction, however, is only one effect of a cool academic emotion culture. Indeed, perhaps the most pernicious legacy of the emotional hegemony reflected in *Freedom and Discipline* and *The National Interest* is the truncated notion of citizenship they promote. As Hollander and Saltmarsh (2000) explained, during the Cold War, U.S. institutions of higher learning saw a radical change as they organized themselves around the political, scientific, and economic demands of the military–industrial complex: "Their structure, administration, and academic culture embraced science and technology, emphasized objectivity and detachment, and elevated the role of the scientifically educated expert over ordinary citizens in public affairs" (p. 30). The very existence of *Freedom and Discipline* and *The National Interest* challenges these new emphases by stressing the humanities' role in creating good citizens. But their notion of "civilized joy," their suggestion that citizenship is a natural extension of lofty, Arnoldian educational goals, reproduced the very objectivity and detachment of scientific inquiry that they sought to oppose. The strong feelings associated with participatory citizenship—with social movements and political engagement—were anathema to the cool affective climate of the classroom. As Clark (2000) illustrated in *Cold Warriors: Manliness on Trial in the Rhetoric of the West*, academics were fully aware of the costs of voicing strong political views: "The Cold War made both complexity and the personal view impossible, reducing everything that touched the issue to the distorted mirror of [McCarthy's] terrorizing campaign. Evidence of the violence showed in accusations, firings, and even jail sentences. But much of the violence operated on the possibilities of discourse, a vast deadening" (p. 127). This "vast deadening" is most apparent in the emotion culture of the academy that remains with us today as postsecondary pedagogy, with notable exceptions, fosters the development of disengaged citizens who feel unentitled or helpless to act in a civic capacity. Indeed, service-learning pedagogies which seek to merge democratic participation and higher education face a central challenge: a kind of affective reeducation which, in helping students feel entitled to act in a civic capacity, undercuts the tradition of cool or affectively disengaged classroom climates.

Processes of emotional hegemony are inherent in any effort to define the relationship between literacy and democratic citizenship. And it is important to acknowledge that there is no "outside" of emotional hegemony: If emotional styles and affective identifications are, indeed, culturally influenced and constituted, then attempts to get at some "natural" expression of emotions are ill-founded. To struggle against oppressive forms of emotional hegemony, to understand how they influence our teaching practices, our conceptions of "good" writing, and our personal and political relationships with colleagues and students, we must resist a search for true emotions unhindered by culture. Instead, we must historicize and recontextualize emotion discourses and experiences. Articulating a politics of affect, making emotions an explicit and central feature of our pedagogical theories, is an integral step in this process.

ENDNOTES

1. Although efforts to distinguish between values, attitudes, beliefs, and other "kinds" of affective states are useful for many forms of research, I conflate *affect* and *emotion* here to reflect common social uses of the terms. See Brand's (1994) discussion of vernacular uses of these terms, such as her claim that "*affect* is a high-brow term for emotion" (p. 151).
2. See Brand's (1989) *The Psychology of Writing: The Affective Experience* for quantitative studies of emotion that reflect cognitive psychology models of empirical studies. Although valuable, these studies rarely take into consideration the cultural influences that shape writing students' affective experiences in the process of composing.
3. Pavletich (1998) illustrated this point with Harriet Beecher Stowe's *Uncle Tom's Cabin*; Stowe ends the book, not with a plan of political action, but with a call to urge people to feel differently about slavery: "There is one thing that every individual can do—they can see to it that they *feel right*" (p. 56).
4. Many postmodern theorists argue that the affective restraint inherent in the concept of *American cool* has intensified in the last three decades as every aspect of lived experience in U.S. culture has become mediated by technologies of mass culture (see Grossberg, 1992; Jameson, 1984; Massumi, 1993).
5. Anger is one of the most frequently studied emotional states, particularly as its expression is channeled or dismissed in the workplace. Worsham (1993), for example, argued that the dictate against expressions of anger works to configure oppressive practices—such as sexual harassment—as the result of individual, rather than institutional, behavior. Also see C. Stearns and Stearns (1986) for a fascinating history of anger in U.S. culture.
6. As one reviewer of this article insists, the term *expressivism* circulates as an underdefined and pejorative concept in much writing about composition studies. Although it is beyond the purview of this chapter to offer a comprehensive history of expressivist pedagogies, my definition of both *expressivist* and *social epistemic* rhetorics stems from Berlin's (1997) delineation in *Rhetoric and Reality*.
7. See Faigley (1992) for discussion of post-Fordist economics and their impact on educational policy.
8. By 1957, 82% of American homes sported at least one television set, stations had shifted from live- to pretaped broadcasts, and national marketing surveys for TV advertising became commonplace. See Spigel (1990) for a particularly interesting discussion of technological changes and their effect on familial and work relations.

REFERENCES

Ball, A., & Lardner, T. (1997). Dispositions toward language: Teacher constructs of knowledge and the Ann Arbor black English case. *College Composition and Communication, 48*(4), 469-485.

Berlin, J. (1987). *Rhetoric and reality: Writing instruction in American colleges, 1900-1985*. Carbondale: Southern Illinois University Press.

Bleich, D. (1995). Collaboration and the pedagogy of disclosure. *College English, 57*(1), 43-61.

Boler, M. (1999). *Feeling power: Emotions and education.* New York: Routledge.

Brand, A. G. (1989). *The psychology of writing: The affective experience.* New York: Greenwood.

Brand, A. G. (1994). Defining our emotional life: The valuative system—a continuum theory. In A. G. Brand & R. L. Graves (Eds.), *Presence of mind: Writing and the domain beyond the cognitive* (pp. 155-166). Portsmouth: Boynton/Cook.

Clark, S. (2000). *Cold warriors: Manliness on trial in the rhetoric of the west.* Carbondale: Southern Illinois University Press.

College Entrance Examination Board. (1965). *Freedom and discipline in English.* New York: Author.

Dolan, D. (1978). *Project English (1961-1968): Conception–birth–life–death—and who cared?* Report prepared for the University of California, Riverside (ED 175 016).

Edmundson, M. (1997, September). On the uses of a liberal education: I. As lite entertainment for bored college students. *Harper's*, pp. 39-49.

Faigley, L. (1992). *Fragments of rationality: Postmodernity and the subject of composition.* Pittsburgh: University of Pittsburgh Press.

Gorzelsky, G. (2002) Ghosts: Liberal education and negotiated authority. *College English, 64*(3), 302-325.

Grossberg, L. (1992). *We gotta get out of this place: Popular conservatism and postmodern culture.* New York: Routledge.

Hairston, M. (1992). Diversity, ideology and teaching writing. *College Composition and Communication, 43*(2), 179-195.

Harris, J. (1991). After Dartmouth: Growth and conflict in English. *College English, 53*(6), 631-646.

Hollander, E., & Saltmarsh, J. (July-August 2000). The engaged university. *Academe*, pp. 29-32.

Jaggar, A. M. (1992). Love and knowledge: Emotion in feminist epistemology. In K. Okruhlik & E. D. Harvey (Eds.), *Women and reason* (pp. 115-142). Ann Arbor: University of Michigan Press.

Jameson, F. (1984). Postmodernism, or the cultural logic of late capitalism. *New Left Review, 146*, 53-92.

Kantor, K. (1979). The revolution a decade later: Confessions of an aging romantic. *English Journal, 68*(8), 28-31.

Kitayama, S., & Marcus, H. R. (Eds.). (1994). Introduction to cultural psychology and emotion research. In *Emotion and culture: Empirical studies of mutual influence* (pp. 1-22). Washington, DC: American Psychological Association.

Langstraat, L. (1996). Hypermasculinity in cultural studies and composition. *Composition Forum: A Journal of the Association of Teachers of Advanced Composition, 7*(1), 1-16.

Lutz, C. (1988). *Unnatural emotions.* Chicago: University of Chicago Press.

Massumi, B. (Ed.). (1993). Everywhere you want to be: Introduction to fear. In *The politics of everyday fear* (pp. 3-37). Minneapolis: University of Minnesota Press.

McLeod, S. (1991). The affective domain and the writing process: Working definitions. *Journal of Advanced Composition, 11,* 95-105.

Mercer, C. (1983). A poverty of desire: Pleasure and popular politics. In F. Jameson (Ed.), *Formations of pleasure* (pp. 84-100). New York: Routledge.

Miller, S. (1991). *Textual carnivals: The politics of composition.* Carbondale: Southern Illinois University Press.

Murray, D. (1982). Teaching the other self: The writer's first reader. *College Composition and Communication, 33,* 140-147.

The National Interest and the Teaching of English. Champaign, IL: Author.

Pavletich, J. (1998). Emotions, experience, and social control in the twentieth century. *Rethinking Marxism, 10*(2), 51-64.

Postman, N. (1985). *Amusing ourselves to death: Public discourse in the age of show business.* New York: Penguin.

Spellmeyer, K. (1996). After theory: From textuality to attunement with the world. *College English, 58*(8), 893-913.

Spigel, L. (1990). Television in the family circle: The popular reception of a new medium. In P. Mellencamp (Ed.), *Logics of television: Essays in cultural criticism* (pp. 73-97). Bloomington: University of Indiana Press.

Stearns, C., & Stearns, P. (1986). *Anger: The struggle for emotional control in America's history.* Chicago: University of Chicago Press.

Stearns, P. (1994). *American cool: Constructing a twentieth-century emotional style.* New York: New York University Press.

Worsham, L. (1993). Emotion and pedagogic violence. *Discourse, 15*(2), 119-148.

16

VISUAL IMAGES IN THE *CHICAGO DEFENDER*

Sponsoring (Counter) Public Literacies

Jill Swiencicki
California State University-Chico

If you see it in the Defender it is so.
—front-page slogan, *Chicago Defender*

Robert Abbott founded the *Chicago Defender* in 1905, and in little more than a decade it emerged as perhaps the most important Black newspaper in the nation. As the chief journal of the Black press, the *Defender* played a crucial role in promoting the Great Migration, the period roughly between 1915–1940 in which more than 1 million Blacks left the southern states to seek opportunity in the north. The paper ran articles, photographs, cartoons, and ads that highlighted the social, economic, and political advantages of moving north, especially to urban centers like Chicago. Indeed, the aggressive position taken by the paper "underscore[s] the extent to which Abbott did everything he could to aid and abet the migration" (Suggs, 1996, p. 27). Spear (1967) observed that the paper "portrayed contrasts between northern freedom and southern tyranny" (p. 52); the north, he argued, was envisioned as offering "not only economic opportunity but a chance for human dignity" (p. 53). More recently, DeSantis (1998) showed how the paper utilized specific genres of the American Dream myth to exploit this sense of discontent among the southern readership. These studies bookend over three decades of research on the rhetorical strategies the *Defender* used to aid the Great Migration. This chapter puts these findings to new ends, asking what the migration rhetoric reveals about the relationship between the *Defender* and its readers.

Along with moving readers with its rhetoric, the *Defender* sponsored them through encouraging specific visual and textual literacy practices. According to Brandt (2001), *sponsors* "are any agents, local or distant, concrete or abstract, who enable, support, teach, model, as well as recruit, regulate, suppress, or withhold literacy—and gain advantage by it in some way" (p. 556). The concept of *sponsorship* that Brandt articulated is useful in understanding literacy practices as always determined by particular contexts, relationships, and needs. Although readers were being encouraged to move north, southerners and others (from urban professionals to politicians to waiters to agricultural workers to housewives) were learning strategies for agential participation both within the dominant culture and against it in the form of agitative counterpublics. This sponsorship aimed for the creation of vital Black public and counterpublic spheres, as well as a richly imagined national Black identity. The *Defender* achieves these aims in multiple ways; in this chapter I focus on its relentless modeling for Black citizens of the practices needed to critically respond to the oppression they face from businesses, governments, and individuals, and to exercise their rights to participate in political processes by modeling and regulating what that participation might look like and what kind of values that citizenry should recognize and uphold. I illustrate this sponsorship approach by focusing on visual images and their accompanying texts from the earliest editions of the *Defender*, roughly from 1909 to 1916, because they appeared on the eve of the migration and offer us a view of the rhetoric that literally moved African Americans to northern urban centers and prefigured an artistic response to the migration by artists, musicians, and writers. I see the visual strategies embedded in political cartoons, lynching images, and illustrations that accompany features on prominent African Americans as promoting visual literacy, "the ability to understand and make visual statements, sensitizing people to the world around them, [and to] the relationships and systems of power of which [subjects] are a part" (Moore, 1994, p. 99). But because sponsors "represent the causes into which people's literacy usually gets recruited," they also "deliver the ideological freight that must be borne for access to what they have" (Brandt, 2001, pp. 556, 557). Although the paper modeled literacy practices aimed at gaining leverage for the race, it at times advocated appropriating the very values and ideals of the dominant culture that obscured its struggle. Through pointed combinations of texts and visual representations the paper challenged and also reproduced complicated notions of gender, nation, and subjecthood in the advancement of a Black public sphere.

At the historical moment of the migration, the literacy practices promoted by the *Defender* were essential to the creation of Black public spheres, or sites of public participation in rational-critical debate in which Blacks set the agenda. The importance of this effort is underscored by Brandt's (2001) observation that, "throughout their lives, affluent people from high-caste racial groups have multiple and redundant contacts with powerful literacy sponsors as a routine part of their economic and political privileges"(p. 559). In *Land of Hope*, Grossman (1989) described how issues of the *Defender* were carried by train south and read aloud in barber shops, churches, and gatherings in homes. This kind of communal readership practice is a crucial part of creating informed public spheres during Jim Crow. As the *Defender* itself stated, the paper helped "to meet the needs of intelligent publics" in large part through the meanings embedded in visual texts, such as political cartoons, illustrations for feature articles, and advertisements. These visuals helped to account for a readership that could not "read" text either because they lacked the skills, or because they were reading it in transit, in secret, or in collaboration with other readers who shared the same paper. But for this readership, and a larger "aspiring" black readership of an emergent middle class, the visuals were deeply persuasive accompaniments to the written articles and captions and served not just as a reinforcement of those texts but as another way to add dimension to the literacy requirements of the paper. These texts and the practices they engendered are made even more remarkable when we consider the assumptions about participation that the notion of the public sphere rests on. Baker (1995) noted that the "emergence of Habermas's public sphere [was] generated by property ownership and literacy" (p. 13). Black Americans "arrived on New World shores precisely as property belonging to the bourgeoisie. They were strategically and rigorously prevented from acquiring literacy. And they were defined . . . as devoid of even a germ in their minds that might be mistaken for reason" (Baker, 1995, p. 13).

The *Defender* does create public and counterpublic sites of participation and information, but it does so not so much by staging debate that readers can weigh in on, but instead by telling them how to enter publics and giving them some literacy skills to do so. In fact, the paper's predominant mode of literacy sponsorship in the period I've investigated can be characterized by its front page slogan: "If you see it in the *Defender* it is so." While read in the contexts mentioned earlier—barber shops, churches, homes—the paper can be seen as a supplement to rational critical debate; but taken on its own, the *Defender* serves to determine the debate's right outcome. This is a sponsorship approach of modeling and regulating response from readers, and examples of this can be seen in the *Defender*'s aggressive stances on local elections for alderman. In "Which One?", an early *Defender* political cartoon about an upcoming Chicago election, the visual is organized in three scenes, each depicting a candidate for alderman who is zealously delivering a campaign speech as their audiences look on with varying degrees of interest. Although the images of the candidates are essentially identical, the cartoonist takes great pains to show the radically different ways in which the same audience responds to each candidate's oration—moving from boredom in the first scene, to belligerence in the second, to vigorous approbation in the third. The cartoon claims to be expressing "the people's wishes," thus the *Defender* serves to visualize a public sphere of rational-critical debate about an issue of civic urgency, in this case political representation. The cartoon, although representing "the people," is also constructing an argument about the proper candidate for representative office for those who have not yet taken part in the debate, thus promoting a visual literacy that tells readers how to imagine their place within public dialogues. In "Which One?" the *Defender* both stages and decides the outcome of a local debate.

This sponsorship approach is best understood in the context of oppression and the need for providing readers with clear roads to action. Consider Peter P. Jones' brief notice "To the Voters of the 2nd Ward" (Fig. 16.1), which actually replaces the headline on the March 30, 1912 issue of the *Defender*:

CHAS. S. DENEEN and The BLACK PHILOSOPHER Page Four

The Home Edition

The Chicago Defender.

If you see it in The Defender it is so

VOLUME VII, NUMBER 11 — CHICAGO, ILL., SATURDAY, MARCH 30, 1912 — PRICE 5 CENTS

To the Voters of the 2nd Ward: Through some trickery while my petition was being circulated to place my name on the ticket as a candidate for Alderman it failed to stand the test. But in order that we may have representation I am still in the race to the finish. You can vote for me by placing a square, thus: ☒ drawing same with your pencil or ink on the ballot under the word "Independent" and cross in same and write *Peter P. Jones*, as inscribed. Enough of these and you will have representation. Signed: **PETER P. JONES**

Fig. 16.1. "To the Voters of the 2nd Ward."

> Through some trickery while my petition was being circulated to place my name on the ticket as a candidate for alderman it failed to stand the test. But in order that we may have representation I am still in the race to the finish. You can vote for me by placing a square, thus X, drawing same with your pencil or ink ballot under the word "Independent" and cross in same and write Peter P. Jones, as inscribed. Enough of these and you will have representation. Signed: Peter P. Jones.

The paper sacrifices the space of the headline for the voice of the candidate who not only critiques the "trickery" of his removal from the ballot, but also then educates readers on how to negotiate the material act of marking a ballot and placing a vote. Here, the *Defender* augments its role as a national news vehicle in order to serve as an instructional guide for local readers who have limited time to act. It is suggested that one needs to learn one's position within the field of competing discourses quickly—with deadlines and real consequences. The paper's role is not to assess a range of debates, but to help readers recognize the right one. In both these examples, the notion of rational-critical debate that is so central to the formation of public spheres and counterpublic spheres is absent, replaced by a modeling of a basic civic literacy practice.

The urgency of this kind of sponsorship—modeling practices to achieve specific outcomes—is not encouraging a refeudalized passivity among readers but rather is the creation of a public representative body to effect change on a large scale. In this period and into the migration years, the *Defender* takes on what Fanon (1963) called the "function of the nation" (p. 21), making Black citizens feel a part of a totality, feeding the passion of the subject to be empowered by collective national identity. The paper invites readers to understand themselves within the scope of images that comprised a turn-of-the-century national symbolic, "the order of discursive practices, icons, metaphors, heroes, rituals, and narratives which effect citizens subjective experience of their political rights, civil life, private life, and the life of the body" (Berlant, 1997, p. 20). To illustrate this, I single out two recurring iconic images: lynching sketches meant to forge critical consciousness and provoke collective action, linking male bodies to the creation of national identity; and visuals that honored the public actions of Black women on behalf of their race.

The lynching of African Americans is a practice that purportedly responded to sexual crimes perpetrated by Blacks and often included torture, burning, and dismemberment. It occurred with regularity from the 1870s to the 1930s, the victims numbering, according to NAACP statistics, somewhere between 4,000 and 10,000 (Gunning, 1996, p. 5). Robyn Weigman (1997) wrote that "above all, lynching is about the law," a statement that makes explicit how black personhood—afforded through enfranchisement and citizenship—disrupts the stability of white male power (p. 81). Indeed, in the years after 1865 White-on-Black violence came to be seen as "hysterically self-defensive"; as Gunning (1996) observed, "the black rapist proved useful for white Americans seeking to come to terms with post-Civil War anxieties over national unity, black emancipation, altered gender roles, growing labor unrest, European immigration, and the continued evolution of the United States into an increasingly multiethnic nation" (p. 6). For Gunning and other historians of lynching, "[t]he black male body, hypersexualized and criminalized, has always functioned as a crucial and heavily overdetermined metaphor in an evolving national discourse on the nature of a multiethnic, multiracial American society" (p. 3).

The *Chicago Defender* intervened in discourse on and instances of lynching in a number of ways: by representing those who fled this terror and succeeded to a life of "true" freedom in northern urban centers; by creating space for rational-critical debate by and for African Americans; by creating and supporting a Black public sphere of arts, letters, politics, and culture related to the paper; and by didactic consciousness-raising about southern "tyranny." One of these overtly didactic spaces in the paper was the political cartoon, which fostered visual literacy in spaces of critical cultural commentary. After surveying the premigration editions of the *Defender*, a sketch that was accessed frequently by editors, both as subject for the articles and in the cartoons, was that of the lynched Black male (Fig. 16.2). It is this image that editors often used to instill a visual literacy in their readers that forged critical consciousness and provoked action.

It is significant that the exact same lynching sketch gets recycled throughout a number of different editions of the *Defender* (December 31, 1910, April 6, 1912, and August 26, 1914 issues). This drawing appears in many different contexts: sometimes it accompanies a feature article or an op-ed piece, sometimes it stands alone, or sometimes it is accompanied by a caption that serves as a kind of meditation. The scene is one of an adult Black male who hangs from a portion of a tree in the foreground of the composition as a group of White men on horseback with guns recede into a barren landscape in the background. The iconography is extremely neutral and spare—it suggests no specific place, space, or region—and this generic quality of figures and landscape may be deliberate. After all, its visual simplicity contributes to the portability of the sketch from one news context on lynching to another. But spare, simple compositions are often a main feature of African-American paintings depicting lynching. As Griffin (1995) observed, in such representations it seems that the body literally *becomes* the landscape. Here we see that its contours, its relation to the tree and its integration to both tree and land via shading, become the most detailed feature of a

Fig. 16.2. Lynched Black male.

scene depicting a landscape and a people wounded by racial violence. This is the image of trauma, a wound inflicted on the body and the mind, one that

> is not locatable in the simple violent or original event in [the] past, but rather in the way that its very unassimilated nature . . . returns to haunt the survivor[s] later on . . . [such representations tell] the "story of the wound that cries out," that addresses us in the attempt to tell us of a reality or truth that is otherwise unavailable. This truth . . . cannot be linked only to what is known, but also to what remains unknown in our very actions and our language. (Caruth, 1996, p. 4)

As representative in part of the national landscape, then, this spare image becomes a statement about collective trauma, as well as a critical statement about a nation that refuses to acknowledge that collective trauma and repair it. Along with providing editorial convenience and critical social commentary, the repeated use of this lynching image offers something more: a focal point for a collective meditation about racial trauma. As trauma theorists suggest, the phenomenon of repetition serves as a way to revisit a racial trauma at a safe distance. In other words, it allows readers to admit and acknowledge the trauma in ways that the oppressive culture may actively repress and disremember. It also offers readers a way to mobilize and take control over the trauma: to derive an activism and a collective identity from the trauma that the symbol references.

In the 1910 New Year's Eve edition of the *Defender*, the editors deploy this sketch of the lynched figure to "look backward and see the bodies of 200 heroes lynched." Here the image is a sociopolitical focal point, the point at which the reader is meant to measure the past and frame the future against a sanctioned climate of random violence and murder. The body of the Black man signifies as the historical past, present, and future for the race, a provocative landmark, part of the landscape of racial violence that has structured the history of America and serves as a point of reflection. The caption reads, "we mourn and hide our faces in shame at a government, the greatest the world has ever seen which would permit such crimes to be instituted in her domain. We look with shame upon our churches for not raising a dissenting voice; and we look with shame on American priests who at no time during a lynching have they tried to stop the mob or offer a prayer for the lynched." This statement shows the openly didactic function of this visual in combination with its caption, as it instructs readers on how to see the sociopolitical climate through the lens of the lynched figure. Readers look in "shame" against government and religious institutions which, instead of being parallel institutions of critical literacy, they argue, have been silent and rendered such lynching spectacles invisible. Interesting too that the same caption also instructs the reader to imagine what is not made visible in public culture, the "5000 innocent girls rushed into motherhood by our southern white friends." Gunning argues that "the very figuration of black women . . . gets lost in the shuffle over black and white male articulations [of lynching]" (p. 8); if this is so, the *Defender*'s illustration and caption combine to form "a site of interpretive intervention within public discourse that might challenge the dominant readings of history and culture" (p. 9). Here, the caption works in tandem with the sketch to visualize what the cartoon alone does not represent; it insists upon rewriting the scene of lynching to include the more historically accurate relationship between White men and Black women than the one that lynching implies between

Black men and White women. Thus, it insists on the larger issues of power and ownership that are at the root of public and private, White-on-Black acts of violence. This may provide an example of what Baker (1995) meant when he argued that "critical memory . . . is the very faculty of revolution: Critical memory judges severely, censures righteously, renders hard ethical evaluations of the past that it never defines as well-passed. The essence of critical memory's work is the cumulative, collective maintenance of a record that draws into relationship significant instants of time past and the always uprooted homelessness of now" (p. 7).

The spectacle of the lynched figure is accessed repeatedly by the *Defender* to elicit action and emotion. It is relevant to contrast it with images like "The President's Waste Basket" (Fig. 16.3) in which we see the

Fig. 16.3. The President's Waste Basket.

issue of national race divisions from the viewpoint of the white power structure. The image is one of President Wilson at his desk, discarding a petition against lynching, while letters about foreign policy sit centrally on his desk. Wilson is represented only as a pair of hands, hands that can barely stand to touch the lynching petition as it hovers above his trash can. The trash can is the largest image of the scene, and is filled to bursting; it, combined with the desk, suggests the vast distance between reader's interests and the interests of those in power. That Blacks are on the wrong side of power is emphasized by the fact that, while Wilson is embodied, the demands of "10,000,000 colored citizens" are flattened into text. With the visual horrors of violence against Blacks represented as a text, the cartoon suggests that their case is seen as flimsy, thin. Unlike real bodies, a text is easier to put aside, or in this case, throw away. Here the *Defender* ensures that its own readers don't normalize their own conditions of terror through the visual refrain of the lynched black man and instead begin to associate that image with critical action. "Better clean your own [waste basket], Mr. President, before you point your finger at someone else," reads the caption. And, as Griffin (1995) showed, the *Defender* frequently published letters from the south, usually anonymously at the request of the writer, such as this one from Troy, Alabama: "'Dear Sirs: I am enclosing a clipping of a lynching again, which speaks for itself. . . . So many of our people here are almost starving'"(p. 23). Griffin showed that fear of violent reprisal was a major catalyst for leaving the south, and it seems that the *Defender* saw itself as a leader in safeguarding these literacy artifacts, bringing to public view the letters and experiences of those hoping to escape terror, letters which elsewhere (such as the president's desk) were unacknowledged or discarded.

Other representations of the scene of lynching are often embedded within intertextual references to heighten irony, pathos, and associative quality such as "Easter Morn in America" (Fig. 16.4).

This sketch shows the Christ figure in robe and halo appearing above a lynching scene, a scene that stands in as the image of the crucifixion that is the hallmark of Easter iconography. The White instigators that swarm the Black male figure at the stake are shown laughing, jeering, and brandishing weapons, and mark an analogy to the mob who hurled vitriol at the figure who, according to Christian belief, died to save humanity from their sins. The cartoon suggests that the lynched figure must be resurrected for the nation to re-emerge as stronger, wiser, martyred, and inspired through his pain. The triangulated figures of Christ, the Black male victim, and the white man (figured with a gun and a raised fist) is presented as the image to be meditated on with the prayer captioned below: "bless the four thousand known who have been lynched and murdered without cause . . . in this country of supposed civilized people." The call to ironize the "supposed

Fig. 16.4. Easter Morn in America.

civility" of the White race is crucial here and is a main argument of the Black public sphere that the *Defender* is trying to constitute. Consider a 1914 *Defender* column "Keeping in the Track," in which the writer discusses the relationship of Blacks to codes of white bourgeois civility:

> Many who come from below the Mason and Dixon line are unaccustomed to the ways of northerners and having heard that there are no restrictions often step in where Angels fear to tread. It must be remembered that there is prejudice everywhere; it only changes in degree in

> the different sections of the country . . . unfortunately large cities attract a greater many of the lower element of the race, people who are shiftless, lazy, and unprincipled; it is this class that make it so hard for the better element. The average white person judges the entire race by the example at hand and usually they come in contact with the lowest or form their opinion after reading a derogatory article concerning a criminal in the daily press. It is imperative that each and every one be as circumspect as possible, live and act above board. We are on trial. As we walk, so, to certain minds, does the entire race walk.

The value in this article lies "not in tracking the conservatism of [the paper's] vision, but in analyzing the meaning of [its] struggle to work through the moral contradictions of the racial politics of their era" (Gunning, 1996, pp. 12-13). What emerges here is instruction about another race's visual literacy, and how Whites use that literacy to "read" Blacks. The *Defender* argues that Blacks are legible to Whites only as crude stereotypes, encouraging an awareness of the limited kinds of visual literacies that Whites operate under—literacies that transcend the geo-political borders of north and south. The paper promoted an awareness of White visual literacies so that Blacks could accommodate it in emancipatory and even subversive ways within the bourgeois codes that proscribed them.

As scholars such as Royster (1997, 2000) have shown, Black women played a crucial role in fostering the kinds of critical consciousness that the *Defender* promoted. Indeed, women were arguably the most vital and vocal members of anti-lynching campaigns. Ida B. Wells and Mary Church Terrell were just a few of the hundreds of black women across the country who labored as reformers, activists, and orators for the cause against the public lynching of African Americans. They made explicit "the connections among the sexual exploitation of black women, the economic exploitation of black people, and the practice of lynching" (Griffin, 1995, p. 25). The premigration issues of the *Defender* represented Black women in such agitative roles, bringing me to the second image explored that represents the *Defender*'s attempts to construct an empowered, national Black identity for readers. An example of this is found in the September 16, 1911 cover story, "A True Race Woman Speaks." Beneath this headline is the photograph of a demure, handsomely dressed woman with the caption, "Miss Eva Claiborne, Hero" (Fig. 16.5).

Claiborne is featured by the paper because, while out one night in Chicago, she refused to capitulate to her male escort's request that she not make a scene in a Chinese restaurant that was rumored to refuse service to Blacks. Here is a section of Claiborne's response to the *Defender*:

Fig. 16.5. Miss Eva Clairborne, Hero.

Do you know, Mr. Reporter, that one-half of our men are no more protection to the women than a baby would be, and you may take it from me, that I will never be caught out in company again with such a young man as he. I was not looking for trouble. My manner was ladylike and my voice was not raised any louder than it is this minute. . . . I tell this to the *Defender* because it is the only paper in Chicago that seems to stand up for the rights of the race and the protection of its women. Tell all the young ladies of our race for me to go right ahead and stand up for their rights and if our men are too cowardly to demand a right given by the constitution of the state of Illinois, then run them home and go out alone.

Such active entrance into the public sphere signified what Berlant (1997) called a diva citizenship; a diva citizen stages dramatic coups in a public sphere in which she does not have privilege (p. 233). She takes on national projects, redefines national values and the notion of what subjects can do for their countries. In the late 19th century, for example, Anna Julia Cooper explained that "the woman of today [must] interest herself in the presence and responsibilities which ramify through the profoundest and most varied interests of her country and race" (Rooks, 1996, p. 67). Such calls for diva citizenship were answered by Ida B. Wells, who waged strong critiques of lynching; Nannie Helen Burroughs, who actively struggled for Black women's rights; and Francis Harper, who insisted on reimagining, through her writing, a just America where neither race nor sexuality existed as a mode of domination.

While imagining a female iconicity that aggressively challenges racist stereotypes, Claiborne's diva citizenship as a True Race Woman simultaneously references the bourgeois lexicon of True Womanhood, which ensconced women in the domain of moral guardianship of family, home, race, and nation. In the excerpt from her testimony to the reporter, Claiborne constructs the public as a male space, one that women need "protection" against from men with courage. While she proudly steps into the role of agitator that her escort abandoned, she takes pains to mention that she did so while keeping her voice and comportment within acceptable feminine range. As a final coup, and referencing an awareness of separate, gendered spheres, she feminizes her male escort by sending him "home" so she can do the just work of nation-building.

Her status as a True Woman is also referenced by her photograph, which shows an extremely fashionable hair and clothing style, and a gentle comportment. Her coding within bourgeois modes of adornment relates to other gendered literacies in the *Defender*, which provided models and information to assist Black women in placing their experiences within meaningful constructions of self that had currency in "respectable" northern Black culture. Hair and beauty advertisements, for example, visualized women in ways that linked their bodies to both economic mobility and social equality. Such equality was contingent on both the *Defender*'s ability to figure women in bourgeois models of womanhood and reader's facility with visual literacies that promoted these models. African-American women's agency was rooted in part in their ability to "make" their bodies accommodate the vision of respectability; Higgenbotham (1993) claimed that this vision of respectability countered racist images, but also condemned what was perceived to be negative practices and attitudes among African-American women: "respectability signified an assimilationist leaning leading to an insistence upon black women's conformity to the dominant society's norms of manners and morals" (p. 187). Such is a reference to the ideological freight that sponsors like the *Defender* channel in their relations with readers.

Along with race women, another iconic representation of black women depicts them as wives and mothers. Like the ads, the photos of women that accompany feature articles connect these bodies to a politics of respectability. The conflation of body and respectability suggests the image of a "proper" Black woman, a woman who, by her very appearance, helps her husband garner social leverage in the public spheres of business and civil society. The feature article on Mrs. Louis Anderson strengthens the claim that a representation of female respectability increases men's public opportunities. The picture here features a lovely, placid Mrs. Anderson, who testifies to her 17 years of good trust in her husband in support of his potential public conduct as alderman. This representation also conflates domesticity, respectability, and body in order to create a trustworthy ethos for Mrs. Anderson and, by extension, Mr. Anderson. The article "Rube Foster his home, and his family" (Fig.16.6) offers a similar image.

At the top of the page Foster sits at his desk; this picture has been positioned directly above the pictures of his wife, his home, and his son. The obvious hierarchical ordering here signifies that Foster has built his authority on a domestic foundation. Mrs. Foster is the embodiment of this foundation as the representation of both home and child, by extension representations of Mr. Foster himself. In the premigration issues of the *Defender*, black women are symbolically constructed as bearers of the black national identity; visualized as True Women and Race Women, black women embodied a public role that derived in part from bourgeois codes of femininity. The *Defender* included diva citizenship in the visual literacies that it offered in combination with images that encouraged women to accommodate to the bourgeois lexicon of true womanhood.

Brandt (2001) argued that an "analysis of sponsorship forces us to consider not merely how one social group's literacy practices may differ from another's, but how everybody's literacy practices are operating in differential economies, which supply different access routes, different degrees of sponsoring power, and different scales of monetary worth to the practices in use" (p. 561). In effect, Brandt argued that literacy sponsorship is a two-way street. It is clear what reader's of the *Defender* gain: a defender. Indeed, in its premigration period, *The Chicago Defender* was invested in creating literacy practices that transmitted information as well as affective indicators and detailed actions for how to respond to that information. The *Defender*'s visuals make connections that encourage readers to read against dominant, traumatic constructions of their geo-physical and racial-somatic situation, and read with the critical and emancipatory logics they offer. What readers gain, however, is accompanied by the interests of the *Defender*, and so these

Fig. 16.6. Rube Foster his home, and his family.

logics were often complicit with bourgeois codes of civility. These kind of privileged codes of publicness were important for the *Defender* to encourage; after all, they benefited from this sponsorship because it meant not only increased revenue for the paper: it meant increased social power for African-Americans politically, economically, and socially, power that would then further enhance the *Defender*. In this way, critiquing the paper's complicity with certain class codes is complicated, for the paper usually reframed those codes as survival mechanisms to make African-American publicity effective. These literacies helped African Americans learn to reconstitute their lived experiences and knowledges against the logics of dominant racial oppression. It also worked to substantiate a rational-critical debate about racial and political relations that further fostered intra-racial alliances, communities, and agencies.

The *Defender* was not just encouraging movement, but position—to take a position within and against competing discourses, economies, political debates, and personal interactions, and provided readers practices on how to do this. This is an intervention into the history of literacy, one that, as Brandt sees it, reveals "a catalogue of obligatory relations. That this catalogue is so deeply conservative and, at the same time, so ruthlessly demanding of change is what fills contemporary literacy learning with their most paradoxical choices and outcomes" (p. 571). Archival work which explores literacy practices in (counter)public contexts offers a counternarrative to the conservative catalogue Brandt calls up. And when linked to contemporary studies of literacy practices, it "points to the importance of examining how literacy . . . fits within the social structure of the community or group in which it functions" (Moss, 1994, p. 3), furthering the sometimes liberatory, always paradoxical, deeply complex outcomes that sponsorship relations demonstrate.

ACKNOWLEDGMENTS

I owe a deep debt of gratitude to Cara Ungar, who collaborated on the early stages of this project and presented it with me at the Watson Conference in 1999. I would also like to thank David Martins and Mark Hall.

REFERENCES

Andrew (Rube) Foster; his family and his home. (1915, February 20). *The Chicago Defender.*

Baker, H. A. (1995). Critical memory and the black public sphere. In The Black Public Sphere Collective (Eds.), *The black public sphere: A public culture book* (pp. 7-37). Chicago: University of Chicago Press.

Berlant, L. (1997). *The queen of America goes to Washington City: Essays on sex and citizenship.* Durham, NC: Duke University Press.

Brandt, D. (2001). Sponsors of literacy. In E. Cushman, E. R. Kintgen, B. M. Kroll, & M. Rose (Eds.), *Literacy: A critical sourcebook* (pp. 555-571). New York: Bedford/St. Martins Press.

Caruth, C. (1996). *Unclaimed experience: Trauma, narrative, and history.* Baltimore, MD: Johns Hopkins University Press.

DeSantis, A. (1998). Selling the American dream myth to black southerners: The Chicago *Defender* and the great migration of 1915-1919. *Western Journal of Communication, 62*(4), 474-512.

Easter morn in America. (1916, April 22). *The Chicago Defender.*

Fanon, F. (1963). *The wretched of the earth.* New York: Grove Weidenfeld.

Griffin, F. J. (1995). "Who set you flowin'?" In *The African American migration narrative.* New York: Oxford University Press.

Grossman, J. R. (1989). *Land of hope: Chicago, black southerners, and the great migration.* Chicago: University of Chicago Press.

Gunning, S. (1996). *Race, rape, and lynching: The red record of American literature, 1890-1912.* New York: Oxford University Press.

Higgenbotham, E. (1993). *Righteous discontent: The women's movement in the black baptist church, 1880-1920.* Cambridge, MA: Harvard University Press.

Keeping in the track. (1914, August 26). *The Chicago Defender.*

Moore, D. (1994). *Visual literacy: A spectrum of visual learning.* Englewood Cliffs, NJ: Educational Technology Publications.

Moss, B. (1994). Introduction. In B. Moss (Ed.), *Literacy across communities* (pp. 1-7). Cresskill, NJ: Hampton Press.

The President's waste basket. (1916). *The Chicago Defender.*

Rooks, N. M. (1996). *Hair raising: Beauty, culture, and African American women.* New Brunswick, NJ: Rutger's University Press.

Royster, J. (Ed.). (1997). *Southern horrors and other writings: The anti-lynching campaign of Ida B. Wells, 1892-1900.* New York: Bedford Books.

Royster, J. (2000). *Traces of a stream: Literacy and social change among African-American women.* Pittsburgh: University of Pittsburgh Press.

Spear, A. H. (1967). *Black Chicago: The making of a negro ghetto, 1890-1920.* Chicago: University of Chicago Press.

Suggs, H. L. (1996). *The black press in the middle west, 1865-1985.* Westport, CT: Greenwood Press.

To the voters of the 2nd ward. (1912, March 30). *The Chicago Defender.*

A true race woman speaks. (1911, September 16). *The Chicago Defender.*

Weigman, R. (1997). *American anatomies: Theorizing race and gender.* Durham, NC: Duke University Press.

17

CONCEPTUAL DIVERSITY ACROSS MULTIPLE CONTEXTS

Student Athletes on the Court and in the Classroom

Julie Cheville
Rutgers University

> *We have bodies connected to the natural world, such that our consciousness and rationality are tied to our bodily orientations and interactions in and with our environment. Our embodiment is essential to who we are, to what meaning is, and to our ability to draw rational inferences and be creative.*
>
> —Mark Johnson (1987, p. 13)

For several decades, qualitative researchers have been aware that cognition is not exclusively intramental. The work of Scribner and Cole (1981) accelerated interest in how the distinct conditions of language use mediate thought. Today, scholarship in situated cognition considers the conceptual significance of socially mediated patterns of activity (Engestrom, Miettinen, Punamaki, & Punamaki, 1999; Kirshner & Whitson, 1997; Walkerdine, 1998; Wertsch, 1995) and community (Lave, 1997; Lave & Wenger, 1991; Rogoff, 1995; Wenger, 1998). And yet, because the central focus of this scholarship has centered on the influence of symbol-making, most notably language, the tradition has not squarely challenged a longstanding philosophical and scientific devaluation of the human body as an avenue to meaning. Given recent accounts of the link between cognition and bodily activity (Damasio, 1994, 1999; Johnson, 1987), there is reason to expand the notion of *situativity* to include the influence of the body on the mind. In this way, cognition might be conceptualized in a way that recognizes both language *and* the human body as mediational tools.

Drawn from a 2-year ethnographic study of female student athletes at an NCAA Division I institution, this chapter examines bodily activity in the context of participants' athletic and academic learning. On the basketball court, players fostered a partnership of mind and body, relying on ritualized activity and apprenticeship to enter into shared understanding. Although their discursive orientation included linguistic mediation, the athletes' daily enactment and rehearsal of bodily activity had consequential effects on thought. In the classroom, these students frequently encountered literacy practices that dismissed the human body, privileging instead the processing of linguistic information abstracted from concrete activity and interaction. This chapter considers the discursive disjunctures characterizing the learning of student athletes and suggests the need for a theoretical construction of literacy that responds to conceptual diversity by acknowledging the mediational influence of the body on literate activity.

EMBODIED COGNITION: THE INTERDEPENDENCE OF MIND, BODY, AND ACTIVITY

In *The Body in the Mind: The Bodily Basis of Meaning, Imagination, and Reason*, philosopher Johnson (1987) insisted that the partnership of mind and body is responsible for an array of mental structures, or schemata, that guide cognition. He suggested that, "any adequate account of meaning and rationality must give a central place to embodied and imaginative structures of understanding by which we grasp our world" (p. xiii). Although the concept of embodiment holds variable meaning across disciplines, Johnson's notion of embodied cognition emphasizes the influence of bodily activity on thought.[1] As he explained, particular spatiotemporal experiences of the body lead to the emergence of distinct schemata that, in turn, guide both concrete and abstract mental operations. Johnson maintained that "imaginative projection," the process by which particular mental structures arise from bodily activity, is vital yet largely ignored.

In the context of their athletic learning, female student athletes reported the considerable influence of "embodied" mental structures (Cheville, 2001), those schemata that emerged from bodily practice. Of these, the *balance schema* was most important. On the court, participants oriented to the diffusion of interrelated bodies with the objective synchronic motion. From the spherical equilibrium of the ball to the equal distribution of a standing player's weight to the integrated motion of five players across court space, systemic balance was central. According to Johnson, the embodied schematic structure that emerges from such activity has a profound effect on cognition. With recurring experiences of balance, an embodied mental structure arises that inclines one to recognize "balanced personalities, balanced systems, balanced equations, the balance of power, the balance of justice, and so on" (Johnson, 1987, p. 87). To achieve systemic balance, players' knowledge-making was distinctly reflexive in nature. Qualley (1997) explained reflexivity this way:

> Reflexivity is not the same thing as reflection, although they are often part of the same recursive and hermeneutical process. When we reflect, we fix our thoughts on a subject; we carefully consider it, meditate upon it. Self-reflection assumes that individuals can access the contents of their own mind independently of others. Reflexivity, on the other hand, does not originate in the self but always occurs in response to a person's critical engagement with an "other." Unlike reflection, which is a unidirectional thought process, reflexivity is a bi-directional, contrastive process. The encounter with an other results in new information or perspectives which we must hold up to our own current conception of things. (p. 11)

Learning on the court necessitated that each player move beyond the reflective mastery of isolated positional knowledge to a deeper sense for all options possible at the other four positions on the court. What mattered was a shared perceptual understanding for an entire system of play. As Jackson and Delehanty (1995) wrote, "Basketball is a sport that involves the subtle interweaving of players at full speed to the point where they are thinking and moving as one. To do that successfully, they need to trust each other on a deep level and know instinctively how their teammates will respond in pressure situations" (p. 17).

The synchronic activity that supported learning and knowing for the female athletes was a product of asymmetrical relations between the coach as teacher, older players as master students, and younger players as apprentices. Even though each position on the court required particular schemata, successful play demanded that players calibrate their perception to achieve a "relational matrix" (Becker, 1995) that defied individualism. Jenny, a junior reserve center, explained the string metaphor that her coach used to encourage collective consciousness:

> Coach teaches guards the "string concept." You're not supposed to get closer than maybe ten or twelve feet. When this person cuts through, you stay on the string. If she cuts away from you, she's pulling you with her. If she cuts over there, you don't stay over here because if she's stuck, she can't pass the ball back to you. . . . After you've been playing with the same people for a while, you almost start to get on the same brain waves. It's comfortable. You get really confident and, "Well, yeah, they understand. They understand what I'm thinking, and I understand what they're thinking." I can lob a pass up to Tan and expect her to catch it. I know her timing on her jump and how high she is going to jump or if she is going to be up higher in the lane when she posts. I think that's what makes a team really successful. If you know that person is going to be there without even having to look at them.

Only by "being there" together in body did players enter into reflexive knowing. For Jenny and her teammates, synchronic bodily activity ensured systemic balance. To this end, learning was necessarily a political process in which coaches and elder players assumed considerable responsibility for facilitating the perceptual processes of younger players. Learning grew complicated on the those occasions when novices resisted adjustments in perception or master students refused to negotiate the process (Cheville, 2001).

Another mental structure, the *containment schema*, originated from concrete experiences of "in" or "out" and guided players' relation to distal or proximal conditions, even in an ideational realm. As Johnson (1987) suggested, "When we actually move from one place to another, we experience ourselves as traversing a path from one bounded area to another. This experience . . . provides a basis for our understanding of negation" (p. 39). In effect, the recurring physical experience of being "inside" or "outside" culturally codified boundaries shapes an individual's abstract, or nonphysical, understanding of him or herself as actor or audience, accepted or negated, insider or outsider.

Containment was considered so fundamental an orientation that players had little excuse for a violation as basic to court sense as "stepping on the line." More specifically, however, the female athletes refined the containment schema in accordance with their designated positions on the floor. Systemic balance necessitated that players understood how containment meant different things at different positions. For post players, the containment schema was primary. As defenders, they denied the ball from entering the lane, where the shooting percentages of opponents were often highest. Containment was achieved when defensive players oriented toward the axial condition "out" by filling passing lanes and interrupting the possibility that opposing players on the perimeter could pass the ball to teammates in the lane. Containing the ball to the perimeter, or keeping it "out," also involved various schemata for force. Players relied on a stable stance, low hips, and solid shoulder blocks as they fronted, played behind, and three-quartered their offensive opponents. Speaking in terms of her post defense, Malikah explained:

> My mindset is that that yellow paint right there is mine. Treat it like it's your house. . . . If somebody's in there scoring, you can't let them do that. You've got to get them out because they're messing with your house.

Here, Malikah acknowledged force and containment schemata as central to her play. A possessive sense for the court as "home" was a frequent figurative connection for players, a fact not surprising given, as Bachelard (1969) noted, "the house is one of the greatest powers of integration for the thoughts, memories, and dreams of mankind" (p. 6). According to Johnson (1987), embodied schemata that hold considerable efficacy often extend into existing networks of figurative meaning, a process he termed *metaphorical extension.* Not uncommonly, one hears basketball players allude to their "house" or "home," a reference either to their positions on the court or to their native arenas. Over the several years that I observed Malikah and her teammates, what struck me about the extension of image schemata into metaphor is that so long as a player felt she contributed to the care and cultivation of the space she inhabited, the metaphor supported the partnership of mind and body. In the wake of injury, however, when Malikah grew tired of practices that did not translate into game time, her metaphorical sense for home disengaged from the image schemata required of her play on court. Malikah's obligatory connection to place-making responsibilities for which she had formerly held deep regard suggested the metaphor was no longer transformative for her.

For Karen, a starting point guard, bodily activity fostered mastery of what Johnson termed the *path schema,* a conceptual structure that guided her orientation along the axes "from" and "toward." Her position stressed the successful progression of the ball from player to player and from player to basket. Additionally, a time clock demanded that Karen advance the ball in a designated period of time. This temporal element became particularly clear to me one practice as she brought the ball up court during a scrimmage. A manager had activated the shot clock several seconds before the start of action, leaving Karen with fewer seconds than her regulation 30. At the sound of the buzzer, a full 3 seconds early, Karen turned to the manager's table with an emphatic "the clock was off." Indeed, it was. And Karen seemed to have "felt" so. Later she explained the moment,

> Part of my responsibility that's been driven into my head over the years, among other things, is how much time you have on the clock. I think after you run a certain number of plays and you run them as many times as we do, knowing you have to be aware of time, I think you know. If a ball has swung around two or three times, then your time has to be running pretty short. You know if it goes off early. There's no way that that's right. It's part of the awareness of the things around you.

Karen's orchestration of ball movement required constant assessment of teammates' performances. Would a player combating a strained muscle sustain the motility she needed to receive the pass at the high post? Would reserves sitting cold on the bench enter the game and adjust quickly to a demanding play sequence? Injuries, associational adjustments, and other dynamic factors affected Karen's schematic orientation.

For novices, the struggle to adjust one's body to new spatial and temporal dimensions was clear. During one practice, the head coach relocated players to foreign positions on the court in a drill designed to test their knowledge of systemic balance. With Tangela, a starting center, looming at the foreign point guard position and Amy, a freshman reserve post, shifted out to an unfamiliar wing position, the coach ordered Stacy, a freshman reserve point guard, to the post position near the hoop. Within seconds of the first offensive play, both freshmen were confused. Later, Tangela spoke with me about the significance of the drill:

> In a sense, everybody has to know what everybody else does. That's why when Stacy and I were on the court, and Stacy was going through the plays in her head like she does before every game, and I said, "Okay, what does the post do in this play?," she said, "I don't know what the post player does!" Karen and I were like, "You're the point guard. You're supposed to know what everybody does." I said, "I know what the guards do when we do the plays, so you gotta know what the posts do." She's like, "Okay. Okay." So I asked her, "Where does the post go in such and such a play?" And she was like, "I don't know!" She didn't even know. It was crazy.

The lesson of the drill was clear; one is never simply a post, a forward, or a guard. She is all three of these positions. The reflexive understanding required of all positions demanded considerable time, negotiation, and practice, as well as collective investment in instructional rituals. In this context participants' cognition emerged from bodily activity through two processes. By means of imaginative projection, players developed concrete and abstract orientations to balance, containment, force, verticality, and motion. When a particular schema extended into existing networks of figurative meaning, players' learning was enhanced by means of metaphorical projection.

In their classroom experiences, the female student athletes had few opportunities to draw on the mental structures they employed on court. Instead, knowledge-making often hinged solely on "propositional" schemata (Johnson, 1987), those cognitive structures mediated by language. Literacy practices in the academic domain were often solitary rather than social. Like many undergraduates, participants in the study spent significant periods of their academic learning in lecture halls. Such a context facilitated the transmission of information to audiences ranging from 50 to 300 hundred students. Rituals associated with language and literacy in these classrooms immobilized the body, making interaction and concrete application of concepts nearly impossible. As Jenny noted, such a context was problematic:

> I cannot sit in a lecture hall and watch the teacher put notes up on the overhead. . . . Just going pretty much from what he's gotten written up there. I can't do it because there's no interaction. If it's a small discussion group, a class of maybe 15 or 20 people, I think I do much better because you can give your point of view and hear what other people say about it. And hearing about what other people think, whatever you're studying, is like, "Oh, God, now I understand. They were confused on that, too, and they figured out a way to understand it."

The partnership of mind and body, as well as the reflexive engagement of self and other, was often denied in the context of participants' classroom learning. At issue is what I call *schematic portability*, which refers to the degree the schemata learners rely on in one context are available to them in another. Concern for schematic portability is a way of identifying the conceptual disjunctures students face as they traverse multiple sites of learning within a single institution. In addition to the disembodied pedagogy that characterized lecture hall formats, student athletes' learning across contexts was complicated by graduate instructors who lacked pedagogical expertise and instructional support, redundant layers of "remediation," and the absence of meaningful encounters with faculty and nonscholarship students (Cheville, 2001).

The lack of schematic portability that characterized participants' learning was ironic in light of the central importance of embodied schemata to intellectual discovery. Robert and Michelle Root-Bernstein (2000) noted the extent to which scholars' cognitive processes rely upon the body: "Creative thinking—the kind of thinking in every discipline that generates and conceptualizes new insights—relies on what the philosopher Michael Polanyi has called the 'personal knowledge': images, patterns, sensual and muscular feelings, play-acting, empathizing, emotions, and intuitions" (p. A64). Here, the Root-Bernsteins point out the curious institutional ideology that insists upon the primacy of propositional structures as the means to understanding when, in fact, creative discovery and imagination rely so often on embodied cognition. Of the irony, they noted, "Those forms of knowledge have almost no place in our universities, where thinking is almost universally presented as if formal logic were its basis, and words and mathematics its language of choice" (p. A64).

AN INSTITUTIONAL DIVIDE: KNOWING VERSUS BEING

Over the course of the study reported here, as well as during my decade of employment in various retention programs, I sensed that an overarching ideological divide between academic and athletic programming contributed to the schematic disjunctures student athletes experienced. In many mid-size and large public universities, the nearly independent function of these domains reinforces a longstanding philosophical distinction between thought and action. In the athletic sphere, student athletes often find their lives temporally and spatially restricted, required by athletic support personnel to enroll in the same courses, eat at the same training tables, study at the same learning centers, and reside in the same dormitories. Removed from nonscholarship students and from opportunities to negotiate their schooling, student athletes have reported significant degrees of alienation. This isolation is particularly acute for student athletes of color.[2] Although distinct by virtue of gender and thereby removed from the particularly insidious cultural assumptions attached to African-American masculinity,[3] female student athletes of color admitted concern for how their athleticism might be interpreted. Nadine, an off guard, remarked:

> I'm a Black woman who plays sports. The Black community is only known for entertainment and sports and not known for being doctors, lawyers, or great minds. I have to fight against that day in and day out. I constantly fight against that, to try to prove that I do have a mind . . . I'm here to learn.

Nadine's "fight" was complicated by her location in an intercollegiate sports enterprise that made her visible to a local campus and broader public only by way of her physical accomplishments. Her athleticism posed little challenge to a predominantly white public that "has historically sought entertainment, profit, and forms of racial reconciliation that do not challenge fundamental assumptions about racial difference" (Hoberman, 1997, p. 4).

Although student athletes understood the interrelation of mind and body as central to their athletic learning, they feared their bodies jeopardized their intellectual status in classrooms. In particular, those of color worried that their race and unmistakably athletic physiques might be interpreted by faculty and peers as evidence of cognitive deficit. Like several of her teammates, Tangela regretted occasions when instructors drew her athleticism to public attention:

> My teacher announced in class, "The women's basketball team has been winning, and we've got an athlete in the class." I didn't want that. I didn't want other students to look at me like that. I didn't want them to be thinking that I was dumb.

Although such acknowledgment may strike instructors as benign, attention that associates student athletes with physicality is particularly dangerous within those institutions oriented ideologically to a mind–body divide. Such contexts rarely challenge the assumption that intellectual activity requires a transcendence of mind over matter. The result is that nonscholarship students and faculty may fail to recognize, or even reject, the bodily dilemmas that situate students' conceptual orientations.

At worst, faculty who view the phrase *student athlete* as paradoxical are guided by what hooks (1994) cited as the "romantic notion of the professor . . . as a mind that . . . is always at odds with the body" (p. 137). A newspaper commentary written by a professor of English at Iowa State University evoked this understanding:

> Every season in the newspaper there's the litany of offenses committed by student athletes: drug possession, forgery, domestic abuse, assault, theft, armed robbery. We continue to make bail. Make excuses. Set them free. A part of us feels betrayed that these kids are messing up the chance that they have to make something of themselves. Aren't we giving them a free education, for crying out loud? (Kupfer, 1995, p. 9A)

Kupfer issued this sweeping indictment before advising, "Get rid of the hired thugs we call student athletes" (p. 9A). In her criticism, she enforced the divide between mind and body with totalizing allusions to physical and property crime that allow her to consolidate ideological power and privilege as an intellectual who must bear the burden of student athletes' criminality. Although the Student Right-to-Know and Campus Security Act of 1990 mandates the disclosure of campus crime statistics, there exists no separate category for intercollegiate student athletes. However, given that hundreds of male and female students represent *each* of more than 1,000 NCAA Division

I, II, and III member institutions, Kupfer's remark may be less an accurate characterization of this constituency than an indication of what student athletes most fear—that their athleticism will be appropriated and used against them by those who have the power to deny or devaluate their presence.

Certainly, faculty members have a legitimate right to scrutinize their athletic budgets, particularly in those institutions where general college funds are diverted to athletic coffers. In addition, both faculty and students have reason to question policies that grant student athletes inordinate residential or academic privileges. What critics must realize, however, is that blame targeted expressly at student athletes, although expedient, is rarely an effectual means of initiating institutional change. As McLaren (1993) warned, claims that localize blame "relieve teachers from the need to engage in a form of pedagogical self-scrutiny or a serious critique of their personal roles within the school, and the school's role in the wider society" (p. 211).

Appreciating embodied cognition challenges a historical devaluation that has had several consequences. First, to the extent that language has been understood as liberating one from bodily "constraints," theories of cognition have accorded exclusive attention to the mediational role of language. Second, for those understood in terms of bodily difference, the devaluation of the body has been the means by which individuals and cultural groups are made to bear the stigma of physicality, what is often a simultaneous indictment of intellect. Concern for how cognition is embodied upends the traditional rhetorical and philosophical insistence that language liberates one's mind from the material conditions of her body. In effect, embodied cognition reasserts how, for all students, denial of the body erases ways not just to be but to think.

LITERACY PRACTICES THAT MIND THE BODY

> Understanding is an event—it is not merely a body of beliefs. . . . Knowledge must be understood in terms of structures of embodied human understanding, as an interaction of a human . . . with its environment (which includes its language, cultural traditions, values, institutions, and the history of it social community). (Johnson, 1987, p. 100)

A central feature of athletic learning for the female student athletes was the emphasis on understanding as primarily a process. On the court, these athletes engendered a "perception-action dialectic" (Crossley, 1996) that was necessarily political, requiring negotiated consensus to arrive at shared meaning. Although language assisted learners to characterize their perceptual fields in brief interludes between play, it was the nonverbal codification of embodied mental schemata that was primarily responsible for the reflexive consciousness learners sought during extensive sequences of action. The reflexive circuit (Siegle, 1986) from self to other and back to self attuned learners to the significance of process and positionality. Growing familiar with this conceptual orientation at the same time I was teaching freshman composition, I began to consider ways that writing might assist students to bridge the physical and the textual. As Reynolds (1993) suggested, recognizing how language is embodied is necessary if writers are to understand their perceptual locations.

> A writer's subject positions are determined by the space of her body, her geographical location, her shifting intellectual positions, her distance or closeness to others, to texts, to events . . . ethos is created when writers locate themselves; it is "a way of claiming and taking responsibility for our positions in the world, for the ways we see, for the places from which we speak." (pp. 335-336)

To accept that understanding is a process and that a writer's textual positions are located in concrete activity is to recognize the significant potential of narrative to both document and bridge one's shifting physical, conceptual, and textual positions. As Holquist (1989) suggested, narrative is the textual genre most oriented to the patterns of stasis and change so characteristic of the relations between mind and body, self and other, and structure and antistructure.

The problem, of course, is that an arbitrary distinction between critical knowledge and personal experience can lead to general disregard for narrative. The genre's very connection to the lived body can be problematic for teachers. In the mid-1990s, the freshman composition program in which I taught involved a two-semester sequence, the first semester devoted largely to narrative-based writing and speech. For inexperienced instructors, the teaching and evaluation of narrative generated concern. Peers in my teaching assistants' advisory group admitted their hesitation, and in some cases resentment, at teaching and assessing personal writing. They recognized the limitations of traditional narrative practices and the problems associated with "possessive individualism" (Shotter, 1989), particularly the failure of conventional narratives to welcome new forms and spaces for subjectivity. For many instructors, forms of autobiographical writing existed antithetically to modes of inquiry they understood as critical. As the first semester progressed, it was clear that this discomfort had led some to proceed directly to argumentative assignments more in line with the second semester curriculum. Although I sympathized with my teaching peers, I also worried about what the extinction of narrative might mean to students, particularly those inclined to think reflexively. At the same time, I was experimenting with a fall course that incorporated narratives of self and other into a semester-long field project that culminated in an ethnographic essay (Chiseri-Strater & Sunstein, 2002).[4] I shared Mahala and Swilky's (1996) view that

> story may be a framework for moving beyond personal narrative. . . . If writers understand how their experience is rooted in various socio-historical processes and community traditions, they can more easily move between them, integrating personal and scholarly ways of knowing the self, others, and the world. (p. 365)

Although I regret that I did not have the occasion in this context to teach intercollegiate student athletes, this opportunity would arise during postdoctoral teaching. Later, as a senior lecturer in the Writing Workshop at Ohio State University, I sensed that those students who were inclined to think reflexively benefited from narrative-based inquiry that allowed them to reconcile the negotiated interaction associated with fieldwork and the textual quandaries associated with representation. An undergraduate basic writing program, the Writing Workshop possessed the autonomy and resources necessary for a post-doctoral faculty to experiment with a host of embodied practices that included oral histories, apprenticeship, portfolios, computer-mediated authoring and communication, service learning, and problem-based inquiry.

The Writing Workshop is one of few basic writing programs in the country that has survived and prospered in ways that affect the retention of those whose literate practices reflect diverse conceptual styles. For several reasons, the program is promising. First, it serves transitional students on their entrance to the university, a time when they are most inclined to struggle with the sensibility of an institution that so often splinters their identity. Second, its faculty are skilled in pedagogies that necessitate reflexive thinking. Course enrollments limited to 15 students are taught in classrooms that allow for a circular setting, an arrangement that invites students and their instructor to maintain visual access to each other during discussions. The orientation is not unlike the ceremonial huddle, a symbolic ritual in team sport that locates each learner equidistant from a center point so that the axial experience of space and other is the same. Schematically, such an arrangement is influential. On the perimeter of the classrooms, individual stations allow for computer-mediated instruction. In this way, oral and written language is an outgrowth of embodied action via direct and technological interactions. Literate practices that support narrative reflexivity recognize the experience of border crossing (Giroux, 1993) and perceptual negotiation (Horner & Lu, 2000) without disassociating these struggles from concrete relations and activities. Political and ethical issues associated with representation are not abstract concepts but are connected directly to one's physical and social location in and across contexts, and become the very subject of one's storying. Put simply, one's embodied activity is the means to language and thought.

RECONCILING THE ACADEMIC–ATHLETIC DIVIDE

In 1969, Jensen, a professor of educational psychology at the University of California, suggested that African-American students are genetically predisposed to cognitive disadvantage and thereby more inclined to learn by doing, or "associational learning," than by abstract thought. His claims remain abhorrent on two counts. First, such a view ascribes intellectual deficit to bodily difference, thereby conferring cognitive status to those who occupy essentialized positions in a host of binaries (White/non-White, *male*/female, *able*/disabled). Second, such a claim sustains the erroneous view that pedagogies requiring students to make concrete connections to content and to each other are inherently less sophisticated than those that transmit information. The insidious implications of Jensen's argument are clear when one understands how participatory action, manifested both linguistically and bodily, supports pedagogies oriented to the dissolution of boundaries between mind–body, self–other, and reflection–reflexivity.

Across the economies of sport and school, all participants—faculty, staff, and students—come to hold conceptual orientations constituted by discursive conditions that locate them. Reconciling multiple contexts of learning will require individuals who are less concerned about defending their respective institutional spaces than about listening and thinking through each other. Committees that investigate intercollegiate athletics must include not only those who can most adequately attest to the dilemmas of schematic portability, the student athletes themselves, but also those faculty and staff courageous enough to sidestep seductive and grand rhetorical arguments that posit blame. Above all, these individuals must consider systemic reforms that challenge the ideological divide between mind and body that infiltrates every dimension of academic life.

The appreciation for literacies as situated, contextual processes requires research methodologies oriented to linguistic and bodily activity. Although discourse analyses have traditionally acknowledged the influence of "ways of being" (Gee, 1999), there has been little attempt, beyond basic descriptions of body image or orientation, to document the distinct influence of the human body on the mind nor to explain how particular forms of bodily activity support shared cognition. Complicating existing notions of literacy will require an appreciation for participatory action as both socially situated and embodied. Like Whitson (1997), I do not see a theoretical disjuncture between current studies of situated and embodied cognition. Rather, I envision a more comprehensive yet delineated framework for understanding how human activity might better support literate practice.

ENDNOTES

1. For accounts of embodiment in anthropology, see Becker (1995), Connerton (1989), Douglas (1966), Jackson (1995), Mauss (1973), and K. Young (1994). For those in biomedicine and medical anthropology, see Csordas (1994), Damasio (1995), Jackson (1994), Lock and Scheper-Hughes (1987), Komesaroff (1995), Olsen (1991), Rothfield (1995), Sacks (1995), and Scheper-Hughes (1993). For critiques of embodiment in cultural, historical, and feminist studies, see Bordo (1993), Brumberg (1997), Butler (1993), Fiske (1993), Foucault (1984), Gallop (1995), Goldenberg (1990), Grosz (1994), Haraway (1991), hooks (1991, 1994), Lorde (1984), Sappington and Stallings (1994), and Sheets-Johnstone (1992). In the area of disability studies, see Davis (1997), Fine and Asch (1988), Mitchell and Snyder (1997), Morgan (1991), Thomson (1996), and Wendell (1996). In education, see McLaren (1993), Payne (2000), and Walkerdine (1997). In philosophy, refer to Jackson (1989), Merleau-Ponty (1962), Welton (1969), and I. Young (1990).
2. In 1987 the Presidents Commission of the National Collegiate Athletic Association sponsored an American Institute for Research study that surveyed intercollegiate student athletes enrolled in 42 of an existing 291 NCAA Division I schools. Based on questionnaire and interview data, the study represented the responses of 292 intercollegiate student athletes in high-profile men's and women's sports. According to the AIR findings, 50% of those interviewed acknowledge a feeling that they lacked control of their academic lives. For an analysis of the study and its racial implications, see Hawkins (1995).
3. John Hoberman (1997) challenges the assumption that sport in the United States has contributed to racial integration. He argues that "the cult of African American athleticism" has only reinforced racist assumptions about the intellectual achievement of African males. While I agree with Hoberman's assertion that sport poses serious conceptual demands for students athletes of color, I reject his claim that African-American males welcome, even cater, the images reserved for them. My experiences with female and male athletes suggests their disdain for the stigma of athleticism.

4. The field project evolved over the course of the semester and included four stages, each requiring a particular phase of research and writing (examining the self, entering the field, interviewing informants, and coming to conclusions).

REFERENCES

Bachelard, G. (1969). *The poetics of space.* (M. Jolas, Trans.). Boston: Beacon Press.

Becker, A. (1995). *Body, self, and society: The view from Fiji.* Philadelphia: University of Pennsylvania Press.

Bordo, S. (1993). *Unbearable weight: Feminism, western culture, and the body.* Berkeley: University of California Press.

Brumberg, J. (1997). *The body project: An intimate history of American girls.* New York: Random House.

Butler, J. (1993). *Bodies that matter: On the discursive limits of "sex."* New York: Routledge.

Cheville, J. (2001). *Minding the body: What student athletes know about learning.* Portsmouth, NH: Boynton/Cook.

Chiseri-Strater, E., & Sunstein, B. (2002). *FieldWorking reading and writing research* (2nd ed.). Boston: Prentice-Hall.

Connerton, P. (1989). *How societies remember.* Cambridge: Cambridge University Press.

Crossley, N. (1996). *Intersubjectivity: The fabric of social becoming.* London: Sage.

Csordas, T. (Ed.). (1994). *Embodiment and experience: The existential ground of culture and self.* Cambridge: Cambridge University.

Damasio, A. (1994). *Descartes' error: Emotion, reason, and the human brain.* New York: Avon.

Damasio, A. (1999). *The feeling of what happens: Body and emotion in the making of consciousness.* New York: Harcourt Brace.

Davis, L. (1997). *The disability studies reader.* New York: Routledge.

Douglas, M. (1966). *Purity and danger: An analysis of the concepts of pollution and taboo.* London: ARK.

Engestrom, Y., Miettinen, R., Punamaki, R., & Punamaki, R.L. (1999). *Perspectives on activity theory.* Cambridge: Cambridge University Press.

Fine, M., & Asch, A. (Eds). (1988). *Women with disabilities: Essays in psychology, culture, and politics.* Philadelphia: Temple University Press.

Fiske, J. (1993). *Power plays, power works.* New York: Verso.

Foucault, M. (1984). *The Foucault reader.* New York: Pantheon.

Gallop, J. (Ed.). (1995). *Pedagogy: The question of impersonation.* Bloomington: Indiana University Press.

Gee, J. P. (1999). *An introduction to discourse analysis: Theory and method.* New York: Routledge.

Giroux, H. (1993). *Border crossings: Cultural workers and the politics of education.* New York: Routledge.

Goldenberg, N. (1990). *Returning words to flesh: Feminism, psychoanalysis, and the resurrection of the body*. Boston: Beacon.

Grosz, E. (1994). *Volatile bodies: Toward a corporeal feminism*. Bloomington: Indiana University Press.

Haraway, D. (1991). *Simians, cyborgs, and women: The reinvention of nature*. New York: Routledge.

Hawkins, B. (1995). *Examining the experience of Black student athletes at predominantly white NCAA division I institutions using an internal colonial model*. Unpublished doctoral dissertation, University of Iowa, Iowa City.

Hoberman, J. (1997). *Darwin's athletes:How sport has damaged Black America and preserved the myth of race*. New York: Mariner.

Holquist, M. (1989). From body-talk to biography: The chronobiological bases of narrative. *Yale Journal of Criticism, 3*(1), 1-35.

hooks, b. (1991). *Ain't I a woman: Black women and feminism*. Boston: South End.

hooks, b. (1994). *Teaching to transgress: Education as the practice of freedom*. New York: Routledge.

Horner, B., & Lu, M. (2000). *Representing the "other": Basic writers and the teaching of basic writing*. Urbana, IL: NCTE.

Jackson, J. (1994). Chronic pain and the tension between the body as subject and object. In T. Csordas (Ed.), *Embodiment and experience: The existential ground of culture and self* (pp. 201-228). Cambridge: Cambridge University Press.

Jackson, M. (1995). *Paths toward a clearing: Radical empiricism and ethnographic inquiry*. Bloomington: Indiana University Press.

Jackson, P., & Delehanty, H. (1995). *Sacred hoops: Spiritual lessons of a hardwood warrior*. New York: Hyperion.

Jensen, A. (1969). How much can we boot, IQ and scholastic achievement? *Harvard Educational Review, 39*, 1-123.

Johnson, M. (1987). *The body in the mind: The bodily basis of meaning, imagination, and reason*. Chicago: University of Chicago Press.

Kirshner, D., & Whitson, J. (Eds.). (1997). *Situated cognition: Social, semiotic, and psychological perspectives*. Mahwah, NJ: Erlbaum.

Komesaroff, P. (1995). *Troubled bodies: Critical perspectives on postmodernism, medical ethics, and the body*. Durham, NC: Duke University Press.

Kupfer, F. (1995, March 17). Football's awesome mythological status is bewildering. *Ames Daily Tribune*, p. 9A.

Lave, J. (1997). The culture of acquisition and the practice of understanding. In D. Kirschner & J. Whiteson (Eds.), *Situated cognition: Social, semiotic, and psychological perspectives* (pp. 17-36). Mahwah, NJ: Erlbaum.

Lave, J., & Wenger, E. (1991). *Situated learning: Legitimate peripheral participation*. Cambridge: Cambridge University Press.

Lock, M., & Cheper-Hughes, N. (1987). The mindful body. *Medical Anthropology Quarterly, 1*, 6-41.

Lorde, A. (1984). *Sister outsider: Essays and speeches*. Freedom, CA: Crossing Press.

Mahala, D., & Swilky, D. (1996). Telling stories, speaking personally: Reconsidering the place of lived experience in composition. *Journal of Advanced Composition, 16*(3), 363-388.

Mauss, M. (1973). The techniques of the body (B. Brewster, Trans.). *Economy and Society, 2*, 70-88.

McLaren, P. (1993). *Schooling as a ritual performance: Toward a political economy of educational symbols and gestures* (2nd ed.). New York: Routledge.

Merleau-Ponty, M. (1969). *The visible and invisible: Followed by working notes* (A. Lingis, Trans.). Evanston, IL: Northwestern University.

Mitchell, D., & Snyder, S. (Eds.). (1997). *The body and physical difference: Discourses of disability in the humanities.* Ann Arbor: University of Michigan Press.

Morgan, K. (1991). Women and the knife: Cosmetic surgery and the colonization of women's bodies. *Hypatia: A Journal of Feminist Philosophy, 6*, 25-53.

Olsen, A. (1991). *Body stories: A guide to experiential anatomy.* New York: Station Hill Press.

Qualley, D. (1997). *Turns of thought: Teaching composition as reflexive inquiry.* Portsmouth, NH: Boynton/Cook.

Payne, M. (2000). *Bodily discourses: When students write about abuse and eating disorders.* Portsmouth, NH: Boynton/Cook.

Reynolds, N. (1993). Ethos as location: New sites for understanding discursive authority. *Rhetoric Review, 11*, 325-339.

Rogoff, B. (1995). Observing sociocultural activity on three planes: Participatory appropriation, guided participation, and apprenticeship. In. J. Wertsch, P. Del Rio, & A. Alvarez (Eds.), *Sociocultural studies of mind* (pp. 139-164). Cambridge: Cambridge University Press.

Root-Bernstein, R.S., & Root-Bernstein, M. (2000, January 14). Learning to think with emotion. *The Chronicle of Higher Education*, p. A64.

Rothfield, P. (1995). Bodies and subjects: Medical ethics and feminism. In P. Komesaroff (Ed.), *Troubled bodies: Critical perspectives on postmodernism, medical ethics, and the body* (pp. 168-201). Durham, NC: Duke University Press.

Sacks, O. (1995). *An anthropologist on Mars.* New York: Knopf.

Sappington, R., & Stallings, T. (1994). *Uncontrollable bodies: Testimonies of identity and culture.* San Francisco: Bay Press.

Scheper-Hughes, N. (1993). *Death without weeping: The violence of everyday life in Brazil.* Berkeley: University of California Press.

Sheets-Johnstone, M. (1992). *Giving the body its due.* Albany: State University of New York Press.

Shotter, J. (1989). Social accountability and the social construction of "you." In J. Shotter & K. Gergen (Eds.), *Texts of identity* (pp. 125-160). London: Sage.

Scribner, S., & Cole, M. (1981). *The psychology of literacy.* Cambridge: Harvard University Press.

Siegle, R. (1986). *The politics of reflexivity: Narrative and the constitutive poetics of culture.* Baltimore, MD: Johns Hopkins University Press.

Thomson, R. G. (1996). *Extradordinary bodies.* New York: Columbia University Press.

Walkerdine, V. (1997). Redefining the subject in situation cognition theory. In D. Kirshner & J. Whitson (Eds.), *Situated cognition: Social, semiotic, and psychological perspectives* (pp. 57-70). Mahwah, NJ: Erlbaum.

Walkerdine, V. (1998). *Counting girls out.* London: Falmer.

Welton, D. (1998). *Body and flesh: A philosophical reader.* Malden, MA: Blackwell.

Wendell, S. (1996). *The rejected body: Feminist philosophical reflections on disability.* New York: Routledge.

Wenger, E. (1998). *Communities of practice: Learning, meaning, and identity.* Cambridge: Cambridge University Press.

Wertsch, J. (1995). The need for action in sociocultural research. In J. Wertsch, P. Del Rio, & A. Alvarez (Eds.), *Sociocultural studies of mind* (pp. 56-74). Cambridge: Cambridge University Press.

Whitson, J. (1997). Cognition as a semiotic process: From situated mediation to critical reflective transcendence. In D. Kirschner & J. Whitson (Eds.), *Situated cognition: Social, semiotic, and psychological perspectives* (pp. 97-150). Mahwah, NJ: Erlbaum.

Young, I.M. (1990). *Throwing like a girl and other essays in feminist philosophy and social theory.* Bloomington: Indiana University Press.

Young, K. (1994). Whose body? An introduction to bodylore. *Journal of American Folklore, 107*, 3-8.

18

MULTIPLYING LITERACY = ADDING NUMERACY

Numbers and the Literacy Educator

Cindy Johanek
Denison University

> *Like language, religion, and music, mathematics is a universal part of human culture.*
>
> —Steen (1990, p. 220)

> *Mathematics has as much to do with computation as writing has to do with typing. Imagine that throughout the course of one's education all one ever did in English class was diagram sentences.*
>
> —Paulos (1992, p. 335)

In his short story, "Subtotals," Burnham (1992) presented an inventory—literally—of one man's life. In short, crisp sentences, all ending in numerals and beginning with "Number," Burnham gives his readers a life as he sees it, play by play, score after score:

> Number of broken bones: 0. Number of Purple Hearts: 0. Number of times unfaithful to wife: 2. Number of holes in one, big golf: 0; miniature golf: 3. Number of consecutive push-ups, maximum: 25 . . . Number of times caught in the act, any act: 64. Number of postcards sent: 831, received: 416. Number of spider plants that died while under my care:

> 34. Number of blind dates: 2. Number of jumping jacks: 982,316. Number of headaches: 184. Number of kisses, given: 21,602; received: 20,041 . . . Number of times fallen off playground equipment, swings: 3; monkey bars: 2; teeter-totter: 1 . . . Number of miracles witnessed: 0 . . . Number of times I forgot what I was going to say: 631. (pp. 97-99)

The entire sudden fiction piece continues in this manner for its own short life of one paragraph that fills a page and a half. By the time we finish Burnham's inventory, we get a sense of who this man is, sharing his successes and limitations, his embarrassments and playfulness, his satisfaction and grief. We see a man possibly hurt to realize that he has been thoughtful enough to send more postcards than he has received, given more kisses than he has been offered. Yet we also see a man inattentive enough to kill several plants, insensitive enough to have been unfaithful to his wife (more than once), and jaded enough to have been unable, perhaps, to see a miracle.

Burnham's inventory, in other words, drives us quickly into the mind of an imperfect and incomplete human being. Although the list (as the title suggests) offers mere "subtotals" of all that has been this man's existence, the tally creates a portrait of a life's journey—a journey that is impossible without the numbers on which it relies for conveying its many layers of meaning, emotion, self-reflection, and images: It becomes, indeed, a "journey toward a sense of mathematical beauty" (Swallow, 1995, p. 572).

NUMERACY AND THE LITERACY RESEARCHER/THEORIST

For most literacy theorists and educators, however, such mathematical beauty has yet to be invited into the discourse on literacies, even in discourse on the inherently (and ironically) mathematically framed *multiple* literacies. For instance, in a composition reader boldly titled *Literacies,* a text designed to "represent many different ways of interpreting experience and the world" (Brunk, Diamond, Perkins, & Smith, 2000, p. xiii), "literacies" are, not surprisingly, limited to standard reading and writing practices focusing on the word, never nearing the number—or the powerful combination of numbers *and* words, numbers *as* words.

Embracing fully a new critique of scientism, literacy theorists have expressed a growing distaste for (and distrust of) numbers and, by extension, the kind of literacy—numeracy—required to fully understand and use numbers well. For Neuleib and Scharton (1994), researchers who rely on experimental designs and gather numerical evidence treat students no better than laboratory rats. For Berthoff (1990), psychological studies deliberately ignore context in the quest for meaningless data. For Lerner (1997), quantitative studies reduce human beings to "manageable integers" (p. 2). For Enos (1996), stories tell more truth than numbers do. And for Elbow (1990), numbers are simply "untrustworthy" (p. 251).

Furthermore, Snyder (1990) suggested that literacy and numeracy are, indeed, two *different* ways of knowing, "based on separate yet complementary cognitive skills . . . learned in specific educational contexts that may sustain one or the other of these modes of thought, seldom both" (p. 233). In Snyder's longitudinal study of 51 MIT graduates, very few (less than one third) were able to engage in nonmathematical modes of thought while they were undergraduates. Twenty-two years after graduation, more than three fourths of the graduates had somehow become more comfortable with more "psychological" or less determined ways of knowing. In the undergraduate curriculum (at least), here is a clear separation between numbers and words, between the sciences and humanities, a distance compounded in part by growing specialization in higher education, imbalanced funding for programs in our schools, and an early 21st-century culture that has come to value math/science/technology/business more highly than reading/writing/art/history.

But for Paulos (1991), a mathematician and a leading numeracy theorist, numeracy—or an ability "to deal comfortably with the fundamental notions of numbers and chance" (p. 3)—is requisite for success in other literacy contexts and acts. Paulos has a keen understanding of what numerous rhetorical theorists have explored for centuries: successful argumentation, communication, and inquiry will sometimes require our understanding of numerical evidence. From Aristotle to Cicero, from George Campbell to George Hillocks, evidence (and what counts as evidence) has been integral to our work. These voices, however, are buried by an explosion of recent scholarship that argues (or even demonstrates) otherwise—a new favoritism toward only qualitative research, a recent surge in acceptance of storytelling as scholarship, a strong commitment to inquiry that is social/political/personal, rather than logical/scientific (see Charney, 1996, for related criticism). Especially revealing is the unexplainable phenomenon of quantitative studies in our field being published as qualitative reports (Johanek, 2000, pp. 60-66).

Although my defense of the "quantitative" will never devalue the "qualitative" (and I object to the dichotomy anyway), any defense of numerical evidence or of numeracy as a much-needed literacy is an unpopular stance. But I agree with Paulos (see also Steen, 1996; Swallow, 1995) when he demands to know why some forms of illiteracy are accepted while others are not: Innumeracy is not only accepted but is *acceptable*. If a student in our classroom were to exclaim, "I hate math" or "I can't even balance my own checkbook," we most likely respond with a chuckle of acceptance (or even empathy) (Paulos, 1995, p. 4). But if that same student were to moan,

"I hate to read" or "I don't read unless it's required," we would feel that all-too-familiar tingle from a great challenge wrapped in insult.

The acceptance of innumeracy results in our inability to become fully literate in other ways: numeracy enables us to more powerfully explore political literacy, workplace literacy, academic literacy, visual literacy, and so on. Consider, for instance, Gale's (1994) *Political Literacy*, in which he explored legal rhetoric and ideology and outlines political literacy as an individual's ability to seek justice—an important ideal to which literacy educators have been strongly committed. Gale's book brings forth two important notions concerning numeracy: the first through argument, the second through demonstration.

First, Gale argued effectively—through theory and common sense—that true political literacy is achieved when individuals critically examine a system in a manner that enables them to secure their individual rights and maintain social justice. To be politically literate is to understand "that as ideology is unself-critical, the rhetoric of theories about legal interpretation may work to undermine justice in the interest of maintaining the dominant ideology" (p. 16). Piercing the veil of this ideology is what political literacy is all about. However, Gale did not address the fact that if we remain innumerate, how will we achieve social justice and secure individual rights if we cannot decipher all of the evidence given to support a legal decision, if we are unfamiliar with some methods of data gathering and analysis (and, indeed, manipulation), or if we refer to those who actually gather and present such data as a collective, vague, and distant "they"?

Second, of interest to numeracy theorists, Gale demonstrated an unfortunately innumerate approach to argument himself (despite his attention to political literacy, interpretation, evidence, and justice). Gale relied almost exclusively on an ethical appeal (we are to believe his claims as a former lawyer and judge). For example, consider that on one page alone, Gale made three specific claims that suggest quantifiable data of some kind. With phrases such as "some legal scholars," "fewer legal scholars and judges," and "much of the commentary" (p. 15), Gale called on quantifiable ideas or differences without any textual or numerical support, such as footnotes/sources, survey results, or specific examples—features many of us would demand, to some extent, in essays from first-year college students.

Readers who have already achieved the political literacy of which Gale spoke should demand more evidence. For those who have not achieved political literacy, Gale paradoxically supported their political *illiteracy* by posing broad, unsupported, veiled claims without the accompanying evidence an individual needs to assess the justice or validity of those claims—accompanying evidence that is *permissible* to omit in a largely innumerate society.

NUMERACY AND OUR READING/WRITING CLASSROOMS

To fully embrace "multiple" literacies and the rich connections between numeracy and other forms of literacy, we must consider the potential dangers of innumeracy—to our students and to ourselves. In my own composition classrooms, I encounter students' basic innumeracy all too often, from an inability to compute a GPA, to grade complaints from students who believe that grades of almost all Bs (but one D and one F), for example, should still average to the most frequent grade, a B (confusing measures of central tendency, the mean and the mode).

When my students use or see numerical evidence, more innumeracy is revealed. For example, when my students conduct research on individually chosen arguments, I present a sample student text to which I believe they will relate. In "To Sign or Not to Sign," a student writer, Carol, attempts to convince readers to think twice before becoming organ donors. Carol has many strengths: She writes with much passion, in a strong voice that is unmistakably her own, and from her own experience as a surgical nurse who has participated in organ harvesting. Carol argues that organ harvesting is a violent act and that organ transplantation is a profit-driven unfeeling enterprise.

Carol's use of numbers, however, is not as strong. To support her claims in one portion of the text, for instance, Carol offers this statistic from a survey of surgical nurses who were invited to give their feelings about organ harvesting: "Nearly a quarter did not like the time involvement" (Kirsch, 1998-1999, p. 59).

When I ask my students about the use of this statistic, they almost always respond in one way: It seems odd for surgical nurses assigned to an organ harvesting team to complain about the amount of time it takes to do the job. Often, students offer an analogy from another line of work: What if teachers complained that they have to spend time with students, for example? I often tell students that they ask a good question, but I challenge them to find another problem, too. After using this sample essay for several semesters (and with numerous students), no student has yet questioned the persuasiveness of "nearly a quarter" in Carol's sentence. As students blink at me, I often explain, "If you have nearly a quarter, and I have over three quarters, who has more?" Usually, they respond with a "light-bulb-OH!"

Frequent use of this example has continued to surprise me in two ways. First, that students have yet to point out that "nearly a quarter" seems an unconvincing statistic for Carol to use. But second, that students need only that one example to make them more critical of how (and why) they read (and write) percentages in text for the remainder of the semester.

Steen (1990) passed on other disturbing observations of innumeracy, such as a 1988 study that found

> about 40 percent of the nation's seventeen-year-olds—can solve moderately more sophisticated problems such as finding 87 percent of 10, or computing the area of a rectangle. And only 6.4 percent of these students—representing only one in twenty of young U.S. adults—can perform simple multistep problems such as calculating total repayment (principal plus interest) on a loan. (p. 215)

In employment situations, required calculations are frequently done by "tricks" or shortcuts created through lore, rather than through school-taught methods (Steen, 1990).

As a result, numeracy theorists such as Paulos, Steen, and Swallow have all put forth a call to end the "mind-numbing way in which mathematics is generally taught" (Paulos, 1995, p. 3) so that mathematics courses, exercises, and tests focus less on isolated, discrete computation skills and more on the conceptually rich contexts in which those skills make sense. After all, sports fans, consumers, medical patients, students of all subjects, parents of all children have their eyes on numbers of different kinds and try to infer meaning from them—for all sorts of reasons, with all sorts of outcomes. The planning of our very futures is inherently numerical, as we invest in retirement plans, pay our debts, estimate time and interest, set goals, and move—month after month—through the rest of our lives.

Math teachers are becoming more aware of the limitations that a skills-oriented, worksheet-dominated course naturally has on the development of numeracy (see, e.g., Whitin & Whitin, 2000). Literacy educators, especially writing teachers, recognize a familiar "paradigm shift" that took place in our own teaching a few decades ago. As literacy educators, we should, with delight, prepare ourselves for and fully support the shift (from skills to concepts, from drills to context) about to unfold in math education.

To begin, we should incorporate an exploration of numeracy in our reading and writing classes, and we can start by taking these six steps:

1. *Confront your own anxiety*. If you suffer from math anxiety, you, too, have limited the kinds of literacy you can attain. It is acceptable to admit such anxiety to students, perhaps in an effort to create a dialogue about the effects of innumeracy. What are innumerate individuals unable to do? How does it affect us? How does it make us powerless over some areas of our lives? If math anxiety is at the core of innumeracy in some way, what do we do about that? Books on math anxiety, such as Tobias' *Overcoming Math Anxiety* (1993) and *Succeed with Math* (1987) could help. Many college learning centers and/or counseling offices also offer guidance for those who face math anxiety. Finally, I find

Paulos to be a delightful, humorous writer who could help reduce anxiety. (I first encountered Paulos' work a few years ago when he appeared on *Dateline* to explain the odds of winning the New York lottery; see Paulos, 1980, 1988, 1991, 1992, 1995.)

2. *Ask for mathematical help if necessary*. Literacy educators often enter the lives of other departments, especially in writing across the curriculum programs (sometimes aggressively, "sticking our noses into other people's business"). Invite other noses into your business by searching your math department, research designers, and statistics courses for someone who is willing to visit your classroom, perhaps someone who is exploring numeracy theory. Possibly the beginning of a strong collaborative relationship, this math expert could help fill in gaps with which you are less comfortable. Even those of us who are numerate in many ways could still have gaps in our knowledge (just like experienced, strong writers who still work to improve themselves). For instance, my brother-in-law, who teaches high school calculus and other math courses (and who was a "math whiz" as a small child), admits a lack of knowledge and confidence in statistics. Despite my studies in statistics and the fun (yes, fun) I have studying statistics, I still find calculus and stocks and bonds to be mind-boggling. We all have gaps in many literacies.
3. *Look for examples in your own reading*. As we read professional publications, newspapers, and popular magazines, all sorts of numerical data appear before our eyes. Start clipping interesting examples to help demonstrate your own numeracy at work—your own critical reading. When I was taking an undergraduate statistics course, our professor clearly explained the difference between a median and a mean when she brought in a newspaper clipping about a possible teachers' strike in our local school district. In that particular community, most residents were outraged to know that teachers who "work only part of the year" and already "get paid too much" with "all those holidays off" would dare strike for more pay (sound familiar?). To make matters worse, the local newspaper, as shown in the clipping we studied in statistics class, printed the surprisingly high "average salary" of teachers in that school district. A numerate eye, however, would have noted that an accompanying graph revealed that the "average" (or mean) included the superintendent's salary (almost four times higher than a teacher's salary). Either the median salary should have been used, or the superintendent's salary removed before computing the mean. (What happens in the

minds of readers unable to read graphs? Well, we already know that, don't we?)

4. *Discuss numbers logically and emotionally*. Numbers can have a strong emotional impact in addition to the logical support they could provide to support an argument or demonstrate a concept. How do we respond to numbers? Even a number as seemingly "static" as 10%, for example, could draw out varied emotions, depending on context. If 10% of the people in my county have chosen not to own a car, I might have no reaction to that news at all. But if I learn, say, that 10% of the children under age 13 in my county have been abused or neglected and are currently in foster care, then 10% seems "higher" emotionally. There are other ways to state numbers, too, which could produce different emotional reactions. For example, if 10% seems small to us, depending on context, perhaps a number like 10,000 would have a greater impact (if we are talking about 10% of 100,000 people, which is 10,000, for instance). Newscasters are often guilty of choosing the most dramatic way to present a number so that it has the greatest effect; however, in this example, 10% and 10,000 are the same thing. Students could also explore (or be asked to write their own) texts that rely on numbers in varied ways (such as the short story that opens this chapter). Through examples such as these, students could become more critical—as readers and writers—of how numbers are used to create an emotional appeal and ask more questions about sample sizes, how data were gathered, how numbers compare to earlier findings, and so on.
5. *Teach survey writing*. Especially in a writing class, learning how to write surveys can be a powerful way to facilitate numeracy in connection to the other forms of literacy we value. As students are asked to become researchers themselves, gathering data, they learn about numbers from the "inside" and from the "beginnings" of first choosing how many questions to ask, whom to ask, how to ask, why they'd ask, what they want to know, and so on. Students will need to decide what kinds of survey questions would be most useful and then how to organize the data once gathered. For example, students should be shown the differences among rank-order questions, multiple-choice questions, likert-scale questions, yes–no (or true–false) questions, open-ended questions, and fill-in-the blank questions. (Most students naturally want open-ended questions, but they find out—too late—how very difficult it is to manage such data. Usually, a blend of question types serves us well.) Consult with research designers or pro-

fessors on your campus for help with writing surveys, and see MacNealy's (1999) chapter on surveys in *Strategies for Empirical Research in Writing.* (And because university Internal Review Board [IRB] guidelines vary, check your own IRB office for its stand on informal, small studies involving human subjects in such a course. If your school requires all studies, even these, to be approved, then no study should be done without IRB approval. In some cases, however, such classroom exercises are exempt from review.)

6. *Discuss numeracy.* Finally, numeracy as a form of literacy should be openly discussed, named, and explored in reading or writing classrooms, especially its connection to other forms of literacy. As literacy educators, we can give numeracy an important seat in our classrooms by making it as important as all other kinds of literacy we teach, study, and value. Like all other forms of literacy, numeracy is never its own "unit" in a classroom, somehow separated from other concepts and skills. It will appear (and become necessary) again and again as our students read, write, and live their lives.

MULTIPLYING LITERACY = ADDING NUMERACY

Truly multiplying literacy by adding numeracy does not require a total and dramatic change in what we, as literacy educators, already do. Critical questions, insightful observations, increased power, careful choices and research, and appreciation of language are already at the core of what we teach and what we hope our students gain. Acknowledging and exploring numeracy as an already integral part of an enterprise devoted to multiple literacies enables our students to read with different eyes, to write with careful evidence, to think more powerfully in the workplace, in the academy, in their own personal lives, and in an ever-changing democracy.

Certainly, as literacy educators and researchers, we should not feel pressured to *become* mathematicians. Yet, in the context of (and in connection to) other literacies we value, we must not deny the power of numeracy or, worse, remove its exploration from our research and our classroom as if it is unconnected or unnecessary to all other literacy forms we teach. To do so ensures that we and our students will read and write less critically, argue less effectively, engage only partially in a democracy, and fragment the individual power on which the fullest blossoming of our work—and our students' work—so urgently depends.

REFERENCES

Berthoff, A. (1990). *The sense of learning*. Portsmouth, NH: Heineman, Boynton/Cook.

Brunk, T., Diamond, S., Perkins, P., & Smith, K. (2000). *Literacies: Reading, writing, interpretation* (2nd ed.). New York: Norton.

Burnham, G. (1992). Subtotals. In J. Thomas, D. Thomas, & T. Hazuka (Eds.), *Flash fiction* (pp. 97-99). New York: Norton.

Charney, D. (1996). Empiricism is not a four-letter word. *College Composition and Communication, 47*, 567-593.

Elbow, P. (1990). *What is English?* New York: Modern Language Association.

Enos, T. (1996). *Gender roles and faculty lives in rhetoric and composition.* Carbondale: Southern Illinois University Press.

Gale, F. (1994). *Political literacy: Rhetoric, ideology, and the possibility of justice.* Albany: State University of New York Press.

Johanek, C. (2000). *Composing research: A contextualist research paradigm for rhetoric and composition.* Logan: Utah State University Press.

Kirsch, C. (1998-1999). To sign or not to sign. In *Ball Point: The Ball State University Writing Program Handbook* (17th ed.). Needham Heights, MA: Simon & Schuster Custom Publishing.

Lerner, N. (1997). Counting beans and making beans count. In *The Writing Lab Newsletter, 22,* 1-4.

MacNealy, M. S. (1999). *Strategies for empirical research in writing.* Boston: Allyn & Bacon.

Neuleib, J., & Scharton, M. (1994). Writing others, writing ourselves: Ethnography and the writing center. In J. Mullin & R. Wallace (Eds.). *Intersections: Theory-practice in the writing center.* Urbana, IL: NCTE.

Paulos, J. A. (1991). *Beyond numeracy: Ruminations of a numbers man.* New York: Knopf.

Paulos, J. A. (1988). *Innumeracy: Mathematical illiteracy and its consequences.* New York: Hill & Wang.

Paulos, J. A. (1992). Math-moron myths. *Mathematics Teacher, 85*(5), 335.

Paulos, J. A. (1995). *A mathematician reads the newspaper.* New York: Basic Books.

Paulos, J. A. (1980). *Mathematics and humor.* Chicago: University of Chicago Press.

Snyder, B. R. (1990). Literacy and numeracy: Two ways of knowing. *Daedalus, 119*, 233-256.

Steen, L. A. (1990). Numeracy. *Daedalus, 119*, 211-231.

Swallow, J. R. (1995). Beautiful numbers. *American Scholar, 64*, 572-578.

Tobias, S. (1987). *Succeed with math: Every student's guide to conquering math anxiety.* New York: College Entrance Examination Board,

Tobias, S. (1993). *Overcoming math anxiety.* New York: Norton.

Whitin, P., & Whitin, D. J. (2000). *Math is language too: Talking and writing in the mathematics classroom.* Urbana, IL: NCTE/NCTM.

V

CRITICAL LITERACIES AND CRITICAL THINKING ABOUT LITERACIES

19

SAVAGE (IL)LITERACIES

Hunting the Realities of Injun Joe

Kevin Ball
Youngstown State University

In early April 1997, CBS rushed its *48 Hours* newsmagazine crew to the Ozark hills in southern Missouri to document the climax of Missouri's largest manhunt in recent history, a manhunt that had lasted more than 6 nerve-wracking months while crisscrossing and backtracking through three counties. Although the size of the manhunt—the number of law enforcement officials swelled to 400 at its peak—and its subject—36-year-old Alis Ben Johns, a suspect in three brutal murders and a string of burglaries—perhaps warranted a snippet on national newscasts, the *48 Hours* crew imagined a different slant on the story of a fugitive featured briefly on *America's Most Wanted,* a story with a wider audience appeal. A scarce 7 minutes and 16 seconds into the broadcast that aired several months later, correspondent Harold Dow elicited, in an interview with Johns' mother, the trope that permeated the media's coverage of the manhunt. "He couldn't read or write, so it made it rough on him," Johns' mother remarked to Dow. "He can't be right if he's doing all what they say he's done." What fascinated the CBS journalists the most (and indeed, what intrigued members of both the local and national media covering the chase), was not Johns' remarkable ability to evade the manhunt through his skills and cunning as a woodsman, but rather his lack of another more civilized skill: "Johns has a sixth- or seventh-grade education and can't read or write."

Nicknamed "Injun Joe" because of his woodsmarts and an affinity for "playing Indian" as a child, Johns was caricatured immediately by the media as the stereotypical hillbilly due to his inability to read or write. Because the assessment of literacy frequently provides the framework within which to evaluate cultural practices, Johns' illiteracy also provided an obvious cultural marker of difference for any reader of a newspaper, alienating Johns as cultural "Other". The public obsession with literacy and its role in the creation and perpetuation of Otherness has been well documented (see Giroux, 1987; Graff, 1987; Scribner, 1988; Street, 1995). For example, in his essay "Representations of Literacy and Region: Narrating 'Another America,'" Mortensen (1994) analyzed popular literary sketches of the genteel Bluegrass to describe how public discourse narrates "another America" through its representations of literacy and region.[1] This chapter examines the modern day public discourse of newspaper and television journalism and their narratives depicting Johns as Ozark hillbilly. The nature of the "sketches" differs, but the narration of "another America" through representations of literacy and region remains just as ideologically insidious. What is perhaps not so obvious about the use of the literacy trope to characterize Johns are the differences in narrative representations of the manhunt between local and national media coverage. The literacy trope was manipulated by various media for different purposes, each striving to reassure or reaffirm the values of their individual audiences.[2] This chapter explores what those distinctions between local and national media representations reflect about public discourse and a culture that consumes such narratives so voraciously.

Johns has a sixth- or seventh-grade education and can't read or write.

THE "REALITIES" OF INJUN JOE

On October 1, 1996, Alis Ben Johns shot and killed his former friend, Tommy Stewart, during an argument the two men were having over Stewart's ex- and Johns' current girlfriend, Beverly Guehrer. According to authorities, all three had been drinking at a party earlier in the evening; the argument ensued after Stewart saw Johns riding in a car with his former girlfriend and confronted the two. Stewart's body was found the next day lying beside the rural Pulaski County road. He had died from seven shots—including one in the back of the head—fired from a .22-caliber rifle.

After the murder, Johns avoided a warrant issued for his arrest by Pulaski County by disappearing into the rugged Ozarks forests. For the next 6 months, Johns lived in the heavily wooded forests, crisscrossing from Miller, Camden, and Morgan counties and gaining a legendary reputation as a skilled woodsman and survivalist. During that time, authorities say he committed two more murders, a string of burglaries, a kidnapping at gunpoint, and firing a gun when discovered during a home burglary. Authorities believe Johns killed his 57-year-old former employer, Leonard Voyles, and stole his truck on February 27, 1997, while on the run from police. He is also accused of killing Wilma Bragg, 69, and stealing her car. Her body was found in her home on March 9, 1997. Both Voyles and Bragg were found bound and shot in the back of the head with a .22-caliber rifle, the gun Johns reportedly had mastered before he was 10 years old.

Authorities say Johns survived by breaking into vacant cabins and ransacking them for food, often cooking his food before retreating to the woods. In the largest manhunt in recent Missouri history, Johns managed to elude as many as 400 local law enforcement officers, national guardsmen, water patrolmen, military police, and members of the Missouri State Highway Patrol, Missouri Department of Corrections, and Missouri Fire Marshal's office. Officers on foot used search dogs to comb the heavily wooded, rocky hill region, bringing in all-terrain vehicles and Humvees when the roads disappeared. Helicopters and planes filled with human spotters and infrared sensors hummed the skies overhead. Water patrolmen searched the coves, docks, and lakehouses dotting the Lake of the Ozarks.

Finally, on April 7, 1997, two state water patrol officers found Johns hiding in a cabin with his girlfriend. Cornered, Johns attempted to escape by holding his girlfriend in front of him with his rifle aimed up her torso to her chin. He was finally captured after one of patrolmen wounded him in the abdomen with a shot from his service pistol.

In a trial that lasted less than 3 days, a jury of seven women and five men found Johns guilty of the first degree murder of Tommy Stewart. On Friday, January 22, 1999, the jury deliberated for less than 4 hours before sentencing Johns to the death penalty.[3]

For 6 months, many of the writers covering the Injun Joe manhunt began and ended their accounts with tales of his various "exploits" and "woodsmarts," repeatedly contrasting those same woodsmarts with Injun Joe's illiteracy and lack of schooling. The woodsmarts were presented not as a valued form of alternative knowledge, but as a marker of difference, proof of a cultural degeneracy, and an assurance of a cultural chasm existing between all Injun Joes and the rest of society. It may have been Johns' nickname, but it was the reporters who were constructing Injun Joe by writing his story.

Johns has a sixth- or seventh-grade education and can't read or write.

REPRESENTATION AND IDENTIFICATION: "HE'S AN ANIMAL"

Invested in the story because of their membership in the Ozarks region and sensitive to its representation, residents as well as local newspapers and their editors and reporters found themselves negotiating reflections of themselves in Injun Joe's Otherness. Mentioned prominently in almost every news story concerning the manhunt, Johns' illiteracy thus served as an obvious and familiar marker for a lack of cultural sophistication and a justification for dehumanizing him. Dominating the coverage of the manhunt, this familiar trope functioned on multiple levels as a force for representation and identification for residents of the region being associated with Johns. The media's representations of Johns not only reflect the values of the local culture but reveal its members reconstructing themselves and their region through language. Brodkey (1986) noted that through literacy tropes, literate members of a society define the position and cultural roles of those deemed illiterate. Use of the literacy trope in the Johns manhunt clearly distanced Johns from the other residents. By excluding Johns, the trope provided a collective regional identity for the area's civilized citizens apart from him; the exclusion clearly distinguished them from Johns, who became cast as Other.

Reporters continued to figure Injun Joe in terms of his illiteracy throughout Johns' recovery in the hospital: "During his 8 days in the hospital, it was, who is illiterate, watched television news reports of his case and asked guards to read him newspaper accounts" ("Feeble," p. A1). Poignantly, it was reported that Johns saved a news clipping with his mother's photograph that accompanied the interview with her. Because he would be unable to read that interview himself, however, the clipping represented a primitive talisman more than a personal momento.

Gee (1996) noted that although language is a large part of what makes us human and what distinguishes us from other creatures on earth, literacy has seemed to many people to be what distinguishes one kind of person from another kind of person. "If language is what makes us human," Gee wrote, "literacy, it seems, is what makes us civilized" (p. 26). Use of the trope reassured local readers that their civilization and local culture are intact while reaffirming their civilized values and regional identity. At the same time, the trope served as a public declaration to the nation, defining Johns as a different kind of person and not of their kind. This public defense of the region carries implied issues of race and class. "*Johns may live within our region*," the representations seem to state, "*but he is not of our class—and perhaps not even of our race*." By continually stigmatizing Johns as the illiterate subject of a statewide manhunt, the media branded him as culturally inferior and uncivilized—renaming and refiguring him instead as Injun Joe, as savage—with his degeneracy defined by his lack of literacy. Eventually, the trope reduced Johns from a person to a subhuman level. Based on interviews with local residents, an article in a local newspaper blared the headline: "Like an Animal." From a bar just down the street from where Johns used to live, one resident offered his advice for the authorities searching for Johns: "He's just an animal. He's thinking like a deer, thinking like an animal. . . . They need to think like a deer."

Other journalists soon adopted this animal theme, weaving it into their stories and the folklore of Injun Joe itself. In another article describing local reactions, one resident described himself as an "experienced outdoorsman" (in contrast to Johns as "woodsman") who had lived in a cave for several years in Colorado. "He's probably using deer skins to cover himself and cover his scent," the outdoorsman deduced. "That kind of odor is strong enough to throw off the dogs. Also, if he knows anything about plants, which he probably did, he knows which ones he can eat." At no point in the article did the reporter address any questions about why this man had lived in a cave for several years, choosing instead to regard his experiences as a source of authority. The choice of terms to differentiate between the two men is especially revealing, as if the shift from woodsman to outdoorsman reflected a refinement of culture that elevated him above his less "civilized" counterpart. Normally a marginalized figure, this outdoorsman found himself momentarily valued for his background and experience hiding in the woods and living off the land. A way of life that would typically have stigmatized him as an outcast in this case served as a credential, enabling him to speak authoritatively and to pronounce judgment on Johns.

"They made a big deal about that raw rabbit he supposedly ate," the outdoorsman added. "I've eaten raw groundhog and raw porcupine. If you're desperate enough, you can eat anything. Shoot, he's nothing but a wild animal himself." His willingness to condemn Johns' behavior as that of an animal illustrates the ways in which authority and credibility were crafted by the media to facilitate Johns' representation.

Like many local residents, one woman mourned the idyllic days before the manhunt intruded on their lives and their town was a wonderful spot for sharing a drink with friends. "You drank beer by the gallons and the bogeyman wasn't sitting out there waiting for you like he is now," she reminisced. By early April, local residents had clearly ceased to think of Johns as human. He was a savage, a bogeyman, and the media's representations reflect that perception.

An interview with Alberta Johns in the *Jefferson City Post-Tribune*, a regional newspaper centered in the state capital, revealed some of the underlying racial and class tensions. Condensed from the Associated Press, the story's headline read: "Johns' mother says her son 'cracked up.'" Alberta's first quote, one of the few quotes included in this article, depicted her son as "cracking up" after he was denied his monthly disability check: "I don't know if he cracked up or what. It doesn't sound like him, killing people execution-style the way they say. I can't picture him doing it. I mean, Joe was a good shot and could shoot you between the eyes from across a room if he wanted. Why would he do it execution-style?"

The authors and editors of this particular story relegated the story of the checks and their origin in a slight mental retardation from early childhood seizures to a paragraph along with other seemingly trivial background information. Instead, most of the article was devoted to the colorful folklore of Injun Joe, how his father was one-half Cherokee and how, as a child, Johns began learning wilderness tricks that would baffle police during the 160-day manhunt. Such a focus diverts attention from any question of the causes of and social responsibility for Johns' illiteracy and subsequent behavior while inflating the racial stereotypes of the Indians and savages of dime store pulp fiction.

"Sometimes Joe would crawl on his stomach through the woods to sneak up on deer," his mother recalled. "He kind of favored the Indians. He did the rain dance sometimes when we had a garden and it wouldn't rain. He could hide in the water and breathe through a reed."

"He'd try anything," she added with a laugh. "I can't get over how he could evade so many people." Alberta's evident pride in her son is followed immediately by a depiction of her life as an abused spouse and her work in low-skill jobs since the age of 15. The parade of details surrounding her beatings and mistreatment at the hands of her husband, coupled with her unstinting labor in menial tasks, types her as representative of a lower social class, someone eligible for readers' pity but not their sympathy or empathy. She is just too different from her readers.

Positioned strategically as the last paragraph at the end of the article is the sentence, "Johns has a sixth- or seventh-grade education and can't read or write, his mother said." Seemingly trivial and almost an afterthought, the line reminds readers of the cultural difference separating them from Injun Joe. The trope comforted them, raising them above Injun Joe, and there is nothing trivial or careless about its presence or positioning in the article to elicit those responses. These final words speak of an irreconcilable Otherness, a difference stemming from and founded on literacy (indeed, Injun Joe would not even be able to read the news stories printed about himself). Yet even these words offer inherent contradictions. Wouldn't a sixth- or seventh-grade education enable an individual to read and write, at least on a basic level? What kind of formal education did he have if he could not read or write? The newspapers uniformly ignored these troubling inconsistencies, avoiding messy distinctions by simply labeling Johns as "illiterate" or as "a barely literate Ozarks woodsman."

Johns has a sixth- or seventh-grade education and can't read or write.

WHISKEY AND BEATINGS (OTHER DETAILS ARE SCARCE)

Another prime example of the public discourse within which Injun Joe was simultaneously being portrayed and constructed by outsiders—by reporters from outside the region—is the interview with Johns' mother conducted by a staff writer from the *Kansas City Star* in mid-April while the manhunt's noose was tightening.

The visual layout of the front-page story creates a powerful covert subtext. Foregrounded beneath the headline, "He is my son, my baby son," is a close-up of Alberta's tearful face. Framing Alberta in the background is the family room wall covered with pictures of Native Americans, coyotes, and panthers. The writer makes a point of mentioning that Alberta weeps for her son "alone except for her collection of cheap art, ceramic animals and a few family photos." The patronizing and condescending photo and story indeed make the wall hangings appear "cheap," tawdry, and lower class. The subjects of these wall hangings—the Native Americans, coyotes, and panthers—and their inclusion in both picture and text contribute to the deliberate construction of Injun Joe and his family as wild, as untamed, as animals.

In the upper right-hand corner are the cliched "before" and "after" photographs of Johns. On the left, a small picture Alberta keeps in a box with other family photographs shows her son as a young boy, his hair cropped short, posing stiffly as if for a school photo. Although he appears uncomfortable in the neatly buttoned dress shirt, he smiles at the camera, his lips curled slightly at the edges to reveal evenly spaced baby teeth.

On the right, the more recent photo used by police in their search, grainy and out of focus, captures a contrast of time. In this photo, the barechested, unshaven Johns slouches with his eyes shifted off to one side, his head hunkered down into his shoulders as if for protection. His hair is long and tangled and greasy, and a black baseball cap sits askew on top of his head. His lips are half-open, frozen somewhere between a smirk and a curse. This second picture captures not only a contrast of time but a contrast of cultures: Juxtaposed with the criminal pose, the icon of childhood innocence documents difference visually, illustrates Otherness, and makes the identity of Injun Joe that much more menacing, evil, and frightening.

Beneath the picture of Alberta in a lower right inset box is a harried picture of Montana McGowan, Alis' sister, her eyes shifted down and away from the camera, with her quote in bold: "He was all right on the beer, but once he got on the whiskey, look out. If he was liquored up, anything was possible." McGowan's quote and shifty-eyed stare complete the subtext for the entire story, painting a garish picture of Injun Joe as hillbilly, alcoholic, and cultural degenerate. "We all knew the woods well growing up," McGowan added later in the same interview, "but he lived in them."

And everyone knows that real humans do not live in the woods.

The staff writer chose to lead his feature story with an often repeated tale of the 14-year-old Johns making himself invisible under a bush to hide from the sheriff. The writer then summed up Johns' entire early life in one brief paragraph. Tied together by ellipses are the sickly 4-year-old stricken with seizures, the 10-year-old who wept every night after school because of knowledge beyond his grasp and mocking peers, and a teenager who coped by fleeing into the timber and away from humans.

Continued on the back page, is the explanation of how Johns came home from the hospital after his seizures wetting himself and unable to feed himself. After that, he was always a slow learner, a condition on which his peers preyed. The feature writer apologizes to the reader for the paucity of detail at this point; after all, he explained, "family history is oral, and details are scarce." No follow-up. No explanation.

Alberta Johns' life story is portrayed in the same folklorish tradition as her son's under the boldface subheading "Whiskey and beatings." As a young woman with an eighth-grade education, Alberta married Alis Johns, a member of an Ozarks family that for 100 years had named one boy from each generation Alis. Her husband drank whiskey, carried a pistol in his boot, and demanded that Alberta give birth to a child each year. Although on most nights he would get drunk and beat her, often threatening to shoot her and throw her body in a brush pile, he never harmed the children.

"They seen some of the beatings he done," she said, the writer attempting to reproduce the Ozark dialect and imperfect English grammar.

"I always loved him," she assured the reporter. "I don't think he returned it, especially in the end, after I had my tubes tied and wasn't a real woman anymore."

Alberta freely admitted that, each month since the Stewart murder, she had taken her son's $435 disability check to him—a check he had received every month of his adult life. In February, officials told her he would have to come into the Social Security office to pick up his own check.

"Well, he was too smart for that. He knew police would be waiting for him. But without the money, he couldn't stay where he'd been, so that's when all the troubles began." Despite Alberta's claims to the contrary, the subtext clearly depicts the woman and her son as the buffoons in this freak show. The combination of Ozark dialect and imperfect grammar coupled with the stigma of Alberta's own eighth-grade education undercuts her credibility, robbing her of any potential for empathy. When the reporter describes how she had, since February, watched with pride as Johns eluded the hundreds of law officers in the Ozark woods, the subtext reduces Alberta to the debased class level of her son. How could anyone, the writer asks behind the writing, feel pride for someone like Injun Joe?

The writer follows "Whiskey and beatings" with the dramatic, boldface subheadings "Victims of a .22" and then finally, "Didn't see a killer" in anticipation of the readers' demand for details about the killings and subsequent manhunt. A choice tidbit from an interview with McGowan, Johns' sister, reveals this perceived thirst. McGowan remembered how as a child her brother would frequently lose his temper and get violent, and once he even stabbed her in the foot with a knife. And as he grew older and found whiskey, he grew crazier, she said. Violence. Liquor. Bloodshed.

The newspaper story ends with Alberta's wish to speak to her son again, to hold him again and "tell him he's still my boy and that I still love him." By this time, the writer has ensured that his readers will share no similar sympathies with the killer. "This whole thing, he was just scared," Alberta explained. "He ran because he didn't know what else to do." Alis ran like an animal, an impression made stronger by the writer's depiction of the final shootout between Johns and the water patrol officers. The writer described the hunt, detailing how, when "cornered," Injun Joe was shot in the "gut" (rather than the "stomach" or the "abdomen") as if he really were an animal. And nowhere in the *Associated Press Style Guide*, a journalist's Bible, will you find "gut" listed as the correct anatomical term for the area of Johns' wound—not even in contexts referring to animals or hunting.

Johns has a sixth- or seventh-grade education and can't read or write.

48 HOURS: WE TAKE YOU THERE

Similar to the local coverage of the manhunt, the national media also fixated on convenient comparisons to savages and animals. Early in the *48 Hours* broadcast, as a local deputy and correspondent Harold Dow walk through the woods, the voiceover reminds viewers: "Some say he lives like Davy Crockett. . . . Others say he lives like an animal."

"Alis can go 4 to 5 days without eating," the officer informs Dow. "We know that he'll eat an animal raw."

"He'll eat an animal *raw*?" Dow gasped incredulously, once again invoking images of Johns as cultural degenerate, savage, and animal. From the outset of the broadcast, the implications needed no further vocalizing.

"It's hard to tell the general public the type of person you're really after unless they've been down here and actually seen how he lived and how he survived," a deputy confessed to Dow. Subtitles such as "Cat and Mouse" spaced throughout the broadcast reinforced the animal imagery while reminding viewers that authorities are battling woodsmarts and cunning, not intelligence. With only a few words, *48 Hours* established Injun Joe as dehumanized Other.

And like the local media, *48 Hours* relied heavily on the literacy trope. Seven minutes and 16 seconds into the broadcast, Dow informed viewers that Alberta said her little boy had a hard time growing up. "They told us he was retarded," Alberta said. "He couldn't read or write so it made it rough on him. . . . He can't be right if he's doing all what they say he's done." If CBS hadn't already done so, illiteracy branded Johns as culturally inferior. And as a bonus for CBS and its story, Dow managed to get Johns' mother to do the branding.

Although they both may have relied on many of the same tropes, the national media had strikingly different agendas than local reporting for telling the story. Distanced from the events, members of the national news media had the least investment in the story and the most to gain by exploiting the hillbilly folklore of the region. Although local reports of the manhunt contextualized the story, providing a sense of region and Johns' Otherness within that region, depictions in national reports such as the *48 Hours* broadcast served the opposite purpose. National coverage strove to elide the particulars of the case in order to simplify it into a single storyline, a storyline underscored by the literacy trope. Using the Injun Joe plot, CBS scripted the action story version of the "literacy myth" (see Graff, 1987) in which civilized, literate individuals vanquish savage illiteracies and restore order to the community.

Such a grand narrative allows viewers to condemn Injun Joe without condemning or even considering social institutions such as family and social services and the health, legal, and educational systems that helped shape Alis Ben Johns' life. The convention of the grand narrative and its standard tropes permits no space for the issues of an individual's life to rework the essential storyline. Indeed, it would be difficult for viewers to enjoy such grand narratives unless the stories were out of context. Once viewers begin questioning why Johns' family life or special needs were never addressed,[4] the narrative loses its intriguing appeal. Instead of reveling in the good guys–bad guy chase scenes, viewers might have to consider cause-and-effect relationships between Johns' childhood and his actions. Or they might be forced to apply the knowledge gained from his fate. When they devour stories out of context, however, viewers find that they are no longer interconnected with the characters, and therefore they are no longer responsible for their actions. Absolved of responsibility, viewers are free to consume such stories at will without regard for reality, truth, or fact.

Although local reports sought to comfort their audience and reaffirm its identity, national coverage aimed to merely shock and tantalize its audience. This melodramatic tone was clear from the first few seconds as Dan Rather welcomed viewers to CBS' version of the story, frowning seriously while solemnly narrating how a "cold-blooded killer lured police into a deadly game of hide and seek in a growing climate of fear and darkness." After the first commercial break, viewers were introduced to Sheriff Glen Spencer—young, handsome, and clad in his crisp uniform—who reminded them: "It's basically a game of cat and mouse." With the hero introduced, the soap opera melodrama continues, the voiceover teasing its audience along, asking: "Will there be other victims? Find out when *48 Hours* returns." Later in the broadcast: "The Shootout . . . when *48 Hours* returns."

CBS' most deliberate narrative manipulation occurs in its portrayal of Spencer, who is cast as the protagonist of this drama. Dow narrated: "And it's all catching up with Sheriff Spencer. It's not just the work. He doesn't have time to see his family either, not even his newborn baby girl." Conspicuously and deliberately, the CBS cameras captured Spencer reading a report handed to him at the command post. Responsible, a family man, and—most importantly—literate, Spencer offered viewers the antithesis of Injun Joe. Dan Rather's final voiceover evoked viewers' concern and sympathy for Spencer and the literate members of a community traumatized by an escaped savage: "It's a high-risk game right to the end."

After manhunt and story are both tidily resolved in 45 minutes, Dow assured viewers: "Sheriff Glen Spencer can finally head home." Close-ups capture Spencer embracing his wife on his safe return to the local community center. Spencer shed a tear as he hugged his daughter while comforting her (and thereby comforting CBS viewers). "Daddy got the bad guy," he reassured her. "Yes, I did. Daddy got him."

In the tradition of cinematography, this story's final scene was captured in slow motion. The final image celebrated Spencer embracing his daughter tightly, patting her on the back, comforting her. And with this single tidy image, CBS restored order, culture, and civilization in the successful return (both literally and figuratively) to hearth and home.[5]

RETURN TO ORDER: A SHADOW OF THE MAN

Ultimately, all of the Injun Joe stories, both local and national, functioned to order their readers' world. Gates (1989) reminded us about the nature of story:

> The stories that we tell ourselves and our children function to order our world, serving to create both a foundation upon which each of us constructs our sense of reality and a filter through which we process each event that confronts us every day. The values that we cherish and wish to preserve, the behavior that we wish to censure, the fears and dread that we can barely confess in ordinary language, the aspirations and goals that we most dearly prize—all of these things are encoded in the stories that, in effect, we live by and through. (p. 17)

National coverage of the case ceased after the manhunt's dramatic climax, the moral of a civilized literacy conquering savage illiteracies suitably encoded. The civilized, literate order of this "other America" restored, Injun Joe had served his purpose by modeling (in their marked absence) the values society cherishes and wishes to preserve as well as the behavior it wishes to censure. Although a quality that fascinated a wide audience, the decontextualized nature of the Injun Joe saga also made it readily disposable.

Although CBS' interest waned, local media narratives persisted (although not as in depth with the frequency as during the height of the manhunt), dutifully documenting the region's return to order in the Other's physical separation from society through imprisonment. As the final punctuation of the literacy trope, reports devoted special attention to the psychiatrist's testimony at the mental competency hearing. The psychiatrist said that Johns told him he had seen ghosts, including the spirit of an Indian who helped him elude authorities. While maintaining that Johns seemed to understand the difference between right and wrong, the psychiatrist explained his "borderline" IQ as "subaverage intelligence, but not mental retardation." The psychiatrist also said Johns didn't know his age, what month it was, or who the president of the United States was. "Because, as he said, he did not keep up with things like that," the psychiatrist reported. Noted on the public record, this professional assessment offered readers a final reassurance of the chasm of difference separating the Savage from them.

A color photograph accompanying a story about Johns' hearing provided a visual illustration of this return to order. In this photograph, Johns sits in the courtroom, his head shaven, his neck and shoulders shrunken and wasted. In the background, a patrolman's looming chest frames

Johns, the officer's black tie, silver badge, and tan uniform contrasting sharply with Johns' white T-shirt, traditional prison garb. His head turned, Johns looks up at the judge, his brow furrowed. His mouth is no longer smirking; he is beaten.

One of the most deliberately crafted images of the denouement comes from the text of the story: "Sickly and meek, triple murder suspect Alis Ben Johns trudged across the courtroom, his shoeless feet barely coming off the carpet—a shadow of the man who for months eluded police with his stamina and savvy." A shadow of a man, Johns does not walk; he trudges. Sickly and meek, Johns no longer eludes the sheriff by disappearing under a bush; he is no longer invisible. The writer has created an unmistakable final message: Ultimately, stamina and savvy pale in comparison to the literate skills and behaviors valued by the rest of civilized society.

Johns has a sixth- or seventh-grade education and can't read or write.

AUTHORS AND AUTHORITIES

The fact that CBS' *48 Hours* continues to operate under the same ideological standard 9 years after depicting Appalachia as its first "another America" offers compelling evidence that a single literacy still provides the framework within which we perceive reality and evaluate cultural practices.[6] The stigmatization of those not "lettered" and "schooled" continues to serve as fodder for the media's stories. Public discourse continues—whether by design or by accident—to equate a narrow range of literacies with culture, intelligence, and even humanity. If narrative compels readers (and listeners) to question their realities and to re-evaluate their beliefs, why is it that we rarely question the narrative representations—especially within the public discourse of the media—of literacy and their creation and perpetuation of Otherness? Is it because the realities seldom matter? Or is it because the stories possess more cultural capital?

Forgotten amidst all these dramatic images is a little boy's seizure as a 4-year-old and the resulting untreated learning disability. Missing are the details about the years of classmates' cruel taunting and ostracism. The loss of a 10-year-old boy's father to a heart attack. A mother unable to cope. The weeks and months spent alone in the woods. As in all such stories, the details are overshadowed by the story's perpetuation. We ignore the little boy in the rush to live the legend. No one misses him, however. After all, the details never really matter. The story's the thing. Even though we know how they will end, we need the legends to keep our heroes elevated in their lofty places above us with folk like Injun Joe lodged safely and securely somewhere below, boundaries as confines mapped firmly in place. Ultimately, it is the stories and not the police officers, the authors and not the authorities, that keep us all in our places.

ENDNOTES

1. Ironically, Mortensen's (1994) essay examines another *48 Hours* production. In 1989, CBS News dispatched a production crew to the mountains of eastern Kentucky to document connections between adult illiteracy and social ills such as unemployment and teenage marriage rates whose numbers exceeded the national averages. According to Mortensen, Appalachia is depicted in this broadcast as different, as "another America," because of its abnormally high adult illiteracy rate. CBS and *48 Hours* seem to rely on such literacy narratives as staples of their programming.
2. Coverage of the manhunt occurred in a variety of local and regional newspapers as well as national attention in Associated Press new stories and an edition of CBS' news magazine *48 Hours*. Local newspapers included the *Lake Sun Leader* and the *Sedalia Democrat* ("Serving the Heart of Central Missouri"). The *Kansas City Star* and the *Jefferson City Post-Tribune* occupied a more tenuous middle ground. The *Star* covered the highlights of the manhunt and assigned a feature reporter to interview Johns' mother. Because of its location in Jefferson City, the state capital, the *Post-Tribune* seemed to foster more of a psychological distance between itself and the chase, relying primarily on Associated Press wire stories for its coverage.
3. In 2002, Johns had been convicted and was on death row for the murder of Tommy Stewart. He was awaiting trial for the murders of Voyles and Bragg.
4. At the trial for Stewart's murder, Johns' public defender argued that Johns was a victim of an unstable family life where he never developed the skills necessary to live a "normal" life. They also presented his "borderline" IQ scores as evidence of brain damage and impaired intellectual capacity.
5. Interestingly, the remaining time in CBS' 1-hour segment was devoted to a story on the Ultimate Fighting Championships, a savage, no-holds-barred fighting contest in which the winner is the contestant left standing at the end of the competition. The segue to this story on Ultimate Fighting and its coupling with the Injun Joe manhunt reveal a great deal about CBS' perception of its audience, but that's another story—and another chapter.
6. Because it provides one of the most deliberate amplifications of the narrative representations of literacy, I wanted to show a segment of the CBS "news story" as part of my presentation on this subject at a recent national literacy conference. Unfortunately, when I contacted CBS, a representative refused to grant permission, explaining that "we usually don't allow excerpting" and that my only option would be to show the "documentary" in its entirety. I found it

ironic that CBS would be concerned with me using their "documentary" out of context considering their "documentary" constructs such a stylized version of reality based on their ideological standard of literacy.

REFERENCES

Brodkey, L. (1986). Tropics of literacy. *Journal of Education, 168*(2), 47-54.

Feeble-looking Johns pleads innocent to murder. (1997, April 17). *Daily Capital News*, p. A1.

Gates, H. L. (1989). Narration and cultural memory in the African-American tradition. In *Talk that talk: An anthology of African-American storytelling* (pp. 15-19). New York: Simon & Schuster.

Gee, J. P. (1996). *Social linguistics and literacies: Ideology in discourses.* London: Taylor & Francis.

Giroux, H. A. (1987). Introduction. In P. Freire & D. Macedo (Eds.), *Literacy: Reading the word and the world* (pp. 1-27). South Hadley, MA: Bergin & Garvey.

Graff, H. J. (1987). *The labyrinths of literacy: Reflections on literacy past and present.* London: Falmer Press.

Mortensen, P. (1994). Representations of literacy and region: Narrating "another America." In P. A. Sullivan & D. J. Qualley (Eds.), *Pedagogy in the age of politics: Writing and reading (in) the academy* (pp. 100-120). Urbana, IL: National Council of Teachers of English.

Scribner, S. (1988). Literacy in three metaphors. In E. R. Kintgen, B. M. Kroll, & M. Rose (Eds.), *Perspectives on literacy* (pp. 71-81). Carbondale: Southern Illinois University Press.

Street, B. V. (1995). *Social literacies: Critical approaches to literacy in development, ethnography and education.* London: Longman.

20

NEITHER DISTANT PRIVILEGE NOR PRIVILEGING DISTANCE

Local Literacies and the Lessons of the Heidelberg Project

Patrick Bruch
University of Minnesota
Valerie Kinloch
University of Houston Downtown
Richard Marback
Wayne State University

On February 5, 1999, city workers were sent for a second time in 10 years to remove the tons of belts, bicycles, broken appliances, car parts, and dolls that Tyree Guyton had painstakingly collected, painted, and arranged on and around the homes and vacant lots of Heidelberg Street on the lower east side of Detroit. Detroit City Council Woman Sheila Cockrel applauded the dismantling of the Heidelberg Project, echoing the claims of some Heidelberg Street residents who consider Guyton's creation to be just a lot of junk. Of course, they are right. The broken appliances, car hoods, and dolls are just a lot of junk taken from the refuse littering the alleys and streets of Detroit. But to the bus loads of high school students, to the automobile executives in town on business, and to the many other visitors who make the Heidelberg Project the third most visited tourist attraction in the Detroit area, the appliances, car hoods, and dolls are much more. People come into Detroit to Heidelberg Street to see the junk that has been transformed into such creations as Noah's Ark, a speed boat filled with worn and discarded stuffed animals; the Hoods, car hoods painted with facial features and propped against trees; and the OJ House, a house on Heidelberg Street covered with advertising images of Black males.

Tyree Guyton started collecting debris, decorating it, and arranging it in 1989 as a response to the abandonment and crime that had decimated his neighborhood. As Guyton later explained in an interview for *Newsweek* (Plagens & Washington, 1990), his art talks "about life here in this area. I want to talk about the craziness. Every now and then someone is going to make it out of this, but the majority of people don't. They're not going to go to an art show. Putting art right here for them has made the people more conscious of themselves. It has made people say, 'I can do art too'" (p. 64). Making the people of Heidelberg Street conscious of themselves, Guyton makes public the reality of life in inner-city Detroit. Widely acclaimed for his art, Guyton has toured Europe with several pieces from the Heidelberg Project and has been the subject of documentary films. For his efforts, city officials have bestowed on him the Spirit of Detroit Award, and he has received grant money from the state of Michigan. Yet, as his fame grew, and as the Heidelberg Project grew, the patience of Guyton's neighbors and the praise from city officials diminished. The visitors still come. But as they leave, they cannot ignore Guyton's neighbors, who hold signs that read, "If you think it's art put some in a plastic bag and take it to your own neighborhood."

Those who pay attention to the signs are made to feel uncomfortably self-conscious about their presence on Heidelberg Street. Of course they think it is art. Of course they wouldn't want it in their neighborhoods. The people who visit Heidelberg Street live elsewhere. If they come in from the suburbs, from Birmingham, Grosse Pointe, Royal Oak, or Southfield, they come from communities where the lawns are green and cut, the trash is picked up regularly, and the homes are well maintained. We cannot imagine these communities tolerating the Dotty Wotty house, a two-story, wood frame house covered with yellow, purple, pink, and blue polka dots. We cannot imagine such communities tolerating the Rosa Parks Bus, a broken down bus that is also painted with polka dots and that sits in a vacant lot at one end of Heidelberg Street. But people come from these communities to Heidelberg Street to see the refuse of urban decline transformed into art. They come not only because here it is (at least for them) tolerable, but also because, here, decline is made remarkable.

The Heidelberg Project makes decline remarkable by physically confronting the privilege that encircles and defines inner cities. Guyton challenges visitors to Heidelberg Street to comprehend the experience of being poor (and Black) and living life among commodities that are always unavailable. As Guyton put it in the *Newsweek* interview, "Most of the things used are things that I didn't have coming up [on Heidelberg Street]. We didn't have a phone, we didn't have toys to play with. So a lot of the stuff that I relate to is stuff that has played a part in my life—stuff that I didn't have, stuff that I wanted" (Plagens & Washington, 1990, p. 64). The objects used in Guyton's art project are objects many inner-city residents still do not have and still desire. The concentrated mass of all the stuff makes visible the overwhelming volume of available commodities as well as the sheer neglect of inner cities. Some of Guyton's neighbors resent having the concentrated mass of discarded objects forced on them in ways that draw public attention to neglect. The signs held by Guyton's neighbors challenge visitors to the Heidelberg Project to consider that making art out of auto parts, broken dolls, and tattered shoes mocks the desires of inner-city residents for commodities, inviting outsiders to blame residents for what they do not have. The signs ask visitors to take stock of their participation in both the indifference to the voices of inner-city residents and a tolerance for inner-city dilapidation.

It is an open question whether visitors to the Heidelberg Project recognize that the presence in Detroit of Guyton's found art installation is correlated to the absence of found art installations elsewhere. It is an open question that raises more general questions about the role of literacy in establishing privilege and location. As literacy acts, the signs that ask visitors to remove the trash and bring order and cleanliness to Heidelberg Street are not critical of the process of suburbanization that has left inner-city blight in its wake. As literacy acts, the signs have meaning for visitors because they express familiar values, values that are used in other places to explain the presence of privilege and plenty. The signs ask, "since we too value cleanliness and order, why can't the affluence of the suburbs be available here as well?" As literacy acts, the signs draw further attention to disparities of privilege because they are written and displayed by people who live right there. They ask why they must live with this stuff. So the signs make an appeal from two directions at once, from recognition of a generalized distant privilege and from an experience of local poverty that necessarily privileges distance.

From where, then, do these signs demanding the redistribution of privilege draw their force? Locally, from Heidelberg Street? From the physical weight of the objects amassed here? From the location of poverty here? Or from somewhere else where privilege is more tangibly present and easily accessible? From the inequities in our nation's distribution of opportunities and resources? From the narratives and histories of urban decline? From the critical contrast of inner cities with the privilege of suburban America? The gap between the appeal from inner-city residents and the appeal to suburban visitors is a physical distance measured by differences in authority and power. But it is not an empty space. It is a space traversed with boundaries that are material as well as rhetorical. It is a space where material objects are spatially arranged, objects we use to ground our narratives of cleanliness and trash, of blight and renewal. It is a distance across which we inscribe poverty and privilege. Whatever sense visitors make of the Heidelberg Project, or of the signs of Guyton's neighbors, is a matter of how acts of reading and writing ground, as they are grounded in, experiences of distance and privilege in the material spaces of Detroit.

Read in this way, the dilemma of the signs becomes a concern for literacy education. Guyton offers a literacy practice that critically examines the distance between privilege and blight. His literacy project suggests that blighted and neglected inner cities are outcomes of the same discourses and practices (materialism, individualism, competition) that define privileged suburbs. But Guyton's vocal neighbors do not experience his critical literacy as supportive of their dreams and senses of themselves. They invest in a literacy of privilege, a literacy of cleanliness and order and work and progress that understands blight as the absence of values rather than the unintended outcome of certain values. What else could the signs say? How else could residents challenge visitors to the Heidelberg Project while also demanding changes in their neighborhood? And, what other ways might visitors have to read the signs? The answers to these questions depend on purpose and method, on why and how we approach uses of literacy. In the remainder of this chapter, we consider several approaches to literacy education and community literacy that represent for us the major trends in theories of literacy, rhetoric, and writing. Although representatives from each of these approaches—Berlin's (1991) cultural studies pedagogy, Goleman's (1995) concept of working theory, and Cushman's (1996) advocacy of community-based literacy—have distinct advantages, each also has limits when put to use on Heidelberg Street. Thinking these approaches through the signs on Heidelberg Street, we are able to think our way to future possibilities for theories and practices of literacy in contemporary urban settings.

Teachers and researchers of literacy, rhetoric, and writing who understand texts and their uses through a critical appraisal of cultural politics would likely locate the signs on Heidelberg Street in dynamics of power. Here, the purpose would be to take stock of how dominant literacies construct objects, spaces, and relationships, keeping privilege away from or out of places like Heidelberg Street. Much as Guyton has claimed for his art, the purpose of such an approach would be to "make people more conscious of themselves" as participants in hegemonic discourses. Berlin (1987) exemplified such an approach to the demands of literacy education. He reformulated the demands placed on literacy education by highlighting its role in perpetuating dominant spatial and political relations, observing that, "The ability to read, write, and speak in accordance with the code sanctioned by a culture's ruling class is the main work of education, and this is true whether we are discussing ancient Athens or modern Detroit" (p. 52).

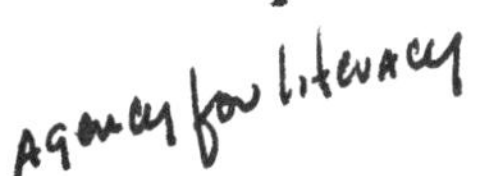

Recognizing that education need not serve the narrow interests of a ruling class, Berlin developed a cultural studies pedagogy to disrupt the dominant narratives that naturalize the material objects and spatial arrangements of late capitalism.

Like Guyton's challenge to his neighbors to critically question their own dreams, and like the signs intended to make visitors to the Heidelberg Project self-consciously uncomfortable, Berlin's (1993) pedagogy is designed to make students and their teachers self-consciously uncomfortable with their participation in the construction of privilege in the mass media. He proposed using literacy education not just to disrupt, but to transform spatial and material relations, by "situat[ing] literacy instruction within the concrete economic, social, and political conditions of late capitalism, doing so in the interests of serving egalitarian ends for education in a participatory democracy" (p. 248). Critically situating dominant representational practices in concrete spatial and material conditions asks students to become more conscious of subject positions that privilege their indifference to inequality. With such self-consciousness, teachers and students could not but feel the challenge to their privilege posed by the signs on Heidelberg Street, a challenge to which they would be obligated to respond (more on this later). In his pedagogy, Berlin sought to make the contradictions of representation and renewal, of distance and privilege, into the central concerns of composition and rhetoric. Just how he brought these contradictions into focus is worth considering in greater detail.

Berlin (1991) established connections among representation, space, and material conditions by drawing attention to material realities and individual identities as interwoven social constructs, where "the medium of construction is cultural discourse" (p. 50). Within this view, separate and distinct representations do more than represent a reality outside of language. Individual representations—such as advertisements, television shows, songs, and movies—manifest dominant as well as subordinate narratives or "cultural codes" that compete to make sense of past, present, and even future attitudes, interactions, and relationships. Understanding any and all signs—Guyton's, his neighbors', art critics', visitors,' the city council's—as invoking thick cultural codes, teachers, researchers, and students of literacy, rhetoric, and writing can map the geographic, social, and economic discourses that distance citizens from each other in contemporary urban spaces. In this way, teachers, researchers, and students can identify justifications for these distances, while at the same time representing those distances as outcomes of practice and thus as subject to change. By drawing attention to the ways representational practices construct rather than simply communicate spatial distances and material privileges, Berlin challenges teachers and students, as Guyton challenged his audiences, to question the ways that normal and natural literacy practices perpetuate unjust relations. Like Guyton, Berlin challenged writers to question the taken-for-granted narratives that claim privileged literacies enable progress for all.

Berlin's (1991) insistence that language represents "the scene where different conceptions of economic, social, and political conditions are contested with consequences for the formation of the subjects of history" (p. 51) can also be used to make sense of the residents' views of both Heidelberg Street and the Heidelberg Project. Opponents of the Heidelberg Project practice a version of critical literacy by drawing attention to the street itself as a sphere of exchange and interaction governed by unspoken conventions and assumptions. The signs of Guyton's neighbors call into question conventions of art, contesting the economic, social, and political conditions that have limited art critics to celebrating the Heidelberg Project as an art object, a discourse that disregards the object's economic meanings and physical consequences for both its local and its distant audiences. Drawing from Berlin, we could read the residents' signs as challenges to mass media representations of inner cities as places where no one cares about cleanliness and order, where complaints and excuses prevail, where residents are disconnected from mainstream economies and values. Valuing the residents' resistance to mass media representations and to Guyton's alternative discourse would enlarge debate about whether the OJ House, the Rosa Parks Bus, or the Bicycle Tree—an elm tree wrapped with the tangled frames of discarded bicycles—offer a viable alternative to privileged literacies or just remain junk. Such a debate would invoke cultural codes available through other discourses. The signs could be read as using the privileged status of discourses of cleanliness and order to encourage visitors to become more self conscious of their own positions within intersecting representational, material, and spatial contexts.

But what can we expect visitors to Heidelberg Street to do with their self-conscious awareness of their own positionality? As Berlin (1991) phrased it, the point is to make people "aware of the cultural codes—the various competing discourses—that attempt to influence who they are . . . [and to] encourage [them] to resist and to negotiate these codes—these hegemonic discourses—in order to bring about more personally humane and socially equitable economic and political arrangements" (p. 50). He made a leap here, from awareness of hegemonic discourses to resistance to those same discourses. On the one hand, the leap is necessary. Creating "more personally humane and socially equitable economic and political arrangements" requires engagement with dominant representations of current relations and the spatial and material conditions those representations justify. On the other hand, Berlin's leap obscures the point that the residents' signs make so eloquently—critique of dominant cultural discourses only sets us adrift without necessarily motivating us to transform our spatially, materially, and representationally grounded senses of what is possible and desirable. Not that Berlin was unaware of this problem. As he put it, critical awareness can produce something other than democratizing resistance. It can also produce "a stiff unwillingness to problematize the ideological codes inscribed in their attitudes and behavior" (p. 52). Recognizing resistance to literacy practices that unsettle who we are, we can think more carefully about the signs Heidelberg Street residents have written, the signs that certain literacy pedagogies might teach them to write, and the social conditions that force them to act.

It is not that neighbors do not appreciate the spatial, material, and representational distance between inner-city struggles and suburban privileges. They already point critically to those dynamics with their signs, asking (and even already knowing the answer to the question), why does the trash belong in their community and not in a more affluent community? The problem for Guyton's neighbors is that neither Guyton's version of literacy nor their signs, by themselves, provide the leverage needed to participate effectively in defining more humane or socially equitable relations. This is because the location of Guyton's critiques in an inner city art installation makes it easy for privileged visitors to resist the message of the signs and to remain unwilling to take some of the project or the message home with them. This unwillingness and distancing of authority reproduce the powerlessness and rage of residents, and further complicates, according to Berlin (1991), "the ideological codes inscribed in their attitudes and behavior" (p. 52).

Farmer (1998) recognized the degree to which the realities of resistance expose weaknesses in a cultural studies version of democratic literacy. According to Farmer, cultural studies pedagogies can slight their own contingency and situatedness, and so can seem to advocate a universal perspective that transcends the inequalities it exposes. The consequences, as Farmer put it, are that "notwithstanding its liberatory aspirations, cultural studies is seen by many as elitist or authoritarian in its methods and goals" (p. 187). Farmer proposed instead a pedagogy that "both respects our students' views and, at the same time, questions the complacencies which too often inform those views" (p. 187). We agree with Farmer that teachers must respect the views of people, like the sign-carrying residents of Heidelberg Street, who embrace the local promises of conventional literacies. But we are also committed to actualizing the promise of critique. The difficulty lies in joining affirmation of different voices to engagement with the spatial and material specificities of those voices.

We could affirm the literacy acts of Heidelberg Street residents while critically engaging the specificities of all our voices by promoting local reflection on the spatial and material conditions of discourse production. Goleman (1995) provided useful guidelines for this practice. Goleman described learning and teaching writing as "working theory," which she explained as the need in literacy education for both students and teachers "to work the theories that are working them toward their own critical becoming as readers and interpreters of discourse's specific effects" (pp. 124-125). To work theory as Goleman proposed demands that teachers and students develop a dialectical awareness of the relationships among the material, representational, and spatial effects of the cultural artifacts we read and write. Here, too, the purpose is to develop self-awareness. This awareness, or, as Goleman (1995) called it, critical effectivity, involves "(1) restoring a cultural artifact to the social dialogue it is a part of so as (2) to understand the specific hegemonic relations that structure the dialogue, and thereby to enable one (3) to read an artifact's form ideologically as a specific way of representing the world" (p. 26). Goleman's argument for learning reading and writing as a form of critical effectivity brings teachers and students, as readers and writers, into direct contact with the contradictory contexts of living with and through texts. We write and read texts out of culturally and historically available meanings, thereby writing and reading ourselves into specific cultural and historic contexts, constraints, and possibilities. The advantage Goleman's critical effectivity has over cultural studies is in minimizing the authority of any one privileged vantage point. As readers and writers, both students and teachers are constantly in positions of conflict and difference; the multiple positions become contexts and contacts out of which cultural artifacts derive significance and into which they infuse meaning.

As a possible framework for learning to read and write the signs asking visitors to Heidelberg Street to take some of the trash with them, Goleman's theory of critical effectivity would demand that we learn to "work on" the Heidelberg Project at the same time that we "work on" writing, by discursively working out the cultural and material effects of commodified and discarded items in the space of inner-city Detroit. Working Heidelberg Street in this way, the signs of residents vie with art critics and cultural theorists for the authority to represent Guyton's installation. Despite Goleman's argument for acknowledging multiple positions, all positions are not equal. Guyton's neighbors have far less access to resources for representing the Heidelberg Project. Such representations include a documentary that won an award at the Sundance Film Festival. The film, by Nicole Cattell, chronicles the life of Tyree Guyton and celebrates the artistic achievement of the Heidelberg Project. Also, in support of the arts in Detroit, Daimler-Benz in 1996 sponsored a German tour of 40 pieces of Guyton's art. In the face of the greater resources available for representing the Heidelberg Project in film festivals and art museums, hand-lettered cardboard signs appear trivial, even unsophisticated in the way they work the

Heidelberg Project. Cleveland artist Kristin Bly characterized the reactions of neighbors as unsophisticated, remarking that "Like Tyree, I make guerilla art . . . and I know the reality of putting things where others think they don't belong. Somehow the community can't accept the idea that one man's trash is another man's treasure." Unable to see the treasure in the trash, Guyton's neighbors are not necessarily less sophisticated. Rather, their signs differently work the Heidelberg Project. They challenge the use of their neighborhood as a site for representational practices critiquing the abandonment of inner cities. They demand a material redistribution of resources. They are asking Guyton to not put "things where they don't belong," claiming that their neighborhood is a place where other things do belong, things like street lights and trash pick up that will improve the condition of their street and the quality of their lives.

At the same time, artists and art critics are not insensitive to the quality of life of area residents; nor are they, as Bly put it, unaware of the "reality of putting things where they don't belong." Working the Heidelberg Project as an intervention in logics of abandonment, critics such as Bly have more faith in the force of aesthetic critique than in the physical activity of resource redistribution. The differences in how Bly works the Heidelberg Project and how Guyton's neighbors work it reduces to a difference in goals. Is it best to change the sense we make of the world by changing our representations? Or is it best to redistribute resources without concern for altering our representations? And who gets to decide where things go and what things get changed?

Because they occupy the space and have to live with the consequences, the residents of Heidelberg Street may at first appear to have the privilege of saying to Guyton, or to Bly, that the bicycles, the shoes, and the polka dots don't belong. Neighbors' decisions about what does and does not belong do matter. But privileging a local vantage point does not lead inevitably to thinking the Heidelberg Project just so much junk. Some neighbors do like it, and Guyton also lives on the street. We simply cannot use the measure of who is closest to say whether Guyton or some of his neighbors are right. The enormity and significance of the debate requires appeal to the critical advantage of perspectives located off of Heidelberg Street. Both proximate and distant criticism of the Heidelberg Project need to take account of differing interpretive conditions, in effect, as Goleman put it, reterritorializing literacy.

Motivated by material desperation and spatial marginalization, various occupants of Heidelberg Street have demonstrated limited patience for reterritorializing their discourses. In the signs they hold, angry neighbors forego Goleman's version of critical effectivity in favor of a foundational interpretation of junk as junk and art as art, interpretations that appeal directly for action and appear to open an avenue for access to redevelopment resources. Unfortunately, the resources made available through any singular interpretation do not connect redevelopment to the conditions of urban decline out of which the current situation was generated. In Goleman's terms, the direct appeal fails because it does not write itself fully enough into a dialogue of urban decline that would "read an artifact's form ideologically as a specific way of representing the world" (p. 26).

How might we invoke critical effectivity to intervene in literacy acts on Heidelberg Street? The problems and possibilities in Goleman's pedagogy are illustrated in her close reading of a student essay. In the essay, a student describes his missionary work in Haiti and the dilemma he faced as he tried to decide whether to temporarily marry the sister of a Haitian friend in order to help her flee from Haiti to the United States. As the student explained in his paper, he cannot marry the woman. As Goleman explains his narrative, the student is limited in the end by "foundational assumptions" about himself, as well as by assumptions about "discourse universality," that conflict with the "techniques of reversal, discontinuity, specificity, and exteriority with which he has begun to work his discourse on Haiti" (p. 133). In the end, Goleman read the essay as a demonstration of a literacy education that facilitates the student further working the language that works him. She concluded by proposing, "perhaps his literacy will have a chance to catch up with his situation so that what actions he chooses to take against repression and what actions he chooses not to take may be part of a larger understanding—an understanding of the specific discursive and cultural reality he is part of as a critical subject of history" (p. 134).

It is unclear whether Goleman was suggesting that, as a consequence of gaining critical effectivity, next time the student would decide differently. More to the point, Goleman was suggesting that without critical effectivity literacy perpetuates the privilege of distance. "In itself, however, the acquisition of a nonfoundational point of view is not enough. As we see, it can be split off and applied to the nonprivileged other, a Third World discourse for the powerless who alone are subjects of history. The discriminatory nature of this split is continuous with the impoverished discourse it leaves the writer for himself" (p. 134). But the split of foundational and nonfoundational discourses cuts both ways. By privileging the discursive and cultural realities that make objects and spaces meaningful to us, Goleman provided no way for us to legitimate the foundational discourses Guyton's neighbors lay claim to. For them, the immediate experience and material significance of the space of Heidelberg Street and the objects of the Heidelberg Project are realities that matter most and that most demand response. And to best effect that response, they write in terms that appeal to dominant, or foundational, discourses: "Trash is trash. And no one wants to live with trash." It is to this appeal that Bly and others respond using a more privileged, nonfoundational discourse. "But it isn't trash, it's art." In effect, critical effectivity doesn't help us cross the divide on Heidelberg Street.

Working the discourses, objects, and theories that work Guyton and his neighbors would commit us to facilitating the acquisition of nonfoundational discourses, encouraging neighbors to understand, in larger, critical terms, why they don't want the trash on their street. This is the case not because Guyton and Bly don't need to understand either themselves as critical subjects or their actions in terms of discursive and cultural realities. It is the case because Guyton and Bly already have expressed this kind of understanding. They understand that these are objects no one wants. That's the point. More importantly, they also recognize what they do as having a larger cultural significance they can communicate through nonfoundational descriptive discourses.

The residents of Heidelberg Street are themselves not unaware of the history of Detroit's decline, even though they may not connect their prospects for urban renewal to the history of abandonment. So the issue is not so much one of their literacies needing to catch up with their situation as much as it is one of our hopes for literacy contradicting, or negating, their situation. Recognizing this, the goal for literacy intervention on Heidelberg Street can be reframed, using Goleman's terms, as working the situation to transform the relationship between competing claims about the status and value of all the appliances, bicycle frames, car hoods, dolls, and shoes.

But we must be careful here. The appeal of residents, who want their conditions changed to catch up with their literacies, and the appeals of outsiders such as Bly, who ask local literacies to catch up with the situation, each oversimplify the effort as well as the promise of working theory. Residents who just want their streets cleared of the junk are simplifying the debate to the extent that their discourses are infused with mass images of what a neighborhood is. Those who do not appreciate why this matters in the face of living with the objects that no one wants also oversimplify. Advocating that others alter their interpretive strategies by emphasizing their embeddedness in the immediate context is not the same thing as visitors taking responsibility for the spatial, material, and representational consequences that their lives elsewhere have on residents of Heidelberg Street. In this sense, standing at a distance from the local investments in working literacy expressed in the signs of Heidelberg Street residents, Goleman's model offers an alternative to local investments and the literacies that embody them. But at the same time, to the degree it is premised on a nonfoundational distance from the spatial and material context of Heidelberg Street and its residents, Goleman's model of literacy catching up with situations only gives us a way of reading the signs as loosened from materially shaped and spatially grounded hopes for literacy that inspire residents to act in the first place.

Working toward a critical effectivity enabling active representational involvement in the material and spatial organization of our lives together, Goleman moved closer to a local involvement that refocuses the global, systemic critique of cultural studies pedagogies. At the same time, however, Goleman's approach does not enable an adequate intervention in literacy practices in places like Heidelberg Street because it does not give enough consideration to the value that remains in foundational discourses for marginalized people. In an effort to take direct action on the declining conditions of inner cities, Cushman (1996) theorized the democratic prospects of literacy in terms of direct involvement that invites community members to reclaim civic space and foundational literacies.

In "Rhetorician as Agent of Social Change," Cushman proposed increased involvement in community relations, refiguring the potential of literacy through a distinction between "missionary activism," which draws its authority from the privileged distance of the university, and "scholarly activism," which builds its authority on proximity to local interests and practices. Cushman argues her preference for scholarly activism on the grounds that it "facilitates the literate activities that *already* take place in the community," whereas missionary activism "introduces certain literacies to promote an ideology" (p. 13). By enacting a scholarly activism within the material conditions of existing community writing, Cushman argued that compositionists can take responsibility for the spatial and material consequences of current distributions of literacy as these effect the lives of specific groups outside the academy.

On Heidelberg Street, the goal of facilitating literate activities already taking place suggests working with Guyton's neighbors to somehow improve the impact of their signs. Attending to the material conditions of writing in an urban space such as Heidelberg Street, attending to the arrangement of physical objects that motivate neighbors to write their signs, attending to the spatial contexts that either support or undermine their writing, requires, in Cushman's view, that literacy teachers and researchers "walk between both worlds, the home and the community center," providing resources for writers to achieve their goals (p. 21). Describing scholarly activism as solidarity with the interests and practices of locally situated people, Cushman provided a way for us to affirm the handwritten signs asking visitors to Heidelberg Street to bag up some of the trash and take it with them. Scholarly activism requires teachers and researchers of literacy, rhetoric, and writing to critically read the signs as interventions in daily realities that encourage passivity, apathy, and silence. Valuing the literate practices of Heidelberg Street residents, scholarly activists turn away from the critical deficiencies of those practices toward the material and spatial deficiencies inhibiting them. Following this emphasis, Cushman's scholarly activism can be used to make sense of the Heidelberg Project by drawing our attention to the material sustenance necessary for all persons in an exchange to feel valued and taken seriously.

In a real sense, Guyton's Heidelberg Project does much the same work as Cushman's scholarly activism. Guyton often claims the greatest achievement of the Heidelberg Project is getting people talking about issues of urban decline and renewal. In circuit court, in city council meetings, on the internet, in Detroit newspapers, in classrooms, as well as on Heidelberg Street, people are talking about issues of urban decline and renewal because they are talking about the Heidelberg Project. But as Guyton pointed out for *Newsweek,* people don't talk as much, or in the same ways, without his intervention. As one example, the owner of a restaurant in Detroit recently remarked that a burned out apartment building near his restaurant has been scaring off business for the last ten years. As the restaurateur put it, "I wish the city would tear down that building instead of this [the Heidelberg Project]. . . . I wish they'd move all this stuff to my corner in place of the abandoned building. This stuff is junk, but it's pretty junk" (Hurt, 1998, p. 6C).

Guyton's art does more than promote a certain discourse and, as he said, a certain consciousness. Like Cushman, Guyton challenges the privilege of distance by marking it as a distant privilege that has disastrous and disabling consequences on life in inner-city Detroit. Privileging the inner city, the vacant lots, the secular materials, and the discarded consumer goods of his community, Guyton infuses new value into the things separating the inner city from other communities. But the act of infusing aesthetic value into a line of worn shoes stretching from one end of Heidelberg Street to the next requires that those shoes, like all the other objects Guyton has collected and assembled, be removed from foundational vocabularies according to which they are simply junk. Working the objects that work us, and that work our discourses, Guyton breaks the links between the material reality of the trash, practices of consumerism and deindustrialization, and discourses of urban blight, white flight, and suburban expansion. Taking Guyton seriously, our literacies lose their uncritical foundational grounding in the objects and places of our lives. Maybe no one wants to live with the trash, but improving the quality of life on Heidelberg Street is more than simply a matter of cleaning the streets because the problem is one of discourses, objects, practices, spaces, and values.

As we have been arguing, grounding literacy acts in objects, practices, spaces, and values hinders the effectiveness of the signs on Heidelberg Street and stymies the intervention of literacy workers in the writing and reading of those signs. In a sense, Cushman addressed the dilemma by avoiding it. As she put it, "the luxury of literacy can easily be transferred from the university to our neighborhoods when we expand the scope of our scholarly activities to include activism" (p. 16). This faith in the transfer of literacy to spaces such as Heidelberg Street too easily glides over the distances across which material resources are distributed in support of the uneven production of texts and the reproduction of specific foundational beliefs in those texts and their values. Perhaps through scholarly activism we can bring to the residents of Heidelberg Street a literacy that would contend effectively with the literacies of art critics, filmmakers, and lawyers. But this would not be the same literacy already taking place in the community. If not changing the content of the message, activism would seem to necessitate changing the technology of the message's delivery. We do agree with Cushman that a democratic literacy must avoid a missionary zeal that imposes our ideology on others. But we are persuaded that scholarly activism cannot avoid ideological engagement because literacy acts already taking place on Heidelberg Street are, like all other literacy acts, interpolated by ideologies. This means we agree that redistributing literacy does have consequences for changing relations of power among individuals, but the redistribution of literacy resources, in and of itself, does not change existing spatial and material conditions of inequality. To use Goleman's (1995) term, redistributing literacy in ways that have consequences for the unequal distribution of material resources requires a reterritorializing of literacy. Reterritorializing literacy involves more than a redistribution of literacy from where it is to where it isn't. It involves a rearticulation of the relationships among literacy acts, social practices, and material objects; it involves as well a reorganization of our lives with each other among acts, practices, and objects.

The need for reterritorialization is demonstrated in Cushman's (1996) explanation of how she helped someone pursue her goal of learning to use language to "sound respectable, you know, white" (pp. 15-16). As the experience of African-American scholars such as Cornel West demonstrates, the simple act of hailing a cab remains overdetermined by race despite individual literacy achievements. Appropriating mainstream cultural practices privileging whiteness does not change the spatial, material, and representational relations among wealth and poverty, whiteness and otherness, privilege and distance, that create conditions individuals must negotiate in urban settings. While sounding privileged may avoid inaction and despair, it nonetheless undertheorizes and disengages the sound of privilege from its material grounding in abandoned and dilapidated places such as Heidelberg Street.

How can we, as teachers and researchers of literacy, engage the debate about the Heidelberg Project? To bring together the empowering foundationalism of scholarly activism with a critical intervention in the social functions of literacy in modern Detroit, we propose an emphasis, on the one hand, on redistribution of literacy and material resources and, on the other hand, on the material and representational conditions of existing distributions. Signs critical of the Heidelberg Project call for scholarly activism that goes beyond merely redistributing the luxuries of mainstream literacies. No, most people really would not want to bring some of the trash back to their own neighborhoods. The belts, shoes, car parts, broken toys, stuffed animals, and household appliances, taken together with the signs of neighbors, the statements of city officials, and the evaluations of art critics, overwhelm our efforts and draw our attention to the inadequacies of literacy theories to the task of negotiating the real practices of everyday life.

Perhaps the first lesson of Heidelberg Street is that intervention in material, spatial, and representational "processes whereby a relative handful of private interests are permitted to control as much as possible of social life in order to maximize their personal profit" (McChesney, 1999, p. 7) is much more complicated than many literacy teachers and researchers have previously realized. Lessons of literacy learned on Heidelberg Street give us an opportunity to understand a variety of positions in literacy studies in terms of new challenges and new opportunities. Heidelberg Street can help us learn lessons about the work we have done and, at the same time, teach us some lessons about meeting the challenges we face. Responding to the ways dominant literacies exaggerate the traversability of distance and privilege through appeals to an individualized meritocracy, critical theorists such as Berlin and Goleman have promoted literacies critically distancing writers from the assumptions embedded in their conventions. However, as we have suggested, critical literacies tend to assume a posture of distant privilege obscuring the organization of representational authority through material and spatial distribution. In this sense, more rigid critical literacies proposing to reveal the truths of inequality fail to offer a model of participation or dialogue that responds to existing demands for equality. More flexible critical literacies, such as Goleman's, do recognize a critical posture involves being simultaneously inside and outside of hegemony. Such formulations represent critique not as an end in itself but as part of a dialectical process of critical effectivity. But theories such as Goleman's tend to strategically overlook the overwhelming coincidence of material, spatial, and representational forces bearing down on transformative negotiations of current conditions. At best, critical literacies highlight the relational nature of meanings and interpretations, creating contexts for new kinds of deliberations.

Community literacy advocates such as Cushman have attempted to use resources of institutional privilege to spatially redistribute literacies and, through this, the material conditions of privilege. However, one of the lessons of Heidelberg Street is that these redistributive approaches minimally engage the relational nature of privilege and distance. For Heidelberg Street residents, the fact that city council members and others listened and responded to their discourses of hard work, cleanliness, propriety, and property, did not shift relations of power. As city workers haul away portions of the Heidelberg Project, the relations among those forced to live in inner cities and those able to live elsewhere has not been changed. The privileged discourse of civic order as competitive individualism continues to exercise its privilege of naming the purpose and value of public space and controlling interventions in it.

Heidelberg Street teaches us that the prospects of a democratizing literacy lie in interventions in the representational, spatial, and material conditions of civic life proximate to and at a distance from local manifestations of global trends. As an alternative to the choice between a redistributive literacy and a critical literacy, we argue for closer attention to the intersection of the material and representational organization of distance and privilege. The privileges distancing the university from the inner city are material as well as rhetorical, and as such are deeply inscribed in the civic literacies of consumer culture, economic development, institutional history, and urban politics and planning. Rearticulating the local possibilities of literacy studies with the global material and representational realities of urban inequality involves taking account of the spatially organized, physically experienced, and forcefully expressed privileges of literacy.

We encourage teachers and researchers in literacy studies to rethink our appeal to distinct vocabularies of critique and renewal. As the signs on Heidelberg Street signify, a postmodern conception of literacy must do more than either critique representations of the inner city or provide textual practices enabling individuals to survive inner-city life. As a material example, the Heidelberg Project challenges representational manifestations of urban despair, consumerism, and White flight, undoing privileges withheld by spatially distant literacies of redevelopment. A postmodern conception of literacy enables citizens and residents by accounting for the inner city in terms of spatial relations of inequality made explicit in material conditions and representational practices of privilege and distance.

REFERENCES

Berlin, J. (1987). Revisionary history: The dialectical method. *Pre/Text, 8*(1-2), 47-61.

Berlin, J. (1991). Composition and cultural studies. In M. Hurlbert & M. Blitz (Eds.), *Composition and resistance* (pp. 47-55). Portsmouth, NH: Boynton/Cook.

Berlin, J. (1993). Literacy, pedagogy, English studies: Postmodern connections. In C. Lankshear & P. McLaren (Eds.), *Critical literacy: Politics, praxis, and the postmodern* (pp. 247-269). Albany: State University of New York Press.

Cushman, E. (1996). Rhetorician as agent of social change. *College Composition and Communication, 47*(1), 7-28.

Farmer, F. (1998). Dialogue and critique: Bakhtin and the cultural studies writing classroom. *College Composition and Communication, 49*(2), 186-207.

Goleman, J. (1995). *Working theory: Critical composition studies for students and teachers.* Westport, CT: Bergin & Garvey.

Hurt, C. (1998, September 18). Heidelberg Project comes down next week. *Detroit News*, p. 6C.

McChesney, R. (1999). Introduction. In N. Chomsky (Ed.), *Profit over people: Neoliberalism and global order.* New York: Seven Stories Press.

Plagens, P., & Washington, F. (1990, August 6). Come on-a my house. *Newsweek,* p. 64.

21

RHETORICS OF RACE IN CONTESTATION

Reading for Written and Visual Literacies in *The New Negro*

Laura Gray-Rosendale
Northern Arizona University

> *The day of "aunties," "uncles," and "mammies" is equally gone. Uncle Tom and Sambo have passed on, and even the "Colonel" and "George" play barnstorm roles from which they escape with relief when the public spotlight is off. The popular melodrama has about played itself out, and it is time to scrap the fictions, garret the bogeys and settle down to a realistic facing of facts.*
>
> —Locke

The Harlem Renaissance has often been characterized in contrasting ways, either as a "marked moment of rupture and reconstruction of black subjectivity *en masse*" or as an "inverted reinscription of the romanticist mythology created by European ideologies" (Mercer, 1994, p. 113). This chapter argues that historical moments such as the Harlem Renaissance need to be taught in this light, as a series of both written and visual rhetorical conflicts, ambiguities, paradoxes, and uncertainties. Drawing from a course I teach titled "Cultural Rhetorics of the Harlem Renaissance,"[1] I detail how my students and I investigate differences and similarities between Aaron Douglas' visual rhetorics and the written texts that appear alongside them in *The New*

Negro (Locke, 1925). As Faigley (1999) and others contend, we increasingly need to discern the relationships between oral and literate aspects of our culture, encouraging an inquiry into the ways in which visual and material literacies influence and impact conventional written forms. In this way, students may better ascertain that visual representations are not solely transparent media forms but rather can generate considerable recastings of written texts, sometimes contradicting their claims, occasionally endorsing them, and other times accomplishing a bit of both.

Teaching visual literacy in our rhetoric classes alongside other kinds of literacy may serve to better help to expose that, as hooks (1995) noted, representation is a "crucial location of struggle for any exploited and oppressed people asserting subjectivity and decolonization of the mind" (p. 3). This may disrupt our views of other texts of the period and therefore challenge the impacts visual media and their historical contexts can have on us. Although there are many other possible and fruitful approaches one might take to reading the rhetorics of the visual in light of the written in our own research, my students and I have tried to observe the following directions while reading the visual and written texts of *The New Negro*:

- *Rhetorical Juxtapositions of the Written and the Visual*: Look carefully at the strategic placement of the visual texts within the written contexts. Examine the juxtapositions of the visual images alongside the written texts. How do written texts such as captions, superimpositions, fine print, or headlines work to shape or change how the visual images work rhetorically? When written texts appear alongside visual ones, do these visual images serve to disrupt, augment, or complicate the written texts and how so? How do issues such as arrangement, emphasis, clarity, conciseness, tone, and ethos operate similarly or differently within the written or verbal texts? What political potentialities do these visual images offer when read in the context of the written texts and vice versa?
- *Rhetorical Readings of the Visual*: Look at how visual texts function rhetorically (Ashwin, 1984; Barthes, 1985; Bernhardt, 1986, 1993; Kostelnick & Roberts, 1998; McQuade & McQuade, 2000). You can look at just a few or all of the following: (a) Audience Construction: How is the audience constructed within this visual text? How and where is audience constructed multiply to account for the mixed identities inherent within the African-American contributors and the White as well as Black middle-class audience members? Do/does it/they differ(s) from the one(s) constructed within the written texts alongside it? (b)

Narrative Construction: Describe the narratives depicted within these visual images. What messages are conveyed rhetorically through the symbols utilized within the visual texts? Who is responsible for the arrangement of these images? In what ways do they reify ethnic, racial, national, and gendered boundaries and in what ways do they transgress them? (c) Character Construction: Who are the characters within these symbol-laden narrative structures? What do we know about them and their potential stories given the visual images depicted? What are the potential rhetorical gains or losses of representing these characters within these particular ways? (d) Setting/Situation Construction: What is/are the setting(s) that is/are constructed through these images? Try to describe how colors, shapes, and textures are utilized so as to accomplish this. What is the tone or mood of the visual image? What colors, shapes, textures, character depictions, narrative constructions, or the like strategically exemplify this? (e) Constructions of Rhetorical Purpose: What are the potential rhetorical purposes of the piece given how it operates and the larger context within which it appears? What motivates the production of the piece (local contextual constraints as well as ones endemic to the Harlem Renaissance as a movement)? (f) Construction of Rhetorical Appeals: How does this image work strategically to appeal to the audience's emotions, sense of themselves as reasonable and rational, as people of ethics and character, or as people with particular political agendas or interests? (g) Rhetorical Constructions in Response to Macro-Issues: How do political, social, economic, and cultural pressures of the text's production shape and impact the images it offers and vice versa?

As I elucidate here, teaching visual literacy in this way may advance stronger, more complex, and more innovative readings of texts (Kaufer & Butler, 1996; Thompson, 1997). It can also grant students a fuller sense of the many rhetorical forces at play within texts, the connections between such forces, and the tangled nature of all forms of textual production. Knowledge about the rhetoric of the visual texts, then, serves to substantially dispute and contest what Derrida (1974) termed the myth of the "full presence" or "plentitude" of the written texts that occur alongside the visual texts. Although such readings of the visual too often remain neglected within rhetorical circles, they are critical to our students' learning as well as to achieving more complete readings of how historical and cultural moments can rhetorically shape and are constructed through and by textual productions.

THE NEW NEGRO: ONE SIGNIFICANT SITE OF WRITTEN-VISUAL INQUIRY

Considered by numerous scholars to be perhaps the most significant text of the Harlem Renaissance period, *The New Negro* (Locke, 1925) initiated the movement and many of its most recurring generic forms. Beginning with theoretical sections that argue for the value of an American Negro literature, *The New Negro* (emerging from an earlier issue of the Survey Graphic) includes fiction, poetry, drama, dramatic criticisms, and critical texts about spirituals alongside poetic forms that echo them, some of which use Black dialect, traditional folk pastoral forms, and primitivist images. The final sections reclaim African-American history and demonstrate the need for African Americans' critical assimilation to White culture.[2] The rhetorical and political complexities of marketing the new volume essentially compelled Locke to make the final version of the text more national in scope rather than Harlem-centered, to address the Black middle class more overtly, and to capture the attention of faculty at colleges who would require the book for their classes (Linneman, 1982; Stewart, 1983). As a result, *The New Negro* contains additions aimed at providing middle-class, Black leaders' accounts. In order to meet the complicated demands of this rhetorical situation, this new volume sought to move away from attempts to be "representative," or to use "racially rhetorical" styles, instead endeavoring to infuse the modernist form with the vernacular or the folk as literary vehicles. The individual written texts of *The New Negro* ultimately reflect this complex rhetorical situation. They are often internally contradictory, containing within them Black nationalist arguments alongside constructions of mulatto identity, as well as calls on behalf of class consciousness aside arguments to maintain middle-class stasis.

Much scholarship has been produced about *The New Negro*. Echoing the general reception of the Harlem Renaissance period itself, *The New Negro* has been largely conceived of as a unified, noncontradictory text, most often in one of two rather narrow, dichotomous ways. First, the text has been characterized as one dedicated to African-American issues, radical in its political motivations, particularly in its concentration upon concerns such as Black nationalism (Baker, 1984, 1987, 1988; Moss, 1978; Wertheim, 1976). In this first view, frequently Locke's editorship is taken to be proof positive of African-American culture's critical revaluation in opposition to White culture. Second, *The New Negro* has been viewed as a sellout. Some scholars have maintained that it was not vernacular enough because its writers tried to transport the rich tradition of African-American values into the conventions and values of White culture, stressing Black exoticism and Black assimilation (Gates, 1987, 1988a, 1988b; Lewis, 1981; West, 1993). In this second view, Locke's prejudices and elitism are oftentimes blamed for the lack of inclusion of more vernacular voices, and often the Harlem Renaissance itself is written off as a sham.

However, when one looks closely at this text's written and visual rhetorical elements, it is apparent that a variety of conflicting discourses are at play. These contradictory discourses each evidence the historical and cultural moments of their productions, the distributions of their knowledges, and the varying ways in which power operates (Awkward, 1995; hooks, 1992). Although this text certainly does provide crucial self-definitions by African Americans, undermining the second critical perspective, the volume clearly also contains conflicts and discontinuities that appear to undermine the first perspective as well. Finally, neither view surfaces as adequately accounting for the multiple contradictions within the text. The first risks ignoring the many interracial and interethnic cultural resources within the volume so as to argue for this as a strictly African-American focused collection. In contrast, the second, aiming to avoid racial essentialism while also distinguishing between White and Black traditions, often disregards the potential of Harlem Renaissance writers realizing critical political goals while concurrently utilizing traditionally white cultural forms.

Since Aaron Douglas' visual texts[3] contribute to and respond to the rhetorical contradictions of the larger *The New Negro* text,[4] my students and I have found that they point at ways to read the rhetorical complexities of the volume in terms of strategic constructions of audience, narrative, setting/situation, rhetorical appeals, and other macro-issues. Douglas' visual representations indeed do portray themes of black nationalism as well as Africanism important to the larger text of *The New Negro*, developing a sense of what the "American Negro's" experience encompassed. On the other hand, they are at times mediated through white perceptions and artistic traditions of exotic primitivism (Dover, 1960; McElroy, 1990; Rubin, 1984). Douglas' visual texts certainly seek to valorize otherness and difference, challenging dominant conceptions of identities constructed through and by white culture. On the other hand, they can also at times depend upon conceptions of Americanism (Black art as "indigenous" art) and motives for self-determination which were already supported by White intellectuals (Bassett, 1992; Bontemps, 1972).

Perhaps most importantly, although Douglas' visual texts appear on the surface to simply support the written texts that appear alongside them, these visual texts also often disrupt the attempts of the written texts to furnish fixed answers to the questions they address. Instead, as my students and I have uncovered, the visual texts seem to both augment and challenge notions of cultural pluralism and national identity, cultural nationalism and the new left, as well as folk images and the high aesthetic, breaking down distinctions between the applied and the fine arts. In particular, Douglas' visual texts that introduce certain sections of *The New Negro* work rhetorically to both confirm and deconstruct the ambiguities of the written texts that they appear next to, revealing a more complex cultural landscape than conventional criticism often acknowledges.

It is particularly important to investigate the rhetorics of Douglas' artwork alongside the rhetorics of the written texts since the largest single difference between the *Survey Graphic* original and the new version centers around the artwork in both. The original version of the book included artwork by Winold Reiss, a White artist known primarily for his portraits of Blackfeet Indians and German working-class actors and actresses. In his pieces, Reiss attempted to focus on the folk character of the individual under the difficulties of modernism (De Jongh, 1990) as well as the persistence of cultural heritage in the face of urbanization, while avoiding the depiction of primitivism. However, believing that an African American should do the artwork, Reiss resisted rendering the African decorations for the new volume, instead paying for Douglas' art schooling, suggesting that he move away from painting the landscapes that were familiar for him and more toward depicting the "kind of world" that a "black artist see[s] and transcribe[s]." As a result of the art within this volume, Douglas would come to be known by many as "the father of Black American art." Although Reiss' works sought primarily to break down distinctions between fine and applied arts, Douglas' work appears to build on Reiss' work by also incorporating the theory of dynamic symmetry. Using a hard-edged, flatly painted style with interlocking rectangles and diagonals, Douglas sought to create a sense of tension and movement within the frame. Not utilizing color until later in his career, Douglas' work frequently employed simple geometric shapes, interlocking circles, triangles, rectangles, and squares.

Although some have argued that Douglas' work centers around European Cubism fostered by Picasso, recently more scholars have suggested that Douglas' work bears the hallmark of American cubism, precisionism, or cubist-realist that does not aim at representing spatial ambiguity of two- and three-dimensional spaces but aims toward reduction (and simplification) of forms to their simple geometry. Like many precisionists, Douglas sought to paint the subjects of grassroots culture. Unlike other precisionists, however, Douglas' aim appears not to be realism but a desire to portray a "symbolic sojourn through time" (E. Johnson, 1997). Douglas' work, then, was not interested in the formalism of European primitivism also popular during the time which plundered African forms for its own artistic purposes. Instead, Douglas labored distinctly against this. Douglas' main motivation, through the use of stylization more akin to Art Nouveau and Art Deco, was to make statements about the conditions under which African-American people lived during the Harlem Renaissance period (Johnson, 1997; Kirschke, 1995; Loomba, 1998). He chose to observe aspects of African rituals expressed in dance and everyday life, incorporating iconography and renderings of masks along with cubist strategies into his work.

As I show through revealing the close, contextualized readings of these visual texts that I have completed with my students, Douglas' illustrations titled "Music" (which comes before the section of the same name), "The Spirit of Africa" (which can be found before the section "The Negro Digs Up His Past"), and "'From the New World'" (which appears before the section "The New Negro in a New World") work to destabilize traditional readings of *The New Negro* text as a whole as well as its specific written contributions.

CONFLICTS IN MUSIC: AMERICAN-NESS, AUTHORSHIP AND HISTORY

Within the "Music" section of *The New Negro*, Douglas' artwork frames rather diverse written texts.[5] These pieces, when examined closely, clearly debate and contest the meaning of concepts critical to the Harlem Renaissance movement. For instance, Locke's own text, "The Negro Spirituals," and J.A. Rodgers' "Jazz At Home" sought to argue for African-American music's "American-ness" from two rather different perspectives. Locke asserted that the spiritual was valuable not necessarily for any religious connotations it had, but because of its uniquely "American response" to the hardships of slavery. On the other hand, Rodgers suggested that while jazz naturally tended toward vulgarities and crudities, under the proper conditions (taken away from the masses and put in the hands of a select few), it could have a democratizing influence upon its hearers and could undermine racial tensions between Black and white people. However, other texts such as Gwendolyn Bennett's "Song," and Claude McKay's "Negro Dancers,"[6] disregarded the concept of "American-ness" entirely in their evaluation of African-American music. As such, they overtly challenged the already contestatory assertions of Locke and Rodgers: Jazz was a uniquely Black response to the evils of slavery. Its cultural and historical relevance remained largely for the African-American community alone. Spontaneous and not linked to one single author, Bennett and McKay argued that jazz exposed the roles of the vernacular, African history, and matriarchal lineage as significant to its communal roots.

My students and I have found that reading Douglas' visual image "Music" rhetorically only highlights and reinforces the conflicts to which the written texts in this section of *The New Negro* seem to point, revealing both relationships that support and critique the production of difference. Strategically utilizing Egyptian and stylized representations, first Douglas' visual text communicates the confluence of competing discourses by offering different conceptions of audience, narrative, and character construction alongside each other. For instance, although Douglas' image distinctly echoes Locke's call for the spiritual over the religious uses of music, it also simultaneously questions the strict "American" heritage of jazz and the blues, evidencing support of both Bennett and McKay's seemingly contradictory assertions. In doing so, Douglas forces audiences, both those who view this music as distinctively American or those who perceive it as distinctly African-American or African, to acknowledge the impacts of the dissonances of their positions. In doing so, Douglas engages in a subversive recoding of values and ideologies. He also challenges the idea that either narrative about African-American music is by itself detailed enough. Finally, Douglas' visual rhetorical choices disclose the complexity of the roles African-American music affords its players and its listeners.

Visually, Douglas accomplishes all of this in a number of crucial ways. First, Douglas disrupts the role of religion in the production of African-American music. Douglas does this by offering an image that exposes the tensions and mergings between Christian-centered religious depictions (American-dominated and monotheistic) as well as pagan ones (African-dominated and pantheistic). At the top left corner of "Music," in place of a representation of the sun, is the stylized portrayal of a seemingly genderless African face drawn iconographically, leaving the question of jazz's lineage open for interpretation and debate. The figure's eye also looks somewhat like an opened padlock, suggesting liberation from strictures. From this head stream beams of light. Whether this face represents the sun as a God or depicts human traits and their presence in the natural world is left ambiguous.

Second, Douglas questions the notion that jazz, blues, or spirituals are strictly African-derived or African-American or American-centered. Douglas achieves this rhetorically by representing the characters in his drawing as ambiguously African or African American.[7] Each of the figures appears faceless, expressionless, forcing the reader of the visual text to confront the possible complexities of the image.

Third, not only does Douglas' illustration reveal the dissonances between the positions held by the writers in this section. Douglas also seems to overtly rhetorically dismantle a number of specific suggestions: (a) That jazz is a strictly American form and that it necessarily has democratizing capabilities (Rodgers), (b) That jazz and the blues are uniquely American responses to the experiences of slavery that challenge the oppressions of slavery itself (Locke), and (c) That jazz is unauthored and spontaneous (Bennett and McKay). Slightly off center in the frame is a stylized drawing of a genderless, black figure, this time in full profile with a horn held to her or his lips, clearly the author/performer of the music. The figure has a long gown and stands on a geometric platform above two other genderless figures whose faces are obscured. One is looking directly downward, the other supporting her or his head in her or his hands. The features of the bodies are angular, appearing contorted and folded over themselves within the tight, cramped space. Although the first figure in the landscape is not on the same level as the other figures since the geometric form separates them, the horn is somehow able to penetrate the expressed boundary, a boundary that ironically also supports the musician standing above.

Through this image, Douglas is able to imply a number of rhetorical possibilities. Although music can permeate the boundaries that exist between the cramped and immobilized figures, it does not appear to free them or to democratize them. However, the horn player appears at least somewhat free and in a position of power within the context of this image. Similarly, although the music arises from the hardships of slavery, it is not evident that it provides any sort of liberation from oppression in this image or whether it further reproduces such circumstances in new, insidious forms. As my students and I concluded, Douglas' visual image serves to highlight the contradictions within the written texts in this section of *The New Negro* by leaving a number of critical rhetorical issues undecided: Is the music (jazz or spirituals) offering a means of spiritual uplift for the masses? Does it emerge from the masses as a means of empowerment? Or, is it filtered down to the masses through a mediating figure who is controlled largely by white interests? Does music offer a transparent representation of the drudgery of African Americans' everyday lives? Or, do the power relations around the production of such music threaten to further oppress or exoticize African Americans of the Harlem Renaissance period? Does this music finally bring solace or elicit greater pain? Who, then, should be thought to be responsible for the language of music, the masses, or a few select artists? In failing to provide ready answers to these questions, Douglas' visual image offers students and other readers of *The New Negro* text the potential to understand the Harlem Renaissance as dominated by intricate ideas and continually disputed terms.

CONTRADICTING HISTORIOGRAPHIES, NEW PASTS

The next section on the history of African-American literature, "The Negro Digs Up His Past," which accompanies Douglas' print "The Spirit of Africa," appears to work in a similar way. The complexity of this written section and Douglas' visual image, for instance, seem to readily disable contemporary criticisms from scholars such as Cornel West who argue that the Harlem Renaissance was "not a true renaissance" because there was no attempt by its writers and artists to reclaim a classical heritage (West, 1993). Clearly, however, many participants saw this classical heritage not in traditional Enlightenment forms but in African ones. This part of the book commences with Arthur A. Schomburg's text also titled "The Negro Digs Up His Past." Schomburg affirms the need to recover African-American history and its African heritage that has been buried, doing so by drawing on the traditional arguments that had been made heretofore by mainly White, Western historians. In direct contrast, Arthur Huff Fauset's essay on recovering the African-American folk heritage from White literary treatments appears next to Schomberg's, subverting his contentions directly. Fauset instead charges that we must begin a scientific study of Negro folklore itself and supports the call for Boasian ethnographic and linguistic approaches to Negro folklore so that it may be better understood. Drawing on Fauset's suggestions, Locke's piece, "The Legacy of Ancestral Arts," centers on the possible lessons to be learned from African art for African-American history. For Locke, the formal qualities created by Europeans as standards by which arts should be judged simply did not do justice to African-American arts themselves.

Douglas' visual text, "The Spirit of Africa," like the earlier visual text we have considered, contains a series of similar rhetorical contradictions and aspires to merge competing discourses about the appropriate heritages, folklores, and histories that should be drawn from in making sense of the present of the Harlem Renaissance. First, it seems to call for a uniquely African or African-American heritage for the history of the Harlem Renaissance as opposed to a caucasian one, just as Schomburg, Fauset, and Locke themselves do. Second, it renders ambiguous how this should be done and the viability of the products that may result from such approaches. Third, in Douglas' own execution of the drawing he does not depend strictly upon one of these heritages alone. Instead, the images in this visual text appear to be stylized more within the Egyptian vein, with hints of African culture, as well as American.[8]

Douglas begins by offering an image of a Black figure at the center of the visual image, clearly suggesting the viability of both African and African-American heritages for constructing histories. This illustration features a human figure again in stylized geometrical drawing, drumstick in hand and drum in lap. The figure's head is raised and her or his other hand reaches out and touches/is touched by one of two geometric shapes that come out of the sky, out of either upper corner. Despite this, the Egyptian motifs and designs within the depiction of the figure suggest a larger legacy from which African-American peoples might pull so as to create their histories. The other images within this visual complicate the rhetoric as well. How are these shapes meant to function? What discourses do they produce about the figure, or the notion of the construction of history? The two geometric shapes in the background are evidently dark, ominous, but behind one of them are softly rolling lines in varying thicknesses, seeming much like the calm behind a storm, waves of sound emanating from the drum, smoke, or water. Both of these geometrical shapes seem to encroach upon the figure, but the figure's expression is again ambiguous, referencing overt defiance as much as prayerful exuberance. The role this character is acting out within the narrative that the drawing offers is again somewhat confusing. Is the character's action one of acceptance/invitation or mere compliance? The outstretched hand indicates a welcoming or a potential call to action. The drumming and upward glance once again call on the merging and/or contradictory impulses within religious discourses that pervade the entire volume, paganism and Christianity.

Beside the figure are two ovals, appearing much like some kind of small bushes or shrubs. As my students and I have looked at the visual depiction alongside these written texts, we have been led to ask, what indeed lies buried beneath this surface that must be investigated? Below the figure and the ground on which it sits are flowers in full bloom, ready to be harvested. Again, the roots of the harvest are uncertain in this representation. Do they emerge organically from African heritages, African-American investments, a conception of pan-Africanism, or an American landscape that has been dominated by White values? In what ways are these ambiguities highlighted through Douglas' reductionist artistic techniques? In offering the reader such images, Douglas complicates Schomburg's notion that "excavation" is what needs to be done since, in Douglas' representation, the blooms have already appeared and are ready to be picked in the present. Douglas' image also challenges Fauset's scientific study of Negro folklore since, according to the image of the figure in the drawing, it may not adequately encompass human emotion and the history of slavery's impact upon African-American peoples. Finally, Douglas seems to disrupt Locke's call for a return to a strict version of Africanism as the mode for writing histories of African-American peoples both in the image of the flowers (fruits of the present in our own culture) and the images derived from Egyptian forms. As such, Douglas appears to call for a larger, more all-inclusive conception of what the many African as well as other heritages of African-

Africans there might be, a larger sense of what should be part of African American history and how it might be written.

DIVERGING CONSTRUCTIONS OF "AFRICAN-AMERICAN" SUBJECTIVITIES

The final section of *The New Negro* my students and I often examine comes in Part II of the volume titled "The New Negro In a New World." Here the appropriate constructions of "African-American" identities are discussed, contested, and challenged. Paul Kellogg's piece commences this section by effectively arguing against Locke's earlier claims for a new Negro subjectivity that would emerge naturally from his own experience. He contends instead that Negroes are becoming more Americanized through their ability to mimic the white experiences of immigration and pioneering, asserting that this should be perceived as a positive outcome. Assimilation of this kind is considered valuable in Kellogg's text whereas within Locke's text, appearing in the earlier section, African-American experience carries its own authority to challenge the limits and boundaries of white culture. Likewise, within Kellogg's text, slavery and African heritage are represented as profoundly un-American and therefore must be discarded rather than integrated into American experience. For this reason, Americanism cannot be regionalist and folk culture can play little part in definitions of Americanism. This new vision of Americanism is oftentimes closely linked to middle-class, Black values over and against the values of the Black masses.

Such a disconnect between Locke's previous claims and the other writers' assertions can also be found in Kelly Miller's "Howard: The National Negro University." This text represents Howard University as a "national Negro University" funded and chartered by the U.S. Congress, which preserved notions about Emersonian ideals and the role of the American scholar. Likewise, E. Franklin Frazier's "Durham: Black Capital of the Middle Class," which links the importance of White middle-class values to a growing Black bourgeoisie. Finally, Melville Herskovits' "The Negro's Americanism" uncontrovertibly asserts the importance of Americanism over the potential African heritages of African-American Harlemites. The Negro subjectivity, Herskovits contends, is not to emerge from Negro experience but through the Negro's "American-ness," specifically the ability to assimilate to a monolithic white culture.

Once again Douglas' illustrated contribution, "'From the New World,'" challenges the views expressed by the writers as well as highlights the contradictions within the volume. This same piece would also be used for the cover of the February 1926 special industrial issue of *Opportunity*.

Unlike Paul Kellogg who views White experiences of immigration and pioneering as the necessary steps for the formation of African-American identity, Douglas exposes why assimilation may not only be impossible culturally and economically but it may also be undesirable because it supports the cultural myths that perpetuate economic (class) and social disparities between Blacks and between Whites and Blacks. Douglas' images make clear that it is impossible to see slavery as "un-American" because the outfall of slavery is what keeps African-American workers oppressed in their working and living conditions within the present. Equally interesting, Douglas' images disrupt and even dismantle the additions of Miller, Frazier, and Herskovits that cater to the middle class black audience's potential sensibilities. Instead, Douglas' visual image works rhetorically to expose the caste system that exists between lower class and middle-class Blacks during the Harlem Renaissance movement.

Douglas' rhetorical choices in constructing his visual images are pointed. The white spaces within the drawing are few and jagged. Again we see two Black figures displayed prominently in the picture. Their angular body parts meld into the geometrical designs that form the outer frame of the picture. Both bodies are in motion, one staring ahead, the other, mallet in hand, with both arms stretched toward the sky. The two figures appear to be centered around a platform, perhaps an anvil. Douglas chooses to represent workers here, ambiguously laboring in a steel mill or another industrial site. One has a poker in hand and seems to be heating it since there are geometrical flame shapes emanating from it. The other figure appears to be in mid-swing, ready to hit the molten metal below. Beyond these figures, however, little about the other shapes is certain. Shapes in the distance appear to be houses with a tree to the side of them, emphasizing that these workers are clearly far away from neighborhoods, families, and feelings of safety and comfort or pastoral landscapes largely associated with middle-class, often White, sensibilities. The image in the left corner appears to be a fan, the kind one might be likely to find in an industrial setting such as a factory, the one source of light and air ventilation within the room.

Although Douglas' visual representation indicates that Miller, Frazier, and Herskovits are partially right, African Americans are a stable part of the American economy, the rhetoric of his visual images seems to be asking questions about at what cost and for whose benefit. The African-American masses stand to gain little from Howard University's Emersonian ideals or Black middle-class values. Although these African Americans that Douglas depicts are indeed contributing to a vision of "American-ness," as the writers in this section argue, Douglas' visual image demands one ask about the nature of this contribution and under what duress it is being offered. What finally is "American-ness," Douglas' visual text seems to query? Is it mere assimilation to white, bourgeois American-ness? Is it determined by white standards or not? The forces that result in these workers' working conditions remain the unsaid of this visual text. Who oversees these workers? What are we to make of their lives of toiling? In whose service is their work performed? And, isn't this image very far removed from the middle-class African-American ethics that the articles would advocate? In that sense, as my students and I have determined, we might read Douglas' illustration as a strategic rhetorical attempt to highlight the differences between the experiences of the masses in African-American culture of the period and those who aspire to Black middle-class values, those fronting the Harlem Renaissance movement itself.

CRITICAL SCHOLARSHIP ON THE HARLEM RENAISSANCE: VISUAL LITERACY AND ALTERNATIVE PERSPECTIVES ON *THE NEW NEGRO*

> What I mean to suggest is that the topic of race and rhetoric should not be limited to, say, studies of African American oratory or Native American rhetorical practices (though we surely must have these), but should include as well canons and histories that take into account, where appropriate, racist and antiracist discourses; patterns of linguistic and cultural displacement and reassertion; essentialist representations of rhetoric and nation; hybrid racial/ethnic identities and discursive practices; the conspicuous absence of the other in treatises or theories that purport universal application; the assumption of raceless or race neutral theories and theorists; and the inexplicable silences about struggle for literacy, humanity, sovereignty, civil rights, and the right to speak. (Campbell, 1999, p. 12)

As Antonette (1998) contended in her book *The Rhetoric of Diversity and The Traditions of American Literary Study,* much contemporary scholarship on the topics of rhetoric, cultural studies, and race has been somewhat problematic. Despite our own best efforts, we have tended to reproduce a "noncritical multiculturalism," introducing difference primarily in order to efface it and reifying homogeneity at the same time as ostensibly embracing difference. These noncritical approaches need to be replaced by what Antonette terms a "critical multiculturalism," one that "attempts to reevaluate the means by which individuals are locked into unified subjectivities" (p. 40). This will allow scholars, teachers, and students to inquire where and how difference acts as a social construction that is dynamic and changing as well as how particular rhetorical practices construct what counts as sameness and difference. Such a perspective aims to work against the commodification of otherness in an effort to demarginalize and apprehends cultural location much as Homi Bhabha recommends, as an articulation of various intersecting and often contesting positions. It operates against the essentializing of difference or forcing its isolation from other positionalities, seeking instead to question containment or static categorizations (Olson & Worsham, 1999). Critical multiculturalism can attain this through an examination of how rhetoric is deployed to define cultural groups as well as how rhetoric is utilized by groups and individuals to disable such categorizations.

As I have tried to expose, one potentially fruitful way to further the project of critical multiculturalism is through bringing together rhetorical issues, visual literacy, and cultural studies. In this view, subjects may be understood to be constructed socially and textually in relation to discourses, and discourses may be conceived of as produced in fragmentation. Such a critical multiculturalism implies that the construction of subjects, power and social control are always at stake in any representation and in its rhetorics. As Brummett and Bowers (1999) affirm in their "Subject Positions As a Site of Rhetorical Struggle: Representing African Americans," contestations take place "over how groups of people are textually represented because those representations are the raw materials for constructing subject positions " (p. 121). Where one finds representations, one confronts contention over appropriate subject positions and endeavors to assert power. Therefore, such representations must be studied thoughtfully for what they impart about how people have been oppressed by representations as well as how people can be liberated by them.

In offering this reading of *The New Negro* and the role of Aaron Douglas' artwork within it I have sought to indicate the crucial paradoxes endemic to the rhetoric of the entire volume and the Harlem Renaissance movement at large. *The New Negro* text is the intersection of a variety of conflicting discourses about issues of race, ethnicity, and class relations. Rather than enabling one to make easy arguments about the success or failure of the Harlem Renaissance, its support of African-American issues, or its undermining of them, this text reveals the differences at play that could not be settled within the historical moment of the text's production, the Harlem Renaissance as a whole, or even in our contemporary critical discourses about how the text functions. Neither merely foregrounding the value of African-American values over White ones nor reproducing a cult of primitivism that foregrounds "Black authenticity," the text, in its written documents and its visual depictions, keeps differences in play. Clearly, the rhetorical ambiguity within this text is also marked by several other crucial elements that connect to the visual texts we have explored that should be investigated further:

1. The complicated nature of the rhetorical situation to which these writers/artists were responding, complete with economic, sociopolitical, cultural, and artistic pressures,
2. The radical discursive differences within the movement that is often falsely thought to be cohesive, coherent, and unified called the Harlem Renaissance, either not subversive enough or radical in its political potentialities (forecasting the Civil Rights movement), discursive differences which might have certainly contributed to its "downfall" but also functioned as part of its critical strength (its recognition of multiple subjectivities and audiences by those both inside and outside the movement),
3. The recognition that such discursive differences existed either explicitly or implicitly across both very similar seeming as well as apparently different texts created by various authors/artists. Even at the moment when it would seem that contradictory views are resolved within specific texts, some of the same ambiguities seem to resurface repeatedly within and across other texts by virtue of the strategic juxtaposition of texts, selection of certain texts, and the exclusion of still others.
4. The role of Douglas' own artistic training and the political and cultural constraints placed upon him through this as well as the ways these aspects might have impacted his textual productions.

Recognizing the internal contradictions within and between the major written and visual texts of the period exposes something about the critical investments of our contemporary scholarship about the Harlem Renaissance as well. There has been a great attempt to fix this period of cultural history, to define it as either a moment of liberation or a moment of co-optation. A close rhetorical examination of the texts in question, however, reveals that neither view by itself is sufficient. As Campbell (1999) has urged rhetoric scholars to understand, rhetorical analyses of texts that take up race as a key term, and those that deny it, reveal layers upon layers of complication. Discourses of racism and antiracism, linguistic and cultural displacement as well as reassertion, appear to operate alongside each other, oftentimes within the same texts. Likewise, hybrid racial and ethnic identities and discursive practices within *The New Negro* text put pressure upon other attempts within the book as well as within American culture to provide only cohesive, fixed conceptions of "blackness" and "whiteness." Exposing students to visual texts of this kind can expose students to these complexities and ambiguities.

As such, a rhetorical reading of *The New Negro* reveals multiple positionalities rather than an essentialist conception of difference, pushing against tendencies toward containment. In doing so, it works against a simple turn to a study of "rhetorical others" without a focus upon the differences within discourses about race. And, although an investigation of *The New Negro* text alone would certainly highlight such discursive contestations within the Harlem Renaissance movement itself, it might not reveal the ways in which visual representation itself can be one critical site in which discourses with strikingly different investments can co-exist simultaneously ("Music" and "The Negro Digs Up His Past") as well as how the unsaid of the written texts can effectively work to silence a whole cross-section of people within the marginalized group ("From the New World"). As a result, rhetorically examining the visual aside the written rhetorical choices seems to provide a richer, more detailed reading of this cultural moment and to expose that not only are visual representations crucial sites where subject positions are constructed and struggled over between groups demarcated as oppressor/oppressed or subject/object. Within this marginalized group operating during the Harlem Renaissance period, the struggle for what the proper identity of the "decolonized other" should be was itself the very subject of discursive conflict. Thus, although Locke's "Introduction to *The New Negro*" could claim that "The day of 'aunties,' 'uncles,' and 'mammies' is equally gone. Uncle Tom and Sambo have passed on, and even the 'Colonel' and 'George' play barnstorm roles from which they escape with relief when the public spotlight is off," the constructions of African-American subjectivities, subjectivities produced among fragmented, contradictory discourses that were being socially as well as textually constituted, were still very much debated. Exposing students to the complexity of this debate, in its written and visual forms, finally offers them a more complete understanding of the Harlem Renaissance, one that resists the easy characterizations that have been made about this period.

APPENDIX: *THE NEW NEGRO* VISUALS AND TABLE OF CONTENTS

By Douglas

"An' the stars began to fall."

The Spirit of Africa

CONTENTS

PAGE

CONTENTS xxi

PAGE

ENDNOTES

1. I have taught this course for several years now to a group of students who include a number of Native Americans (both Hopi and Navajo), African Americans, Chicano/Chicanas, and caucasians. As a female teacher of this class who comes from a somewhat varied yet predominantly Anglo background I have struggled to interrogate my own subject position and called on my students to do the same. For a more detailed discussion of this course, its assignments, student responses to assignments, and issues of teacher-student subject position, see Gray-Rosendale (in press).
2. See the appendix for "Table of Contents."
3. The drawings and decorative designs that Douglas completed for this volume are many. They include the following: "Meditation," "Rebirth," "Sahdji," "The Poet," "The Sun-God," "'Emperor Jones,'" "Roll, Jordan, Roll,'" "'An' the Stars Began to Fall,'" "Music," "The Spirit of Africa," and "'From the New World.'"
4. For excellent discussions of race and rhetoric, see Gilyard (1999) and Worsham and Olson (1999). I have also found bell hooks' video "Cultural criticism and transformation" to provide a critical perspective on such matters.
5. For Douglas' artwork, see appendix.
6. Many texts like McKay's were printed in *The New Negro* despite their requests that they not appear there. This reveals something about the rhetorical pressure on Locke to include certain kinds of work as well as the extent to which various Harlem Renaissance authors saw the representation of their work in this book to be politically and artistically problematic.
7. Although we do read these visual images as a class, one or more students are responsible for researching biographical and critical information about Douglas. In these presentations students usually reveal the extent to which Douglas saw himself to be offering images in his work that both spoke to African as well as African-American history. It was this connection that Douglas hoped to highlight in his work, and this, students have reasoned, may be one of the reasons for the ambiguity of his figures.
8. This same illustration by Douglas would also be reprinted in the February 1926 issue of *The Crisis* where it would be retitled "Invincible Music, the Spirit of Africa" with the misleading caption, "Drawn for The Crisis by Aaron Douglas."

ACKNOWLEDGMENTS

I would like to thank the audience who first responded to this paper and offered feedback when it was delivered at the Thomas R. Watson Conference in 1998. Thanks also go to Jean Boreen, Sibylle Gruber, Cynthia Kosso, and Randi Reppen for their useful insights.

REFERENCES

Antonette, L. (1998). *The rhetoric of diversity and the traditions of American literary study*. Westport: Bergin & Garvey.

Ashwin, C. (1984) Drawing, design, and semiotics. *Design Issues, 1*(2), 42-52.

Awkward, M. (1995). *Negotiating difference: Race, gender, and the politics of positionality*. Chicago: University of Chicago Press.

Baker, H.A., Jr. (1984). *Blues, ideology, and Afro-American literature.* Chicago: University of Chicago Press.

Baker, H.A., Jr. (1987). *Modernism and the Harlem renaissance.* Chicago: University of Chicago Press.

Baker, H. A., Jr. (1988). *Afro-American poetics: Revisions of harlem and black aesthetic.* Madison: University of Wisconsin Press.

Barthes, R. (1985). The rhetoric of the image. In *The responsibility of forms: Critical essays on music, art, and representation* (pp. 21-40). New York: Farrar, Straus, & Giroux.

Bassett, J. E. (1992). *Harlem in review: Critical reactions to Black American writers, 1917-1939.* Selinsgrove: Susquehanna University Press.

Bernhardt, S. (1986). Seeing the text. *College Composition and Communication, 37*, 66-78.

Bernhardt, S. (1993). The shape of text to come: The texture of print on screens. *College Composition and Communication, 44*, 151-175.

Bontemps, A. (1972). *The Harlem renaissance remembered.* New York: Dodd & Mead.

Brummett, B., & Bowers, D. L. (1999). Subject positions as a site of rhetorical struggle: Representing African Americans. In T. Rosteck (Ed.), *At the intersection: Cultural studies and rhetorical studies* (pp. 117-136). New York: Guilford.

Campbell, K. E. (1999). Race and rhetoric: An unlikely tandem? In C. J. Swearingen (Ed.), *Rhetoric, the polis, and the global village* (pp. 11-13). Mahwah: Erlbaum.

De Jongh, J. (1990). *Vicious modernism: Black Harlem and the literary imagination.* Cambridge: Cambridge University Press.

Derrida, J. (1974). *Of grammatology* (G. Spivak, Trans.). Baltimore, MD: Johns Hopkins University Press.

Dover, C. (1960). *American negro art.* London: Studio.

Faigley, L. (1999). Material literacy and visual design. In. J. Selzer & S. Crowley (Eds.), *Rhetorical bodies* (pp. 171-201). Madison: University of Wisconsin Press.

Gates, H.L. Jr. (1987). *Figures in black: Words, signs, and the "racial" self.* New York: Oxford.

Gates, H.L. Jr. (1988a). *The signifying monkey: A theory of African-American literary criticism.* New York: Oxford University Press.

Gates, H.L. Jr. (1988b). The trope of *The New Negro* and the reconstruction of the image of the black. *Representations, 24*, 129-155.

Gilyard, K. (Ed.). (1999). *Race, rhetoric, and composition.* Portsmouth, NH: Boynton Cook & Heinemann.

Gray-Rosendale, L. (in press). The ambiguous cultural rhetorics of race and difference: Teaching the harlem renaissance. In A. Tarver & P. Barnes (Eds.), *New perspectives on the Harlem renaissance.* Boston: St. Martin's Press.

hooks, b. (1995). *Art on my mind.* New York: The New Press.

hooks, b. (1992). *Black looks: Race and representation.* Boston: South End Press.

hooks, b. (1997). *Cultural criticism and transformation.* Amherst, MA: The Media Education Foundation.

Johnson, E. E. (1997). *Rediscovering the Harlem renaissance: The politics of exclusion.* New York: Garland.

Kaufer, D., & Butler, B. (1996). *Rhetoric and the arts of design.* Mahwah, NJ: Erlbaum.

Kostelnick, C., & Roberts, D.D. (1998). *Designing visual language: Strategies for professional communicators.* Boston: Allyn & Bacon.

Kirschke, A. H. (1995). *Aaron Douglas: Art, race, and the Harlem renaissance.* Jackson: University of Mississippi Press.

Lewis, D. L. (1981). *When Harlem was in vogue.* New York: Knopf.

Linneman, R. J. (1982). *Alain Locke: Reflections on a modern renaissance man.* Baton Rouge: Louisiana State University Press.

Locke, A. (Ed.). (1925). *The new Negro.* New York: Atheneum.

Locke, A. (Ed.). (1968). *The new Negro.* New York: Arno Press & The New York Times.

Locke, A. (1992). *Race contacts and interracial relations: Lectures on the theory and practice of race.* (J.C. Stewart, Ed.). Washington, DC: Howard University Press.

Loomba, A. (1998). *Colonialism-postcolonialism.* New York: Routledge.

McElroy, G. (1990). *Facing history: The black image in American art, 1710-1940.* San Francisco, CA: Bedford Arts & Washington, DC: Corcoran Gallery of Art.

McQuade, D., & McQuade, C. (2000). *Seeing and writing.* Boston: Bedford St. Martin's.

Mercer, K. (1994). *Welcome to the jungle: New positions in black cultural studies.* New York: Routledge Press.

Moss, W.J. (1978). *The golden age of black nationalism, 1850-1925.* Hamden: Archon Books.

Olson, G. A., & Worsham, L. (Eds.). (1999). Staging the politics of difference: Homi Bhabha's critical literacy. In G. A. Olson & L. Worsham (Eds.), *Race, rhetoric, and the postcolonial* (pp. 3-42). Albany: State University of New York Press.

Rubin, W. (Ed.). (1984). *Primitivism in 20th century art: Affinity of the tribal and the modern.* New York: Museum of Modern Art.

Stewart, J. C. (Ed.). (1983). *The critical temper of Alain Locke.* New York: Garland.

Thompson, G. (1997). *Rhetoric through media.* Boston: Allyn & Bacon.

Wertheim, A. F. (1976). *The New York little renaissance: Iconoclasm, modernism, and nationalism in American culture, 1908-1917.* New York: New York University Press.

West, C. (1993). *Keeping faith: Philosophy and race in America.* New York: Routledge.

Worsham, L., & Olson, G. (Eds.). (1999). *Race, rhetoric, and the postcolonial.* Albany: State University of New York Press

VI

REFLECTIONS

22

TRAVELING TO LITERACIES

A Journey Deep, Wise and Hard

Carole Pfeffer
Bellarmine University

> *. . . and such a long journey:/The ways deep and the weather sharp . . ./ A hard time we had of it. . . .*
>
> —Eliot (1964, p. 27)

It seems, even to me, a bit pretentious to begin this discussion of literacy with a reference to Eliot's poetic rendering of the Magi's journey, given the historical and religious theme of the work, as well as its somber tone. Nevertheless, the more I reflect on my own journey through the terrain of literacy studies, the more cognizant I am of the import of my travels and the ways in which my sojourn resembles the trek Eliot versified. Like the figures in this poem, I have found my journey "long" and "hard" and "the ways deep."

Its beginning was innocuous enough. In attendance at a composition conference in 1992, I found myself in an afternoon session, the topic of which escapes me. At one crucial juncture in the presentation, however, the speaker noted the importance of meshing classroom pedagogy with "one's own definition of literacy." My reaction to her admonition was one of complete confusion, and I can still vividly recall my sense of outrage at what seemed then to be the woman's flippancy, even blasphemy, in opening for discussion a concept I had always viewed as closed. Her suggestion that teachers of reading and writing might actually disagree on the definition of what for me was a foundational, sacrosanct term seemed not only preposterous but dangerous. Even then, I realized that the power of naming and defining is a grave endeavor; as Freire and Macedo (1987) noted, to name the world is to change it. Knoblauch and Brannon (1993) similarly emphasized the seriousness of such activity, describing the process of renaming (an endeavor the conference speaker had audaciously undertaken) as an "attempt to negotiate the substance of social reality and contest prior meanings in favor of new or different ones" (p. 3). While sitting in an auditorium that October afternoon in 1992, something deep within me realized that any attempt to rename/reframe literacy posed an affront to my conceptual framework—the matrix from which I operated on a daily basis in writing and reading classrooms. I left that conference badly shaken, having begun a journey now in its seventh year: moving toward a conception of multiple literacies.

Reflecting on my initially vehement reaction at the conference, I now realize that exposure to such disquieting ideas about literacy constituted for me what could be called a critical incident, an occurrence that allows us to see with new ideas some aspect of what we do and who we are. Stars from the East, Bodhi trees, and snippets from a conference presentation: all can serve as beacons to look more deeply, to move from familiar topography and travel to new lands. In a very real sense, this one speaker's words served as a clarion call, heralding as they did the beginnings of my journey to "re-envision," in the words of Rich (1979), my understanding of literacy as, in fact, a concept plural at its core.

Truth be told, I had never consciously explored the concept of literacy, certain, I suppose, that it was self-explanatory, thereby warranting no scrutiny on my part. Having now spent years immersed in literacy studies, I still marvel at how literacy tends to render itself a deceptively straightforward and transparent concept. Indeed, argued Knoblauch and Brannon (1993), the danger in literacy studies rests in our glib acceptance of a definition that appears to reveal "simple and stable truths" (p. 24). That I had fallen prey to this pitfall for most of my teaching career of nearly two decades is an admission I make with both embarrassment and distress, aware as I now am that within simplistic and blithely articulated definitions of literacy inhere potentially devastating consequences for students.

Early on in my journey, however, I lacked this profound comprehension. In fact, in my righteousness, I agonized about students being academically "short-changed" by other "radicals" like the conference presenter, individuals no doubt "dumbing down" the sacred activities of reading and writing in classrooms throughout the nation by veering from the model of academic literacy that had guided me throughout my life as student and teacher. Despite my fears, however, I found myself unable to silence a persistent inner voice clamoring for attention, calling me to explore other definitions of literacy that might be floating around. Still, it would be erroneous to suggest that my initial commitment to this educational quest was marked by real integrity or a genuine passion for learning; my motivation instead stemmed from a desire to better comprehend new ideas so that I might more effectively refute them.

Such combativeness was certainly reinforced by various colleagues at the time, many of whom had been educated within traditional liberal arts institutions, similar to the one in which we were teaching. At the commencement of my journey into literacy studies, our mutual outrage at the notion of literacy as a topic for intellectual query and debate only heightened my growing alarm that something was seriously amiss in the Academy. Eventually, however, as I delved more deeply into the topic and began what can truly be termed an intellectual pilgrimage, I found the lack of serious conversational opportunities extremely disappointing and isolating. Such dialogic encounters should lie at the heart of academic life, argued Graff (1987), who suggested that the "real enemy of tradition is the kind of orthodox . . . study that neglects theoretical ends, values, and definitions in the hope that they will take care of themselves" (p. 3). It is now all too clear to me that my initial forays into literacy studies were compromised due to the paucity of professional discussion on the topic at my institution. In fact, I often wonder if I might have succeeded in my earliest attempts to dismiss altogether the concept of multiple literacies had I not been facing a doctoral dissertation.

Riddled with questions and fears but also more and more intrigued by the topic, I committed myself to a case study addressing the ways in which students and professors in a teacher education program for English majors defined literacy. Given my journey at the time, as well as my previous 13-year stint as a secondary English teacher, this venue appeared ideally suited for the pursuit of my questions. Fortunately, my work was preceded by an immersion in texts addressing the many facets of literacy or I am quite sure I would have underestimated the complexity of the topic as I engaged in the study. In fact, the sheer number of related books and articles nearly overwhelmed me; I remember my incredulity as I continually discovered more texts to be read. Of course, given my previous conviction that the concept of literacy was transparent, I had never availed myself of any resources on the topic; indeed, I had been oblivious to the wealth of information addressing it. Imagine my humility while reading of "literacy wars" that had been raging for years while I, righteous and innocent, had remained hunkered down in a veritable bunker of ignorance.

When I finally took the plunge into literacy studies, however, I gradually began to comprehend the intricacies of the topic. Brodkey (1986) introduced me to the concept of literacy as a "social trope" with its various definitions serving as "cultural Rorchachs" (p. 48). An encounter with a text by Knoblauch and Brannon (1993) echoed this observation, with the authors arguing that any definition of literacy necessarily involves "multilayered significations . . . of social reality" (pp. 3-4). And moving from the sublime to the more light-hearted, a character from Carroll's (1960) *Through the Looking Glass* (1960) perhaps put the matter most succinctly for me as I read the various definitions of literacy being posed: "'When I use a word,' Humpty Dumpty said in a rather scornful tone, 'it means what I choose it to mean, neither more nor less.'" And when Alice responds, in a tone as haughty as my own during my initial questing, "'The question is . . . whether you *can* make words mean so many different things," Humpty Dumpty remains unruffled in his reply: "The question is . . . which is to be that Master, that's all" (p. 179).

"That's all," indeed. For as my study of the literature made vividly clear, numerous individuals and organizations have "weighed in" with definitions of literacy, each arguing passionately for primacy within various arenas. Functional literacy, cultural literacy, academic/essayist literacy, personal literacy, computer/technological literacy, multiple literacies, family literacy, meta-literacy—the number of competing definitions, as observed by Knoblauch and Brannon (1993), is nothing short of "astonishing" (p. 24). And, they argued, the process by which these representations of literacy come to be is as important to scrutinize as the definitions themselves. A given definition assumes prominence, these authors insist, through its articulation by individuals possessing the authority to name/define literacy: "definitions don't tell with metaphysical certainty what literacy is, but only what somebody with the power to speak wants or need it to be" (pp. 23-24).

At this point in my journey I was confronted with an unnerving reality: My definition of literacy had been socially constructed by mere human beings with vested interests, who "wanted" it or "needed" it to be so fashioned, not handed down from on high by a supreme being to whom I owed unquestioning allegiance. This statement may sound melodramatic, but it nevertheless captures the intellectual *angst* plaguing me at the time. In fact, this realization is pivotal in my literacy autobiography, for it marks nothing short of an ontological shift in my thinking. Just as troublesome was my realization that I had, in fact, willingly offered mindless and enthusiastic assent to the definition of literacy that had always been, it seemed to me, part and parcel of my very being. How, I wondered, had I failed early on to comprehend this process of defining, and how/why had I relinquished my right—indeed, my professional responsibility—to question others' definitions of a concept so integral to my teaching?

Once again, Knoblauch and Brannon (1993) offered some insight, noting that those individuals with the authority to define literacy can also "compel unconscious assent," engaging in a "form of colonizing, a way of making others more like themselves" (p. 24). Deliberate efforts are made by proponents of various definitions to make a particular representation of literacy "appear invisible, at least transparent, a window on the world" (p. 24). The articulation of literacy I had embraced had indeed appeared transparently correct because of my failure to "scrutinize" and "critique" it, the "only safeguards human beings have if they are to participate freely in negotiating the world" (p. 24).

Having first acknowledged my "colonization" by others' ways of articulating literacy, I next had to admit an equally vexing actuality: Just as I had been taken hostage by others' definition of literacy so too had I undoubtedly coerced countless students into adopting my version of "literate truth," implying to them that the concept was penultimate and closed for discussion. At one particularly low point in this journey of self-awareness, I remarked to a colleague that I shuddered to think of the students I had wounded through failing to exercise my professional responsibility of deliberately and carefully considering my theoretical framework of literacy.

An article by Schuster (1991) I happened onto at this point powerfully challenged me to better blend theory and practice in my professional life. He persuasively argued that, stripped of each other, both theory and practice suffer: "The opposite of 'theory' is not 'practice' but rather 'thoughtlessness' or even 'mindlessness.' Theory is not opposed to practice; it is opposed to muddled thought, to confusion. Similarly, the antonym of 'practice' is not 'theory' but rather laziness, inertia, lack of accomplishment" (p. 42). My "mindlessness" had become all too apparent to me, as each text I read pulled me further into the complex landscape of literacy issues.

If the only consequence of my voluminous reading had been a familiarization with a body of literacy definitions, of course, this journey would have been merely another trek into the world of memorization, downloading information into my cranial database. Through mindful reading, however, I perceived that within each articulation of literacy inhered a paradigmatic framework/theory laden with educational, social, and political ramifications. I gradually conceded that the lens through which literacy is viewed determines the atmospheres created and nurtured in classrooms, the types of reading and writing assigned and valued, assessment procedures established to measure individuals' rate of "progress," the praise accorded to those persons deemed literate, and the devastating censure meted out to the unfortunate ones branded illiterate. Clearly, I was wrestling with matters of substance where the stakes are enormous.

And there was at the time no way for me to simply ponder these realities as an aloof researcher or a novice anticipating a teaching career; not only had I been an educator for twenty years when I began my doctoral program, I continued teaching full time throughout my studies. As I struggled to reconcile new information with old ways of being and teaching, I had not the luxury of withdrawing and weaving the pieces together in some coherent whole before resuming my work in composition and literature classes. Instead, I was dragging myself (literally, it often seemed) into the classroom each day, uncomfortable with many of my previous beliefs and a great many of my former pedagogical practices, but still confused as to a new definition of literacy to embrace, much less how to use it to inform my everyday teaching. This experience resonated all too well with my reading of Eliot's Wise Men, who find themselves at home with neither their new vision nor their previous belief system: "We returned to our places, these Kingdoms, / But no longer at ease here, in the old dispensation." And like them, I too often lamented (and still do, at times) the loss of surety I had once felt, a sense of being grounded and confident, with no need to follow stars or bibliographies on literacy. Most of my teaching career had been characterized by ease and a near absolute clarity (however misinformed and naïve) regarding such concepts as reading, writing, literacy, students, and teachers. As I traveled more deeply into literacy studies, confusion and fear replaced any sense of assurance I had once possessed in terms of my teaching, and I identified with Eliot's Magi who admit: "this Birth was / Hard and bitter agony for us, like Death."

The death of what, you might ask? Nothing short of a way of being and acting in classrooms. For, having at the commencement of my career limited my definition of literacy to the academic or essayist model (the only approach I had experienced), I had—subtly at times, pointedly at others—taken it on myself as a teacher of reading and writing to rid the Academy of inferior texts and to correct students' informal and incorrect language practices. A "terminator" armed with red pens, I had passionately committed myself to saving Standard English, preserving the canon, maintaining decorum in the activities of reading and writing, and protecting students from the negative linguistic influences of family and friends. My activities flowed naturally from my perception of literacy at the time; indeed, they make perfect sense when I consider my literacy mindset at that point in my teaching. Having embraced a single, autonomous definition of academic literacy, it never occurred to me to question how the exclusive role of Standard English in classrooms might silence students, how a canonical approach to literature might overlook countless writers students would love to read, how any definition of "decorum" with regard to reading and writing might reflect a poorly conceived theory of literacy, how relentless criticism leveled at students regarding the linguistic patterns they share with family and friends might serve to distance them from arenas central to their development of self and the activities of reading and writing, or how a "school" definition of literacy might ignore crucial literacies necessary in today's increasingly technical and technological careers. I was, quite simply, too confident in my singular definition of literacy and my role as its protector to question any pedagogical, perhaps even ethical, impropriety in my teaching. Acknowledging these discomforting realities was an important leg of my journey, but, as noted earlier, my admission was not accompanied by an immediate, intuitive flash—a "new and improved" vision of literacy and appropriate classroom practices. In essence, I knew at this point who I no longer was but not who I was to become, and therein lies the real anguish of such interior travelling of which Eliot's narrator speaks.

This sense of emotional and intellectual displacement is also poignantly depicted in the writings of such individuals as Rodriguez and Hoggart. In his literacy autobiography *Hunger of Memory*, Rodriguez (1982) described the journey from his Catholic, working-class, Mexican-American culture into the middle-class, secular, Anglo world of school. He spoke of the pain experienced by individuals like himself as they are forced to shed their identities when moving between the worlds of home and school that are so often polar opposites with regard to language.

Hoggart (1957) made a similar argument in *The Uses of Literacy*, wherein he wrote of the interior sojourn of British working-class students as they enter the middle-class world of academia. Often, insisted Hoggart, individuals are unable to integrate these two different environments (home and school), remaining suspended, as it were, unable to live intimately in either. Even when a person manages to master the literate forms of both school and home, he or she is likely to reside on the fringes of both, neither comfortable with his or her own linguistic style nor fully assimilated into the world of school and its particular style of literacy.

These texts now speak eloquently to me in ways they could not on my first encounters with them, unable as I was at that time to comprehend such divisions within one's core. Building as it had on my familial/cultural background, my previous education had never created such a traumatic fissure within my being. School had been simply "more of the same" for me—until my doctoral studies. My study of literacy effected within me the same sorts of alienation and confusion that Hoggart and Rodriguez described among those attempting to master academic/essayist literacy. For, as I learned, doctoral work it is not merely an experience of expanding one's rhetorical and linguistic repertoire, which is stressful enough as writers who in the past might have felt proficient to some degree now find themselves subdued and bewildered in the face of writing a dissertation. This academic endeavor also plunges students into new worlds, much like the individuals described in Rose's (1989) *Lives on the Boundary,* who—despite various intellectual talents—often find themselves without an academic map or guideposts. The frustration is only heightened by one's inability to share this journey with friends and family who are often unfamiliar with these new universes, thereby creating the isolation described by Rodriguez, Hoggart, and Eliot: displaced, in a very real sense, in both landscapes.

Under the tutelage of wonderful professors, I gradually acquired the knowledge and skills I needed to successfully complete the rigors of my degree but these talented individuals could not, obviously, walk the even more difficult journey for me, that of redefining myself (both as a person and educator) in light of a new model of literacies that had taken embryonic root within me. In many ways I am still wrestling with how to bring new concepts to fruition, embodying a new theory of multiple literacies in the classroom. For while my attempts at fostering a multiple literacies learning environment are at times both exciting and energizing, they are always accompanied by a nagging worry that I have somehow abandoned my professorial responsibilities and my students' needs. And the fact that I have an intellectual rationale/theory for my pedagogy does not fully eliminate the anxiety I experience. The former representation of literacy as monolithic and academic continues to haunt me in my work, so strong was its hold on me. While I continue to grow more comfortable within this paradigm that has called me to radically rethink and redefine the terms reading, writing, student, and teacher, I suspect that the suspension between competing theoretical frameworks articulated by Rodriguez and Hoggart will continue to plague me, representing as it does my own journey through two different worlds of literacy.

And therein lies one of the great benefits of my journey: its ability to increase my understanding of students' literacy travels. At long last I grasp, at a visceral level, some sense of learners' dislocation, confusion, and fear when faced with a new way of being in school. At long last I better comprehend the ways in which reading, writing, and speaking are dramatically linked to one's self and identity. Of course I claim only partial identification with students' feelings; I am well aware that my experiences in a doctoral program while already well established in a career are not commensurate with younger students' journeys on entering elementary, secondary, or even collegiate programs where linguistic practices differ vastly from those in the individuals' social and familial environments. Factors such as my age, my "literacy capital" (Stuckey 1991), and my previous success in navigating the demands of essayist literacy no doubt enable me to negotiate this difficult journey with more aplomb. Still, the travelling has not been without hardship.

The writing of my dissertation and this essay represent ongoing attempts to address the struggles and harness the power of writing to both record and make sense of my travels. The great value of literacy narratives, notes Soliday (1994), is their ability to provide "sites of self-translation" as individuals struggle to articulate "their passages between language worlds" (p. 511). As I have become active scribe of my own narrative, I have found myself passionately interested in hearing others' stories, as well. In the case study I conducted, I interviewed prospective high school English teachers who were completing a master of arts in teaching degree and three tenured professors who had been instrumental in shaping the program in which the students were enrolled. When I initially designed the study, I was still being fueled by the need to defend literacy as I had always understood it; I therefore very much hoped I would find a "traditional" program credentialing future teachers who would be reliable custodians of all that was good and true within reading and writing classrooms, individuals promoting a single representation of literacy as academic/essayist. As the study evolved, however, I became more interested in the ways in which literacy was being named/defined in the program and how students had either embraced or resisted this naming process. Were they, I wondered, engaged in journeys similar to mine at the time? If so, how were they faring in their travels?

The results were fascinating, as I discovered a program where numerous guideposts pointed to a definition of literacy that was very inclusive. Department handouts, class discussions, and various assignments all spoke of diversity and a capacious definition of literacy. Conversations with the professors also underscored this commitment to a multiple literacies model, with literacy defined as "the greatest use of the greatest number of dimensions of the written and spoken language," a "huge spectrum of possibilities" with regard to symbolic representation, and "code-switching" to address "diverse situations." Although these professors acknowledged some level of tension with regard to the pedagogical implications of their definitions (an admission that sustained me during my own frustrations within the classroom), they were confident that a coherent conceptual framework was in place within the program and that, as Knoblauch and Brannon (1993) might say, the approach was "transparent." But was it?

By this stage in my work on literacy, I was prepared for contradiction and dichotomy; I had, after all, served as "poster child" for confusion and consternation during my doctoral work on the topic. Consequently, I was not altogether surprised by the results of my interviews with the student subjects, all of whom mirrored back, to some extent, various questions, opinions, and concerns I had previously articulated in my own journey.

Most surprising to the professors was the fact that students were initially stymied when asked to define literacy. My requests were greeted by looks of dismay, confusion, and embarrassment, followed by an apology of some sort: "I'm sorry, but I'm not sure what you're asking . . ."; "I know I should know this, but nothing comes to mind right off the bat. . . ."; "I can't tell you how stupid I feel; here I am an English major and I've never really thought about this before. . . ."; "Literacy . . . Hmmmm. . . . give me a minute; this is a tough one. . . ."; "It must seem like such a basic question to you [hardly!] but—I swear—I haven't really thought it through . . . let me think . . ."; and, perhaps my favorite: "You're not gonna tell the professors around here that I don't have clue about this, are you?" It is difficult to express the empathy I felt for these student respondents, a semester away from student teaching and desperate to feel "in control," as they grappled mightily with the same question that had so long intellectually engaged me. Their emotions betrayed my same journey as these prospective teachers moved from confusion, to dismay, to embarrassment, and even to a bit of anger while talking with me about the topic.

Once they regained some measure of composure, however, their definitions of literacy were forthcoming, and these future teachers' primary concern was their students' ability to read and write with enough proficiency to succeed in the arenas of work and society at large. However, when I nudged these interviewees a bit more and asked them to consider literacy in terms of their future teaching careers, an interesting trend emerged: the academic/essayist model surfaced as a superior literate expression. As I asked for some reflection on this shift in thinking, these prospective teachers were refreshingly honest in articulating their own "literacy travels." One student admitted that "all of this is very confusing at times. . . . It's hard to fit it all together and I get overwhelmed at times . . ." Another respondent acknowledged that "my ideas are newly formed" and that the program in which she was enrolled "really forced me to rethink this whole topic, and it's been difficult. . . ," while one of her peers said, simply, "I'm just not sure what literacy is, I guess, when I try to think about it in terms of both school and society as a whole; there seems to be lots of different kinds of literacies. . . ." Like Eliot's figures, these individuals were speaking of a "long journey: the ways deep." One young man wondered, in fact, "if I won't spend my whole career trying to figure this issue out."

Perhaps that is the lesson in all of these literacy sojourns: an acknowledgement of complexity that requires thoughtful, faithful, and wise traveling. Brandt (1995) observed: "The piling up and extending out of literacy and its technologies give a complex flavor even to elementary acts of reading and writing today" (p. 651). Eschewing any facile approach to literacy, Brandt instead bluntly insisted that "Literacy is always in flux. . . . Indeed . . . literate ability has become more and more defined as the ability to position and reposition oneself amidst literacy's recessive and emergent forms" (p. 666). The students in my study were years ahead of me in "positioning" and "themselves," struggling to make sense of the "cacophonous mix" (Brandt, 1995) of literacies. And, although no one could make the intellectual journey for them (or any of us, for that matter), we can, within our profession, work deliberately to assist one another in such travels.

One of the clearest lessons from both my own and my student subjects' experiences with literacy is that we all would have profited immensely from carefully planned opportunities to reflect upon and discuss literacy as a concept throughout our educational and professional journeys. As Minter, Gere, and Keller-Cohen (1995), noted, "learning about literacies is a long-term intellectual project" (p. 684) so it is imperative that "in classes across the academy" professors "encourage and enable" (p. 684) students to engage in this process. These same authors address the ways in which their students were "confronted with multiple and often competing conceptions of literacy arising out of the conflicting goals, practices, and systems of beliefs inherent in [the] different contexts in which they [the students] worked—the school, the after-school program, and the on-campus seminar" (p. 672). Often, the writers admit, "These multiple enactments of and expectations surrounding literacy clash" (p. 673), but these professors had chosen to throw their students headlong into the chaos. Confusing? No doubt. Unnerving? Most assuredly. Yet there is no alternative route if the students are to encounter literacy in its many forms. To allow for debriefing, however, Minter, Gere, and Keller-Cohen created seminars wherein their students could talk not just of their experiences but the ways in which these events were shaping their understanding of literacy, learners, and teachers. These classroom meetings became "meta-literate" occasions during which everyone was assisted in developing a vocabulary to converse about literacy in all of its complexity, to give voice to questions and frustrations, to talk of intellectual conflicts and interior confusion.

Such an approach well reflects Brandt's (1990) definition of literacy, as she argued against a text-based model of literacy and instead describes it as "knowledge embodied in doing, a knowledge in which what is made is not separate from the making of it. In that sense, literate knowledge resembles craft knowledge, know-how, knack" (p. 89). Brandt ultimately chose to describe literacy as an "act of involvement," implying that the passive acceptance of someone else's definition of it is anathema to authentic literacy. All learners must actively engage in the coming to know; all of us must make the journey ourselves. It is this reality that leads Salvio (1990) to talk of literacy as "intimate."

The destinations are multiple, and the sojourns often "deep and hard." But like Eliot's wise men, those of us who have traveled far admit that, despite the often difficult terrains, we "would do it again" And we do, every time we walk into another classroom, another conference, another learning experience. Yet make no mistake about it: while learning the computer for composition classes, encompassing vernacular in academic classrooms, moving from a verbo-centric model or literacy to a more artistic approach (Chesiri-Strater 1991), fashioning activities related to the world of work, and creating classrooms where literacy is addressed deliberately and thoroughly as a concept are challenging activities when addressing multiple literacies for the 21st century, they are less taxing and unnerving than that part of the journey which precedes these shifts in pedagogy: a reconceptualization of how we define literacy. As we pursue this sojourn we find that, like the Magi, our wisdom and humility deepen.

REFERENCES

Brandt, D. (1990). *Literacy as involvement: The acts of writers, readers, and texts.* Carbondale: Southern Illinois University Press.

Brandt, D. (1995). Accumulating literacy: Writing and learning to write in the twentieth century. *College English, 57*(6), 649-68.

Brodkey, L. (1986). Tropics of literacy. *Journal of Education, 168*, 47-54.

Carroll, L. (1960). *Alice's adventures in wonderland & Through the looking glass.* New York: New American Library.

Chiseri-Strater, E. (1991). *Academic literacies.* Portsmouth, NH: Boynton/Cook.

Eliot, T.S. (1964). *Journey of the magi. Selected poems.*New York: Harcourt.

Freire, P., & Macedo, D. (1987). *Literacy: Reading the word and the world.* New York: Bergin & Garvey.

Graf, G. (1987). *Professing literature.* Chicago: University of Chicago Press.

Hoggart, R. (1957). *The uses of literacy: Aspects of working-class life, with special references to publications and entertainment.* London: Chatto & Windus.

Knoblauch, C.H., & Brannon, L. (1993). *Critical teaching and the idea of literacy.* Portsmouth, NH: Boynton/Cook.

Minter, D. W., Gere, A. R., & Keller-Cohen, D. (1995). Learning literacies. *College English, 57*(6), 669-687.

Rich, A. (1979). *When the dead awaken: Writing as re-vision. On lies, secrets, and silence* (pp. 33-50). New York: Norton.

Rodriguez, R. (1982). *Hunger of memory.* Boston: Godine.

Rose, M. (1989). *Lives on the boundary: The struggles and achievements of America's underprepared.* New York: The Free Press.

Salvio, P. (1990). The world, the text, and the reader. In A.A. Lunsford, H. Moglen, & J. Slevin (Eds.), *The right to literacy* (pp. 269-275). New York: Modern Language Association.

Schuster, C.I. (1991). Theory and practice. In E. Lindemann & G. Tate (Eds.), *An introduction to composition studies* (pp. 33-48). New York: Oxford University Press.

Soliday, M. (1994). Translating self and difference through literacy narratives. *College English, 56*(5), 511-526.

Stuckey, J. E. (1991). *The violence of literacy.* Portsmouth, NH: Boynton/Cook.

23

A REFLECTIVE MOMENT IN THE HISTORY OF LITERACY

Charles Bazerman
University of California–Santa Barbara

The 1998 Watson Conference and the related chapters presented in this volume represent but one moment in the complex and emergent history of literacy. More specifically, these documents represent one moment in the history of reflection on literacy.

It is hardly surprising that we should reflect about literacy, for literacy is an overwhelmingly reflective activity. We think when we read and when we write, as meanings play out in our mind, and we frequently think about what it means to read and to write and to be caught up in the meanings mediated by reading and writing. One reason we think about these things is that we are constantly making choices as we read and write—about what to read and write, how to do it, what meanings we should take from our own and others' texts, how these meanings should affect our understanding and action. As literacy educators it is even less surprising that we should reflect on literacy, for our profession demands we think about what it is we are teaching, how it may be taught and developed. Moreover, we constantly look on students grappling with the tasks of literacy and wonder what is happening with them, what their difficulties are, and what we can do to help them.

The history of literacy extends about 5,000 years, the history of inscription even longer. And the history of articulate reflection on literacy goes back to the earliest extant texts. The Epic of Gilgamesh, dating to the middle of the second Millennium BC, reports the hero's inscription of knowledge as one of his accomplishments:

> the lord of wisdom, he who knew everything, Gilgamesh,
> who saw things secret, opened the place hidden,
> and carried back word of the time before the Flood—
> he travelled the road, exhausted, in pain,
> and cut his works into a stone tablet.
>
> (ll.4-8)

We know how much the inscription, education, and knowledge industries have expanded since then. Currently, 3 to 4 billion people are literate, and most of them were taught by somebody, using some kind of teaching book. In the United States alone, the publishing industry in 1997 had $117 billion in shipments, with more than $6 billion of that being textbooks—primary through university (U.S. Census Bureau, 1999).

So three October days in Louisville, near the end of the fifth millennium of literacy and the first millennium of printing, in the middle of the sixth century of printing and publishing in the west, and the second century of expanding public education is indeed just a small spot on a very large map.

That map is a very rapidly changing one, however, with the Internet being only the most recent of a series of transformative technologies in the last two centuries—including steam and rotary presses, cheap paper, pencil, fountain and ball point pens, railroads to carry books and newspapers rapidly to distant markets, telegraphy, paperback books, the filing cabinet, and paper clips—that have made the written word cheap, convenient, and ubiquitous, transforming the economy, government, politics, knowledge, religion, entertainment, and education.

The material technologies that mediate literacy have changed the conditions of literacy and enabled expanding and creative uses of the written word. The earliest clay counters that are believed to be the precursors of literacy early elaborated into business accounting and commercial contracts, both of which took on new forms as they became the heart of the commercial system in early Renaissance Italy. Early letters to agents elaborated into the modern world of corporate and bureaucratic records and files. Inscribed laws and decrees became complex systems of governance and adjudication, with volumes of legislation, regulation, court records, precedent, and commentary. Early letters of useful news led to newsletters and newspapers, news commentary, and news magazines, and now the entire complex of news media. Scriptures beget commentary, scholarship, and prayer books. Transcriptions of public performances become poetry and drama and narratives and novels and detective potboilers and Harlequin romances (Bazerman, 2000a, 2000b).

Each of these elaborating documentary forms are part of elaborating social systems, roles and activities. Written law has spawned judges and appellate judges and Supreme Court justices, lawyers and clients and paralegals, law librarians and law professors and law students, and fundraisers for law schools. Financial records and financial instruments created professions of accountants, bookkeepers, clerks, typists, bankers, middle-level managers, and IRS agents. And for each field, complexes of activities and roles become built on the spine of written genres that stabilized and regularized relations within increasingly differentiated and elaborated activity systems (Bazerman, 1997). As literate artifacts grew in complexity and variety, tied to increasingly specialized activities and forms of knowledge, schooling became crucial for the maintenance of social systems and the fates of people whose lives were ever more caught up within those systems. The literacies, literate practices, and literatures of schooling become accordingly extensive and complex in relation to the multiple literacies of societies that they prepared people for.

Each area of social activity—law, business, finances, government, politics, entertainment, education, knowledge production—is now creating new presences on the internet and other electronic media. In turn, each of the new presences are changing the activities and social organization of these worlds of social action, creating new forms of life for us to live in and through.

This dazzling growth and articulation of new literate practices has created the information age. For several centuries our lives have been increasing tied up with literate practice—so that we live not only in the built world of cities and roads and electric grids, but in a built symbolic world of inscriptions. These inscriptions now move so fast, are so ubiquitous and cheap, proliferate so rapidly, and are becoming so essential for the activities of our lives, that the manipulation of these symbols is seen as the defining characteristic of the foreseeable future—the information age.

One of the talmudic commentaries on Genesis asks when exactly Adam and Eve ate of the tree of knowledge and began sinning. The commentary answers, early in the morning of the eighth day. People seem in a headlong rush to eat of the fruits of knowledge and live the life that knowledge will give us. Comedian George Burns died shortly after his 100th birthday. Within his life he saw the development of the internet, computers, television, radio, the expectation of universal literacy and universal secondary education, and wide access to the universities. The lives of two George Burns span the development of modern journalism and cheap printing, mass education, and the modern research university. Six George Burns would have seen Gutenburg, only 50 George Burns the birth of writing, and

500 George Burns perhaps the very origins of language. What will be the world of literacy that the George Burns born today will see? And what will the schooling be like to prepare people to participate in that world? And what will the writing instruction be to support these students in their schooling and in the social literate worlds beyond school?

So what are the parts of literacy that we reflect on at this moment in this volume? This is to ask what parts of literacy are we now building and rebuilding. What adjustments are we contemplating between the social orders we live in and the literate activity that sustains those orders and provides means for individuals to participate? What are we foreseeing as the literate needs of coming generations?

A major theme in this volume, and the conference it comes out of, has been an issue with us since the beginning of literacy: the power that comes with literacy and who should have access to it. Even though the earliest scribes were slaves or others low in social power, they served the powerful who used literacy to extend their military, political, religious, and commercial empires. No matter how low their origins, scribal classes soon learned how to use their monopoly on communicative power-at-a-distance to entrench their place and extend their authority, within the bureaucracies of state, church, commerce, or later, schooling—as lawyers, civil servants, priests, accountants and economists, corporate managers, professors, and all the other literate professionals that hold sway over the dominant institutions of modern life. As literacy has increasingly become the lifeblood of almost all aspects of life, access is no longer just about who will have the good fortune to rise, but has become about whether all people will have the ability to carry out day-to-day interactions, to protect themselves within those literate systems which encompass their lives, and to make a living in an information economy. Even athletes now need the information, habits, and regimen that are associated with modern literate practice. Chapters in this volume note with disapproval the stigmatization of those who remain unlettered and the way those stigmatizations serve to entrench the interests and ideology of the lettered (Gleason, Chap. 2; Ball, Chap. 19). But they also note approvingly and with interest those who gain literacy despite not being historically favored with direct access to extensive formal literacy education (Branch, Chap. 1; Gleason, Chap. 2; Hogg, Chap. 4). By such negative and positive tales we reaffirm our commitment to universal access to literacy—seeing it as a fundamental human right and necessity in the modern world.

As professional literacy educators, all the authors in this volume realize their commitment to access to literacy through teaching. Questions of teaching underlie most of the essays here and are the explicit focus of a large number of them. What to teach? How to teach? How to organize classrooms? How to develop and train teachers? Such questions also have a long history, but they gained force and focus in the last century as those employed in schools became recognized as professionals requiring specialized knowledge and training. The teaching of writing became such a research-based profession only in recent decades. Now the range of teaching concerns and approaches include the development of rhetorical reading (Wardle, Chap. 5), large group discussions (Beach, Eddleston, & Philippot, Chap. 7), ESL students in writing classrooms (Leki, Chap. 6), the use of portfolios in GTA training (Bell, Chap. 3), the use of technology to enhance learning (Tannacito, Chap. 9; Schendel, Neal, & Hartley, Chap. 10; Pence, Chap. 13), and disciplinarily specific forms of writing (Patton & Nagelhout, Chap. 8).

The great value placed on literacy currently has, several authors in this volume recognize, resulted in other realms of human knowing and accomplishment being inappropriately demoted in value. At stake is the worth of people who have pursued paths alternative to or in addition to literacy, our support of these other forms of development, and an understanding in the way the development of these other capacities may influence literacy learning. Chapters in this volume recover the forms of knowing associated with sports (Cheville, Chap. 17), music (Sohn, Chap. 14), the visual arts (Swiencicki, Chap. 16; Bruch, Kinloch, & Marback, Chap. 20; Gray-Rosendale, Chap. 21), and mathematics (Johanek, Chap. 18). To increase the value of these skills authors label them as forms of literacy—which ironically maintains letters as the paradigm of skills. One chapter also recovers the role of affect in what is sometimes mistaken to be the rational and cognitive world of literacy. The chapter explores the regimes of emotion and relation that pervade and constrain writing. If we remain emotionally undeveloped and unaware, our writing becomes limited and enlisted into ideologically driven regimes of meaning and social order (Langstraat, Chap. 15).

Literacy has, since the 18th century, been viewed as a tool of critical consciousness, closely associated with democratic revolution and reform. Modern democracies based as much on literacy as rhetoric have a different cast than classical rhetorical democracies, with a new emphasis on widespread information, rational bureaucratization, and critical inquiry (sometimes carried out through specialists in journalism or the academy). Chapters here examine the role of journalism in expressing critical consciousness (Swiencicki, Chap. 16; Gray-Rosendale, Chap. 21) and the role of the literacy classroom in developing critical consciousness (Gleason, Chap. 2); other chapters take on the direct role of critical analysis of our culture (Ramey, Chap. 11; Wysocki, Chap. 12; Langstraat, Chap. 15; Bruch, Kinloch, & Marback, Chap. 20).

Literacy has always developed hand in hand with the technologies by which it is realized—whether clay tablet, printing press, or microchip—

and people have almost always immediately wondered about and commented on how the newest technology might be used and its consequences. The latest technological changes of the electronic revolution have, however, come at a time when a large class of literacy education professionals have developed, there are large schooling responsibilities for literacy, the technological changes are being adopted widely and rapidly in society, and schools have for internal and external reasons been reasonably quick in responding to (or at least worrying about) the increasing pace of changes. Whether or not technology is the most fundamental issue literacy professionals must address over the next few decades remains to be seen, but it is certainly the most pressing. Chapters in this volume examine the meanings being enacted within these latest transformations of literacy (Wysocki, Chap. 12; Ramey, Chap. 11) and how the technology is changing the practices of literacy learners (Tannacito, Chap. 9; Schendel, Neal, & Hartley, Chap. 10).

Literacy and literacy education are ongoing processes, caught up with the power, institutions, practices, technologies, and other forms of communication and practice of the time. Literacy is always recreated with every act of reading and writing, always local, always of the moment, but also always part of past and future literate acts for texts travel through time. If we were to put this volume in the time capsule to be opened at the Watson Conference on Literacy in 2100, the particulars of literacy would certainly be different, maybe substantially different, perhaps because of the way in which technology and the accompanying social changes will have rearranged power and access, institutions and practices, and opportunities. But I suspect the themes will be recognizably continuous with the issues we worry about now—unless literacy educators are not there to be pondering over them. I wouldn't put my money, though, on literacy education going out of fashion for some time.

REFERENCES

Bazerman, C. (1997). Discursively structured activities. *Mind, Culture and Activity* *4*(4), 296-308.

Bazerman, C. (2000a). Letters and the social grounding of differentiated genres. In D. Barton & N. Hall (Eds.), *Letter writing as a social practice* (pp. 15-29). Amsterdam: John Benjamins.

Bazerman, C. (2000b). A rhetoric for literate society: The tension between expanding practices and restricted theories. In M. Goggin (Ed.), *Inventing a discipline* (pp. 5-28). Urbana, IL: NCTE.

U.S. Census Bureau. (1999). *1997 economic census*. Washington, DC: U.S. Department of Commerce.

ABOUT THE CONTRIBUTORS

Kevin Ball is assistant professor of English at Youngstown State University where he teaches undergraduate and graduate courses in composition/ rhetoric in addition to co-directing YSU's Early English Composition Assessment Program (EECAP) project. His current research interests include the risks of composing identity for inner-city student writers, the intersections of the composition class and working-class studies, and the political rhetoric of Ohio's Mahoning Valley. He continues to closely monitor Injun Joe's case.

Charles Bazerman, professor and chair of the Department of Education at the University of California, Santa Barbara, is interested in the social dynamics of writing, rhetorical theory, and the rhetoric of knowledge production and use. His most recent book, *The Languages of Edison's Light*, won the American Association of Publishers' award for the best scholarly book of 1999 in the History of Science and Technology. Previous books include *Constructing Experience*; *Shaping Written Knowledge: The Genre and Activity of the Experimental Article in Science*; *Textual Dynamics of the Professions*; *Landmark Essays in Writing Across the Curriculum*; *The Informed Writer: Using Sources in the Disciplines*; and *Involved: Writing For College, Writing for Your Self.*

Richard Beach is Wallace Professor of English Education at the University of Minnesota. He is author of *A Teacher's Introduction to Reader Response Theories* (NCTE) and co-author of *Inquiry-based English Instruction: Engaging Students in Life and Literature, Teaching Literature in the Secondary School, Journals in the Classroom: Writing to Learn.* He is a former president of the National Conference on Research in Language and a former member of the Board of Directors of the National Reading Conference.

Kathleen Bell is associate professor of English at the University of Central Florida in Orlando. Over the past 20 years, she has directed writing programs at the University of Miami (FL), Old Dominion University (VA), and the University of Central Florida where she also directed the Learning Communities Program. She authored the texts *Developing Arguments: Strategies for Reaching Audiences* and *Writing Choices: Shaping Contexts for Critical Readers.* Her current research involves the reconstruction of arguments that influence the careers of women in the arts.

Pat Bruch is assistant professor in the General College at the University of Minnesota. He has published articles on basic writing, writing theory, and writing pedagogy. He has also published a composition reader, *Cities, Cultures, Conversations,* with Jill Eicher and Richard Marback. He is currently doing research in the area of language rights.

Julie Cheville is assistant professor of literacy education at Rutgers University. Her research interests include situated and embodied cognition, reflexive ethnographic methodologies, and contemplative practice in teacher education.

Sharon Eddleston taught high school English for 33 years at Armstrong High School, Robbinsdale, MN. She received her PhD in Curriculum and Instruction at the University of Minnesota in 1998, and has a strong interest in inquiry-based instruction and whole-class discussions of literature.

Barbara Gleason, associate professor of English at the City College of New York, currently teaches writing, autobiography, language, and literacy courses at the City College Center for Worker Education. She is co-editor—with Mark Wiley and Louise Wetherbee Phelps—of *Composition in Four Keys: Inquiring into the Field Through Nature, Art, Science and Politics* and has published essays on basic writing/college composition in *Journal of Basic Writing, College Composition and Communication*, and *College English.* Her recent publications on returning adult learners and their literacies appear as chapters in *Attending to the Margins: Writing, Researching, and Teaching on the Front Lines*; *Mainstreaming Basic Writers: Politics and Pedagogies of Access*; and in *CompCity: Identities, Spaces, Practices.*

Laura Gray-Rosendale is associate professor of rhetoric and composition and co-chair of the Commission on the Status of Women at Northern Arizona University. She teaches graduate and undergraduate classes in cultural studies and visual rhetoric, the history of rhetoric, gender studies, and literacy theory. Along with various articles and book chapters, Gray-Rosendale has published *Rethinking Basic Writing: Exploring Identity, Politics, and Community in Interaction* and *Alternative Rhetorics: Challenges to the Rhetorical Tradition* with Sibylle Gruber. Her new books, *Fractured Feminisms* with Gil Haroian-Guerin and *Radical Relevance* with Steven Rosendale are forthcoming.

Cecilia Hartley collaborated on the article "Toward a Theory of Online Collaboration" as a graduate student at the University of Louisville. Her scholarship on teaching with technology has appeared in *Computers and Composition* and several edited collections. She currently lives in Alabama and is the owner and proprietor of Writerspace (www.writerspace.com), a company that develops and maintains Web sites for published writers.

Charlotte Hogg is assistant professor at Texas Christian University. Her chapter in this volume is part of a larger book project on the literacies of older women in western Nebraska; other work from this project is forthcoming in *Western American Literature*. She also has an article forthcoming with Robert Brooke in *Protean Ground: Critical Ethnography and the Postmodern Turn.*

Brian Huot is professor of English and Director of the Composition Program at the University of Louisville. His work has appeared in *College Composition and Communication*, *College English* and other journals and collections devoted to literacy and its teaching.

Cindy Johanek, assistant professor of English and Writing Center Director at Denison University, teaches first-year and advanced writing courses and seminars in composition theory, pedagogy, and history. She has published in the *Writing Center Journal*, the *Writing Lab Newsletter*, and *Computers and Composition.* Her book, *Composing Research,* won the 2001 International Writing Centers Association Outstanding Scholarship Award. She currently serves as treasurer for the East Central Writing Centers Association and the International Writing Centers Association.

Valerie Kinloch is a assistant professor of English at the University of Minnesota. She has published in the areas of African-American literature and composition studies. Her current research is on multiculturalism and urban literacies.

Lisa Langstraat is associate professor of English and director of composition at the University of Southern Mississippi where she teaches in the graduate program in Rhetoric and Composition. She has published articles on cultural studies and composition in journals such as *JAC, Composition Forum,* and *Works and Days*. She is currently working on two book-length projects: a textbook, *Writing In Public: A Rhetoric for Community Service Composition* (with Michelle Comstock), and a study of emotion culture in writing theory and pedagogy, *Where We Live: Toward a Politics of Affect for Composition Studies*.

Ilona Leki is professor of English and director of ESL at the University of Tennessee. She co-edits *Journal of Second Language Writing* (with Tony Silva), is author of *Academic Writing: Exploring Processes and Strategies* and *Understanding ESL Writers: A Guide for Teachers*, and co-editor (with Joan Carson) of *Reading in the Composition Classroom: Second Language Perspectives*. She is winner of 1996 TESOL/Newbury House Distinguished Research Award. Her research focuses on second language writing and reading, academic literacy, and the literacy experiences of English learners.

Richard Marback is an associate professor of English at Wayne State University. He has published in the areas of history of rhetoric, rhetorical theory, and teaching writing. His current research is in the areas of language policy and civic rhetoric.

Ed Nagelhout is an assistant professor at Indiana University Purdue University–Indianapolis, where he helps administer the English department's concentration in writing and literacy. His research interests include writing program administration, commuter students, and literacy practices in urban and postsuburban spaces. He has published numerous articles in journals such as *Technical Communication Quarterly* and *Business Communication Quarterly*.

Michael Neal is assistant professor of English at Clemson University. He earned his doctorate in rhetoric and composition at the University of Louisville, where he studied writing assessment and social consequences resulting from their educational (mis)uses. His research and teaching interests include assessment, writing technologies, writing program administration, composition theory and pedagogy, rhetoric, and service learning. In addition to teaching composition, business writing, and technical writing to undergraduate and graduate students, he is currently the editor of an online undergraduate research journal in engineering as well as the managing editor of the *Journal of Writing Assessment.*

Martha D. Patton is assistant director of the Campus Writing Program and adjunct professor of English at the University of Missouri–Columbia. Her research focuses on writing in the disciplines, particularly in the sciences. She has published in *Language and Learning Across the Disciplines*, *Contemporary Issues in Technology and Teacher Education*, and *Humanistic Mathematics Network Journal.*

Lucretia E. Penny Pence is assistant professor of language, literacy, and sociocultural studies at the University of New Mexico. Her interest in representation of teacher knowledge and ability began with her work in developing performance assessments for the National Board for Professional Teaching and in developing standards and portfolios for the Inter-State New Teacher and Assessment Consortium.

Carol C. Pfeffer is associate professor of English at Bellarmine University, in Louisville, KY, where she has taught since receiving her doctorate in rhetoric and composition from the University of Louisville in 1998. Chairperson of the English department, she specializes in the teaching of composition, and her interest in this area has resulted in her active involvement in Bellarmine's freshman seminar program, which provides a vehicle for working with colleagues from other disciplines in the teaching of writing to freshman. She also directs a curriculum-based leadership program at the university, where she studies writing and literacy issues among scholarship students. Prior to her arrival at Ballarmine in 1990, she taught English at the secondary level for 13 years.

Raymond Philippot is assistant professor of English at St. Cloud State University (MN). He received his PhD in Curriculum and Instruction from the University of Minnesota. Prior to graduate school, he taught high school English in Wichita, KS, and Fergus Falls, MN. His research interests include response to literature and preservice teacher education.

John W. Ramey is assistant professor of English at Coastal Carolina University, where he teaches composition, technical writing and professional communication courses, document design courses, literature survey courses, and poetry writing workshops. He received his MA and PhD from the University of Louisville. He has published two volumes of poetry, *The Future Past* and *Death Sings in the Choir of Light*. Currently he is revising a novel and working on a book about the intersection of verbal and visual rhetoric.

Ellen Schendel is an assistant professor of writing at Grand Valley State University in Michigan, where she teaches courses in professional and academic writing. Her scholarship has been published in *Computers and Composition*, *Assessing Writing*, and *WPA: Writing Program Administration*, among other places. Her current research interest is writing assessment theory and practice.

Katherine K. Sohn is assistant professor of English, and Writing Center coordinator at Pikeville College (KY). In 1984, she initiated and directed the Pikeville College Center for Continuing Education, teaching college composition. Her dissertation, "Whistlin' and Crowin' Women of Appalachia: Literacy Development Since College," won the 2001 College Composition and Communication Conference James Berlin Outstanding Dissertation Award. She is presently working to publish the dissertation.

Beth Stroble is the dean of the College of Education and professor in the Department of Curricular and Instructional Studies at the University of Akron. She has served on the faculties of Northern Arizona University and the University of Louisville. Her studies of leadership, literacy, and school and teacher education reform have appeared in *English Education*, *The Peabody Journal of Education*, *Research in the Teaching of English*, and the *Journal of Technology and Teacher Education*. She currently serves on the Executive Committee and Policy Board for the Ohio Resource Center for Mathematics, Science, and Reading, a "virtual" best practices center for Ohio educators.

Jill Swiencicki is assistant professor of English at the California State University, Chico, where she teaches courses in rhetoric, writing, and women's studies. She is currently at work on a book-length project titled "Eloquent Identities: Rhetoric, the Public Sphere, and Social Difference in Antebellum America."

Terry Tannacito is assistant professor of English at Frostburg State University (MD), where she teaches general professional writing courses to students from a variety of majors and concentrations. She received her PhD from Indiana University of Pennsylvania in English rhetoric and linguistics, and has been concentrating in teaching professional writing: business writing, multimedia design, and editing/production. She has published articles on the topics of teaching professional writing online and electronic peer response groups.

Elizabeth Wardle is a doctoral student in rhetoric and professional communication at Iowa State University. Her dissertation project examines over 400 students in three different types of FYC courses in order to answer questions about student motivation, attitudes, and writing improvement. She has a BA in philosophy and an MA in English, both from the University of Louisville.

Anne Frances Wysocki teaches undergraduate courses in visual communication, web development, and interactive media, as well as graduate courses in technology studies and theories of new media in the Humanities Department at Michigan Technological University in Houghton, MI. Her research into visual rhetorics and the rhetorics of interactivity focuses on the relationships that writers/designers/composers construct with their audiences through various kinds of texts when they use a wide range of textual and cultural compositional strategies.

AUTHOR INDEX

R

S

SUBJECT INDEX

A

B

C

D

E

Printed in the United States
46579LVS00003BA/23

9 781572 735378